HD
6061
.W64
1992

Women's work and
women's lives.

$49.95

DATE			

Women's Work and
Women's Lives

WOMEN'S WORK AND WOMEN'S LIVES

The Continuing Struggle Worldwide

edited by

Hilda Kahne and
Janet Z. Giele

WESTVIEW PRESS

Boulder • San Francisco • Oxford

Copyright © 1992 by Westview Press, Inc.

Published in 1992 in the United States of America by Westview Press, Inc., 5500 Central Avenue, Boulder, Colorado 80301-2847, and in the United Kingdom by Westview Press, 36 Lonsdale Road, Summertown, Oxford OX2 7EW

Library of Congress Cataloging-in-Publication Data
Women's work and women's lives : the continuing struggle worldwide /
    edited by Hilda Kahne and Janet Z. Giele.
        p. cm.
    Includes bibliographical references and index.
    ISBN 0-8133-0636-1
    1. Equal pay for equal work. 2. Women—Employment. 3. Women—
Economic conditions. 4. Women—Social conditions. I. Kahne,
Hilda. II. Giele, Janet Zollinger.
HD6061.W64   1992
331.4–dc20   92-12157
                                                                             CIP

Printed and bound in the United States of America

The paper used in this publication meets the requirements
of the American National Standard for Permanence of Paper
for Printed Library Materials Z39.48-1984.

10   9   8   7   6   5   4   3   2

Contents

Preface

This book about the changing lives of women around the world was conceived in winter 1987–1988 at a time when neither of the editors could have imagined the momentous events of the next five years. Who would have predicted the Tiananmen Square repression of 1989 in China, the democratic revolutions in Eastern Europe during the same year, the dismantling of apartheid in South Africa in 1990, or the August coup that resulted in toppling the Soviet Communist Party in 1991? Our global society, marked not only by change but also by growing interdependence, throws into sharp relief the similarities and differences among nations as well as in the lives of the individual women and men who inhabit them.

For Hilda Kahne, who was a Wheaton College faculty member in Kenya in summer 1985, the idea for this book was sparked by attendance at the Nairobi Conference that concluded the UN Decade for Women (1976–1985). The deep sense of sisterhood that prevailed at the conference, even across national boundaries, led to a consideration of the common elements in women's experience and mutual support. One wanted to understand more fully the distinct nature of women's place in society that produced a sense of connectedness despite major differences in geographic location, levels of economic development, political structures, cultural and religious traditions, and personal lives.

For Janet Z. Giele, many of the same issues had arisen in an earlier book, *Women: Roles and Status in Eight Countries*, which appeared in 1977.[1] At that time a central question involved the relative status of women: Why did women experience near equality with men in some countries, whereas in other countries their life options were severely limited? An obvious sequel was to consider how women's roles and status had changed by the last decade of the twentieth century.

The present book thus grew out of both of our interests in understanding women's changing roles around the globe. To provide a baseline for comparison, we agreed that a primary focus of the book should be women's paid work. Then, as each contributor's interests and expertise dictated, the country chapters also could sketch a larger picture of women's lives, showing the relationship of paid work to education, family life, and the larger social, economic, and political contexts.

In getting started, our challenge was to select a group of countries and regions to be included and to locate top-ranking social scientists whose work focused on these areas and coincided with our research interests. Although not all desired countries could be included for study, the book that emerged provides a wide range of descriptive detail on a variety of countries and regions around the globe. In addition, the resulting content gives a basis for comparison among developing regions, nations of the former Communist bloc, and Eastern and Western industrial democracies.

We are pleased that a number of disciplines are represented among the contributors of the country and regional studies: an anthropologist (Safa), two economists (Rudolph and Weil), a historian (Ohta), two political scientists (Lapidus and Wolchik), two psychologists (Kauppinen and Pleck), three sociologists (Cordilia, Haavio-Mannila, and Moghadam), and a British Labour Party research officer (MacLennan) working on policies for social protection and equal opportunity. Although these specialties are not reflected in the organizational structure of the book, the variety of the contributors' backgrounds and training is both a characteristic and a strength of the contemporary study of women's lives. In addition, half of these twelve authors currently live and work in countries other than the United States.

To set the stage for examining women's situation in each country, the two opening chapters consider the fundamental similarities across nations in the general factors that influence women's work roles and general status. Coeditor Janet Z. Giele, a sociologist, introduces the book with a critical review of the modernization theories that, until recently, predicted a gradual improvement of women's status with economic development. She develops a revised conceptual framework that gives a larger place to noneconomic factors such as religion and culture, race and class, and women's access to power. She then shows how women's situation is related to the structure of the state, the economy, and family life.

Economists Francine D. Blau and Marianne A. Ferber provide a broad overview of women's economic status in all parts of the world. Using quantitative data on labor force participation, occupational distribution, earnings, education, and time allocated to housework, they provide a sound basis for the international comparison of women's economic position relative to that of men. Nowhere have women achieved full equality with men. But in the advanced industrial nations, there is some evidence of declining gender difference in job distribution and pay.

At the heart of the book are the ten chapters on women's work and lives in ten different regions or countries of the world. Brief summaries introduce each of the three sections on modernizing, socialist transitional, and advanced industrial societies.

In the book's concluding chapter, coeditor and economist Hilda Kahne returns to the key questions that launched the book. She finds several common features in women's roles and status around the world. Women everywhere share the experience of occupational segregation, pay inequity, and the double burden. These conditions are explained by economic structure, state policy, and traditions and social policies governing women's work and gender relations. Yet women's situation also varies because of market arrangements or distinctive religious or cultural traditions. In addition, social, economic, and political influences can alter the larger context that surrounds women's lives. Kahne concludes on a cautiously optimistic note by listing such positive trends as rising labor market experience and better working conditions and more education and training, all of which can improve women's position. In the end, however, a strong combination of international agencies, national and state governments, private-sector initiatives, and grass-roots community organizations will be needed to achieve greater equality for women at work and more support for their contributions to the home.

Hilda Kahne
Janet Z. Giele

NOTES

1. Janet Z. Giele and Audrey C. Smock (eds.), *Women: Roles and Status in Eight Countries* (New York: Wiley, 1977).

Acknowledgments

No book is complete without a note of thanks to the many persons who contributed along the way. As editors, we owe our principal thanks to the colleagues who participated as contributing authors. Each chapter is an up-to-the-minute account of countries and regions, some of which have changed profoundly since the book was launched. The resulting detail and depth of interpretation go far beyond the ordinary. In addition, we enjoyed a sense of shared enterprise with our contributors, who remained enthusiastic while they gave unstintingly of their expertise. They cheerfully accepted the tedious tasks of revision and correction and met the necessary deadlines. Several also served as reviewers and critics by responding to our own and others' chapters.

Many individuals contributed to the publishing process, especially our editor at Westview Press, Barbara Ellington, who from the beginning saw the potential for such a book and advised and supported us along the way. Production editor Jane Raese and copyeditor Cheryl Carnahan provided thorough, knowledgeable, and meticulous guidance throughout the production process. In the early months of the project, Hanna Papanek was helpful in steering us toward potential contributors. Midway in the process, as we considered courses that might use the book, Kathleen Cloud of the University of Illinois provided us with a detailed list of courses and teachers.

Each of our institutions gave us both material and moral support. For Hilda Kahne, President Alice F. Emerson and Provost Hannah Goldberg of Wheaton College made possible a summer faculty internship in Kenya in 1985 and followed this with continued support for bringing that experience into research and teaching. A mini-sabbatical from teaching in fall 1990 helped bring the project to fruition. For Janet Z. Giele, the support and resources of the Heller School at Brandeis University, especially the Family and Children's Policy Center, allowed her to communicate easily with our international authors and circulate chapters among all the contributors. Berne Webb was an indispensable assistant in that effort, and Cindy Fenichel helped locate and check a number of bibliographic sources. Nancy Shepardson at Wheaton College gave the tables a unified format and monitored other details of production. Marshall Henrichs transformed the tables and figures into their attractive and finished form.

We shared our thinking and our chapters with others and always benefited from their suggestions. Both of us want to express special thanks to Merton

Kahne and David Giele, whose understated comments about substance and publishing (made with characteristic humor and insight) kept us focused on central issues and how best to convey them.

Finally, each of us as editor and author probably owes her greatest debt to the other. We have been professional and personal friends for over twenty years. Yet we continue to learn from each other and to benefit from our mutual interests as economist and sociologist. We strive to understand both the changing work of women and how to improve the quality of their lives.

H.K.
J.Z.G.

PART ONE
Overview

1

Promise and Disappointment of the Modern Era: Equality for Women

JANET Z. GIELE

Over the past century, women who live in modern nations have generally seen an improvement in their political, economic, and social status. Before 1900 women had the right to vote in only a few western U.S. states and New Zealand; by 1960 women voted in every major country of the world. U.S. and European women could not enter colleges and universities until the mid-nineteenth century, but by 1985 they constituted at least half of all secondary school students in many industrialized nations and almost half of college and university students. Women's participation in the paid labor force of many industrial countries steadily rose from about 20 percent in 1900 to over 50 percent by 1990 (United Nations 1991: 108). Marital and civil rights also expanded to encompass rights to divorce, child custody, marital property, and reproductive control (Sivard 1985).

The contemporary world has come to expect that these trends will continue. Women's equality and freedom of choice have become identified with modernism and oppressive patriarchy with traditionalism because greater societal differentiation and complexity increase the individualism and autonomy of women. Value systems have become secularized and religious traditions more diverse to encourage greater reliance on individual belief and interpretation. Political systems have overturned hereditary class and castes and moved toward democracy (Parsons 1966). Ancient extended family and patriarchal kinship systems have lost their grip; and nuclear families, single-parent families, and single-person households form the overwhelming majority of living arrangements in the modern world (Goode 1963).

Clear improvements have resulted in women's educational and employment opportunities. In just twenty-five years, between 1960 and 1985, women's worldwide literacy rate rose from 59 to 68 percent. In the developed world women's labor force participation rose from 42 to 57 percent; and in the decade between 1968 and 1977, the female earnings differential improved an average of 10 percent (Sivard 1985; Cook, Lorwin, and Daniels 1984). Parental leaves and child care facilities that were almost inconceivable in the 1950s era of the "feminine mystique" had become the norm in the Scandinavian countries by 1980, and a child care act was mandated by the U.S. Congress in 1990.

But several tendencies challenge the connection between modernization and women's equality:

1. *Despite feminist efforts on behalf of women, industrialization does not necessarily guarantee sex equality.* Japan's highly educated female citizens are steered away from demanding professions and managerial posts. Instead, they are encouraged as young office workers to turn their talents to purely decorative and expressive functions and after marriage to motherhood and homemaking. The socialist state, although it once appeared to hold greater promise for gender equality, in Central and Eastern Europe has pursued a gender policy of full employment for women that many women—even with socialized child care—now feel is oppressive.

2. *Increased participation in the modern paid labor force does not necessarily bring full economic equality for women.* The U.S. and Nordic countries, with their relatively high rates of labor force participation, still report overall rates of occupational segregation around 50 percent (Cook, Lorwin, and Daniels 1984). In highly industrialized Japan, even though women's labor force participation in nonfamily enterprises has increased dramatically since World War II, it is still extremely difficult for women to have careers without completely forgoing marriage and family life. Nor do women in the Third World necessarily benefit by joining the paid labor force. Rural women may become seasonal wage laborers to produce crops for market and as a result neglect their traditional subsistence role as food producers for family needs. Urban women may have no other choice than a three-shift day that combines low-paying work in sweatshops and after-hours piecework in the home with their usual domestic duties (Nash 1983a, 1983b).

3. *Enlightened social policies for child care, parental leave, and equal employment opportunity do not necessarily produce gender equality in public life, the workplace, or the home.* The Nordic countries, which have the most favorable public policy in support of gender equality, report underrepresentation of women in top business and professional positions relative to men and noticeable sex-typing of male and female jobs. Central and Eastern Europe, which likewise have had official state policy supporting sex equality, have not been able to avoid underrepresentation of women in positions of leadership, job segregation, and overburdening of women on the home front.

These hard facts call for a reexamination of modernization theory as applied to women. Do current trends in women's political, economic, and family roles fit the theory?

MODERNIZATION THEORY AND
THE STATUS OF WOMEN

Since 1970 a unified, if still largely implicit, sociological theory of women's equality has emerged. Social scientists have argued that societies vary in gender equality because of key elements in their social structures. The optimum combination for equality between the sexes has been assumed to be the following: (1) a technologically advanced or industrial economy; (2) a kinship system based on a nuclear rather than an extended family; (3) a democratic state and an egalitarian class structure; and (4) a secularized or "protestant" religious tradition or world view. Such are the propositions one might derive from a close reading of the sociological classics of Emile Durkheim (1933, [1893]), Max Weber (1958 [1904–1905]), or Talcott Parsons (1966).

Beginning around 1970, however, scholars who were studying women's actual experience in development discovered a more complex pattern than the rising line of gradual progress that had been implied by classical sociological theory. First, they found that the relationship between economic development and women's status was curvilinear, with a distinct decline during the early stages of rural and industrial development. Second, religious and cultural tradition explained much of the difference in women's situation among societies that were economically similar. Third, women of different race, class, and residential origins within the same society could be thought of as being at different stages of development depending on whether they worked at menial jobs or in the technologically advanced sector. Finally, women's power at the micro level was not necessarily reflected at the macro level. These key elements, added to the earlier version of modernization theory, actually help to explain the uneven correlation between women's emancipation and the modernization process.

A Curvilinear Relationship

By 1970 efforts to help the developing nations had been under way for several decades when Ester Boserup published her ground-breaking analysis, *Woman's Role in Economic Development*. Boserup, an economist, shattered the linear progress model of women's emancipation and linked women's work patterns to mode of subsistence (horticulture, agriculture, and irrigation systems). Women's roles in production were very important in family farming systems such as those found in West Africa, Oceania, or Central and South America, whereas their roles were fairly limited in the male farming systems of China or India.

Boserup predicted that women's overall status would not necessarily improve with development. In fact, their future appeared to depend on whether they were currently in a male or female farming system and whether current development schemes paid particular attention to their productive roles or were aimed primarily at men. Throughout the 1970s various scholars probed the questions Boserup had raised (Gallin, Aronoff, and Ferguson 1989). By 1990 there appeared to be considerable consensus that a curvilinear relationship existed between women's status and economic development, with neither a straight line of improvement nor of decline but with a valley in women's economic status during the transition from a traditional to a modern economy. Several sociologists have compared this pattern of gender inequality to what Gerhard Lenski (1966) demonstrated for class inequality: *In*equality is greatest at intermediate levels of development, whereas equality appears to flourish in both the earliest and simplest and the most complex and modern of societies (Giele 1977; Blumberg 1979; Chafetz 1984).

Religion and Culture

A second discovery of the 1970s was that religious and cultural traditions had their own independent effects on women's status over and above the impact of economic roles. Again Lenski's (1966) work proved a useful model. His curvilinear graph of class stratification, although it predicted an overall increase in class equality in modern society, envisioned a wide band of variation on either side of the central tendency that was due to cultural and ideological variation.

In her comparison of Middle Eastern and Latin American women's roles in economic development, Nadia Youssef (1974: 19–20) was one of the first to demonstrate the impact of cultural differences on women's economic roles. In 1970 the participation of women in the nonagricultural labor force in Latin America averaged around 20 percent, whereas it was only 4 percent in the Middle East. Yet both regions were at roughly equal stages of economic development at the time.

Since Youssef's pioneering work, a number of other studies have upheld her general observation about the independent effect of cultural tradition on women's roles. In a comparison of women's roles and status in eight countries, I found the greatest sex equality in the socialist and the least in the Muslim countries (1977); other work has supported my broad distinction among socialist, western democratic, and Muslim traditions in their degree of support for gender equality. Janet Chafetz (1984: 115–116) also distinguishes between cultural traditions less favorable to women (among which she classifies Judaism, Hinduism, Christianity, and Islam) and those with more positive views (that tend to be animist, as in the simplest societies) or with a secular outlook (as in socialist or postindustrial capitalist societies).

Race, Class, and Rural Origins

A third refinement of gender and modernization theory has surfaced in the last decade. Obstacles to women's equality became apparent both in reports of the United Nations (UN) Decade for Women (1976–1985) and in the actual experience of the Third World as the development process unfolded. Mechanization of agriculture and export cash crops such as flowers or luxury foods drew women out of subsistence production and resulted in increased food imports and a food crisis in a number of African and Latin American countries. Nor did women's status improve as they entered the informal sector or took on marginal jobs in the cities, where their pay and security were very low (Nash 1983a, 1983b; Deere and Leon 1987).

As scholars and feminists began to rethink the impact of development on women, they recognized the great importance of race and ethnicity, class, and rural or urban location as factors in how women fared. Although a society as a whole might be considered developed, women within that society who were employed as migratory field workers, domestics, or street vendors did not enjoy the same life chances as middle-class women employed as clerical workers or professionals (Tiano 1987). The restricted opportunities of the less-favored groups to enter the more "modern" occupations were heavily influenced by their race, ethnicity, or class background.

The global economy also is differentiated between the urban and industrial First World countries at the core and the developing countries at the periphery, which provide raw materials and cheap labor to the core. What most disturbs the women-in-development scholars is the worsening condition of Third World women who have been forced off the land by the need to earn wages. These women join the migratory or urban labor force. Not only has aggregate food production suffered but also the individual woman's ability to ensure having enough food for herself and her family (Nash 1983a, 1983b; Deere and Leon 1987).

Such difficult conditions are more likely to be encountered by those who are already poor than by those who own land or who come from the middle class. Thus, rather than fostering equality, contemporary development appears to exploit the most vulnerable women at the economic periphery, whereas it serves the interest of those with wealth or education who inhabit the modern core (Nash 1983a: xv). The UN Decade for Women reflected these trends in the call by scholars and feminists for a better and more equitable *redistribution* of the rewards of development (Gallin, Aronoff, and Ferguson 1989; Ward 1990).

Power

After redistribution, *empowerment* was the second watchword to come out of the UN Decade for Women (Gallin, Aronoff, and Ferguson 1989). Power as used by the women-in-development scholars refers not to relations in production that are defined by race or class background but to the pervasive tendency to subordinate *all* women to men in their opportunities for educational, political, or economic achievement.

Thus, the fourth refinement of modernization theory is that women's economic or political power at the household level does not necessarily translate into power at the community or national level. Lack of female power at the higher levels can work as a disincentive to female productivity and reinforce the skewed reward system that privileges men and overburdens women. Rae Lesser Blumberg (1989) has used the theoretical distinction between female power at the *micro* and *macro* levels to call attention to the disincentives for women's participation in production. In the Kibbutz, women's preference for service jobs results in a need to employ foreign labor. Similarly, the overburdening of women in Central and Eastern Europe leads to their withdrawal from the labor force while raising young children. Blumberg suggests that if more women were in positions of power at the societal level, their overburdening in the household would likely abate, and they would once again be eager for employment.

Women's empowerment presumably results in a reordering of rewards to give relatively more compensation and value to reproductive work. Rather than overburdening and underpaying women for their work in child care, social work, teaching, subsistence food production, or the home, society could provide greater rewards for their contribution.

Summary

In sum, we have seen that the linear theory of modernization to promote women's equality has undergone a number of refinements so that it can now accommodate multiple possible paths of development. First, modernization produces no clear linear pattern of upward progress in women's equality; instead, the pattern is curvilinear, with low points associated with peasant agriculture and early industrialization. Second, religious, ideological, and cultural traditions act over and above economic development as dampers or facilitators for women's equality. Third, race, class, and other background characteristics act differentially on a woman's opportunities and rewards in the development process; women in modern and developing nations also experience the modernization process differently. Fourth, the degree of women's power and representation at the highest levels of government has a bearing on how benign the development process will be for women.

Using these propositions, I now review the remarkable recent political, economic, and social developments in women's lives that are described in this book.[1] Does feminist consciousness emerge with political development? Does women's entry into the paid labor force improve their economic position? Do advanced social policies (child care, parental leave, and flexible work arrangements) encourage equality and ease women's lives?

FEMINISM, CITIZENSHIP, AND THE STATE

Our first question concerns women's own consciousness of themselves and their liberation and empowerment. Is there a correlation between the structure of the state and the emergence or presence of feminism?

History shows a very rough association between modernization and women's attainment of citizenship. Between 1890 and the mid-1920s, the first countries to give women the vote were the non-Catholic Western democracies, various European colonies, the Soviet Union, and the United States. Next came Eastern Europe, Western European Catholic countries such as France and Italy, and the most developed countries of the Third World, which granted women suffrage between 1930 and 1950. Finally, since 1950 a variety of African, Muslim, or newly independent countries such as Kenya, Pakistan, and Indonesia have adopted woman suffrage (Pharr 1981; Sivard 1985).

Since World War II, efforts to realize women's equality have had to address a whole new set of social and material conditions, including the further democratization and industrialization of Japan, Southeast Asia, Latin America, and Central and Eastern Europe. Between 1975 and 1985, the resolutions of the UN Decade for Women (Fraser 1987) repeatedly called for changes in the laws to assure equality for women. But subtle barriers persisted. Despite equal opportunity laws, strong cultural expectations continued to give women primary responsibility for the household.

Definition of Women's Equality

In the face of these rapidly changing circumstances, how shall we define women's empowerment and women's equality? At the macro level, women's equality implies significant representation in the leadership and management of both government and industry. At the micro level, women's equality concerns both productive and reproductive work. Equality in productive work implies equal education, job opportunities, and pay. Equality in reproductive work implies support for women's family roles as mothers in ways that neither confine them exclusively to the home nor overburden them with household work.

By these standards, the most developed societies appear to have made considerable progress on the reproductive side, as reflected in men's increased help with the household tasks and the greater availability of household conveniences to relieve women of household drudgery. But women in these societies are still fighting subordination in the workplace and in a number of countries are strikingly underrepresented in elective office. Women in Central and Eastern Europe and the former Soviet Union have the opposite problem. They are expected to be men's equals in the workplace, but they are grossly overburdened at home. Women in the Third World seem to be doubly oppressed. In their productive roles, they have been proletarianized as they are increasingly integrated into the world economy. They also are heavily burdened with family responsibilities that range from child care and cooking to obtaining water and firewood and growing their own food. As a result, women in each type of society have responded with women's movements or a version of feminism that is aimed at improving their particular situation.

Feminism in the Industrialized Nations

After World War II, the industrial nations experienced an unprecedented growth in the service occupations that typically employed women. Women's labor force participation rose sharply, particularly among women in middle and older age groups (Oppenheimer 1970). A second wave of feminism combined a critique of personal life with active efforts to expand women's rights and opportunities. Sweden in particular adopted far-reaching policies for sex equality and began a review of its employment and family policies to encourage women's advancement (Liljestrom, Mellstrom, and Svensson 1978). Feminists in the United States and Canada created women's liberation groups and feminist political organizations in the 1960s. Informal support groups established communication and trust among women from diverse backgrounds. Formal groups investigated women's educational and job opportunities, documented sex segregation and discrimination, and began to develop an agenda for change (Giele 1990). Even in Japan, where women are still much more likely to seek jobs than careers, a women's movement emerged in the 1960s that included consciousness-raising groups and formal organizations working for equal opportunity laws (Pharr 1981).

By the 1990s considerable progress had been made toward the goal of gender equality in the industrial countries described in this volume. The Nordic countries with their explicit and official policy for sex equality clearly had a sizable number of women in the labor force (70–80 percent), a better record on pay equality (77–93 percent), and more women as elected national officials (over 30 percent) (Sivard 1985). Although starting from a lower base than the Nordic countries, women's labor force participation in the United States rose 20 percentage points in thirty years (from 38 to 57 percent between 1960 and 1990), and pay equity in hourly earnings has steadily improved (from 64 to 74 percent between 1979 and 1988) (Kahne 1990; U.S. Department of Labor 1989: 160–161, 1990: 2). The recent unification of the two Germanies brings together the socialist East with its past record of a large percentage of women in the labor force (although unemployment is currently high) and the capitalist West, in which only slightly more than half of women are in the labor force. Yet the thrust of future policy and of feminism for Scandinavia, the United States, and Germany seems clear: to focus on affirmative action and social policies that will close the gap between women's and men's attainments. Social policies in all of these countries now appear to be primarily oriented to supporting a dual role for women as both paid workers and family members, although this is a recent development in the United States and appears only about to occur in the new unified Germany.

Great Britain and Japan, by contrast, appear much more ambivalent in their attitudes toward the ideal woman's role and in fact still tilt toward the traditional home-based role for women. Thus, official British policy is only grudging in its support of child care centers. And in Japan, young college women find it difficult to envision any long-term career other than that of wife and mother.

Will the British and Japanese experiences eventually replicate the Nordic pattern or recent U.S. trends? It is difficult to say. What is perhaps most significant is the fact that the terms of the feminist debate are very similar in all of the industrial countries—whether to choose family, career, or a combination of work and family roles. The dominant trend since 1970 has been toward a pattern of multiple simultaneous roles (Giele and Gilfus 1990).

The Socialist Experience

In socialist and Communist countries, the first wave of feminism stemmed from different sources and took a different course. The tradition of socialist feminism has not been so much concerned with women's suffrage or higher education as with economic and political power for laboring people. Russian revolutionaries criticized women's isolated work in the middle-class household and advocated women's full involvement in work outside the home. In 1918 the new Soviet government instituted far-reaching reforms that guaranteed legal equality of husband and wife, equal education, equal employment, and the right to vote and hold public office. Women in Russia since 1918 and in the German Democratic Republic since 1950 also have had some form of maternity leave and child care (Mandel 1975: 55; Ecklein 1982: 187).

Because of heavy wartime losses, women have been greatly needed in industry and the professions just to keep the society running. During the 1950s in the Soviet Union, there were only fifty-nine men to every one hundred women in the 35 to 59 age group. A strong tradition of women's labor force participation emerged, combined with women's normal family duties.

Within the Eastern bloc countries, however, women protest the "double burden" of employment and family responsibilities—a condition that is particularly acute in socialist societies. Men's roles appear to have changed less as a result of women's employment than has been the case in the West. Moreover, conveniences such as washing machines, indoor plumbing, and well-stocked supermarkets are still less available in the Eastern bloc than in Western societies. As Central and East European countries are turning toward democracy and a Western-style economy, women look for relief in two forms. They hope for an increase in the supply of household conveniences and consumer goods. They also imagine a time when they will be able to work only part time or not at all in order to spend more time with their families. For the time being, feminist protest takes the form of lower fertility rates, which have the effect of linking population policy to the need for more supportive social policies for children and families.

How shall we interpret this interest in the homemaker role? Rather than term it antifeminist, I am inclined to see it as a different form of feminism— what in the West has been called domestic, or maternal, feminism. Women in socialist societies, in claiming the right to choose the wife-mother role, appear to be addressing an issue that was bypassed when women gained equal employment opportunity in the socialist revolution. They are now revisiting it in the context of political and economic changes that put more emphasis on individual choice and the private sector. Frankly, I will be surprised if there is much turning "back" to the traditional homemaker role because women and their families have already become accustomed to a reduced role for household production and face the necessity of women's added outside income to maintain the standard of living. The future debate will probably revolve around flexibility and the right to choose one's work and family roles at different stages of the life course.

It is interesting and probably not accidental that in the socialist countries, the frustration of the homemaker role is the opposite of the problem in Western countries, which is the frustration of women's career achievement. The nature of the problem stems from the peculiar history of each tradition. Socialist societies privileged the productive aspect of women's role and must now address the strains on the reproductive side. Capitalist societies, which had no trouble justifying women's time in reproductive roles, are now trying to give full support to women's work outside the home.

Women's Movements in the Third World

Because political and cultural traditions of developing countries are quite diverse, they are not easily characterized with respect to feminism and women's empowerment. Muslim women in the Middle East and North Africa are traditionally secluded and their activities strictly segregated from those of men. Latin American women combine traditions derived from the strong female roles of native Indian society as well as the cultural patterns of male domination, or machismo, derived from Spanish and Portuguese colonization. Women in East and West Africa have long had independence as food producers and traders.

Nevertheless, several forms of feminism have emerged in developing countries. These movements parallel the three forms of feminism found in both the developed nations of the West and the socialist societies of the Eastern bloc (Jacquette 1982). From my reading of recent reports of women's movements in the Third World, I believe that something akin to domestic feminism is found when women mobilize neighborhood and community resources to make their daily household chores less difficult. The analog of equal rights feminism appears as protest when gender is the basis for excluding women from democratic rights of citizenship that are becoming available to men. Finally, a form of women's mobilization somewhat similar to socialist feminism can be found where historically gender was not so important as working-class solidarity in obtaining rights of employees to organize and bargain for better hours, pay, and job security.

Domestic, or maternal, women's movements in Latin America provide one of the best examples of collective action in support of women's domestic or maternal roles. Such feminist movements have emerged where there is a breakdown in the domestic economy that in a number of instances was triggered by the debt crisis of the 1980s. Women developed local communal dining, health, and child care cooperatives to meet their heavier work load, which resulted from the economic crisis and a triple burden of domestic responsibility, paid work, and informal market work (cottage industry, domestic service, and street vending). In one nation after another, these women's movements have demanded help from the state (sometimes with the support of women candidates) to provide for such improvements in the infrastructure as drinking water, electricity, housing, sanitation, and transportation (Acosta-Belen and Bose 1990; Deere 1987; Nash 1990; Safa 1990). Other popular feminist movements, such as that represented by Las Madres del Plaza de Mayo in Argentina, have protested human rights violations and the disappearance of loved ones in repressive regimes. Again, women's foray into the public sphere is based primarily on their traditional roles as mothers and guardians of the home rather than on an ideology of equal rights.

Equal rights women's movements, on the other hand, are oriented primarily to securing equal rights for women in the public sphere. In Chile in the 1970s, for example, a group of twelve women's organizations was able to draft the Demands of Women for Democracy, which included a constitutional guarantee of equality between women and men (Lago 1987). In Brazil, a National Council on Women's Rights has presented women's proposals for the new Brazilian constitution (Safa 1990). This type of feminism appears to have more chance of developing when there is already a trend toward democracy and men have already attained major rights of citizenship.

Socialist feminism emerges in those situations in which both women and men organize to resist oppression along class or racial lines. Such was the case, for example, in South Africa during the 1940s and 1950s in the canning and food processing industry (Berger 1990). Unionization of the industry skipped the stage of feminism that focuses on practical gender interests and moved directly to challenging the corporate owners and the state. Such movements seem most likely when, as in the South African case, women and children as well as men are involved in the labor force and benefits to workers are benefits to the community and family as well (Acosta-Belen and Bose 1990).

WOMEN'S CHANGING ECONOMIC ROLES

In the past, experts on women in development believed that if more women could find paid jobs, they would be able to escape patriarchal control and gain greater access to education, fertility control, and equal rights of citizenship. By the end of the UN Decade for Women, however, the connection between women's work and women's status appeared to be more complicated. Industrial nations had seen a continued rise in women's labor force participation and improvements in pay, occupational distribution, education, and fertility that seemed consistent with earlier projections. But a darker picture of women's overburdening and continued lag behind men in sharing the fruits of development emerged from the Third World countries (Gallin, Aronoff, and Ferguson 1989). Women's work took somewhat different forms and had different results depending on whether it occurred in an already industrialized nation or in a subsistence economy just beginning the development process.

Key Trends and Descriptive Indicators

Participation Rates. The contrast between the experience of the industrialized and developing countries is perhaps clearest with respect to women's labor force participation. Since 1950 the percentage of women employed in the industrialized market economies gradually rose from around 40 percent to near 60 percent in 1990 and is predicted to rise to 70 percent by the year 2000. The age curve for labor force participation in these capitalist countries changed from an M shape to a curve resembling the inverted U of men's rates, thereby indicating more continuous participation between the ages of 20 and 55. In general, socialist countries have had high women's participation rates (averaging 70 to 80 percent), which not only have remained at that level since World War II but have changed little with respect to age, remaining virtually level from ages 20 to 55. The USSR, for example, saw its women's labor force participation rate rise from over 60 percent in 1950 to over 90 percent in 1985 (Standing 1981; Nuss 1989: 27).

In contrast with both capitalist and socialist industrialized nations, developing countries show great variety in work rates, depending on the region. A decade ago, Guy Standing (1981: 24) reported somewhat lower and *falling* rates of participation in less-developed regions (from over 50 percent in 1950 to around 45 percent in 1980), with age curves similar to the socialist countries—virtually flat between ages 20 and 55 with no time out of the work force in early to middle adulthood for household or child care. By the end of the 1980s, however, Standing (1989) observed rising women's participation rates in virtually all countries, whereas men's rates were declining. Shirley Nuss (1989: 26–27) reports trends that illustrate the variety among the developing countries. East Asian countries show high and rising rates (80 to 90 percent), which are predicted to persist through the year 2000. The next-highest rates occur in sub-Saharan Africa, but these are expected to fall from over 60 percent in 1950 to around 50 percent by 2000. The lowest rates appear in middle-south Asia (India, Pakistan, the Middle East), which averaged roughly 40 percent in 1950 but had fallen to 30 percent in 1985 and are expected to go even lower by the year 2000. East Asian and Latin American nations are the two major groups of developing countries in which women's participation rates actually *rose* about 10 percentage points between 1950 and 1985, from 80 to 90 percent in East Asia and from 20 to over 30 percent in Latin America and the Caribbean.

Over two decades ago, Ester Boserup (1970) predicted a withdrawal of women from the labor force during the initial stages of modernization when families move from village to town. Not only are girls and women insufficiently trained to take up modern-sector work, but industrial or clerical jobs are generally regarded as men's work and therefore are unsuitable for women. In East Asia the pattern is notably different because women are accepted in industry; in Latin America the petty vending and domestic service sectors are regarded as acceptable way stations for women who are making the transition from rural to urban life.

Occupational Distribution and Pay Equity. Differences between modern and developing nations also are evident in women's job opportunities and pay. The mature industrialized economies (whether market or centrally planned) all have a relatively high degree of job segregation by sex, typically around 40 percent in North America and Western Europe. Women's hourly earnings are typically around 70 percent of men's, although Nordic women clearly are better off, with earnings of around 90 percent of men's (Cook, Lorwin, and Daniels 1984: 9).

In the developing nations, the most commonly used indicator of job distribution is the proportion of each sex employed in the agricultural, manufacturing, and service sectors of the economy. In general, there are many more women in agriculture and service jobs than in manufacturing. Between 1950 and 1980, the share of women employed in the agricultural sector fell from 87 percent to 71 percent, whereas their proportions doubled in industry and services. Males' representation in agriculture, industry, and services changed in a similar fashion (Nuss 1989: 40). Income comparisons are difficult because more women than men are employed in agriculture and the informal sector, and they often are not paid in cash.

Mixed Results in the Industrial Nations

Modernization theory predicted that with control of fertility, rising levels of education, and more continuous work histories, most women would be better off both economically and socially. What comes as a disappointment is the persistence of both occupational segregation and pay differences, despite the fall in the birth rate, women's enormous advances in education, and the continued rise in women's labor force participation. How can these patterns be explained, and will they ultimately disappear? Three major competing theories give somewhat different answers to the questions (Stevenson 1978).

Neoclassical Theory (human capital). Neoclassical theory emphasizes the quality of individual performance, which is affected by education, training, and a disciplined attitude toward work (Standing 1981: 227–228; Roos 1985: 3–5). According to this theory, women's access to good jobs will improve as they have fewer children and invest their human capital in their own training, education, and work experience—thereby lengthening their work attachment across the life span. As a result, we would expect to see increased representation of women at the top and an improvement in their pay relative to men's, reflecting their increased productivity.

A variety of evidence supports the neoclassical theory. The proportion of women in the highest-paid professions has risen. For example, in the United States, the proportion of lawyers and judges who are women nearly tripled between 1975 and 1988, from 7 to 20 percent (Rix 1990: Table 19). Women's hourly earnings have increased relative to men's: in the United States, from 64 to 74 percent of those of men between 1979 and 1988; in Sweden, from 74 percent in 1950 to 90 percent in 1987. When pay is compared for women and men within occupations, the picture is even better. Women's wages were between 80 and 100 percent of those of men in the United States in 1989, representing an improvement of several percentage points just since 1983 (U.S. Department of Labor 1990: 3–4).

Institutional Theory (internal labor markets). Institutional theory emphasizes the importance of the type of job structure and cultural norms for determining both access and rate of return. Men are given access to the most rewarding jobs in the stable, well-paid primary sector of employment, with higher status and better career opportunities, whereas women are shunted into the less secure, less well-paid secondary sector in jobs that have little opportunity for advancement. It is assumed that family obligations will interfere with women's work attachment and make them less likely to be committed workers (Standing 1981: 227–228; Roos 1985: 5–6).

Persistent job segregation by sex continues to be characteristic of advanced industrial societies. In her comparison of twelve industrialized nations, Patricia A. Roos (1985) discovered little support for the human capital explanation (which predicts differences based on individual choice and work attachment) when she compared returns to married and never-married women. There was virtually no difference in the pay received by these two groups of women, although the never-married women were similar to men in their full-time continuous work history. Roos concluded that differences in job structure (crowding of women into a few female-typed occupations and lower pay for these jobs) and not human capital investment was the major explanation of the economic inequalities between men and women.

Radical Alternatives (capitalism and patriarchy). Radical theorists focus on the category of gender itself and the association of being female with the experience of discrimination. Socialist feminists blame capitalism, which exploits women's unpaid reproductive labor to care for children and support the male work force but which at the same time sets up barriers to women's paid labor and rewards them poorly for what they do (Anderson 1983: 263–282). Radical feminists focus on fundamental patriarchal values that privilege men and devalue women. The combination of patriarchy and economic exploitation is particularly damaging to women (Hartmann 1976; Sokoloff 1980; Green 1983). In socialist as well as capitalist societies, women's jobs—no matter how much training they require—pay less than men's; and experienced and competent women—even in exacting nontraditional jobs in which men predominate—are less well paid than their male counterparts.

Many observers also have noted the patriarchal elements of the new industrial estates located in export-processing zones. Young women from sixteen to twenty-two years of age are selected as workers because of their docility and willingness to be subjected to long hours and tight discipline, whereas men are found to be insubordinate and restless and unable to sit still eight hours a day to do one boring repetitive task (Lim 1981: 184–185).

Global Restructuring and the Developing World

Observers of the role of women in development now imply that the process experienced by the industrial economies of the West is unlikely to be repeated in many other countries (Ward 1990: 4). Since World War II, the world economic system has become more tightly integrated. Export-manufacturing zones located in Third World nations are controlled by giant transnational corporations based in the industrialized nations of the First World. The question as put by Linda Lim (1983: 70) is whether "the employment of women factory workers by multinational corporations in developing countries [is] primarily an experience of *liberation*, as development economists and governments maintain, or one of *exploitation*, as feminists assert, for the women concerned" (see also Tiano 1987; Standing 1989).

What has changed since the industrialization of the First World is the emergence of a new division of labor in the world system. During the 1970s, international flow of capital multiplied tenfold (Joekes 1987: 29–30). Lender nations in the industrialized core invested in the developing nations at the periphery. In many instances they built capital-intensive rather than labor-intensive industries. In addition, they repatriated well over half of their profits. As a result, the developing nations experienced debt dependency, underdevelopment of their industry, and a distorted growth in their service sectors

(Ward 1988: 24). Rather than experiencing the autonomy and improved status usually associated with wage earning, women workers in the Third World seem to have become trapped in marginal jobs that exploit their class and gender.

The dynamics of this transformation differ by region. In Asia, where industry has been the most dynamic sector, women's employment grew, due in part to international exchange. Latin America, however, saw capital-intensive development in both agriculture and industry, which discriminated against women and encouraged their employment as service workers. The predominance of agriculture in Africa has made entire populations vulnerable to food shortages and falling prices on international markets, a situation that is increasingly disadvantageous to women and children (Joekes 1987: 35).

Effects of Global Integration. Rather than the gradual improvement of women's status, which historically has been associated with industrialization, global integration appears to have brought a hierarchical system in which Third World women are kept permanently at the bottom of the pyramid. Young women with jobs in the export-processing zones typically are subject to low wages, unstable temporary employment, and virtually no legal protection or benefits (Deere and Leon 1987). When their eyes are weakened from the microscopic work of electronics or textile or garment manufacturing, often by the age of twenty-five, they are considered superannuated and leave or are expelled from their jobs with few other options before them (Nash 1983a: x).

In the past, during industrialization in the West, young female workers were inducted into factory jobs, then (after a generation or two) moved into clerical and professional jobs. Now in the developing countries, there is a danger that "footloose" factories will settle briefly where there are tax breaks and a ready labor supply but then depart when conditions become more favorable elsewhere, leaving women unemployed and once again economically dependent (Nash 1983a). A further danger is that experienced workers will be let go because they are eligible for higher wages; they, too, face unemployment because their skills are not transferable to other jobs (Ward 1988).

Importance of Age, Class, Race, and Gender. What has happened in effect is that the world economy has institutionalized age, class, race, and sex hierarchies on a global scale. The new international economy rewards workers differentially according to their current location in life. In the case of industrial work, age is a critical feature. Very young women workers are sought out for labor in the export-processing zones, and even among young women aging proves a hazard to their continued employment as their wages improve with productivity and experience or their eyesight and docility decline. Other age-graded life events such as marriage, childbearing, widowhood, desertion, or divorce also take their toll on women's time that is available for employment and work in the home (Ozawa 1989).

Socioeconomic class, or racial and ethnic minority status, is a second perennial factor (Janiewski 1987). Middle-class women have a choice of remaining outside the labor force or working at professional jobs congruent with their education and status; frequently they rely on the domestic help of poor and minority women (Ferree 1987). Rural or working-class and minority women also are subject to becoming the domestic workers or informal labor force who service the modern sector (Tiano 1987). Gender, or sex typing, is another key feature of "women's" occupations that presupposes low pay, insecurity, and subordinate behavior. Exploitation is built on the premise that women will take jobs that men reject and accept work at the bottom of a pyramid controlled by men.

Thus, it is poor young women especially who have found a niche in the new global economy. They are sought after, if only for a brief period in their lives, as the cheapest and hardest-working labor supply. Jobs that leave the First World because of high labor costs often go to them. For Third World women who do not find industrial employment, the prospects are even bleaker. In Latin America, for example, if men or older daughters have migrated, adult women are left with the responsibility for young children and domestic animals as well as subsistence farming. Some are pulled into the seasonal wage labor force as agricultural laborers picking fruit in Chile or strawberries in Mexico or tending carnations in Colombia (Deere and Leon 1987). Others drift into the informal labor market as domestics, prostitutes, street vendors, or subcontractors doing piecework at home. In Africa, where agriculture is the predominant sector, the brunt of the debt crisis, crop failures, and famine has fallen most heavily on poor women and children (Joekes 1987: 122).

These trends make it difficult to see how there will ever be a time when women's employment patterns in the developing countries will replicate those of the Western industrial world. Instead, U.S. and European scholars are finding parallels between the situation of immigrants and minorities in their own countries and that of poor women in the developing world (Fernandez-Kelly 1989).

POLICIES IN SUPPORT OF WOMEN AND FAMILIES

There are several types of social and economic policies to relieve women's disadvantage at work and in the home. Western Europe and North America have experience with equal employment policies and a variety of measures termed work-family policies. In the developing world, it is structural adjustment policies that particularly affect women's well-being as both workers and family members.

Equal Employment Policies

In many socialist nations, equal rights and equal pay laws preceded women's widespread entry into the paid labor force. In Western countries, the laws generally came later. In both instances, the laws officially banned but did not actually eliminate discrimination against women. In Eastern Europe and the Soviet Union, women are officially assured of employment equality; yet Soviet and Central and East European women's earnings are 65 to 75 percent of men's, and women are bearing a disproportionate share of the household duties. The United States, Great Britain, and Japan all have equal pay laws and legislation prohibiting sex discrimination, yet occupational segregation and the wage gap continue.

Affirmative action is an equal opportunity strategy to increase women's representation in nontraditional jobs, a policy that has been tried with some success in Sweden (Roos 1985). Comparable worth extends affirmative action by taking account of the fact that women and men often work in different occupations and promotes equality by upgrading women's pay scales and basing remuneration on the skills required (Cooke, Lorwin, and Daniels 1984). Progress in establishing standards of comparable worth seems to have had limited success in the United States. Although adopted for some state employees, comparable worth was less readily accepted in the private sector. The European community shows a continuing expansion of the strategy, as evidenced by the 1984 European Court ruling that Great Britain should amend its equal pay act to include comparable worth.

Family Policies

Given the disappointing results of antidiscrimination laws, feminists lately have turned their attention to developing policies that concern the interface between work and family life. Work-family policies expanded greatly during the 1970s and 1980s and generally include child care and flexible schedules, including parental leaves. The development of these policies bears out a prediction by Sheila B. Kamerman and Alfred J. Kahn (1981) that family policies would emerge as soon as the majority of mothers of young children were in the labor force. In the United States, the number of employed mothers of children under a year old passed the 50 percent mark sometime in the late 1980s (Hayes, Palmer, and Zaslow 1990: 17).

Family policies are a modern political and economic invention to handle the changing relationship of work to family life. Although there is wide cross-national variation, all modern family policies challenge three assumptions from the early industrial period: (1) that child care and family work are women's principal or only occupation; (2) that family work necessarily conflicts with paid employment; and (3) that child care and dependent care are exclusively family responsibilities rather than efforts to be shared with employers and the community.

Western countries have generally developed their family policies in response to women's increasing labor force participation. Eastern bloc countries, however, began with official acceptance of women's equality and full-time employment but unofficial dissatisfaction with what this meant in terms of women's second-class citizenship and overburdening. Soviet and Central and East European proposals for child care and flexible work schedules have tended to provide child care support or periods of time off for maternity leave or for raising children in their early years.

Child Care. There appears to be a rough correlation between public commitment to the provision of child care outside the home and the proportion of mothers in the labor force. For example, the Scandinavian countries, with almost three-quarters of adult women in the labor, force, provide municipally funded child care. But the extent of public provision is also affected by political culture. In the United States, where over half of the mothers of preschool children also are working, the tendency is to rely on private arrangements, the costs of which are born primarily by the parents with some help from a child care tax credit. In Central and Eastern Europe and the Soviet Union, public child care facilities appear more likely to be supplemented by informal care in the extended family or lengthy maternity leaves.

Alternative Work Schedules and Parental Leave. A second innovation to accommodate working mothers is the development of a variety of work schedules, including part-time work and parental leaves. In Western nations, part-time work has been the norm for mothers of young children, but unfortunately, it is associated almost everywhere with women's low pay and little opportunity for advancement. In Communist countries, part-time work has been politically despised in official circles as being associated with the bourgeois homemaker's role. Yet working women in the Eastern bloc are calling for increasing part-time work as a liberating opportunity rather than an oppressive threat. Paid parental leaves of twelve to fifteen months such as those found in Sweden and Finland constitute a model that advocates are trying to institute in other industrial countries. The challenge facing all of these programs is to help families and children without hurting women's employment. To the extent that child care arrangements or parental leave become sex typed to serve women primarily, they are likely to intensify occupational segregation and pay inequality. The principal safeguard against this tendency is a policy that is gender-neutral in its consideration of working parents.

Social Policies in the Developing Nations

In modernizing countries, the employment and family policies of the advanced industrial nations have their analogs in the economic recovery policies known as structural adjustment. In some societies, structural adjustment policies are critical influences on women's work and the well-being of children and families. These macroeconomic instruments were instituted in the late 1970s and early 1980s by the International Monetary Fund to help debtor nations balance their import and export accounts, cut government spending, and repay their international loans.

The effects on women have not been altogether benign. In many parts of Africa and Latin America, unemployment has risen. Education, health, and other social programs funded by the state have deteriorated because of shrinking funds. Women's access to land and credit, rather than expanding, in some instances has actually worsened as free-market policies strengthen the large landowners (who are mostly men) and further weaken the small holders (who are mostly women).

Yet for true economic recovery to occur, women need to be well integrated into the development process. Urban women should be better prepared to work in the modern sector, and rural women should have the opportunity to increase their efficiency as food producers (Joekes 1987: 139). The needed policies fall into two categories that are similar to those for the developed world: (1) equal opportunity policies in employment, training, and access to capital; and (2) social policies to enhance the quality of women's domestic and reproductive lives.

Equal Access to Education, Employment, and Capital. In many developing countries, female education and training are blatantly discriminatory. Girls are channeled into domestic arts, whereas boys have access to mechanical and industrial training. Women's entry to modern-sector jobs is also severely limited. For rural women, agricultural extension training is often unavailable (Blumberg 1991). In Africa, 60 to 80 percent of all food for domestic consumption is produced by women, but because many rural development projects have bypassed women and put control in men's hands, yields have actually been *decreasing* in recent years. Rae Lesser Blumberg (1991: 116–119) attributes a major part of the African food crisis to inequity of rewards and incentives to women. The provision of equal access to training, jobs, and credit is a major potential strategy for reversing these trends.

Support for Women's Domestic and Reproductive Activities. According to several research studies independently carried out in Latin America, Africa, and India, it is women's higher income particularly that benefits the health and nutritional status of children. Women typically use a greater part of their income (90 to 100 percent) for food and family needs, whereas men generally reserve about 25 percent for their own use (Blumberg 1991: 102–103). A Guatemalan study reports that women's higher income from local food crops has a substantially greater positive impact on children's height and weight than male-controlled income from the new export crops (Von Braun 1989: 208).

The well-being of families and children also is linked to women's improved education and productivity. Two of the most powerful factors in limiting population growth and providing sufficient food are women's education and women's paid work and food-producing activities (Leslie 1989: 40). Thus, the revision of structural adjustment programs to recognize women's key roles in child spacing and family nutrition should take high priority.

Pricing policies also indirectly affect families' and children's well-being in the relative value placed on women's work (such as household food production) compared with the goods produced by men (usually cash crops or tradables). Improving women's food crops such as cassava, yams, and sorghum is a powerful strategy for effecting major gains in children's health and survival (Joekes 1987: 139). Sadly, however, national policies such as military spending, servicing of chronic external debt, and inefficient use of women's productivity are often both wasteful and detrimental to women and families.

CONCLUSION: HOW TO JOIN FEMINISM WITH MODERNITY

At last we return to earlier questions: Why did modernization bring such anomalous results, and what is the outlook for the future? In general, it appears that the tendencies of modern society are at times on a collision course with women's equal rights and the good of their children and families. Women have historically been associated with the values of caring and interdependence that govern the family, whereas men and modernity have stood for the values of mastery and independence that predominate in the workplace. Society needs both functions in order to survive and has managed in the past by allocating the primary caring responsibilities to women and excusing them from paid employment.

The UN Decade for Women articulated the following general ideals in its World Plan of Action published after the 1975 meeting in Mexico City: "The primary objective of development is to bring about sustained improvement in the well-being of the individual and of society and to bestow benefits on all. . . . The integration of women in development will necessitate widening their activities to embrace all aspects of social, economic, political, and cultural life" (Fraser 1987: 36–37).

The modern juxtaposition of work and family life has produced two broad types of social change. The first, a shift in family forms, stems in part from women's overburdening and unequal role sharing with men. The second, a critique of modern culture, points to the need for valuing the quality of life as well as economic advancement and access to power. Both these movements reach beyond women's increased employment or the emergence of family policy. They prefigure change in the very fabric of societies and cultures in which people live.

Changing Patterns of Work and Family Life

Throughout the modern world, divorce rates have risen, fertility has declined, and the number of single mothers has increased (Kamerman and Kahn 1989). Mary Ann Glendon (1989), in her comparative analysis of changes in family law, concludes that these trends result from women's growing representation in the workplace combined with their continued responsibility as primary caregivers for children and families. In Central and Eastern Europe and the Soviet Union, high divorce rates and low fertility appear in part to be women's safety valves against the double burden of paid work and housework and a defense against the alcoholism and dependence of men. Many highly educated contemporary Soviet women, according to Francine Gray (1990), take the view that a husband is an "elective obligation" who is needed for little more than procreation because a woman and her own mother are the ones most likely to bear the real responsibilities for the family.

Women in the developing world also become single parents for somewhat different reasons. Woman migrants, often older daughters, leave kinship ties and a community of informal support to find city jobs or seasonal farm work. The mother who stays behind is further burdened by household and child care chores, animal husbandry, or additional work for cash income that might have been provided by her husband or older daughter (Crummett 1987). Peggy Antrobus (1989: 16) contends that many government programs are predicated on the "super-exploitation" of women's time. When governments shift expenditures away from assisting women in their multiple roles of production and reproduction, they assume that women will continue to serve as caretakers and fill the gaps created by spending cuts to health, education, care of the elderly, and other essential services.

Suzanne Gordon (1991) recently proposed a new U.S. "national care agenda" that would give a greater place to leisure and family life, as in European countries, by restoring the norm of working no more than forty hours a week and guaranteeing at least one-month paid vacation. For the developed nations, the challenge is to protect time in which to enjoy the fruits of one's labors. For all countries, Martha N. Ozawa (1989: 206–207) articulates two objectives that should be on national agendas in the future: (1) the principle of economic and social parity between the sexes; and (2) the principle of sharing the economic costs of raising children between families with children and those without. Neither women nor men would then have to pay a price for gender, and children would be considered a public treasure—the cornerstone of a nation's survival.

Role sharing between men and women and between the generations is the principal way to relieve the continued overburdening of women. One strategy is to reschedule paid work and caretaking work over the life course in alternating spells of primary responsibility. Fathers and mothers might switch off in their primary responsibilities for children, an idea that has been received with some skepticism by those who are concerned that women's careers will suffer more than men's. Time studies from the United States and Europe show some small but encouraging progress in men's assumption of household and family tasks. In general, it appears that the more educated and urban men help more, even in the former Soviet Union where men still enjoy 50 percent more leisure than women.

Incorporation of Women's Traditional Values

To implement role sharing or a national care agenda requires a major attitude change to give more value to reproductive and caring work. The gender gap in recent U.S. voting patterns expresses these values in women's greater support than that of men for peace, economic equality, health, and social needs (Piven 1990). Women are beginning to assert that traditional family values are *public* values.

Yet women's and family values are at odds with the value system of the modern economy. Free-market economies and capitalism are based on a technical or calculating type of rationality, which uses universalistic impersonal means (the market) to reach the goal of making a profit. Classical social theorists such as Sigmund Freud or Max Weber implied that informal claims of family or community were *ir*rational or *non*rational and thus were to be pushed aside as regressive forces (Bologh 1990: 251). In fact, however, the socialization of children has its own rationality, that of nurturing individuals in an intimate human family so that they will become the productive and moral adults expected by modern society. Without families and women's everyday work in families, no modern state can live beyond the present generation (Okin 1989).

Women's future challenge, then, is to extend principles of justice and gender equality into the home. Modern women have gained rights to citizenship, education, control of their own earnings, and headship of families. They now must be protected against oppression in the home (Bourque and Warren 1989).

At the same time, women's humane concerns for giving care to others should be extended to the world at large. Only by coupling women's liberation with human caregiving will it be possible to create a sense of world interdependence that challenges exploitation by the "global assembly line" (Nash 1983a). With interdependence given a larger place in the modern pantheon, women and men will be able to engage in a form of modernization that is liberating for all, a modern world that is sustainable and replicable over time, and a world that makes possible true equality for women.

NOTES

1. Note that this chapter draws on the succeeding chapters for many of its themes but does not cite them specifically.

BIBLIOGRAPHY

Acosta-Belen, Edna, and Christine E. Bose. "From Structural Subordination to Empowerment: Women and Development in Third World Contexts." *Gender and Society* 4, no. 3 (September 1990): 299–320.

Anderson, Margaret L. *Thinking About Women: Sociological and Feminist Perspectives.* New York: Macmillan, 1983.

Antrobus, Peggy. "The Empowerment of Women." In *Women and International Development Annual*, vol. 1, Rita S. Gallin, Marilyn Aronoff, and Anne Ferguson, eds., 189–207. Boulder: Westview Press, 1989.

Berger, Iris. "Gender, Race, and Political Empowerment: South African Canning Workers, 1940–1960." *Gender and Society* 4, no. 3 (September 1990): 398–420.

Blumberg, Rae Lesser. "A Paradigm for Predicting the Position of Women: Policy Implications and Problems." In *Sex Roles and Social Policy*, Jean Lipman-Blumen and Jessie Bernard, eds., 113–142. Newbury Park, Calif.: Sage Publications, 1979.

————. "Toward a Feminist Theory of Development." In *Feminism and Sociological Theory*, Ruth A. Wallace, ed., 161–199. Newbury Park, Calif.: Sage Publications, 1989.

————. "Income Under Female Versus Male Control: Hypothesis from a Theory of Gender Stratification and Data from the Third World." In *Gender, Family, and Economy: The Triple Overlap*, Rae Lesser Blumberg, ed., 97–127. Newbury Park, Calif.: Sage Publications, 1991.

Bologh, Roslyn W. *Love or Greatness: Max Weber and Masculine Thinking—A Feminist Inquiry.* London: Unwin Hyman, 1990.

Boserup, Ester. *Women's Role in Economic Development.* New York: St. Martin's, 1970.

Bourque, Susan C., and Kay B. Warren. "Technology, Gender, and Development." In *Learning About Women: Gender, Politics, and Power*, Jill K. Conway, S. C. Bourque, and Joan W. Scott, eds., 173–197. Ann Arbor: University of Michigan Press, 1989.

Chafetz, Janet Saltzman. *Sex and Advantage: A Comparative, Macro-Structural Theory of Sex Stratification.* Totowa, N.J.: Rowman & Allenheld, 1984.

Cook, Alice, H., Val R. Lorwin, and Arlene Kaplan Daniels, eds. *Women and Trade Unions in Eleven Industrialized Countries.* Philadelphia: Temple University Press, 1984.

Crummett, Maria de los Angeles. "Rural Women and Migration in Latin America." In *Rural Women and State Policy: Feminist Perspectives on Latin American Agricultural Development,* Carmen Diana Deere and Magdalena Leon, eds., 239–260. Boulder: Westview Press, 1987.

Deere, Carmen Diana. "The Latin American Agrarian Reform Experience." In *Rural Women and State Policy: Feminist Perspectives on Latin American Agricultural Development,* Carmen Diana Deere and Magdalena Leon, eds., 165–190. Boulder: Westview Press, 1987.

Deere, Carmen Diana, and Magdalena Leon, eds. *Rural Women and State Policy: Feminist Perspectives on Latin American Agricultural Development.* Boulder: Westview Press, 1987.

Durkheim, Emile. *Division of Labor in Society.* 1893 (reprint). Trans. George Simpson. New York: Macmillan. 1933.

Ecklein, Joan. "Women in the German Democratic Republic: Impact of Culture and Social Policy." In *Women in the Middle Years,* Janet Zollinger Giele, ed., 151–197. New York: Wiley, 1982.

Fernandez-Kelly, M. Patricia. "Broadening the Scope: Gender and International Economic Development." *Sociological Forum* 4, no. 4 (December 1989): 611–635.

Ferree, Myra Marx. "She Works Hard for a Living: Gender and Class on the Job." In *Analyzing Gender: A Handbook of Social Science Research,* Beth B. Hess and Myra Marx Ferree, eds., 332–347. Newbury Park, Calif.: Sage Publications, 1987.

Fraser, Arvonne S. *The U.N. Decade for Women: Documents and Dialogue.* Boulder: Westview Press, 1987.

Gallin, Rita S., Marilyn Aronoff, and Anne Ferguson, eds. "Introduction: Women and International Development: Creating an Agenda." *The Women and International Development Annual,* vol. 1: 1–22. Boulder: Westview Press, 1989.

Giele, Janet Zollinger. "Introduction: Comparative Perspectives on Women." In *Women: Roles and Status in Eight Countries,* J. Z. Giele and A. C. Smock, eds., 1–31. New York: Wiley, 1977.

———. "Women's Movements." *World Book Encyclopedia* 21: 385–390. Chicago: World Book, Inc., 1990.

Giele, Janet Z., and Mary Gilfus. "Race and College Differences in Life Patterns of Educated Women." In *Women and Educational Change,* Joyce Antler and Sari Biklen, eds., 179–197. Albany: SUNY Press, 1990.

Glendon, Mary Ann. *The Transformation of Family Law: State, Law, and Family in the United States and Western Europe.* Chicago: University of Chicago Press, 1989.

Goode, William J. *World Revolution and Family Patterns.* New York: Free Press, 1963.

Gordon, Suzanne. "A National Care Agenda." *Atlantic Monthly* 267 (January 1991): 64–68.

Gray, Francine du Plessix. "Reflections: Soviet Women." *New Yorker,* February 19, 1990, 48 ff.

Green, Susan S. "Silicon Valley's Women Workers: A Theoretical Analysis of Sex Segregation in the Electronics Industry Labor Market." In *Women, Men, and the International Division of Labor,* June Nash and Maria Patricia Fernandez-Kelly, eds., 273–331. Albany: SUNY Press, 1983.

Hartmann, Heidi. "Capitalism, Patriarchy, and Job Segregation by Sex." *Signs* 1, pt. 2 (Spring 1976): 137–169.

Hayes, Cheryl D., John L. Palmer, and Martha J. Zaslow, eds. *Who Cares for America's Children: Child Care Policy for the 1990s.* Washington, D.C.: National Academy Press, 1990.

Jacquette, Jane S. "Women and Modernization Theory: A Decade of Feminist Criticism." *World Politics* 34, no. 2 (January 1982): 267–284.

Janiewski, Dolores. "Flawed Victories: The Experiences of Black and White Women Workers in Durham During the 1930s." In *Decades of Discontent: The Women's Movement 1920–1940,* Lois Scharf and Joan M. Jensen, eds., 85–109. Boston: Northeastern University Press, 1987.

Joekes, Susan P. *Women in the World Economy: An INSTRAW Study.* New York: Oxford University Press, 1987.

Kahne, Hilda. "Civilian Labor Force, 1950–1990." Unpublished table from combined U.S. Department of Labor statistics. Norton, Mass.: Wheaton College, Economics Department, 1990.

Kamerman, Sheila B., and Alfred J. Kahn. *Child Care, Family Benefits and Working Parents.* New York: Columbia University Press, 1981.

_____ . "Single-Parent, Female-Headed Families in Western Europe: Social Change and Response." *International Social Security Review* 42, no. 1 (1989): 3–34.

Lago, Maria Soledad. "Rural Women and the Neo-Liberal Model in Chile." In *Rural Women and State Policy: Feminist Perspectives in Latin American Agricultural Development,* Carmen Diana Deere and Magdalena Leon, eds., 21–34. Boulder: Westview Press, 1987.

Lenski, Gerhard. *Power and Privilege: A Theory of Stratification.* New York: McGraw-Hill, 1966.

Leslie, Joanne. "Women's Work and Child Nutrition in the Third World." In *Women, Work, and Child Welfare in the Third World,* Joanne Leslie and Michael Paolisso, eds., 19–58. Boulder: Westview Press, 1989.

Liljestrom, Rita, Gunilla Furst Mellstrom, and Gillan Liljestrom Svensson. *Roles in Transition: Report of an Investigation Made for the Advisory Council on Equality Between Men and Women.* Stockholm: LiberForlag, 1978.

Lim, Linda Y. C. "Women's Work in Multinational Electronics Factories." In *Women and Technological Change in Developing Countries,* Roslyn Dauber and Melinda L. Cain, eds., 181–190. Boulder: Westview Press, 1981.

_____ . "Capitalism, Imperialism, and Patriarchy: The Dilemma of Third World Women Workers in Multinational Factories." In *Women, Men, and the International Division of Labor,* June Nash and Maria Patricia Fernandez-Kelly, eds., 70–91. Albany: SUNY Press, 1983.

Mandel, William M. *Soviet Women.* New York: Anchor Books, 1975.

Nash, June. "Introduction." In *Women, Men, and the International Division of Labor,* June Nash and Maria Patricia Fernandez-Kelly, eds., vii–xv. Albany: SUNY Press, 1983a.

_____ . "The Impact of the Changing International Division of Labor on Different Sectors of the Labor Force." In *Women, Men, and the International Division of Labor,* June Nash and Maria Patricia Fernandez-Kelly, eds., 3–38. Albany: SUNY Press, 1983b.

_____ . "Latin American Women in the World Capitalist Crisis." *Gender and Society* 4, no. 3 (September 1990): 338–353.

Nuss, Shirley, in collaboration with Ettore Denti and David Viry. *Women in the World of Work: Statistical Analysis and Projections to the Year 2000.* Geneva: International Labor Office, 1989.

Okin, Susan Moller. *Justice, Gender, and the Family.* New York: Basic Books, 1989.

Oppenheimer, Valerie K. *The Female Labor Force in the United States.* Berkeley: University of California, Population Monograph Series no. 5, 1970.

Ozawa, Martha N., ed. *Women's Life Cycle and Economic Insecurity.* Westport, Conn.: Greenwood Press, 1989.

Parsons, Talcott. *Societies: Evolutionary and Comparative Perspectives.* Englewood Cliffs, N.J.: Prentice-Hall, 1966.

Pharr, Susan J. *Political Women in Japan: The Search for a Place in Political Life.* Berkeley: University of California Press, 1981.

Piven, Frances Fox. "Ideology and the State: Women, Power, and the Welfare State." In *Women, the State, and Welfare*, Linda Gordon, ed., 250–264. Madison: University of Wisconsin Press, 1990.

Rix, Sara. *The American Woman, 1990–91: A Status Report.* New York: W. W. Norton, 1990.

Roos, Patricia A. *Gender and Work: A Comparative Analysis of Industrial Societies.* Albany: SUNY Press, 1985.

Safa, Helen Icken. "Women's Social Movements in Latin America." *Gender and Society* 4, no. 3 (September 1990): 354–369.

Sivard, Ruth. *Women . . . A World Survey.* Washington, D.C.: World Priorities, 1985.

Sokoloff, Natalie J. *Between Money and Love: The Dialectics of Women's Home and Market Work.* New York: Praeger, 1980.

Standing, Guy. *Labor Force Participation and Development.* Geneva: International Labor Office, 1981.

———. "Global Feminization Through Flexible Labor." *World Development* 17, no. 7 (July 1989): 1,077–1,095.

Stevenson, Mary Huff. "Wage Differences Between Men and Women: Economic Theories." In *Women Working: Theories and Facts in Perspective*, Ann H. Stromberg and Shirley Harkess, eds., 89–107. Palo Alto, Calif.: Mayfield Publishing Co., 1978.

Tiano, Susan. "Gender, Work, and World Capitalism: Third World Women's Role in Development." In *Analyzing Gender, A Handbook of Social Science Research*, Beth B. Hess and Myra Marx Ferree, eds., 216–243. Newbury Park, Calif.: Sage Publications, 1987.

United Nations. *The World's Women 1970–1990: Trends and Statistics.* New York: United Nations, 1991.

U.S. Department of Labor. *Employment and Earnings.* Washington, D.C.: Bureau of Labor Statistics, January 1989.

———. *Facts on Working Women.* Washington, D.C.: Women's Bureau, October 1990.

Von Braun, Joachim. "Effects of New Export Crops in Smallholder Agriculture on Division of Labor and Child Nutritional Status in Guatemala." In *Women, Work, and Child Welfare in the Third World*, Joanne Leslie and Michael Paolisso, eds., 201–216. Boulder: Westview Press, 1989.

Ward, Kathryn, ed. "Women in the Global Economy." In *Women and Work: An Annual Review*, Barbara A. Gutek, Ann H. Stromberg, and Laurie Larwood, eds., vol 3: 1–17. Newbury Park, Calif.: Sage Publications, 1988.

———. *Women Workers and Global Restructuring.* Ithaca, N.Y.: ILR Press, 1990.

Weber, Max. *The Protestant Ethic and the Spirit of Capitalism.* 1904–1905 (reprint). Trans. Talcott Parsons. New York: Charles Scribner's, 1958.

Youssef, Nadia Haggag. *Women and Work in Developing Societies.* Berkeley: University of California, Population Monograph Series, no. 15, Institute of International Studies, 1974.

2

Women's Work, Women's Lives: A Comparative Economic Perspective

FRANCINE D. BLAU
MARIANNE A. FERBER

The status of women has many varied dimensions, some not directly measurable. We focus on a number of important measurable indicators that primarily reflect women's economic position: labor force participation, occupational distribution, earnings, education, and the allocation of time between the labor market and the household. Although we do not believe that these indicators summarize all that is of interest or that is sufficient for improving women's status in the larger society, we believe progress in the economic sphere is a necessary, although not sufficient, first step for progress in other respects.

In each case, attention is focused on women's status relative to men's so that data are presented, for instance, not merely on women's jobs and wages but on gender differences in occupations and earnings. This approach implicitly controls for differences across countries that affect men and women similarly and highlights the more significant gender differences that are apt to affect women's control over their own lives as well as their influence in the family and the larger community. Large differences are found among countries and regions in the size of the gender gap with respect to these measures. Two generalizations hold, however. First, women have not achieved full equality anywhere. At the same time, particularly in the advanced industrialized countries for which data on the relevant variables are more readily available, there is evidence of a reduction in gender differences in economic roles and outcomes.

LABOR FORCE PARTICIPATION

Women's labor force participation is an important determinant of their economic position and therefore is examined first. Women who do not work outside the household benefit from whatever standard of living their families reach, but they cannot expect to achieve status in their own right and rarely will have their own sources of income or enjoy economic independence. As Susan P. Joekes (1987: 21) observes,

> It is increasingly accepted that receipt of direct money earnings does indeed mark an improvement in status. . . . Paid work is perceived to make a higher contribution to the family's channeling of money to the household and so goes along with a larger say in household decisions; also, payment of money can carry conversely a threat of withdrawal of that money, which gives the earner greater bargaining power within the household. Increased status confers better material provision, that is, increased claims on the share of consumer goods within the household, and so the link is established between employment status and economic benefit. Aggregative empirical analysis confirms this, in the . . . contrast between Africa and Asia, between Southeast Asia and South Asia, and between South and North India, for example, where in each case the relative material position of women is better in the first place than in the second, in association with a higher rate of female participation in the recorded labor force. Numerous case studies point to the importance of outside employment in improving the treatment that women get in society in general and in the household in particular.

Research in the United States also has confirmed the relevance of labor force participation for women's position in the family (Nieva 1985: 164). Gainful employment thus may be regarded as a step in the direction of equality.

Almost all countries publish data, at least intermittently, on the proportion of women who are economically active. But comparing these statistics can produce misleading results. Published data on labor force participation are influenced by such factors as the age range of the population included, the number of years young people spend in school, the typical retirement age, the age distribution of the population, and whether workers in subsistence agriculture are included. For comparative purposes, it therefore is advisable to use the ratio of women's to men's labor force participation.[1] Distortions still result, however, because of differences in the treatment of men and women. For example, women working in family enterprises, who often are classified as "unpaid family workers," must work more hours in order to be included in the labor force than men who are generally classified as self-employed.[2] Because the countries in which female labor force participation is relatively low are also the ones that tend to relegate women to the category of unpaid family workers rather than classifying them as self-employed, it is possible that differences in women's work between countries are overstated.[3] Nonetheless, there can be little doubt that these are substantial.

Table 2.1 shows the data on participation for 1950, 1980, and 1985 to 1987 for countries grouped by region because of generally similar characteristics. The range within each of the groups also is indicated. As measured by the official statistics, labor force participation of women by region varies from about 20 percent to almost 80 percent of that of men. The evidence is consistent with the proposition that both economic and noneconomic factors help to determine women's role in the labor market.

TABLE 2.1 Ratio of Women's to Men's Labor Force Participation by World Region, 1950-1988[a]

Group	1950[b] Mean	1980[b] Mean	High	Low	1985 to 1988[c] Mean	High	Low
I Eastern Europe	56.7	75.1	85.4	59.5	79.4	88.9	62.1
II Caribbean	53.6	63.7	82.8	32.2	63.0	76.8	40.5
III Sub-Saharan Africa	65.8	62.5	96.7	19.6	—	—	—
IV East Asia	45.8	56.6	89.5	38.2	60.9	81.2	47.4
V Advanced industrialized nations	36.8	55.6	81.2	29.8	64.3	94.5	43.6
VI Latin America	21.5	33.1	44.3	16.4	44.7	66.3	29.4
VII North Africa, Middle East, South-Central Asia	15.0	19.2	55.7	7.1	20.7	43.5	11.3

[a] With the exception of Sub-Saharan Africa, only countries that provided data for all three years are included.

[b] Data are for the economically active population age ten and over, relative to the total population.

[c] Data are for the most recently available year between 1985 and 1988, in most cases for the population age ten and over. Data for Sub-Saharan Africa are not included because they were available for only a few countries and tended to vary erratically relative to previous values. Data for Eastern Europe are from the last year before the dramatic changes of 1989.

Sources: Years 1950 and 1980 from *Economically Active Population: Estimates and Projections 1950-2025* (Geneva: International Labour Office, 1986); Years 1985-1988 from ILO, *Yearbook of Labour Statistics,* 1988, 1985-1989, and 1989-1990; and United Nations, *Demographic Yearbook* (New York: United Nations, 1988).

A number of models have been developed concerning the relationship between economic development and women's labor force participation. One particularly plausible model suggests that female labor force participation declines in the early stages of economic development, then rises at later stages (Durand 1975). Relatively high participation by women may occur in preindustrial economies because of women's participation in family farms and enterprises. With industrialization, the shift of the locus of employment out of the home and into the factory and office tends to be associated with a relative decline in women's participation. However, with further development women are drawn increasingly into market employment.

At least two reasons can be identified for this positive association between female labor force participation and economic development in later stages. First, research in the United States and elsewhere has shown that an increase in the wages women can potentially earn in market employment increases the probability that they will enter the labor force (Layard and Mincer 1985). The tendency of women to substitute market work for housework as their wages rise outweighs the positive income effect on the demand for leisure of their husbands' higher earnings. Thus, the rising real wages of both men and women that occur in the course of economic development tend to induce increasingly more women to work for pay. Rising educational attainment of women and shifts from goods-producing to service economies tend to have similar effects because they increase the potential wages women can earn in the market.

Second, female labor force participation has been shown to be negatively related to the number of children present, especially in industrialized countries where paid work is not readily combined with child care. Hence, as birth rates decline in the course of development, female labor force participation tends to increase. An additional factor is that the market increasingly provides many of the goods and services that formerly were produced in the home. Both of these changes tend to decrease the value of women's time spent in the home and to encourage labor force participation.

The data in Table 2.1 are broadly consistent with this view of the relationship between economic development and labor force participation. Between 1950 and 1980, the ratio of economically active women to economically active men declined somewhat in sub-Saharan Africa, which is composed of countries at very early stages of economic development, whereas it increased in varying degrees in the rest of the world. Particularly large increases in the ratio occurred in the advanced industrialized nations. It appears that with the exception of the Caribbean countries, the trend toward rising participation has persisted into the 1980s.

Government policies also appear to play a role. For instance, when there is a progressive tax system, women married to men with high incomes have more incentive to enter the labor market when husband and wife are taxed as individuals—so the tax rate of each is not influenced by the earnings of the other—than when they are taxed as a couple. As another example, when child care is subsidized by the government, mothers of young children are more likely to seek employment. Such features of government policy most likely contribute to the exceptionally high ratio of female to male labor force participation in Sweden. In the late 1980s the ratio was 94.5 percent in Sweden compared with an average of 65.3 percent overall for the advanced industrialized countries.

The implication of such analyses is that the allocation of women's time between work at home and work in the market is a rational response to economic conditions. This is not the whole story, however. To the extent that education and fertility are influenced by labor force participation, they do not provide an independent explanation; to the extent that they are independent and influence labor force participation, the question remains why they as well as government policies differ as much as they do across countries. No such problems arise with respect to wage rates as explanatory variables because they are presumably determined by economic conditions, including the stage of economic development. The influence of wage rates on labor force partici-pation, however, varies considerably among countries (Mincer 1985). Simi-larly, there are substantial variations in women's labor force participation among countries with economies at roughly similar stages of economic devel-opment. For example, the ratio of female to male participation is considerably higher in the Caribbean (63.0 percent) and East Asian countries (60.9 percent) than in Latin America (44.7 percent) despite roughly similar levels of devel-opment. As another example, the participation ratio is higher in Eastern Europe (79.4 percent) than in the advanced industrialized nations (64.3 percent), although the level of development of the former is lower on average. Finally, the Group VII countries—those in North Africa, the Middle East, and South-Central Asia—have an average participation ratio (20.7 percent in the late 1980s) far below that of any other group.

Some of these differences may be related to the nature of economic development. This might explain, for example, the high ratio of labor force participation of women to men in the Caribbean (63.0 percent), where tourism is a major industry, and the low participation ratio in such countries as Iran (11.9 percent) and Kuwait (37.4 percent), whose economies are dominated by oil production. However, it is also likely that noneconomic factors such as ideology and religion exert a considerable influence on women's labor force status (Blau and Ferber 1986; Ferber and Berg 1991).

Universalist egalitarian standards, such as are professed in socialist coun-tries, generally appear to be positively related to women's role in the labor market. Thus, a more equal distribution of income (Semyonov 1980) and a larger share of resources allocated to social welfare (Weiss, Ramirez, and Tracy 1976) have been found to be associated with higher levels of labor force participation of women—as, for example, in the Scandinavian countries. Similarly, Marxist ideology, which strongly advocates women's entry into the work force, helps to explain the high participation ratios that have existed in Eastern Europe.

On the other hand, Group VII countries, with an average participation ratio of only 20.7 percent, consist entirely of Muslim countries, which have emphasized women's roles as wives and mothers to the virtual exclusion of activities outside the home. Similarly, Catholicism is the prevalent faith in Latin America, where the participation ratio also is relatively low (44.7 percent). For the most part, women also are less likely to be employed in the Catholic countries of Southern Europe than in the Protestant countries of Western Europe. The unweighted average of the ratio of women's to men's labor force participation in the eight countries in which 80 percent or more of the population is Catholic is 57.6; in the seven countries in which 80 percent or more are Protestant, it is 72.2.

OCCUPATIONAL SEGREGATION

Women's economic status is undoubtedly influenced not only by their labor force participation per se but also by their occupations and how much they are paid, two facets that are not unrelated. Again, women's occupational distribution compared with that of men is of interest. Table 2.2 shows the extent of occupational segregation by sex, measured by an index that equals the percentage of men or women who would have to change jobs in order for the distribution of men and women by occupational category to be the same. The index is computed across the seven broad occupational categories for which data are available: professional, technical, and kindred workers; administrative, executive, and managerial workers; clerical workers; sales workers; farmers, fishermen, loggers, and related workers; craftsmen, production-process workers, and laborers (not elsewhere classified); and service, sports, and recreation workers.

The degree of segregation varies widely, but it is substantial in most of the countries. U.S. studies suggest that the extent of measured occupational segregation is greater when a more detailed occupational breakdown is used (e.g., Beller 1984; Baron and Bielby 1984). Thus, the highly aggregated nature of the occupational classification scheme used in Table 2.2 would tend to understate the magnitude of segregation. A particular problem is that the category "farmers, fishermen, loggers, and related workers" continues to include a large proportion of the economically active men and women in many developing countries. For instance, the percent of the labor force in this sector is 64 in Thailand, 56 in Indonesia, and 54 in Ghana. As a result, the index of occupational segregation is very low in these countries, ranging from 10 percent in Thailand to 21 percent in Ghana. At the same time, agricultural work encompasses many different kinds of tasks. The data do not show the extent of gender differentiation among these tasks.

It is also interesting to examine two of the advanced industrialized economies with very low segregation indexes. In Japan 10 percent of economically active women, compared with 7 percent of men, are in agriculture. In Portugal this is true for 27 percent of women and 18 percent of men. It may be due to this tradition of participation in physical work in the farm sector that women in these countries constitute a relatively large minority among production workers. In Japan 26 percent of women and 42 percent of men and in Portugal 21 percent of women and 43 percent of men are in the production sector compared with 41 percent of men and only 11 percent of women in the United States.

Among the four countries with unusually high indexes of occupational segregation, the three Middle Eastern countries of Bahrain, Qatar, and the United Arab Emirates have highly unusual economies, with virtually no agricultural sectors and a heavy concentration in the oil industry in which virtually no women are employed. The situation in the fourth country, Panama, is somewhat different. The high degree of segregation there is due to the low representation of women among both agricultural and production workers, the two categories that contain 65 percent of male workers.

We know little about what causes the wide variations in occupational segregation shown in Table 2.2. The data show no clear tendency for segregation rates to be smaller in the countries in which women's labor force

TABLE 2.2 Occupational Segregation by Major Occupational Category for World Region, 1980s[a]

Region	Occupational Segregation Index	Region	Occupational Segregation Index
I Eastern Europe	31.3	Belgium	38.5
Bulgaria	26.2	Canada	39.8
Czechoslovakia	32.7[b]	Denmark	48.0
Hungary	34.8	Finland	42.7
Poland	30.7[b]	France	38.4
Yugoslavia	32.1	Germany, Federal Republic	36.9
		Gibraltar	42.4
II Caribbean	41.7	Greece	25.4
Bahamas	41.0	Ireland	49.3
Barbados	31.6	Israel	42.1
Belize	55.9	Japan	23.2
Bermuda	41.7	Luxembourg	48.9
French Guyana	39.8	Netherlands	38.5
Grenada	32.8	New Zealand	41.5
Guyana	47.1	Norway	46.3
Haiti	35.3	Portugal	26.0
Montserrat	49.2	South Africa	45.6
Netherland Antilles	50.6	Spain	36.4
St. Christopher and Nevis	33.1	Sweden	41.7
St. Lucia	34.2	Switzerland	39.3
St. Pierre and Miquelon	45.6	United Kingdom	44.5
St. Vincent and the Grenadines	39.0	United States	36.6
Trinidad & Tobago	46.7		
Turks and Caicos	34.2	**VI Latin America**	43.5
Virgin Island (British)	57.1	Chile	49.4[c]
Virgin Islands (American)	36.3	Colombia	32.4
		Costa Rica	42.5
III Sub-Saharan Africa	20.5	Cuba	45.7
Botswana	27.0	Dominica	46.7
Burundi	10.1[b]	Dominican Republic	48.6
Cameroon	22.2[b]	Ecuador	46.5
Central African Republic	18.6[b]	Guatemala	57.2
Comoros	14.8	Mexico	39.0
Gambia	22.3	Panama	53.2
Ghana	20.8	Paraguay	46.4
Liberia	25.1	Peru	30.2
Togo	11.9	Puerto Rico	36.1
Zambia	29.7	Uruguay	30.8
Zimbabwe	23.2	Venezuela	48.6
IV East Asia	17.9	**VII North Africa, Middle East,**	
China	9.7	**South Central Asia**	43.0
Hong Kong	15.0	Bahrain	57.9
India	19.8	Brunei	41.7
Indonesia	13.7	Egypt	24.6
Korea, Republic of	17.8	Iraq	47.8[b]
Malaysia	16.0	Kuwait	51.1
Philippines	35.8	Pakistan	18.6
Singapore	26.6[c]	Qatar	62.3
Sri Lanka	14.7	Syria	45.9
Thailand	9.9	Tunisia	19.3[b]
		Turkey	43.2
V Advanced Industrialized Nations	39.5	United Arab Emirates	60.2
Australia	31.9		
Austria	44.5		

[a]Data are for the 1980s, unless otherwise indicated. Data for Eastern Europe are from the period before the radical changes of 1989. Bangladesh was omitted because the data for 1981 show occupational segregation of 0.1 percent, entirely out of line with data for earlier years.
[b]Data are from the 1970s.
[c]Employees only.

Source: Calculated from data in International Labour Organization, *Yearbook of Labour Statistics* (Geneva: International Labour Office, 1988, 1989-1990 and 1945-1989).

participation is greater, although it would be reasonable to expect male and female occupational distributions to be more similar in countries in which their patterns of labor force participation are more alike. For example, among advanced industrialized countries, the segregation ratio is relatively high in the Scandinavian countries; the participation ratio is 81.2 percent in Denmark, 81.5 percent in Finland, and 94.5 percent in Sweden. But it is equally high in countries with considerably lower participation ratios, such as Austria with 58.9 percent, the United Kingdom with 67.0 percent, and Ireland with 43.6 percent. Similarly, among developing countries occupational segregation is very low both in Thailand, where the ratio of women's to men's labor force participation is 81.2 percent, and in Indonesia, where it is 63.0 percent.

Although occupational structure plays a part in determining the extent of occupational segregation, there also are considerable variations in the representation of women in the same occupation, and these are not necessarily explained by differences in technology. For instance, the agricultural sector is heavily mechanized in both North America and Eastern Europe, yet women constitute a much larger proportion of agricultural workers in the latter. Similarly, there is a very large representation of women among clerical workers in most developed countries, whereas they are a small minority in many developing countries. Neither economic factors alone nor inherent differences between women and men can explain these incongruities. Again, traditions, norms, and even religious beliefs appear to play a part.

What is the likely future of occupational segregation? There is, on the one hand, evidence of some decline in such segregation over the last fifteen to twenty years in the United States and other industrialized countries (Beller 1984; Blau and Hendricks 1979; Blau 1988; OECD 1985). On the other hand, some occupations that have experienced rapid influxes of women are now in danger of becoming segregated again because they are becoming increasingly female (Reskin and Hartmann 1986; Strober 1984). Overall, a reversal of recent downward trends appears to be unlikely, but so does acceleration of the slow decline.

EARNINGS GAP

How much women earn compared to men is one of the main determinants of women's status. Unfortunately, obtaining comparable information for men's and women's earnings for different countries presents a number of difficulties. Among those nations that provide earnings data, some apply to workers in all nonagricultural sectors; others apply to manufacturing only; and they variously provide hourly, daily, weekly, or monthly wages. Additionally, especially for some of the developing countries, the ratio of women's to men's wages varies so erratically over time that one must discount the reliability of the information.[4]

A number of advanced industrialized nations, however, have published reliable hourly earnings for male and female workers in manufacturing over the past several decades. These data, shown in Table 2.3, provide comparisons

TABLE 2.3   Ratio of Women's to Men's Hourly Earnings in Manufacturing, 1950-1987

	1950	1978	1987
Australia	.66	.80	.80
Belgium	.60	.71	.74
Denmark	.64[a]	.86	.84
Finland	.65	.75	.77
France	n.a.	.77	.79
Germany (F.R.)	.64	.73	.73
Greece	.65[b]	.69	.78
Ireland	.58	.64	.67
Luxembourg	.55[c]	.60	.61
Netherlands	.61	.76	.79[d]
New Zealand	.63[a]	.73	.72
Norway	.66	.80	.84
Sweden	.70	.89	.90
Switzerland	.65	.66	.67
United Kingdom	.60	.69	.68
United States	n.a.	.61	.71[e]

[a]1953,   [b]1961.   [c]1966,   [d]1986.   [e]1983.

Sources: Data for 1950 and 1987 are from ILO, *Yearbook of Labour Statistics* (Geneva: International Labour Office), various issues. U.S. data are for weekly wages adjusted for hours (O'Neill 1985). Data for 1978 are from OECD, *Economic Outlook: Historical Statistics 1960-1987* (Paris: Organisation for Economic Co-operation and Development, 1988).

for sixteen countries for 1950, 1978, and 1987. Although in each instance men earn more than women, the earnings gap is far from uniform even among this relatively homogeneous set of countries. But they do have one thing in common: Between 1950 and 1987, the ratio of women's to men's wages rose in every instance for which data are available, albeit by no means to the same extent. Estimates for the United States go back only to 1955, but no sign of progress is evident prior to the late 1970s or early 1980s (Blau and Ferber 1986). Thus, unlike the other countries in which most of the change took place before 1978, for the United States and Greece the increase in the ratio occurs largely after 1978.

The timing of the decline of the earnings gap in the United States—which did not occur until the late 1970s or early 1980s—has led James P. Smith and Michael P. Ward (1984) to argue that it did not reflect the impact of the government's antidiscrimination efforts initiated ten to fifteen years earlier. The implication of this line of argument is that government interference is neither necessary nor desirable. The facts, however, are open to the alternative interpretation that it was earlier legislation in part that encouraged and enabled women to improve their position in the labor market. Further, a number of studies of some of the countries in which the earnings gap closed much more rapidly, including the United Kingdom and Australia, conclude that government policies were clearly instrumental in bringing about this improvement in women's wages (Chiplin, Curran, and Parsley 1980; Gregory, Daly, and Ho

1986; Kessler 1983; Sullerot 1975; Vansgnes 1971; Zabalza and Tzannatos 1985).

An additional factor affecting intercountry differences in the gender earnings gap is the extent of wage inequality in each country. A recent paper by Francine D. Blau and Lawrence M. Kahn (1992) finds that although U.S. women compare favorably with women in other industrialized countries on several measures of skill relative to men, their earnings relative to men are reduced by the much larger wage penalty the U.S. labor market places on those with below-average levels of market skills. The higher level of wage inequality in the United States fully accounts for the lower gender ratio in comparison with the Scandinavian countries and Australia, the countries with the smallest gaps.

EDUCATION

Women's labor force participation, occupations, and earnings are all expected to be related to their level of education. There are a number of determinants of cross-country differences in educational levels. Because more-highly educated women tend to get better jobs, to earn more, and to be less likely to become unemployed, women who plan to be in the labor force have more incentive to acquire education. Thus, the ratio of girls to boys in secondary schools would be expected to vary by labor force participation. Also, in the more affluent countries, education at the primary and secondary levels often is universally available and compulsory. In such instances there is likely to be little gender difference in educational attainment at these levels regardless of women's work roles. In fact, when labor force participation is low, education for girls in these countries is often rationalized as good preparation for their roles as wives and mothers. In the United States, historically girls were more likely to complete high school than boys (Blau and Ferber 1986), probably because their opportunity cost of attending school was lower due to their generally lower market wages. This gender difference was narrowed, however, as labor market options for individuals without a high school diploma have greatly diminished. There may, of course, be differences by gender in field of specialization that are related to the substantial differences in occupations discussed earlier.[5]

As can be seen in Table 2.4, there are large variations in the ratios of boys to girls in secondary school both within and across regions. Our discussion above suggests that some of this variation is related to level of income. The fact that this is the case may be seen in Table 2.5, where countries are grouped by level of per-capita gross national product (GNP). Although 94 percent of countries with a per-capita GNP of $10,000 or more had a ratio of girls to boys in secondary school of 90 percent or more, this was true of only 34 percent of countries with per-capita GNPs below $2,000. Similarly, whereas none of the high-income countries had a ratio below 70 percent, this was true of 41 percent of the low-income countries. There is also considerable variation among low-income countries, however. As Table 2.5 shows, among these

TABLE 2.4   Ratio of Girls to Boys in Secondary School by World Region, 1980s

	Region	Mean	High	Low
I	Eastern Europe	103	127	92
II	Caribbean	100	105	92
III	Sub-Saharan Africa	68	118	37
IV	East Asia	85	108	43
V	Advanced industrialized nations	100	105	93
VI	Latin America	100	107	86
VII	North Africa, Middle East, South-Central Asia	78	120	50

Source: Calculated using data from United Nations, Statistical Yearbook (New York: United Nations, 1988).

countries gender differences in education, like those in labor force participation, appear to be related to religion and tend to be largest in Muslim and Animist countries. Although the ratio of girls to boys in secondary school was 90 percent or more in 64 percent of the Christian countries and 60 percent of the other countries, this was the case in only 5 percent of the Muslim countries and none of the Animist countries.

HOUSEWORK

Thus far, we have discussed work that is included in official labor force statistics, which is work done for pay or profit and in most countries also includes subsistence farming. Housework is excluded, however, even though it provides goods and services that add greatly to the comforts of life and often are crucial to its maintenance. Some information is available that shows women tend to do most of the housework and that the total amount of time expended on it is considerable.

Table 2.6 shows the pattern of time spent on housework and market work by men and women in eight industrialized countries in various years for which data are available. The pattern is broadly similar across countries. Men spend considerably more time on market work and women spend far more on housework, although the total amount of time spent on both together is generally roughly comparable. Unfortunately, these data are not available separately by women's employment status. However, data from the United States suggests that although employed women spend less time on housework than women who do not work outside the home, they continue to do the bulk of the housework and to spend a considerable amount of time on household tasks. At the same time, a husband's time spent on housework does not vary according to the work status of the wife. To the extent that this pattern is generalizable, and anecdotal evidence strongly suggests that this is the case,

TABLE 2.5 Ratio of Girls to Boys in Secondary School by Per-Capita GNP and Religion

	GNP	
Ratio of Girls to Boys	$10,000 or more (%)	Less than $2,000 (%)
100 or more	62.5	21.6
90-99	31.2	12.2
80-89	6.2	10.8
70-79	0.0	14.9
60-69	0.0	16.2
59 or less	0.0	24.3
	(n=16)	(n=74)

	Religion (GNP less than $2,000)			
	Animist (%)	Christian (%)	Muslim (%)	Other (%)
100 or more	0.0	46.4	0.0	30.0
90-99	0.0	17.9	5.3	30.0
80-89	23.5	7.1	5.3	10.0
70-79	11.8	10.7	31.6	10.0
60-69	23.5	10.7	15.8	10.0
59 or less	41.2	7.1	42.1	10.0
	(n=17)	(n=28)	(n=19)	(n=10)

Sources: Data on GNP from *World Military Expenditures and Arms Transfers 1986* (Washington, D.C.: U.S. Arms Control and Disarmament Agency, 1987); data on education from United Nations, *Statistical Yearbook* (New York: United Nations, 1988); data on religion from *World in Figures* (Boston: G. K. Hall, 1988).

it is reasonable to assume that the disparity in men's and women's time spent on housework revealed in the aggregate figures prevails, although to a lesser extent, for families with employed wives. This is of concern because the additional time and energy women spend at home is likely to inhibit their progress in the labor market, particularly if they accommodate household demands by working part time.

There are considerable cross-country differences, however, in the ratio of men's to women's hours of housework ranging, for the most recent year, from 11.3 percent for Japan to 56.9 percent for Sweden. Swedish men spend nearly 15 hours more per week on housework than do Japanese men, whereas average hours of housework are similar for women in the two countries. In addition, in each of the five countries for which data also are available for a year ten to twenty years earlier—Denmark, Japan, Norway, the United States, and the USSR—the amount of time men spent on housework increased to some extent over the period, whereas their time spent in market work

TABLE 2.6 Time Spent on Housework and Market Work in Eight Industrialized Nations (hours per week)

		Total Work		Housework		Market Work	
		Men	Women	Men	Women	Men	Women
Denmark	1964	45.4	43.4	3.7	30.1	41.7	13.3
	1987	46.2	43.9	12.8	23.1	33.4	20.8
Finland	1979	57.8	61.1	13.8	28.6	44.0	32.5
Hungary	1977	63.7	68.9	12.9	33.8	50.8	35.1
Japan	1965	60.5	64.7	2.8	31.5	57.7	33.2
	1985	55.5	55.6	3.5	31.0	52.0	24.6
Norway	1971	53.2	54.6	15.4	41.3	37.8	13.3
	1980	51.0	50.6	16.8	33.0	34.2	17.6
Sweden	1984	57.9	55.5	18.1	31.8	39.8	23.7
United States	1965	63.1	60.9	11.5	41.8	51.6	18.9
	1981	57.8	54.4	13.8	30.5	44.0	23.9
USSR[a]	1965	64.4	75.3	9.8	31.5	54.6	43.8
	1985	65.7	66.3	11.9	27.0	53.8	39.3

[a] Sample from city of Pskov.

Source: Adapted from F. Thomas Juster and Frank P. Stafford, "The Allocation of Time: Empirical Findings, Behavioral Models, and Problems of Measurement," *Journal of Economic Literature* 29, No.2 (June 1991): 477.

decreased. With the exception of Japan and the USSR, the opposite trends prevailed for women.

These findings of cross-country variations and intertemporal trends suggest that the allocation of housework between men and women is responsive to some extent to changes in women's labor force roles as well as to government policies. In most of the countries for which data are available, there appears to be some movement—albeit to varying degrees—toward greater equality in the household, corresponding to the gradual increase in women's opportunities in the workplace (Juster and Stafford 1991). Only as this movement continues will women be able to take advantage of these opportunities more fully.

Information on developing nations is considerably more sparse; perhaps the best source is various essays in Luisella Goldschmidt-Clermont (1987), although even here data are provided for only Bangladesh, Cameroon, Mexico, Nepal, and Venezuela, and these are based mainly on small local or regional surveys. The number of hours per week women spend on domestic work ranges from 18.9 in Cameroon to 49.0 in Mexico. The figures for men again are considerably lower, varying from 1.4 in Cameroon to 18.9 in Mexico. Overall, there seems to be no reason to doubt that throughout the world, women do the bulk of the housework. On the other hand, women's labor force participation everywhere also tends to be lower than men's.

SPECIAL PROBLEMS OF WOMEN
IN DEVELOPING COUNTRIES

Just as girls constitute a smaller proportion of students in secondary schools in countries with lower levels of income, a number of studies in developing countries in which women have low status show that girls receive particularly inadequate care and nutrition (Ravindran 1986; Waldron 1986; Weinberger and Heligman 1987). These are only two examples that indicate that women tend to be better off at a higher level of per-capita income, whether or not they have achieved a high degree of equality with men, and that they tend to be doubly disadvantaged in poor countries when they are also the objects of sex discrimination. Thus, the issue of equality is not merely an indulgence of middle-class women in affluent societies but can be a matter of great urgency for poor women in developing countries as well. At the same time, the wasted potential of women who are not given the opportunity to develop and fully use their productive capacity is a particularly serious loss in these nations.

A recent study of 144 countries (Ferber and Berg 1991) confirmed earlier research that showed a positive relationship between women's labor force participation and the ratio of women to men in the population. Unlike other authors who have emphasized that it is a surplus of women as compared to men that causes women to seek employment (Guttentag and Secord 1983; Grossbard-Shechtman 1985; Ward and Pampel 1985), this study points out that women, when they are primarily "only" wives and mothers and not seen as economically active, are so shortchanged in the allocation of resources that their chances for survival are reduced. To the extent that these conclusions are correct, they suggest that women's economic status is likely to be better when they are employed than when they are full-time homemakers.

CONCLUSION

This chapter has provided a broad overview of women's economic status, examining specifically such important issues as labor force participation, occupational segregation, earnings, education, and the amount of time spent on housework. The picture that emerges is complex. Large differences among countries and regions make generalizations difficult. Nonetheless, two conclusions are warranted. First, nowhere have women achieved equality with men. However, particularly in the advanced industrialized countries in which data on the relevant variables are more readily available, there is evidence of a reduction in gender differences in economic roles and outcomes. It is likely that these changes will continue and possibly accelerate over time as alterations in women's and, to a lesser extent, in men's work and family roles reinforce each other. Nonetheless, there also is reason for concern with the slow pace of change and with how it has everywhere fallen far short of the ultimate goal of equality.

It appears that basic attitudes about gender roles and especially about the roles of men and women in the family are deep-seated and difficult to change. Economic conditions and laws, where appropriately enforced, have increased women's opportunities in the labor market, improved their access to education, and reduced the earnings gap. The division of household responsibilities and resources within the household, on the other hand, is not as readily amenable to change. As long as women but not men have household responsibilities, whether or not they also are wage earners, the goal of equality for women in the economy as well as in the home is likely to remain elusive.

NOTES

1. This is preferable to using the proportion of the labor force that is female because it is not influenced by the sex ratio of the population.

2. It has been suggested that persons producing goods and services for use within their own households also should be included in the labor force (Beneria 1981). A case can be made, of course, that providing goods and services directly is no less productive than earning money to purchase commodities. However, as is suggested in our discussion above, labor force participation as conventionally defined confers greater relative status on women because it enables them to gain control over money. It is this enhancement of relative status that we wish to measure. Hence the conventional definition is most appropriate for our purposes.

3. It may be that women's participation in all types of family enterprises tends to be understated especially in societies in which any role other than that of wife and mother is frowned on. However, Gunnar Myrdal (1968) observed that in Muslim countries such as Pakistan, where measured female participation is very low, women also play a less active role outside the home, even in agricultural work. Similarly, Nadia H. Youssef (1971) suggested that women tend to avoid activities to which a stigma is attached. In sub-Saharan African countries, on the other hand, where measured participation is higher, women do a large share of farm work (Boserup 1970).

4. For instance, the ratio was 82.4 in 1976, 96.9 in 1977, and 86.9 in 1978 for Burma; 63.1 in 1977 and 91.7 in 1978 for Egypt; and 77.4 in 1976 and 55.6 in 1977 in Kenya (International Labour Organization Yearbook, various issues).

5. These points are illustrated by a recent Organization of Economic Cooperation and Development (OECD) (1985: 10) study, which found that in the advanced industrialized countries covered in the study, there has been marked and near-universal growth of female enrollments in higher education but that in many countries, rigid division by gender in terms of field of specialization continues to be apparent. In some countries, however, such as the United States, there recently has been a significant influx of young women into career-oriented fields, presumably as their labor force attachment has increased.

BIBLIOGRAPHY

Baron, James N., and William T. Bielby. "A Woman's Place Is with Other Women: Sex Segregation in the Work Place," in Barbara F. Reskin, ed., *Sex Segregation in the Workplace: Trends, Explanations, and Remedies*, 27–55. Washington, D.C.: National Academy Press, 1984.

Beller, Andrea H. "Trends in Occupational Segregation by Sex and Race: 1960–1981," in Barbara F. Reskin, ed., *Sex Segregation in the Workplace: Trends, Explanations, and Remedies*, 11–26. Washington, D.C.: National Academy Press, 1984.

Beneria, Lourdes. "Conceptualizing the Labor Force: The Underestimation of Women's Economic Activities," in Nici Nelson, ed., *African Women in the Development Process*. London: Frank Cass and Company, 1981, 10–28.

Blau, Francine D. "Occupational Segregation by Gender: A Look at the 1980s." Paper presented at the American Economic Association meetings, New York, December 1988.

Blau, Francine D., and Marianne A. Ferber. *The Economics of Women, Men, and Work*. Englewood Cliffs, N.J.: Prentice-Hall, 1986.

Blau, Francine D., and Wallace E. Hendricks. "Occupational Segregation by Sex: Trends and Prospects." *Journal of Human Resources* 14, no. 2 (Spring 1979): 197–210.

Blau, Francine D., and Lawrence M. Kahn. "The Gender Earnings Gap: Learning from International Comparisons." *American Economic Review* 82, no. 2 (May 1992): 533–538.

Boserup, Ester. *Women's Role in Economic Development*. New York: St. Martin's Press, 1970.

Chiplin, Brian, M. M. Curran, and C. J. Parsley. "Relative Female Earnings in G. B. and the Impact of Legislation," in Peter J. Sloane, ed., *Women and Low Pay*. London: MacMillan, 1980, 57–126.

Duncan, Otis Dudley, and Beverly Duncan. "A Methodological Analysis of Segregation Indexes." *American Sociological Review* 20, no. 2 (April 1955): 210–217.

Durand, John D. *The Labor Force in Economic Development*. Princeton: Princeton University Press, 1975.

Ferber, Marianne A., and Helen M. Berg. "Labor Force Participation of Women and the Sex Ratio: A Cross-Country Analysis." *Review of Social Economy* 49, no. 1 (Spring 1991): 2–19.

Goldschmidt-Clermont, Luisella. *Economic Evaluations of Unpaid Household Work: Africa, Asia, Latin America, and Oceania*. Geneva: International Labour Office, 1987.

Gregory, R. G., A. Daly, and V. Ho. "A Tale of Two Countries: Equal Pay for Women in Australia and Britain." Paper presented at the 1986 meeting of the American Economic Association, New Orleans.

Grossbard-Shechtman, Amyra. "Female Labor Supply, Marriage, and Sex Ratios." Paper presented at the 1985 meeting of the Population Association of America, Boston.

Guttentag, Marcia, and Paul F. Secord. *Too Many Women? The Sex Ratio Question*. Beverly Hills, Calif.: Sage Publications, Inc., 1983.

International Labour Office. *Economically Active Population: Estimates and Projections 1950–2025*. Geneva: ILO, 1986.

International Labour Office. *Yearbook of Labour Statistics*. Geneva: ILO, various issues.

Joekes, Susan P. *Women in the World Economy: An INSTRAW Study*. New York: Oxford University Press, 1987.

Juster, F. Thomas, and Frank P. Stafford. "The Allocation of Time: Empirical Findings, Behavioral Models, and Problems of Measurement." *Journal of Economic Literature* 29, no. 2 (June 1991): 471–522.

Kessler, Sid. "Comparability." *Oxford Bulletin of Economics* 45, no. 1 (February 1983): 85–104.

Layard, Richard, and Jacob Mincer, eds. "Trends in Women's Work, Education, and Family Building." *Journal of Labor Economics* 3, no. 1, part 2 (January 1985).

Mincer, Jacob. "Intercountry Comparisons of Labor Force Trends and of Related Developments: An Overview." *Journal of Labor Economics* 3, no. 1, part 2 (January 1985): S1–S32.

Myrdal, Gunnar. *Asian Drama: An Inquiry into the Poverty of Nations*. New York: Twentieth Century Fund, 1968.

Nieva, Veronica F. "Work and Family Linkages," in Laurie Larwood, Ann H. Stromberg, and Barbara A. Gutek, eds., *Women and Work*, vol. 1. Beverly Hills, Calif.: Sage Publications, Inc., 1985, 162–190.

OECD. *The Integration of Women into the Economy.* Paris: OECD, 1985.

O'Neill, June. "The Trend in the Male-Female Wage Gap in the United States." *Journal of Labor Economics* 3, no. 1, part 2 (January 1985): S91–S116.

Ravindran, S. "Health Implications of Sex Discrimination in Childhood." Geneva: World Health Organization, UNICEF/FHE 86.2, 1986.

Reskin, Barbara F., and Heidi I. Hartmann, eds. *Women's Work, Men's Work, Sex Segregation on the Job.* Washington, D.C.: National Academy of the Sciences, 1986.

Semyonov, Moshe. "The Social Context of Women's Labor Force Participation: A Comparative Analysis." *American Journal of Sociology* 86, no. 2 (November 1980): 534–550.

Smith, James P., and Michael P. Ward. *Women's Wages and Work in the Twentieth Century.* Santa Monica, Calif.: The Rand Corporation, October 1984.

Strober, Myra. "Toward a General Theory of Occupational Sex Segregation: The Case of Public School Testing," in Barbara F. Reskin, ed., *Sex Segregation in the Workplace: Trends, Explanations, Remedies*, 144–156. Washington, D.C.: National Academy Press, 1984.

Sullerot, Evelyne. "Equality and Remuneration for Men and Women in the Member States of the EEC." *International Labour Review* 112, nos. 2–3 (August-September 1975): 87–108.

United Nations. *Statistical Yearbook.* New York: United Nations, 1988.

Vansgnes, Kari. "Equal Pay in Norway." *International Labour Review* 103, no. 4 (April 1971): 379–392.

Waldron, Ingrid. "What Do We Know About Causes of Sex Differences in Mortality? A Review of the Literature." *Population Bulletin of the United Nations*, no. 18-1955 (1986): 57–59.

Ward, Kathryn B., and Fred C. Pampel. "Structural Determinants of Female Labor Force Participation in Developed Nations, 1955–1975." *Social Science Quarterly* 66, no. 3 (September 1985): 654–667.

Weinberger, Mary Beth, and Larry Heligman. "Do Social and Economic Variables Differentially Affect Male and Female Child Mortality?" Paper presented at the 1987 annual meeting of the Population Association of America, Chicago.

Weiss, Jane, Francisco Ramirez, and Terry Tracy. "Female Participation in the Occupational System: A Comparative Institutional Analysis." *Social Problems* 23, no. 5 (June 1976): 593–608.

Youssef, Nadia H. "Social Structure and the Female Labor Force: The Case of Women Workers in Muslim Middle Eastern Countries." *Demography* 8, no. 4 (November 1971): 427–450.

Zabalza, Anton, and P. Zafivis Tzannatos. "The Effect of Britain's Anti-Discriminatory Legislation on Relative Pay and Employment." *Economic Journal* 95, no. 379 (September 1985): 679–699.

PART TWO
Modernizing Regions

Each of the three chapters on modernizing nations reaches well beyond the boundaries of a single country to include a whole region. It is quite a feat for an author to be able to work on such a scale, yet such regional accounts offer excellent opportunities for comparative study by showing how shared cultural themes can interact with different political or economic conditions to produce a varied set of outcomes for women.

Economist Gordon Weil, in his chapter on sub-Saharan Africa, shows how women's active roles in production are shaped by patriarchal gender relations in such a way as to limit women's productivity and access to income. The result is a dangerous economic dependence in which women have important responsibilities but little control over resources. Of particular interest is his focus on economic recovery programs, or "structural adjustment" policies, of the International Monetary Fund and the World Bank. These programs provide a form of cooperative lending to help nations revive their economies, but they often have had adverse effects on the position of women.

In her chapter on Latin America and the Caribbean, anthropologist Helen I. Safa shows how women's rising labor force participation and the growing importance of women's income to the household economy have increased their sense of importance and made them feel frustrated by exclusion from the seats of political power. New women's movements in several Latin American nations began with demands for protection of human rights and provision of more social services in the domestic sphere. These movements promise eventually to transform women's roles in both the home and the state. Clouding this picture of progress, however, is a continuing economic crisis in which high levels of government debt and structural adjustment policies have led to a heavy burden on women to meet the rising cost of living and to an uncertain direction in their future economic status.

Sociologist Valentine M. Moghadam shows how a common cultural theme of sheltering women is found throughout the twenty-two countries she includes in her chapter on the Middle East and North Africa. Although women's total labor force participation in the Middle East remains low in comparison to the rest of the world, there nevertheless has been an increase in modern-sector employment, particularly in government work and other services. Paid work in the formal sector of the economy has become one important path to women's empowerment, even as a great deal of unpaid family labor continues in agriculture, rural craft work, and informal-sector activities such as home-based sewing, food preparation, or hawking of wares. In addition to cultural and economic determinants of women's status and work opportunities, a third important factor is state policy, which has been affected by both the cultural imperatives of Islamic fundamentalism and the economic requirements of servicing national debt.

Through these three modernizing regions one finds several common themes. Cultural traditions do vary markedly—from the expectation that women will be major producers in sub-Saharan Africa, to the growing political voice of women in Latin America, and finally to the sheltering of women in the Middle East and North Africa. But what seems shared by all is the experience that economic development is not necessarily improving women's economic situation or enlarging their sphere of control. Two avenues hold the most promise for change: social movements that will mobilize women for domestic and political empowerment, and economic recovery programs that will give greater attention to supporting women's productive activities in the current economic crisis.

3

Caught in the Crisis:
Women in the Economies
of Sub-Saharan Africa

GORDON WEIL

Women's standard of living in sub-Saharan Africa (SSA) depends largely on two factors. The first is the general economic conditions in the region; these are reviewed in the first section of this chapter. The second factor is the underlying gender relations, which are crucial in determining how the work loads and benefits of development are shared; these are discussed in the second section of the chapter. The last section of this chapter examines the adjustment policies, or economic recovery programs, now pursued by many sub-Saharan African nations. The impacts of these programs on women are analyzed through a model that assesses how they influence economic conditions, which in turn affect women in both productive and reproductive activities.[1]

Figure 3.1 provides the organizing framework for this chapter and emphasizes these concerns. According to the model, women's welfare increases with income and decreases with work loads. Gender relations and economic conditions largely determine women's division of labor between productive and reproductive activities (i.e., maintaining the household), and gender relations are important in determining how much income remains under women's control. Within reproductive activities, the interaction of economic conditions and gender relations determines the opportunities open to women, the technology to which women have access, the environmental conditions in which they work, and the amount of human capital (i.e., their understanding of nutrition, health care, literacy, and similar issues) they possess. These factors determine the effectiveness with which reproductive work is converted into income. Because the fruits of women's reproductive work can come in the form of goods (food and fuel for their families or clothes for their children), this income sometimes takes nonmonetary forms. Reproductive activities also

FIGURE 3.1 Determinants of Women's Welfare

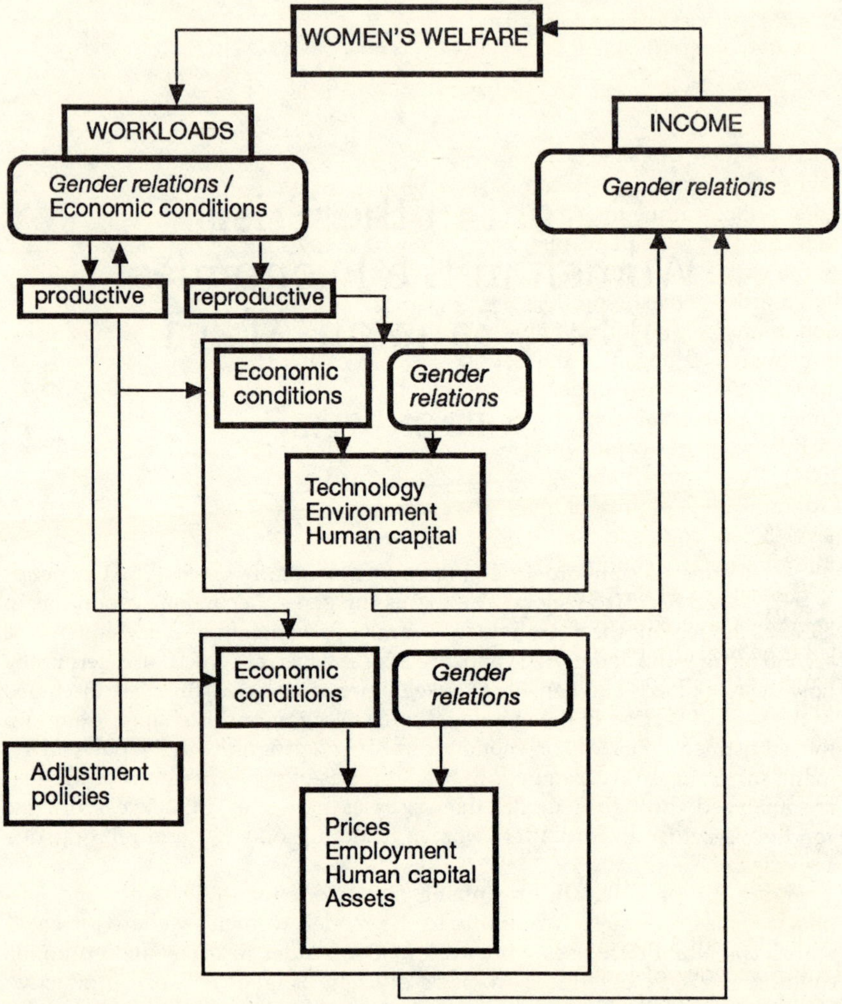

generate monetary income when, for instance, women trade or sell food for cash that can be used to buy cooking oils or utensils to support the household.

In women's other sphere of activity, productive work, the opportunities available and the effectiveness with which work is converted into income also depend on the interactions of economic conditions and gender relations. These factors in turn influence women's access to assets (both physical and financial), employment, human capital (education and skills), and the prices of goods and services they produce. These factors most directly determine women's income.

ECONOMIC CONDITIONS IN SUB-SAHARAN AFRICA

The problem of women's development in Africa is inextricably bound up with the problem of African poverty. And it cannot be solved outside the attack on that poverty.
—Julius Nyerere, 1984

The extent of poverty in SSA today has reached alarming proportions.[2] Signs of economic crisis can be seen almost everywhere.[3] In 1987 thirteen nations (accounting for about one-third of the region's population) were poorer in terms of income per capita than they were at the time of their independence in the early 1960s. In 1987 sub-Saharan Africa, with 450 million inhabitants, had a gross domestic product nearly equal to that of Belgium, with a population of only 10 million (World Bank 1989). This current crisis reflects a decline in growth that began in the mid-1970s. During the 1960s, annual per-capita income grew at just under 1.5 percent; in the 1970s, growth slowed to just under 1 percent; and in the first half of the 1980s the region experienced a shrinkage in per-capita income of 4.9 percent per year (Green and Singer 1984). Even though the World Bank and the United Nations Development Program (1989: 6) present more optimistic data for the 1985–1988 period, they nevertheless conclude that "sub-Saharan Africa continues to lag well behind other developing countries."

The nations of SSA are primarily agricultural, and agricultural growth also has fallen precipitously (World Bank 1988b). Since 1973 agricultural output has grown at the barely noticeable pace of 0.2 percent per year, much less than any other region of the developing world, but population growth between 1980 and 1986 was 3.1 percent per year, the highest of any major world region. This has led to falling per-capita incomes for the nearly 80 percent of the population that lives in the rural sector. Because women are the major agricultural workers in SSA, accounting for about 70 percent of staple food production (World Bank 1989), they have been particularly hard hit by this decline.

On the basis of the World Bank's index of per-capita cereal production (e.g., rice, maize, sorghum, millet) between 1979–1980 and 1984–1986, food production fell 3 percent in SSA, although it rose by 14 percent for the World Bank's category of low-income countries. A new pattern of world food aid provides additional evidence of deteriorating food availability. In 1986 SSA received around 35 percent of world food aid, up from 11.5 percent in 1974 (World Bank 1988b). The areas hardest hit and the women who suffered the most are those in the Sahel (the region just south of the Sahara extending across the continent), the Horn, and Southern Africa, where drought and civil strife have decimated food-production capacity. The lack of food has had a particularly severe impact on nursing mothers and their children.

Slow growth in agriculture (and industry) have been matched by a contraction of international trade. During the first half of the 1980s, exports from SSA diminished at an average annual rate of 2.1 percent, whereas import spending declined by 7.5 percent per year (World Bank 1988b). Although this average glosses over much variation, in the early 1980s little more than half of SSA's imports were financed by export sales. The contraction in import spending causes further falls in income because SSA imports much of its capital equipment, which acts as an engine for economic growth. Even with severe import contraction, SSA as a whole ran a balance-of-trade deficit throughout the 1980s. Although that did not translate into trade deficits for each nation, the World Bank (1988b) reports that in 1986, around two-thirds of the nations of this region ran trade deficits.

Beyond the difficulties experienced in the balance of merchandise trade, many SSA nations also feel the pinch of debt-service payments. Debt in SSA has grown faster than in any other developing region—particularly since 1980—with the result that from 1983 to 1987, debt-service payments took over 20 percent of export proceeds (this peaked in 1988 at 47 percent) (World Bank 1989). With over one-fifth of export proceeds earmarked for debt service, the foreign currency available for imports to promote economic growth or to help feed the growing population is further reduced. Unfortunately, the low-income countries of SSA face the highest debt-service obligations.

Decreasing exports and imports have contributed to state budget deficits in most of sub-Saharan Africa. Because a large portion of government revenues comes from taxes on exports and imports, the deterioration in the trade accounts has reduced government revenues and required reductions in spending. We see this reflected in Zambia as diminished spending on education and in Tanzania as reduced spending on immunizations for children. In almost all nations it has meant a more difficult life for the most vulnerable, particularly poor women.

The widening gap between SSA and the World Bank's group of low-income countries also is evident in higher infant mortality rates, higher childhood death rates, and lower levels of life expectancy (World Bank 1988b). In addition, maternal death rates are higher in this region than in other parts of the world. Furthermore, although Africa has only one-tenth of the world's population, it houses over one-third of the world's refugees. The situation, however, is even worse because official refugee figures do not include another 12 million persons who have been displaced within their own countries due to drought or political instability. The majority of displaced persons and refugees are women and children (World Bank 1989). Finally, by 1983 drought conditions in Africa were reportedly the worst in a century in many parts of the Sahelian region of Western Africa and the Kalahari region in Southern Africa. At the end of the decade, drought still affected many parts of Western Africa and areas of Ethiopia.

R. H. Green and H. W. Singer (1984: 287) conclude that "the recent past, present, and short-term future evolution of the state of Africa's children cannot be described as other than grim." The grim future for Africa's children is in large part a reflection of the bleak lives of Africa's mothers.

The economies of the nations of SSA are in a state of deterioration. It is in this environment of deepening poverty that the women of this region seek to increase their incomes. The shrinking "economic pie" makes it ever more crucial, particularly for women, that the adjustment programs (or economic recovery programs) so widely adopted in this region be successful.

PRODUCTION, REPRODUCTION, AND GENDER RELATIONS

Yet just as women's development in Africa is dependent upon national economic development, so national development is dependent upon the women of Africa and cannot easily take place without them.

—Julius Nyerere, 1984

The current role of African women cannot be understood without reference to their traditional activities as producers, mothers, and traders. Women have always been important producers throughout Africa. In most parts of Africa (Nigeria, Sudan, and Ethiopia may be exceptions), women have long been responsible for producing food for themselves and their families. According to Ester Boserup (1970) and others (Bryson 1981; Newman 1984), more women than men are cultivators, and women have tended to work longer hours than men. Official statistics (FAO 1982) and subsequent revisions made by Ruth Dixon (1985) report that women make up almost half of Africa's rural labor force, compared with about one-third in the rest of the world, and contribute around 80 percent of agricultural labor. One time-use study of 720 rural households in the Ivory Coast reports that women's work loads were twice those of men (UN 1986).

While contributing to production, women continue to hold responsibilities in the private sphere, caring for their children and maintaining the household. These reproductive activities are labor-intensive and, along with women's productive activities outside the home, constitute a double burden of work.

Traditional gender relations have always influenced women's roles in production and reproduction by shaping the way new opportunities are shared between men and women. Gender relations or rights, responsibilities, and customary expectations of men and women vary widely throughout SSA. In most cases women gain access to land (the most important asset) through a male—a husband, brother, uncle, or father. In addition, a woman's access to surplus produce usually is secondary to that of a man and often depends on her bargaining power. The result is a dangerous economic dependence in which women have important responsibilities but little control over resources. This has led women to search for an independent source of income to provide security, status, and authority to influence the family's decisions regarding work and consumption. This is especially important for the almost 30 percent of rural households that are headed by women.[4]

Two broad questions regarding the changes in women's standard of living are raised by Figure 3.1: What has happened to women's work loads, and what has happened to women's income?

Work Loads

Because husbands' household work has not significantly reduced women's reproductive chores, technological progress is the main source of relief. The overall effect of technological progress on women's reproductive work is not clear, however. Ann Whitehead's (1985) review of the effects of technology on women begins with the proposition that although it is still an underresearched field, more and more evidence suggests that women suffer negatively from technological change. For instance, drilling wells in villages could make fetching the family's water easier. But in one example from Kenya (ISIS 1984), men were placed in charge of the new wells, removing control over water from women. Furthermore, because men viewed water control as women's work, they did not maintain the wells. Thus, a large part of the potential benefits was lost, and women's status also was reduced. In another example, Marilyn Carr (1978) explains that the introduction of solar-powered cooking stoves failed to reduce the burden of collecting fuel. Because most cooking is done early in the morning or late in the evening to avoid the direct rays of the noonday sun, solar-powered cooking stoves had limited effectiveness. These are not isolated examples. Some also argue that the reason new technologies have not reduced women's work has been men's control over the development of these technologies (ISIS 1984).

The introduction of new technologies and cash crops also has affected women's productive work loads outside the home. According to Jane I. Guyer (1986), whereas men's tasks have been declining in importance as deforestation has progressed, women's tasks have grown and become more difficult. For instance, the environmental deterioration caused by cutting trees and bush to open new lands for crops indirectly increases women's work loads because women must search longer and walk farther to gather fuel. When land becomes more scarce and the fallow time is shortened, more weeding—a woman's job—is required. As population pressures cause fields to become more fragmented and distant, the demands of transport—usually a woman's responsibility—increase. And as populations increase, more food has to be grown, processed, and prepared by women. Urbanization also has increased women's work loads in the countryside because as men leave for the city, women are left behind to farm alone.

On the other hand, Christina H. Gladwin and Della McMillan (1989) point out that in parts of Africa, the effect of agricultural intensification has been to displace women. They argue that a shift to the plough increases men's participation in farming because ploughing is almost universally done by men. The number of hired laborers often increases; they tend to be males and to be supervised by men. The same authors also report that development projects from Malawi to Nigeria to Sierra Leone have been conceived for men's work. They conclude, however, that only in the more densely populated areas of Africa (such as Senegal, Benin, Togo, or Swaziland) is agricultural intensification likely to push women out of farming activities as it has done in the densely populated parts of Asia. Women, however, do so many different jobs that even as their role in farming per se is reduced, their jobs in marketing or food processing expand along with increases in output. Judy C. Bryson (1981) reports that considering both farming and household activities, the hours worked by women in rural Cameroon actually have increased since the early days of the twentieth century.

In sum, gender relations have not supported a reduction in women's work loads. Rather, the interactions of population growth, environmental deterioration, and some technological advances have tended to increase women's work loads. Women are likely to remain overburdened until men start to assume more of the reproductive chores. According to Agnes Akosua Aidoo (1985: 210),

> The sexual division of labor has made their [women's] tasks at home, in the farms and marketplace more tedious, time consuming, and drudgery-filled than those of their male partners in development. According to the ILO young African girls start working at an earlier age (from 10 years of age) and old women (over 65 years of age) continue to work longer than their age groups anywhere else in the world.

Income

In addition to work loads, women's standard of living also depends on the size and security of their income. As seen in Figure 3.1, women's income depends most directly on three factors: access to income-earning assets (physical and financial assets), access to human capital (through extension services and education), and access to employment (prices are discussed in the next section).

Access to Assets. Although women traditionally gained access to land through a husband or a member of his family, since independence many African nations have made changes in family law and land law. Many of these changes have harmed women. For example, new reforms in Kenya, including land registration, have transferred land to an almost exclusively male-individualized tenure system (UN 1986). This system works against women who traditionally had use rights (more technically, usufructuary rights) to part of their husbands' land in the case of marital breakup. Today, when marriages dissolve, women's access to land is determined by "custom," and few women sit on the tribunals that make decisions concerning wives' access to land. The potential for trouble is illustrated by one study of around 1,700 female farmers in Ghana (UN 1986). Approximately 60 percent of these women lost the farms they had worked for one of three reasons: marital dispute (24 percent), husband's migration to a city (20 percent), or loss of husband (16 percent). These women either had to leave farming altogether or seek employment as farm laborers.

In some places women have lost access to land through another route—new economic opportunities. In the Ivory Coast, for instance, an emphasis on the production of cash crops, including coffee, palm oil, and rubber, has led men to transfer land that previously was used for food production into production of these crops. Women then are left to grow food with less and poorer-quality land. Yet demands on their labor rise as they also are expected to contribute to cash crop production.

Land's productivity depends on several factors, including fertilizer, pesticides, and water control; but women's access to these complementary inputs is limited. Men have greater knowledge about these inputs and access to credit to purchase them. For instance, although women in northern districts of Sierre Leone have cultivated lands planted in both food and cash crops, many have not earned income from these crops. Without complementary inputs, their lands were not sufficiently productive to make cash crop farming profitable. In the same region, women did not have access to the World Bank's integrated Rural Development Project loans because these loans were designed for larger farms, which were owned by men. This is not an isolated example.

Jean M. Due and Rebecca Summary (1982) cite women's lack of access to credit as one of two major factors that constrain women's ability to participate equally in the benefits of development. Traditional practices of lending only to men provide another barrier for women. Women's access is further restricted, as in Kenya, when land registration places titles in men's names, creating collateral not available to women. One study of 123 small-scale farmers who received loans from the Zambian Agricultural Finance Company reported that only two were made to women (Due and Summary 1982). As a consequence, women were forced to seek credit in the informal capital market where local money lenders charge interest rates that are fairly high by formal credit market standards.[5]

Furthermore, with less access to credit, it is more difficult for women to generate increases in productivity. Gladwin and McMillan (1989) provide empirical evidence showing that because women generally have less access to credit, they apply less fertilizer and consequently realize lower yields per hectare. Due to women's importance in food production, the discrimination women face in formal credit markets results in reduced availability of food. Today, this is reflected in the increased amount of food aid received by SSA nations.[6]

Access to Education and Training. Innovative husbandry practices in SSA most often are spread through extension agents, only about 3.5 percent of whom are women (Newman 1984). They have helped to make commonplace such techniques as using oxen for ploughing, growing hybrid maize, and planting in straight lines. The services of extension agents are provided through farm visits and through visits of farmers to training centers. Either way, women have been disadvantaged. One statistical study (Staudt 1982) revealed that about half of the farms sampled, managed by women alone, had never been visited by extension agents, compared to only a quarter of farms jointly managed by a man and a woman. Female farm managers were only about one-fourth as likely to visit training centers as men from jointly managed farms. Furthermore, women who visited these centers devoted most of their study time to home economics rather than agricultural innovation. Studies of Zambian and Malawian farm institutes note the same pattern (Guyer 1986). It is ironic, or more accurately a reflection of gender relations, that in a continent on which women bear so much responsibility for growing food, they receive so little help in improving their husbandry. The immediate impact of this bias against women in the dissemination of knowledge is that women's income and economic security are less than they might be. But more than this, given women's crucial role as food producers, everyone suffers. Gladwin and McMillan (1989) make the point that without women's contribution, there can be no turnaround in Africa's food production in the realistic future.

In urban areas, access to formal education can be a stepping-stone to employment in the modern sector. When there is an excess supply of labor for jobs in the modern sector, educational attainment often is used to ration the positions and then becomes an important factor influencing income levels.

The record of women in formal education is not entirely bleak. In 1980 women made up about 43 percent of all primary school enrollments throughout SSA, with some variation within the region (Newman 1984). In a few countries—Botswana, Cameroon, Lesotho, Mauritius, and Swaziland—girls made up over 50 percent of primary school enrollments. (Newman 1984). Although total enrollments at the secondary level continue to climb, women have not made the gains relative to men that they have at the primary level. The relative advantage to men becomes even larger at the postsecondary levels, due primarily to women's greater drop-out rate caused largely by family responsibilities.[7]

The curriculum offered to women in formal education generally does not prepare them as well as men for modern-sector employment. For instance, one curriculum introduced in Ghana in the mid-1970s offered girls electives in beauty culture, tailoring, dressmaking, and catering but offered boys woodworking, masonry, technical drawing, and automotive practice. In Lesotho, where girls made up 58 percent of the enrollments in technical and vocational schools in 1979, they primarily studied domestic arts (Newman 1984). The differences in curriculum are reflected in the underrepresentation of women in math and science courses as well. Also, because women are a minority of those holding jobs in industry, fewer women than men can take advantage of on-the-job training programs.

Until educational opportunities for women match those of men, women will continue to be disadvantaged in gaining access to modern-sector employment and society's resources. Given SSA's deficit in an educated and trained labor force (World Bank 1981), it is counterproductive to erect barriers to the full participation of half of its population.

Access to Employment. Economic development has fostered both growing urbanization and industrial employment. But between 1960 and 1980, as the percentage of the population living in cities increased from 11 percent to 21 percent (World Bank 1981), the proportion of the labor force employed in industry increased only from 8 percent to 9 percent. The faster pace of urbanization than industrialization has contributed to a growing informal sector, which I discuss below.

With the exception of the Middle East, Africa has the smallest percentage of women employed in industry of any developing region. Although data on women employed in industry are not very reliable or even widely available, according to one UN report (UN 1986), in 1960 women made up 17.2 percent of industrial workers in Africa; by 1980 that figure had increased to only 19.7 percent. This underrepresentation of women's industrial employment may reflect the fact that the rapid growth in textile production and electronics assembly, two industries that typically are female dominated, has occurred much more in Asia and Latin America than in Africa.

Women's employment patterns in industry have tended to reflect gender segregation similar to that found in the rest of the world. According to data analyzed by Richard Anker and Catherine Hein (1986), women make up less than half the employees in all major nonagricultural occupation groupings and are most heavily represented in sales and service employment. This supports Boserup's (1970) earlier finding that women make up a larger number of service and bazaar workers than modern-sector workers. Women also are relatively heavily represented among professional and technical workers because many work as teachers and nurses. Within any occupational grouping, women tend to be underrepresented in jobs that carry decision-making responsibilities. This is so even in industries such as textiles and food processing, which tend to be female dominated, and in countries such as Ghana and Mali, which have a tradition of women's working in these areas.[8]

As in agriculture, industrial technological change has acted both to displace and to provide additional employment for women. For instance, women have been displaced as imported lager beer has replaced the traditional beer brewed by women, and in West Africa, cheaper imported soap has replaced soap long made by women from palm oil and wood ash (UN 1986). On the other hand, although still relatively rare in Africa, the export-processing zone in Mauritius has provided additional employment for over 22,000 workers, around 80 percent of whom have been women (Hein 1986). In this case the predominance of female workers may reflect womens' subordinate position because in Mauritius, the minimum wage for women is lower than that for men. The fact that women can be paid lower wages than men and the belief that women are a more docile labor force are two reasons for the high proportion of women employed in these labor-intensive industries. Whether this additional employment is viewed as exploitation or as an opportunity to earn added income, it should be recognized that jobs closely integrated into world markets often provide unstable employment reflecting world market instability. This instability can create even more problems for women than for men because of their reduced flexibility in work location and in working hours due to domestic responsibilities.

Urbanization also has had the effect of pushing women out of traditional occupations. For instance, trading is an important area of female employment. The women traders of Ghana and Nigeria provide the best-known examples. The growth of urban areas has helped provide a larger market for women who sell handicrafts and textiles as well as food. In fact, a few women have become successful traders. The growth of contract trade, however, in which a few specified goods are provided in large quantities to institutions such as schools, hospitals, hotels, and restaurants, has increasingly drawn men into trading activities. Men have a comparative advantage at this type of work, which requires many contacts and maneuvering within the modern sector where men predominate and substantial amounts of capital to which women usually do not have access. This example illustrates the important fact that income-earning opportunities are more easily captured by those who are more mobile and who have access to complementary inputs such as credit and equipment.

As women are pushed out of trade, and as migrant women enter cities but are unable to secure formal-sector employment, they are forced to work in the informal sector. The informal sector is part of the urban economy characterized by small individual or family firms, petty retail trade and services, and labor-intensive methods of production. In describing women traders in Lusaka, Zambia, Ilsa Schuster (1982) argues that these women are marginal because they make no substantial contribution to the economy of the town, nor do they have the status in the eyes of society that goes with formal-sector employment. The majority of women traders in towns throughout SSA work with little capital and enjoy no security. They sell home-brewed beer or gin, fresh fruits and vegetables, hand-made utensils or handicrafts, or sometimes themselves as prostitutes (Little 1976). In some states (e.g., Zambia) they are harassed by police who make "swoops" to control street trade by detaining or fining those women who have not purchased a license to trade. The large number of traders drives down prices and limits profits. As a result, most women forced into informal-sector activities—such as selling prepared foods, handicrafts, or services—work long hours with little capital, enjoy little security or status, and earn very little income (Clark 1988).

In sum, gender relations have acted as an obstacle to women's equal access to productive assets, human capital, and employment. The consequence of this is twofold. First, women have not benefited from development to the same extent as men. Their work loads have not been reduced, and they continue to be greater than men's; their incomes have not grown substantially or become more secure. Second, SSA has not made full use of its resources in its fight against poverty. Given the existing harsh economic conditions, full use of all resources is critical. Overall, although gender relations have acted as obstacles to women in their pursuit of higher standards of living, more generally they have also contributed to SSA's stagnation.

ADJUSTMENT PROGRAMS AND WOMEN'S WELFARE

In response to the economic decline that began in the mid-1970s, the International Monetary Fund (IMF) and the World Bank began a new form of cooperative lending to help nations revive their economies. Although these "adjustment" loans have different maturities, come from different sources, and are used in different ways, they all have policy conditions attached to them that have had direct impacts on women's lives—on their work loads and on their income.[9] Only a few studies have addressed the impact of adjustment on women (Commonwealth Secretariat 1989; Joekes et al. 1988), although there has been a good deal of work about their impact on the poor (Zuckerman 1989; Heller et al. 1988). Since 1979–1980 at least thirty-one SSA nations have received one or more of these loans and have adopted the policy prescriptions upon which they are conditioned.

At the most general level, the thrust of the policies has been to encourage market liberalization (e.g., an expanded role for markets) and a reduction in government intervention. The adjustment policies most commonly recommended can be grouped into four categories (World Bank 1988a): (1) trade policies, including currency devaluation and tariff reductions; (2) agricultural policies, which increase the role of markets; (3) budget policies, including spending cuts and tax increases; and (4) policies to "rationalize" public enterprises (which involve reducing their scope and increasing their efficiency). Policies in each of these categories affect women through their impacts on the variables cited in Figure 3.1. I examine the effects of adjustment policies on the women of this region by considering the ways adjustment affects the prices of goods and services produced by women, their employment opportunities, women's access to education and training, and women's access to assets.

Prices

Adjustment policies that raise the prices of the goods and services produced by women can raise their income. Prices are affected primarily, although not exclusively, by two sets of policies: exchange-rate devaluation, which is central to trade policies, and agricultural policies designed to increase the role of markets in setting prices. Some have argued that price policy is "gender neutral" in that women stand to gain equally with men. We need to look more closely at the way these policies work before a conclusion is drawn.

Consider first the effects of exchange-rate devaluations. This raises the domestic currency market price of tradables relative to the prices of nontraded goods (nontradables). Tradables include goods that enter international trade (exports and imports) as well as domestically produced substitutes (e.g., domestic beer or shoes) that can be bought instead of their foreign counterparts. As the price of exportable goods rises, there is an incentive to produce and sell more exports; similarly, as the price of imported goods rises, there is an incentive for consumers to substitute domestically produced goods for imports. In this fashion devaluation raises the incomes of tradables producers relative to those of nontradable producers. Most agricultural products women grow (with the exception of cassava and other root crops grown largely for subsistence) are traded internationally and are considered tradables.

Agricultural policies also have strong price effects. These policies call for a reduced role for government agencies (state-owned farms, marketing boards, and distribution facilities) in setting agricultural prices and for a greater reliance on markets. In the aggregate, in the early 1980s around two-thirds of SSA nations fixed the price of food; now about two-thirds rely on markets to set prices (Humphreys and Jaeger 1989). The consequence of expanded reliance on markets has been an increase in prices received by both exporters and food producers. Hence, trade and agricultural policies have tended to reinforce each other by raising the price of exports and most food crops.

At first glance we might conclude that women who produce cash crops such as cotton in Cameroon and Senegal, tea and coffee in Kenya, or tobacco and sugar in Malawi potentially stand to gain as these policies drive prices upward.

This conclusion must be qualified, however, to recognize the special conditions faced by most women in the agricultural sector. Women generally do not have access to complementary inputs such as credit, which allows them to purchase additional inputs so they can expand production of crops that fetch a higher price. In several countries such as Malawi and to some extent Kenya, export crops are produced predominantly on large estates rather than by small landholders. When women are involved in this production, it is usually as hired laborers performing labor-intensive and low-paying tasks. Although expanded production of these crops may increase the demand for hired labor and thus provide added employment for women, women are not the primary beneficiaries of currency devaluations. These beneficiaries are the owners of large estates and plantations, who may be wealthy local landowners or transnational corporations. Again, because women have less access to complementary inputs, they are less able to respond to the incentives of higher prices.

From the perspective of costs, devaluations can hurt women as their costs of inputs rise. For instance, the costs of imported high-yielding wheat or rice seeds will rise following devaluation, as would the costs of imported equipment, fuels, or fertilizer. Such cost increases tend to reduce profits. The profit squeeze can be particularly severe when farmers do not have access to credit enabling them to afford higher-priced inputs. Large estates, often run by transnational corporations, do have access to credit and will be able to afford more costly inputs. On the other hand, small farmers and women who do not have easy access to credit will be hurt by rising costs. In addition, the costs of goods women purchase in their reproductive roles tend to rise. One study in Malawi (Elson 1989) revealed that although the selling prices of agricultural products rose following the adjustment program, so did input costs and the costs of consumer goods. The net result was declining income and nutritional status for smallholders. In the context of African traditions where household budgets generally are not pooled, rising prices for export crops may add to men's income even as rising food costs reduce women's income and children's welfare.

Roots and tubers, such as cassava, are primarily women's crops and also to a large extent are nontradables. Following a currency devaluation, the prices received from the sale of these food crops tend to fall relative to prices received for cereals (a good that enters trade). This relative price change threatens the profitability of crops such as cassava and provides an incentive to switch to cereal production. To the extent that women do shift into cereals, they are drawn more fully into international trade relations in which they experience all the instabilities that go with that trade. They produce for an international market in which they have no economic power rather than for the smaller local market where they may have some power. In addition, given the strong growth in cassava production in the past, such a shift could undermine what has become a safety net of locally produced food for many poor rural families.

More likely, though, women will not be able easily to shift their production from roots and tubers into cereals or other export crops. To do so requires access to seed and other inputs many women do not have.

The direct price effect of devaluation for the large number of women who produce primarily for home consumption rather than for markets is negligible. Even though higher market prices have replaced low government-established prices in much of SSA, in truth little domestically produced grain was actually purchased and sold by marketing boards. One estimate (Hopcraft 1987) suggests that only 10 to 15 percent (and nowhere more than 25 percent) of grain production went through official channels. Furthermore, an even smaller percentage of roots and tubers, which are almost exclusively produced by women, was purchased by government marketing boards. In these cases, rising prices have few positive impacts on women. In food-deficit areas, such as Rwanda and Burundi, rising food prices have reduced family welfare and pushed people into the informal sector of nearby towns, selling home-produced foods or handicrafts (Green and Singer 1984). Overall, the evidence of falling export revenues and continuing food imports implies that incomes have not increased substantially in the agricultural sector. Thus, it is unlikely that women's incomes have risen relative to those of men.

Nonetheless, women may benefit in other ways from market liberalization. In several countries—for instance, Guinea, Ethiopia, and Zambia—government monopolies were supported by laws prohibiting trade across certain regions. Market liberalization eliminates this prohibition and allows more trade to take place. To the extent that that leads to higher prices, lower costs, or increased sales, food producers—who are largely women—benefit.

A potential problem associated with market liberalization policies also must be considered. When government monopolies are eliminated, individuals controlling private monopolies may fill the vacuum and become monopoly middlemen. Women are unlikely to be in these monopoly positions. The result could be that low monopsony prices (prices set in a market in which there is only one buyer) would replace low government prices. In that case, incomes would merely be redistributed from the government to the larger and wealthier traders. Neither the general economy nor women specifically are likely to benefit. A vigilant government is needed to prevent this.

Increased reliance on markets can affect women by altering the relative price between export crops and food crops. If the relative price of export crops rises, there will be a redistribution of income away from women—the main producers of food crops. A World Bank study (1988a) suggests that up to 1986, the price of food rose relative to export prices, but since 1986 the price of food has fallen relative to that of export crops (Humphreys and Jaeger 1989). If this trend continues, there will be an incentive to reallocate land once used for food crops into export crop production. As noted above, in the Ivory Coast women have been hurt by such a shift. Increased production for export has not historically benefited women and often has resulted in a worsening of their position (Elson 1989).

Agricultural and trade policies also affect women in urban sectors of the economy (Tripp 1992). Exchange-rate devaluation may help some women who work in the informal sector. For instance, women who produce domestic beer or soap but who have found much of their market taken over by imports benefit from devaluation that raises the prices of those imports. On the other hand, women are disproportionately represented in bazaar and service-sector employment, which are nontradable areas. Devaluation reduces the incomes of these workers relative to the incomes of those who produce goods for trade. An important impact of devaluation is to raise the price of cereals and other foods. This lowers the real (inflation-adjusted) value of the earnings of urban women who produce nontradables and must purchase most of their family's food.

Policies aimed at reducing budget deficits also have price effects. These policies often include reductions in food price subsidies. In Zambia food price increases led to riots, causing the government to back down from its adjustment program. Another possible outcome as food subsidies are reduced is that a relative price change may lead to increased consumption of roots and tubers such as cassava. If people are willing to change their diets to include more root crops when the price falls, then roots and tubers are truly tradables. In that case, women who produce and sell these crops will experience a rise in their income. However, because these crops have relatively lower nutritional value than do grains, consumers tend to suffer.

Deficit reduction policies also have price effects through tax policy. In some countries, such as Ghana and Nigeria, increased reliance on indirect taxes and user fees (individual payments of school fees or charges for receipt of medical treatment) has reduced women's welfare. These taxes tend to raise the price of goods and services that women purchase in their reproductive roles. Like the elimination of food subsidies, they reduce the value of urban incomes and make reproductive activities more difficult and time-consuming, as women seek out bargains and form networks to locate alternate sources.

As these remarks make clear, the prices of products purchased and sold by women are affected by different adjustment policies in complex ways. Nevertheless, given women's typical economic activities, a strong case can be made for the fact that the effects of prices are not gender-neutral.

Access to Employment

With only a few exceptions, adjustment programs have reduced employment opportunities rather than increased them. Adjustment programs aimed at reducing the fiscal deficit have had the most direct impact on employment. These policies cause economic contraction and employment reductions through reduced government spending and credit contractions. In addition, reductions in tariffs and export taxes, which reduce revenues, necessitate further spending cuts.

Reduced opportunities for employment affect women both directly and indirectly. In Togo, Niger, the Ivory Coast, Guinea, Senegal, the Gambia, and Ghana, adjustment policies have led to closures and liquidations of public enterprises and rising unemployment. In the Gambia between 1985 and 1986, around 2,600 workers were laid off from government payrolls, and in Guinea retrenchment eliminated the jobs of about 3,000 workers (Demery and Addison 1987a). Women are directly affected when they lose their jobs in these retrenchment efforts. Furthermore, because women's mobility is less than men's, it is more difficult for them to find alternative employment. This effect is sometimes offset, as in Mauritius, by the expansion of labor-intensive industries such as textiles and electronics in which the percentage of female labor is high although employment is unstable. Women are affected indirectly when their husbands are laid off and family income falls. Then women must work harder to earn money to make up for the lost income and produce more necessities themselves to provide for their families. This is a clear example of how women's double burden of work and family makes them vulnerable to economic contraction.

In response to retrenchments brought on by these adjustment policies, external aid agencies have funded a few programs to provide new opportunities. For instance, in Ghana the Program of Action to Mitigate the Social Costs of Adjustment (PAMSCAD) includes employment generation through public works and food-for-work projects. In Guinea the World Bank supports a program to provide severance pay to laid-off public-sector workers and lines of credit for small-scale enterprises. The data are not adequate to determine the effect of these programs on women, but given the lack of special efforts to ensure that women benefit equally with men, one cannot be too sanguine.

Within the framework of current adjustment programs, there appear to be relatively few opportunities for women to expand their employment opportunities and thereby secure added income.

Access to Human Capital

Government spending in areas such as health, education, skills, and training of sub-Saharan Africa's labor force (i.e., investments in human capital) contributes to productivity and regional economic growth. Unfortunately, these investments run counter to adjustment programs that require reductions in public expenditures. Lionel Demery and Tony Addison (1987b) report that reductions in defense spending have been much smaller under adjustment programs than reductions in spending on social programs and infrastructure, such as roads, ports, and telecommunications. Reduced spending on road maintenance, for instance, makes it more difficult to transport crops to market and thus has hurt women. Across the continent, cuts in spending on health care have reduced the availability of vaccines and drugs, and cuts in education have resulted in fewer books and supplies.

Although reductions in social services are not targeted specifically to women, they do tend to hurt the poor, and women make up a disproportionate share of the poor (Zuckerman 1989). Furthermore, to the extent that cuts in social services make it more difficult to provide for the health and welfare of children, these cuts not only directly hurt children but also make women's lives more difficult. Cornia, Jolly, and Stewart's (1987) study *Adjustment with a Human Face* makes a strong argument that reductions in spending on social programs have had a particularly detrimental effect on children. Governments need to be more selective in the budget-cutting process. For instance, reductions in subsidies to airlines rather than to education or medicine will have less of an effect on women and children.

There are, however, some positive signs that governments recognize the importance of focusing attention on women. For instance, Ghana has established the Women Farmers Unit under the Secretary of Agriculture. The unit is charged specifically with looking after the interests of female farmers. Ghana uses both male and female extension workers and teaches women new techniques in farming, processing, and storing food (Novicki 1988). This type of program can be a part of structural adjustment packages and can help women boost their productivity.

Assets

What might be the greatest contribution to women's security could come through expanded access to assets, including physical assets (such as land or capital equipment) and financial assets (such as credit). Nevertheless, adjustment programs have done little to promote this. Consider land reform. Women could benefit tremendously from land reform that specifically recognizes their rights to land and its produce. In fact, land reform has not been part of adjustment programs. The World Bank and the Kenyan government planned a discussion of land reform in conjunction with the receipt of a structural adjustment loan, but the subject was never broached. Land reform is a highly charged political subject and can proceed only if a government is fully committed to it. Land reform that directly recognizes and promotes the status of women is extremely rare.

Adjustment policies focused on the rationalization of government enterprises could be another avenue through which women could gain control of productive assets. To date, however, government decontrol of enterprises has not been linked with women's control over them. This could be promoted by targeting financial credit to women to help them, rather than governments, supply goods and services. In fact, the primary effect of adjustment programs through the contractionary aspects of stabilization has been to reduce the amount of credit available. Without special attention, women tend to be crowded out of formal credit markets. In this case, too, free-market policies are biased against women.

CONCLUSION

The future does not look bright for women of sub-Saharan Africa. In the past, nations have not given enough attention to the status and productivity of women and hence have been at least partly responsible for the deteriorating economic conditions in which SSA and the women living there must function. Consequently, most SSA nations have adopted comprehensive adjustment programs, which often are called economic recovery programs. With advice from the IMF and the World Bank, these programs enhance the importance of markets.[10] Markets can be efficient institutions (under certain well-known conditions), but they tend to shift economic power toward the economically strong at the expense of the weak.

The influence of unequal gender relations has made it difficult for women to gain access to employment, human capital, and assets. Consequently, it is difficult for women to earn high and secure incomes. Hence, women are disproportionately represented among the economically weak. Therefore, it is not clear that the increased reliance on markets will work to women's advantage. Although prices themselves may be gender-neutral, as we have seen, gender does greatly influence access to assets and hence the ability to produce for the market. Furthermore, given the division of labor in which men focus on export crops and women bear the responsibility for maintaining family consumption, increasing prices act primarily to raise men's incomes even as they make it more difficult for women to fulfill their responsibilities.

In the long run, market-based policies are not enough. What will most effectively provide income security for women and simultaneously help reduce poverty in SSA are increases in productivity, particularly in agriculture. Pricing policy alone will not accomplish this. Price policy must be coordinated with aggressive programs to build infrastructure, provide credit to smallholders and women in the informal sectors, and develop appropriate new technologies. Furthermore, women need to become more secure in the control of income earned from their own labor. This requires a change in basic gender relations that will not be easily accomplished but that will be facilitated by increases in women's productivity. All of these tasks require active government involvement. The trick is to get governments involved in appropriate ways.

A focus on women can be consistent with adjustment programs. In Kenya, for instance, a recently instituted national agricultural extension system specifically targets women as well as men. Barbara Herz (1989: 44) reports that "while the effort is still quite new, more than half of the farmers actually met by agents . . . are women." Kenya's experience in reaching women farmers has influenced efforts in other nations including Cameroon, Nigeria, Somalia, and Zimbabwe. In Zimbabwe banks specifically make loans directly to women without a male guarantor. Here, small-scale women farmers produce over 65 percent of the marketed maize. At the least, governments must explicitly consider the likely impact on women of different ways of implementing adjustment policies. This may be facilitated by the creation of a governmental Women's Bureau. In the end, in some cases productivity may be stimulated most effectively through the continued existence of marketing boards, as J. Kadyampakeni (1988) argues for Malawi; in others, markets should replace monopoly marketing boards (Lele 1989).

The model that underlies this chapter can be helpful to governments that seek policies to promote women's status through an increase in their productivity. Because the model is focused on production, it highlights the ways women earn incomes; and because it explicitly recognizes gender relations, it highlights ways women have been denied that ability. By considering specifically women's access to physical and financial assets, employment, and human capital as well as the prices of the products women sell within the context of existing gender relations, governments may be able to anticipate the effects of adjustment policies on women. Finally, because the model explicitly recognizes reproductive activities, it helps to reveal the way adjustment policies affect women through that avenue as well as through their productive roles.

Some would question whether a focus on women can make a significant difference within the context of current gender, class, race, and international relations (Mbilinyi 1987). For them, the solution is the destruction of the present order and the creation of a new one. In the final analysis, that may be necessary, but such a plan is not currently on the agenda in sub-Saharan Africa. Adjustment programs are on the agenda, however, and every attempt should be made to get them to work to the benefit of all people of the region.

NOTES

1. Of course, this model like all others is an abstraction from reality. It does not explicitly incorporate class or race relations. Class relations often interact with gender relations to create barriers for women. Nor does the model give enough attention to the interplay between gender and economic conditions in determining the size of women's work loads or the division between productive and reproductive work. (See Cook and Kerner [1989] for an insightful case study of Tanzania.)

2. There is little direct evidence on women's incomes; hence, much of what follows draws inferences from more general data.

3. This section outlines the dimensions of the economic crisis in SSA but does not discuss its causes. For three very different perspectives on the causes of the crisis, see World Bank (1981); Samir Amin (1982); and Cheryl Payer (1983).

4. In Perdita Huston's (1979) interviews, the needs for cash and increased marital instability are recurrent themes. Yet it is Jane I. Guyer (1984) who emphasizes most clearly the importance of a focus on income for understanding the position of women. Because families do not traditionally pool their incomes, a woman has access to income only when it accrues directly to her.

5. Capital markets that are segmented in this way are not efficient because funds are not necessarily directed to their most productive uses. Keep this in mind when I discuss the economic adjustment programs.

6. Formation of women's credit associations is one positive step rural women have taken to improve their access to credit. See Coumba Cesay-Marenah (1982) for a discussion related to the Gambia or Mark DeLancey (1987) for examples from Cameroon.

7. For an analysis of women's role in education in Tanzania that explicitly incorporates class and gender issues, see Donna O. Kerner (1986).

8. Few data are available on women's relative wages. One UN study (1986) reports that Kenyan women earn 63 percent and Tanzanian women 79 percent of men's wages.

9. Strictly speaking, structural adjustment loans come from the World Bank, whereas the IMF largely makes stabilization loans. Stabilization loans are used in conjunction with contractionary monetary and fiscal policy (and currency devaluation) to restore internal and external balance in the short run. Structural adjustment loans are intended to help promote a restructuring of the economy to yield a more efficient allocation of resources and promote long-run growth while also helping to restore external balance. Despite their different purposes, because the two loan programs are usually coordinated, I will use the term adjustment to cover both programs.

10. There remains the question of whether outward-looking policies supported by the World Bank and the IMF are necessarily in SSA's (not to mention women's) best interest. H.

W. Singer and P. Gray (1988) provide evidence that shows it is not so much outward-looking policies as favorable world economic conditions that are most important.

BIBLIOGRAPHY

Aidoo, Agnes Akosua. "Women and Development in Africa: Alternative Strategies for the Future." In *Economic Crisis in Africa*, A. Adedeji and T. Shaw, eds., 201–217. Boulder: Lynne Rienner, 1985.

Amin, Samir. "A Critique of the World Bank Report 'Accelerated Development in Sub-Saharan Africa,'" *African Development* 7, nos. 1–2 (1982): 23–29.

Anker, Richard, and Catherine Hein. "Sex Inequalities in Third World Employment: Statistical Evidence." In *Sex Inequalities in Urban Employment in the Third World*, Richard Anker and Catherine Hein, eds., 63–115. New York: St. Martin's Press, 1986.

Benería, Lourdes, and Shelley Feldman, eds., *Unequal Burden: Economic Crises, Persistent Poverty, and Women's Work*. Boulder: Westview Press, 1992.

Boserup, Ester. *Women's Role in Economic Development*. New York: St. Martin's Press, 1970.

Bryson, Judy C. "Women and Agriculture in Sub-Saharan Africa: Implications for Development (An Exploratory Study)." *Journal of Development Studies* 17, no. 3 (April 1981): 29–46.

Carr, Marilyn. "Technologies Appropriate for Women." In *Women and Technological Change in Developing Countries*, R. Dauber and M. Cain, eds. Boulder: Westview Press, 1978.

Cesay-Marenah, Coumba. "Women's Cooperative Thrift and Credit Societies: An Element of Women's Programs in the Gambia." In *Women and Work in Africa*, E. Bay, ed., 289–295. Boulder: Westview Press, 1982.

Clark, Garcia, ed. *Traders Versus the State: Anthropological Approaches to Unofficial Economies*. London: Westview Press, 1988.

Commonwealth Secretariat. *Engendering Adjustment for the 1990s*. London: Hobbs the Printers of Southampton, 1989.

Cook, Kristy, and Donna O. Kerner. "Gender and Food Shortage in Tanzania." *Feminist Issues* 9, no. 1 (Spring 1989):57–72.

Cornia, Giovanni Andrea, Richard Jolly, and Frances Stewart. *Adjustment with a Human Face*. vol. 1. Oxford: Claredon Press, 1987.

DeLancey, Mark. "Women's Cooperatives in Cameroon." *African Studies Review* 30, no. 1 (March 1987): 1–18.

Demery, Lionel, and Tony Addison. *The Alleviation of Poverty Under Structural Adjustment*. Washington, D.C.: World Bank, 1987a.

———. "Food Insecurity and Adjustment Policies in Sub-Saharan Africa: A Review of the Evidence." *Development Policy Review* 5 (1987b): 177–196.

Dixon, Ruth. "Seeing the Invisible Women Farmers in Africa: Improving Research and Data Collection Methods." In *Women as Food Producers in Developing Countries*, J. Monson and M. Kalb, eds. 19–35. Los Angeles: UCLA African Studies Center, 1985.

Due, Jean M., and Rebecca Summary. "Constraints to Women and Development in Africa." *The Journal of Modern African Studies* 20, no. 1 (1982): 155–166.

Elson, Diane. "How Is Structural Adjustment Affecting Women?" *Development* 1, (1989): 67–74.

Food and Agriculture Organization of the United Nations. "Follow-up to WCARRD: The Role of Women in Agricultural Production." Rome: United Nations, 1982.

Gladwin, Christina H., and Della McMillan. "Is a Turnaround in Africa Possible Without Helping African Women to Farm?" *Economic Development and Cultural Change* 37, no. 2 (January 1989): 345–369.

Green, R. H., and H. W. Singer. "Sub-Sahara Africa in Depression: The Impact on the Welfare of Children." *World Development* 12, no. 3 (March 1984): 283–296.

Guyer, Jane I. "Women's Work and Production Systems: A Review of Two Reports on the Agricultural Crisis." *Review of African Political Economy* 27–28 (1984): 186–192.

———. "Women's Role in Development." In *Strategies for African Development*, Robert J. Berg and Jennifer S. Whitaker, eds., 393–421. Berkeley, Calif.: University of California Press, 1986.

Hein, Catherine. "The Feminisation of Industrial Employment in Mauritius: A Case of Sex Segregation." In *Sex Inequalities in Urban Employment in the Third World*, Richard Anker and Catherine Hein, eds., 277–311. New York: St. Martin's Press, 1986.

Heller, Peter S., et al. "The Implications of Fund-Supported Adjustment Programs for Poverty." Washington, D.C.: Occasional Paper 58, International Monetary Fund, 1988.

Herz, Barbara. "Women in Development: Kenya's Experience." *Finance and Development* 26, no. 2 (June 1989): 43–46.

Hopcraft, Peter. "Grain Marketing Policies and Institutions in Africa." *Finance and Development* 24, no. 1 (March 1987): 37–41.

Humphreys, Charles, and William Jaeger. "Africa's Adjustment and Growth." *Finance and Development* 26, no. 2 (March 1989): 6–8.

Huston, Perdita. *Third World Women Speak Out.* New York: Praeger Publishers, 1979.

ISIS. *Women in Development: A Resource Guide.* Philadelphia: New Society Publishers, 1984.

Joekes, S., et al. *Women and Structural Adjustment.* Washington, D.C.: Organization for Economic Cooperation and Development, 1988.

Kadyampakeni, J. "Pricing Policies in Africa with Special Reference to Agricultural Development in Malawi." *World Development* 16, no. 11 (November 1988): 1,299–1,317.

Kerner, Donna O. "Reading at Home Is Like Dancing in Church: A Comparison of Educational Opportunities in Two Tanzanian Regions." Lansing: Working Papers no. 123, Michigan State University, September 1986.

Lele, Uma. "Managing Agricultural Development in Africa." *Finance and Development* 26, no. 1 (March 1989): 45–49.

Little, Kenneth. "Women in African Towns South of the Sahara: The Urbanization Dilemma." In *Women and World Development*, I. Tinker and M. B. Bramsen, eds. 78–87. Washington, D.C.: Overseas Development Council, 1976.

Mbilinyi, Marjorie. "'Women in Development' Ideology and the Marketplace." In *Competition, A Feminist Taboo?* Valerie Miner and Helen E. Longino, eds. New York: Feminist Press, 1987.

Newman, Jeanne S. *Women of the World: Sub-Saharan Africa.* Washington, D.C.: U.S. Department of Commerce, Bureau of the Census, Office of Women in Development, 1984.

Novicki, Margaret. "Ghana: Balancing Food and Export Production. Interview with Steve G. Obimpeh." *African Report* (September-October 1988): 24–28.

Nyerere, Julius. Speech at Arusha, Tanzania, October 1984. Cited in Agnes Akosua Aidoo, "Women and Development in Africa: Alternative Strategies for the Future. In *Economic Crisis in Africa*, A. Adedeji and T. Shaw, eds. Boulder: Lynne Rienner, 1985.

Payer, Cheryl. "Tanzania and the World Bank." *Third World Quarterly* 5, no. 4 (October 1983): 791–813.

Schuster, Ilsa. "Marginal Lives: Conflict and Contradiction in the Position of Female Traders in Lusaka, Zambia." In *Women and Work in Africa*, Edna Bay, ed., 105–126. Boulder: Westview Press, 1982.

Singer, H. W., and P. Gray. "Trade Policy and Growth of Developing Countries: Some New Data." *World Development* 16, no. 3 (March 1988): 395–404.

Staudt, Kathleen A. "Women Farmers and Inequities in Agricultural Services." In *Women and Work in Africa*, Edna Bay, ed., 207–224. Boulder: Westview Press, 1982.

Tripp, Aili Mari. "The Impact of Crisis and Economic Reform on Women in Urban Tanzania." In *Unequal Burden: Economic Crises, Persistent Poverty, and Women's Work*, Lourdes Benería and Shelley Feldman, eds. Boulder: Westview Press, 1992.

United Nations. *World Survey on the Role of Women in Development.* New York: Department of International Economic and Social Affairs, 1986.

Whitehead, Ann. "Effects of Technological Change on Rural Women: A Review of Analysis and Concepts." In *Technology and Rural Women: Conceptual and Empirical Issues*, Iftika Ahmed, ed., 27–64. London: George Allen and Unwin, 1985.

World Bank. *Accelerated Development in Sub-Saharan Africa: An Agenda for Action.* Washington, D.C.: World Bank, 1981.

_____ . *Adjustment Lending: An Evaluation of Ten Years of Experience.* Policy and Research Series, no. 1. Washington, D.C.: World Bank, 1988a.

_____ . *World Development Report 1988.* Washington, D.C.: World Bank, 1988b.

_____ . *Sub-Saharan Africa: From Crisis to Sustainable Growth.* Washington, D.C.: Oxford University Press, 1989.

World Bank and the United Nations Development Program. *Africa's Adjustment and Growth in the 1980s.* Washington, D.C.: World Bank, 1989.

Zuckerman, Elaine. *Adjustment Programs and Social Welfare.* Washington, D.C.: World Bank Discussion Paper no. 44, 1989.

4

Development and Changing Gender Roles in Latin America and the Caribbean

HELEN I. SAFA

Recent research on gender roles in Latin America and the Caribbean belies the image of the passive, dependent woman, which is a legacy of popular stereotypes as well as of the earlier social science literature. Latin American and Caribbean women are emerging out of the isolation of the home and becoming increasingly important social protagonists in the public sphere. Women are increasing their participation in the labor force, assuming greater economic responsibility for their families, and challenging the state, unions, and other institutions to become more responsive to women's needs.

In part, these changes in gender roles may be explained by the socioeconomic transformations Latin America and the Caribbean have undergone in the postwar period, which have had a special impact on women. Although there were variations by country, the period from 1950 to 1980 in Latin America and the Caribbean was characterized by considerable economic growth, with total product increasing fivefold and per-capita product doubling. Industry expanded and diversified, with manufacturing output increasing sixfold between 1950 and 1987 and the tertiary sector growing at an even faster rate, whereas agricultural employment declined.

Population more than doubled from 1950 to 1980, and there was a marked shift toward urban areas, where the percentage of total population increased from 40.9 percent to 63.3 percent in the same period. Urban growth, which concentrated in large cities, was due largely to internal migration—particularly of women and young adults—and contributed to sharp declines in fertility as well as mortality and infant mortality. As a result, life expectancy increased to over sixty years in most countries, with a growing percentage of aged—especially women. Household size fell, particularly after 1960, and the percentage of households headed by women grew to about 20 percent. Educational levels and employment rates increased for both sexes during this period, but at a faster rate for women than for men (ECLAC 1988b: 1–3; ECLAC 1988a: 7–9).

Although Latin American and Caribbean women clearly benefited from these changes in terms of lower fertility, smaller household size, and increased educational levels and labor force participation, they also continue to suffer from poverty and income inequality, which varies substantially from one country to another. The degree of poverty also varies within countries and is more concentrated in rural areas and among black or indigenous Indian populations.[1] Despite an overall increase in average income from 1965 to 1975, the rich benefited more from economic growth, and the poor constituted about 40 percent of the population in 1970. The percentage of poor increased in urban areas from 1970 to 1980, which can be explained largely by the incapacity of the modern urban sector to absorb the large numbers of persons entering the labor force; this has resulted in persistently high rates of unemployment and underemployment in most countries. Although the role of governments expanded, attempts at income redistribution were limited (ECLAC 1988a: 9–10).

Level of development also affects the gains made by women and results in considerable variation among countries in the region. In general, women in the more advanced and industrialized countries such as Brazil, Cuba, Panama, Argentina, and Chile[2] made greater gains in terms of rising labor force participation and educational levels between 1960 and 1980 than women in countries in which the level of development remained low such as Paraguay and Guatemala (ECLAC 1988b: 9). Fertility levels also showed a sharper decline in the more advanced countries, whereas life expectancy increased for women in all countries except Bolivia and Haiti (ECLAC 1988e: 6, 14).

The economic crisis that hit most of Latin America and the Caribbean in the 1980s threatened to overturn the progress of the previous three decades and to halt all attempts at income redistribution. The crisis was brought on by rising prices of imports, particularly oil; a decline in both the quantity and price of exports, particularly agricultural products and minerals such as bauxite and nickel; and a steep rise in interest rates on the foreign debt, which totalled US$410 billion in 1987 (ECLAC 1988a: 11). The proportion of those living in poverty grew during the crisis as a result of a steep decline in gross domestic product, with negative growth rates in most countries; increased unemployment, which increased 48 percent between 1980 and 1985; and a decline in real wages of between 12 and 18 percent in the same period (ECLAC 1988b: 16). In desperation, several countries were forced to implement structural adjustment programs designed by the International Monetary Fund (IMF) to cut government expenditures, improve the balance of trade, and reduce the foreign debt. These policies, however, often resulted in greater hardship for the poor because they included devaluation of the currency, which accelerated the rate of inflation and the cost of living; the elimination of government subsidies for basic foods and subsidized credits to farmers; cuts in government expenditures, particularly for social services; and the freezing of real wages (Cornia 1987a: 27). The philosophy behind structural adjustment policies is to shift all responsibility for survival from the state to the individual and the family by forcing families to absorb a greater share of the cost of living by reducing government policies aimed at redistribution.

The impact of the economic crisis has been particularly severe on women in Latin America and the Caribbean and threatens to undermine their newly won gains. Most analysts agree that women (along with children and the elderly) constitute a more vulnerable group than men because, as I will show, their occupational distribution and access to resources is more limited (Cornia, Jolly, and Stewart 1987; ECLAC 1988a). At the same time, the crisis is increasing the importance and visibility of women's contribution to the household economy as additional women enter the labor force to meet the rising cost of living and the decreased wage-earning capacity of men. The increased economic importance of women coupled with the rise of female-headed households is weakening the image of men as the principal breadwinners in Latin American and Caribbean households.

This chapter examines the causes and consequences of these changes in gender roles in Latin America and the Caribbean. Because of the scope of information required in an overview, variations between and within countries and between ethnic groups have been minimized, although greater attention has been paid to class differences, which affect the entire region. I focus on three main areas: (1) increasing labor force participation due to economic changes accompanying the growth of urbanization and industrialization; (2) the impact of these changes on family structure, especially the growth of female-headed households and the increased contribution of women to the household economy; and (3) the increasing participation by women in social movements demanding the provision of basic services, the recognition of human rights, and other issues that are politicizing women in Latin America. Considerable attention also will be given to the impact of the current economic crisis on women in these three areas.

INCREASING LABOR FORCE PARTICIPATION

Although there is still a debate regarding the effects of paid employment on women's status, paid work seems to be an essential step in breaking women out of the isolation of the home and increasing their presence in the public arena and their consciousness about public issues. However, because women are relatively recent entrants into the formal labor force in most Latin American countries, they tend to be regarded as supplementary workers[3] and are paid lower wages than men, who are considered the primary breadwinners. Low wages for women reflect the common misconception that their wages are only a supplement to the family income and therefore need not be adequate to support their dependents. This suggests that there are ideological as well as structural obstacles to women's equality in the workplace.

Nevertheless, the size of the female labor force increased threefold in Latin America between 1950 and 1980, with overall participation rates rising from almost 18 percent to over 26 percent in the same period (ECLAC 1988a: 15).

Participation rates for women grew faster than those for men and included all age groups, although single women between the ages of twenty and twenty-nine continued to be the most active (ECLAC 1988b: 5–7). Because of economic need and higher investment in education, particularly among the middle class, many women do not withdraw from the labor force when they marry and have children. For example, the number of women in higher education rose from 35 percent to 45 percent between 1970 and 1985 (ECLAC 1988b: 3).

Higher education levels are a key factor in increased female labor force participation because education prepares women for a wider range of jobs. Women's educational levels rose at an even faster rate than those of men as part of the enormous expansion in primary and particularly secondary education from 1950 to 1970, after which the rate of growth slowed. This contributed to an increase of women in white-collar work between 1960 and 1980, particularly in the more developed Latin American and Caribbean countries. However, even relatively privileged white-collar women face a highly segmented labor market and are found principally in such feminine occupations as clerical work, sales, teaching, and nursing.[4]

Declining fertility levels also contributed to increased female participation rates and can be explained by increased urbanization and educational levels as well as improved access to contraceptive methods and family planning programs in some Latin American and Caribbean countries. Between 1980 and 1985, only three Latin American countries had fertility rates in excess of six children per woman, whereas eight experienced rates of less than four children per woman (ECLAC 1988b: 2).

Latin America and the Caribbean were characterized by rapid rural-to-urban migration from 1940 until 1970, when the rate slowed somewhat. Women predominated in this migratory flow due to the limited employment opportunities available to them in the rural areas. Many migrants are young single women between the ages of ten and twenty-four—often the eldest daughters in large rural families who are sent into the city to work as domestic servants (ECLAC 1988c: 17–18). Lourdes Arizpe (1982) has documented the process of relay migration in Mexico whereby the migrant father is gradually replaced by his sons and daughters in order of age because their remittances contribute to the viability of an impoverished peasant economy. Migrants are impelled by agricultural stagnation and population pressure as well as the expulsion of peasants and tenant farmers due to the introduction of capitalist production methods in agriculture. Rural women who remained behind continue to work as unpaid family members on peasant farms, migrate to new areas of colonization, or hire themselves out as seasonal agricultural laborers (Deere and Leon 1987).

Due to the recent growth of agribusiness in Latin America and the Caribbean, women are assuming increasing importance as agricultural day laborers, both as producers of traditional crops such as coffee and new export crops such as flowers, vegetables, and fruits. In both the traditional and new export agriculture, women command lower wages, work harder, and are less organized than men. Their situation illustrates the "comparative advantage of women's disadvantages," to use Arizpe's (1981) term in a study of women workers in the strawberry export-processing plants in Mexico. Verena Stolcke's (1988) ethnohistorical study of the *volantes*, or day laborers, employed in coffee-growing near São Paulo shows that women's disadvantage is due partly to the greater job alternatives open to men and partly to the increasing need for women's wage labor to help maintain the family.

Domestic service is still the largest occupational group among women in Latin America, although the proportion has fallen markedly from over 37 percent of the economically active female population in some countries in 1960 to a maximum of 22.9 percent in 1980 (ECLAC 1988c: 22). Domestic service also has modernized in the most developed countries of the region, with a changeover from resident to nonresident employees and in some countries, increases in social security coverage, regulation of hours worked and days off, and paid vacations (Chaney and Castro 1989). Domestic service is often the first job rural women find in the city, but as they have children and can no longer live in the employer's home, they move to other activities such as street and market vending (Bunster and Chaney 1985). Street traders range from rural indigenous women in Mexico and the Andes selling their own produce or craft specialties in the city (Arizpe 1975) to "higglers" in Jamaica, Haiti, or the eastern Caribbean who travel among the islands and as far as Miami buying and selling food, clothing, appliances, and other consumer goods (ECLAC 1988d).

Domestic service and street vending are traditional jobs in the informal sector, which is characterized by small-scale, unregulated forms of production and distribution without a formal wage-labor contract. Jobs in the informal sector lack protective labor legislation, minimum wages, social security, or other benefits. Many of the workers in the informal sector are self-employed, but some are what Alejandro Portes (1983) has termed "disguised wage workers." In an effort to cut labor costs and avoid unions and other labor legislation, manufacturers are increasingly subcontracting part of their production process to home workers who are not entitled to any of these benefits. Most of these home workers are married women who must do piecework at home because of child care responsibilities or because their husbands will not allow them to work outside the home. This allows for greater flexibility in working hours for women and also for employers, who can scale the volume of work up or down with market fluctuations. Thus, there is no stability of employment, and the piecework rates workers receive generally fall below the minimum wage, as a recent study of home workers in Mexico City demonstrated (Benería and Roldán 1987). Even service industries such as data processing are turning to subcontracting as a way of cutting their labor costs to meet international competition.

The growth of the informal sector also may reflect state policy, which with international support has encouraged the growth of microenterprises in Latin America and the Caribbean. Because of its capacity for labor absorption and cost advantages in a highly competitive international market, the informal sector is receiving increased support from both the public and private sectors in terms of credit, access to raw materials and foreign exchange, and other privileges formerly reserved exclusively for the formal sector. Income-generating programs for women in both rural and urban areas are a favorite mechanism for setting up these microenterprises, and may simply become another way of cutting labor costs (Safa 1987). These programs have proliferated throughout the region and are generally set up by external sources with minimal funding because the numbers of women involved in each project are small. For example, in Chile in 1984, 700 grass-roots economic organizations were registered for both sexes, involving approximately 100,000 women in Santiago and San Antonio alone (ECLAC 1988c: 29). As in the case of industrial home work, the products of microenterprises, which include agricultural products, clothes, footwear, and other consumer items, often are marketed by multinational corporations.

The percentage of women factory workers in Latin America and the Caribbean remained relatively stable or even declined in some countries with the adoption of import-substitution policies and increasingly capital-intensive techniques of production after 1950. The application of neoliberal economic policies in countries such as Chile also led to deindustrialization and the decline of the industrial labor force. Only in São Paulo, Brazil, did the spectacular industrial boom of the 1970s lead to an appreciable growth in female employment in manufacturing, which increased 181 percent between 1970 and 1980 (Humphrey 1987). However, women workers were largely concentrated in exclusively female and inferior jobs, which shows that the sexual division of labor in the workplace may be reinforced rather than weakened by development and industrialization.

Industrial employment for women in a few Latin American and Caribbean countries has increased as a result of the growth of export processing,[5] particularly since the economic crisis of the 1980s referred to earlier. Export promotion has been favored by governments and international agencies as a way of alleviating unemployment and of earning desperately needed foreign exchange to redress the balance-of-payments crisis. In many countries, export promotion has replaced import substitution as a development strategy. Export processing also represents a decided advantage for the United States and other advanced industrial countries, which cut their labor costs by exporting the labor-intensive stages of the manufacturing process to these low-wage countries and by paying only a low value-added duty when these assembled goods are reimported.

Export manufacturers have shown a preference for women workers because, like agricultural day workers, they are cheaper to employ and less likely to unionize, and they have greater patience for the tedious, monotonous work involved in the assembly-line production of clothing and electronics—the most popular export-processing items. Wage reductions resulting from currency devaluation during the economic crisis have increased the attractiveness of investment in export processing in Mexico, the Dominican Republic, and other areas. In the Dominican Republic, the number of workers quadrupled between 1985 and 1988 to an estimated 85,000, approximately 80 percent of whom are women (Abreu et al. 1989: 142). At the rate of exchange prevailing in August 1986, the average wage in export processing was approximately US$90 monthly (Joekes 1987: 55). Although not officially proscribed, there are no unions in the Dominican export-processing plants; and workers are fired and blacklisted with other plants if any organizing activity is detected. Workers complain of the lack of public transportation, proper eating facilities, adequate medical services, and child care in the free-trade zones in which these export-processing plants are located. Workers with grievances receive little support from the state, and most women simply quit when they can no longer withstand the pressure of high production quotas, strict discipline, and long hours. As a result, labor turnover is high, and factory managers have indicated a preference for women with children because they feel these women's need to work ensures great job commitment (Joekes 1987: 59). A high percentage of Dominican women workers in export-processing zones are married or female heads of households, which departs from the global pattern in which there is a predominance of young single women employed in export processing (Safa 1990).

Many of these married women have entered the labor force because of falling household income and the rising cost of living, and some have become the principal breadwinners in the family. Women throughout Latin America and the Caribbean have adopted a variety of strategies to add income and cut expenditures. Households are doubling up, which increases the number of extended families; in the Dominican Republic, this number is higher in urban than in rural areas, which runs counter to most demographic predictions (Duarte 1988: 19). This appears to be happening in several countries in the region, reversing the trend toward smaller households that occurred prior to the crisis (Gonzalez de la Rocha 1988). Thus far, these survival strategies have enabled consumption patterns in some households to remain relatively stable, although in many countries the nutrition and health situation in the poorest sectors is deteriorating (Cornia, Jolly, and Stewart 1987).

Governments have done little to help the poor meet the rising cost of living, although there are food aid programs in some countries. However, the share of expenditures on social services fell in the majority of the countries of the region between 1980 and 1985 (ECLAC 1988a: 12). Educational deterioration throughout the region is shown primarily through declining primary school enrollments and an increasing loss of teachers. The closure of public health facilities; a lack of medical personnel, medicine, and vital equipment; and growing health care costs have contributed to a sharp increase in infant mortality rates in some Latin American countries (Cornia, Jolly, and Stewart 1987). These cuts in government services add to the cost of living and increase the pressure on women to join the labor force. The cuts also reflect the pressure put on Latin American and Caribbean governments to reduce state policies aimed at alleviating the poverty that results from structural adjustment and other neoliberal economic policies.

Guy Standing (1989) has argued that "global feminization through flexible labor" results from both structural adjustment policies and the need to cut labor costs in order to meet increasing international competition from developing as well as advanced industrial societies. He cites a number of factors such as the growth of export processing, labor market deregulation through subcontracting and the use of the informal sector, and cuts in government expenditures that contribute to the rising participation rates of women and the falling participation rates of men. If, as Standing suggests, women are being substituted for men in various occupational categories (although much less so in Latin America than in other regions), then their increasing incorporation into the labor force may be further weakening the power of organized labor in these regions. Women constitute a cheap labor reserve that is difficult to organize because many women work in the informal economy or in areas such as seasonal agriculture or export processing, where labor unions are prohibited or politically controlled. However, organized labor in the region also has neglected women workers, who are regarded as supplementary workers in comparison to men. On the basis of recent studies conducted among export-processing workers in the Dominican Republic and Puerto Rico, I maintain that women's lack of bargaining power in the workplace lies less with the women themselves than with the lack of support they receive from unions, the state, and political parties (Safa 1990). At present these women workers have no adequate vehicles through which to express their grievances or to transform their sense of exploitation (which is very real) into greater class solidarity. Until the claims of women workers are given the same legitimacy as those of men and not regarded as supplementary or subsidiary, women will continue to be treated primarily as a source of cheap labor.

FAMILY PATTERNS AND THE HOUSEHOLD ECONOMY

As a result of their increased labor force participation in both the formal and the informal sector, women are taking more responsibility than ever for the economic support of their families, whereas the man's role as principal breadwinner is weakening. In place of the patriarchy of the past, a more egalitarian pattern is emerging in which women and men share responsibility for the maintenance of the household as well as participating jointly in making decisions and in some household tasks. The extent of change depends on many factors, but a key factor is the importance of the woman's contribution to the household economy.

In my comparative studies of women factory workers in export manufacturing in the Caribbean, where women are major contributors to the household economy, I have found that women use their earnings and the family's increased dependence on them to bargain for increased authority and sharing of responsibility within the household (Safa 1990). The changes are more marked in Puerto Rico than in the Dominican Republic because the Puerto Rican industrialization process started earlier and in the initial labor-intensive stage, offered more jobs to women than to men, particularly in the garment industry. This type of industrialization plus the growth of employment for women in the service sector helps to explain why 90 percent of respondents in my Puerto Rican sample said it is easier for women to find jobs than men. In Puerto Rico, unemployment rates are higher for men than for women; and as in other countries in the region, participation rates for men have been declining, whereas those for women have steadily increased. In no case in my sample does the woman's wage represent less than 40 percent of the household income; and it is even higher in the case of married women and female heads of household, who constitute a majority of my respondents (Safa 1985: 91–92). Men no longer feel threatened by their wives' working because it is recognized that families can no longer survive on a single wage. For the same reason, most women now continue to be employed even if they are married and have young children, although this places a heavy burden on them.

As in the rest of Latin America, the increased employment of married women in Puerto Rico and the Dominican Republic has not led to any appreciable increase in the male share of domestic work; thus, women with families typically face a "double day." Housework and child care still are conceived of as women's responsibility, even when women also are making a major contribution to the household economy.[6] However, the employed, married Puerto Rican women in my sample now share more decisions with their husbands and have greater control over the family budget. Most maintain that both husband and wife are now the head of the household. In contrast, in Dominican households, the man's role as breadwinner still is more intact, and 80 percent of the employed married women interviewed considered their husbands to be the head of the household (Safa 1990: 86). Although most Dominican women agree that their wage is essential to the family's survival, the ideological dependence on a male provider is stronger. The Dominican women in this sample were generally younger with small children to support, had worked a shorter time, and had fewer alternative sources of income than Puerto Rican women. In Puerto Rico, working women are entitled to unemployment insurance; and unemployed female heads of households with young children can receive welfare assistance, whereas no such transfer payments exist in the Dominican Republic. In both cases, however, female heads of household are the poorest in the sample because they are dependent primarily on the woman's wage, which in export processing is very low.

The failure of men to fulfill their role as economic provider is contributing to the increasing rate of female-headed households in both the Dominican Republic and Puerto Rico and in the region generally since the 1970s. Either men leave on their own accord because they are unable to support their families, or their wives force them out. Partial figures for 1982 show that the number of female heads of household fluctuates between 18 and 23 percent in Latin America and 24 and 46 percent in the Caribbean (ECLAC 1988a: 15). Historical and cultural differences between countries help to account for these variations because there is a long tradition of female economic autonomy in the English-speaking Caribbean. Throughout the region, however, there is a growing importance of socioeconomic factors, such as male unemployment, migration, urbanization, and the recent economic crisis, in the formation of female-headed households. Female-headed households consistently fall into the lowest income categories, even though these women are more likely to be employed than are married or single women. Their low income reflects the disadvantages women face in the labor market and the fact that often fewer household members are employed in female-headed households due to the absence of a male partner. Female heads of households try to cope with this problem by incorporating other adult kin such as siblings or cousins as additional wage earners in the family or as caretakers for children. Poverty is particularly acute among young women with small children, and their numbers are increasing due to the high level of teenage pregnancy in the region (ECLAC 1988a: 26). Most of these teenage mothers continue to live in their parents' households.

Women in poor Latin American and Caribbean households have commonly sought to stretch family income by producing goods at home rather than purchasing them in stores, adding additional wage earners to the household, or developing networks of mutual aid among extended kin and neighbors. With the economic crisis, these patterns have intensified. Newly married couples are doubling up with parents and other adult wage earners are incorporated into the household, with a resulting increase in household size in some countries (Gonzalez de la Rocha 1988; Duarte 1988). The domestic burden is increased as household possessions such as a refrigerator are sold and expenditures are reduced on transportation, utilities, clothes, and even food. Changes in consumption and dietary patterns have resulted in increasing dependence on cheap sources of calories such as rice and potatoes and declining protein intake from milk or meat (Cornia 1987b: 99). Women and young children are most likely to be affected by declining food consumption because preference is given to feeding male wage earners. In both the Dominican Republic and Jamaica, the level of malnutrition among children under four years of age reached 41 percent in 1984 and 1985 (Cornia and Stewart 1987: 115; Ramirez, Duarte, and Gomez 1986: 12).

The extreme economic pressures the poor in Latin America and the Caribbean are now experiencing helps to explain why many women continue to look to men as the principal economic providers. They realize their serious disadvantages in the labor market and are aware of the extreme poverty in which most female-headed households live. The social identity women gain from their role as wives and mothers also is important in explaining the "ideology of domesticity" and women's attachment to their domestic role. As Verena Stolcke (1984) notes in her study of Brazilian agricultural laborers, men have become more demoralized than women over the transition to wage labor and their increasing difficulty in fulfilling their role as breadwinner. The result is an erosion of men's authority in the household. According to Stolcke (1984: 287), "Whereas men have to, literally, 'earn' their rightful place in the household, women's 'natural' place is in the home." This strong identification with their domestic role also helps to explain why some married women may choose poorly paid industrial homework over more remunerative factory employment (Roldán 1985).

In short, the redefinition of gender roles within the family in Latin America and the Caribbean depends on a variety of factors such as the domestic cycle, household composition, and the economic contribution of husband and wife—all of which vary within as well as between countries. My data on Caribbean women workers suggest that women have been more successful in negotiating change within the household than at the level of the workplace or the state, where their needs still are not given the same legitimacy as those of men. Women are breaking through this ideological barrier to gain greater legitimacy in the public sphere; but they still have more leverage within the private sphere of the family, which is their traditional locus of responsibility.

WOMEN AND SOCIAL MOVEMENTS

The 1970s and 1980s witnessed a marked increase in participation by women in social movements in Latin America—as workers in trade unions, housewives in squatter settlements, and mothers defending human rights against state repression. Women's social movements in Latin America are commonly seen as a response to authoritarian military rule and the current economic crisis, through which women organized to defend their families against state repression and threats to their livelihood. However, these movements also can be seen as an outgrowth of a breakdown in the traditional division between the private and public spheres in Latin America. Industrialization and urbanization have weakened the role of the family and strengthened the role of the state. The private sphere has always been considered the domain of women, but it is increasingly threatened by economic and political forces, which threaten its viability and sanctity.

Latin American women are not just defending the private domain against increasing state and market intervention. They also are demanding incorporation into the state so that their rights as citizens will be fully recognized (Jelin 1987). In the process, they are redefining and enlarging their domestic role from one of private nurturance to one of collective public protest, and in this way they are challenging the traditional confinement of women to the private sphere.

Many factors contributed to the increased participation of Latin American women in social movements. Women have long been active at the neighborhood level through both informal networks and more organized forms of collective action such as squatter settlements and barrio committees. These collective activities took on added importance due to the economic crisis and received the support of important groups such as the Catholic church and other nongovernmental agencies. Increased educational and occupational opportunities made women more vocal and contributed to the growth of the feminist movement, which gained visibility during the UN Decade for the Equality of Women from 1976 to 1985. The attention given to poor women by largely middle-class feminists made working-class women more receptive to feminism and to issues of gender inequality.

As a result of their frustration in working through such recognized channels as political parties and labor unions, Latin American women have chosen to confront the state directly in voicing their demands. These institutions have neglected women and continue to regard men as the primary spokespersons to the outside world. In São Paulo, for example, during the industrial boom of the 1970s, despite their increasing labor force participation, women had to struggle to make industrial unions more responsive to their needs. In the case of the important metallurgy union, female union committees were formed and individually active women were integrated into the union hierarchy. Nonetheless, the union continued to regard women as supplementary workers whose needs did not have the same priority as those of men (Souza Lobo forthcoming). Political parties also are seen as a male sphere in which the poor play essentially a client role, exchanging votes for political favors such as improving roads or setting up a day care center. This fosters *asistencialismo* (aid dependency) and may lead to the cooptation of women's groups for partisan political ends. In addition, labor unions and political parties in countries such as Brazil, Argentina, and Chile were greatly weakened due to strong government repression during the years of authoritarian military rule. Thus, the attempt of these regimes to limit legitimate political action contributed to the politicalization of nontraditional groups such as women (Jelin 1987).

Most of the demands women make on the state arise out of their immediate perceived needs and experience and do not question the existing division of labor. One of the principal demands concerns the provision of public services such as running water, electricity, and transportation—all of which are sorely lacking in the squatter settlements in which most of these poor women live. Women's reproductive role as housewives and mothers has tended to push them into the foreground as champions of these collective consumption issues, which include protests against the high cost of living and the lack of day care, health services, and even food. One of the most successful and unique collective consumption strategies to combat the growing economic crisis is the *comedores populares*, or communal kitchens, organized by women in Lima, Santiago, and other Latin American cities. Groups of fifteen to fifty households buy and prepare food collectively for the neighborhood, with each family paying according to the number of meals requested. Many of these *comedores* sprang up spontaneously, whereas others have been started or at least supported by the church, the state, and other local and international agencies. In Lima in 1985, their number was estimated at 300 (Cornia 1987b: 99), whereas more recent estimates give the figure as 1,000–1,200 (Blondet 1989). Their growing number is evidence of women's collective response to the increasing severity of the economic crisis in Peru and other Latin American countries in the last few years.

Some feminists have been critical of these women's self-help organizations because they focus almost exclusively on traditional female tasks and continue to identify women with their domestic role. They arise out of what Maxine Molyneux (1986) has defined as women's practical gender interests in contrast to strategic gender interests, which question or transform the sexual division of labor. However, I would argue that the collectivization of private tasks such as food preparation and child care is transforming women's roles, even though such tasks are not undertaken as conscious challenges to gender subordination.

In contrast to some middle-class feminists, these poor women never reject their domestic role but use it as a base to give them strength and legitimacy in their demands on the state (Caldeira 1987: 97). By politicizing the private sphere, women have redefined rather than rejected their domestic role and extended the struggle against the state beyond the workplace into the home and community.

Nowhere is this more apparent than in the demands Latin American women have placed on the state for the recognition of human rights. One of the best-known cases in contemporary Latin American society is the Mothers of the Plaza de Mayo in Argentina, who played a decisive role in the defeat of the military dictatorship in that country. Composed mostly of older women with no political experience, the group members were able to use their traditional role as mothers as a defense and turn against the state to protest the disappearance of their children and other loved ones during the military dictatorship. In order to maintain their legitimacy, they refused any identification with political parties of feminism. In their own words, *"Nosotros no defendemos ideologias, defendemos la vida"* ("We don't defend ideologies, we defend life") (Feijoo and Gogna 1987: 155). Human rights movements involving women similar to the Argentine mothers have arisen in Uruguay, Chile, Brazil, Honduras, El Salvador, Guatemala, and other Latin American countries under military rule.

The transformative potential of women's social movements in Latin America has been questioned by those who feel they cannot outlive the immediate crisis situation such as the opposition to military rule or the economic crisis. Elizabeth Jelin (1987) maintains that women participate more in short-term, sporadic protest movements than in long-term, formalized institutional settings. In Argentina, the Mothers of the Plaza de Mayo, who played such an important role in the defeat of the military dictatorship, have lost popular support and split into two groups—partly over conflict regarding the democratically elected government's human rights policy and prosecution of the military, which fell far short of their goals.

Most social movements have lost strength as the locus of power has shifted back to political parties with the transition to democratic rule in countries such as Argentina, Brazil, Uruguay, and Chile. Elections rekindle old political divisions between rival political parties and fragment social movements that have arisen not only among women but among youth, the urban poor, and broader-based human rights groups. Nevertheless, certain gains have been made and even institutionalized into legal codes. Women have made the greatest inroads into state power in Brazil through the São Paulo Council on the Condition of Women, which implemented a family planning program and established a special police precinct staffed by women to deal with crimes of sexual abuse and domestic violence (Alvarez 1989: 55–56). The subsequent National Council on Women's Rights successfully promoted a woman's agenda in the new Brazilian constitution adopted in 1988, which facilitates divorce, extends maternity leave, and eliminates the prohibition on abortion (without legalizing it). Argentina also has legalized divorce and modified *patria potestad* to give women more equality in the family and joint custody of children (Jaquette 1989: 199–203). Despite concerted efforts by the Pinochet dictatorship to court women's support in the 1988 plebiscite, 52 percent of Chilean women rejected his continuation in power, reflecting in part the effectiveness of opposition women's groups.

Women's social movements have accelerated the transformation in gender roles in Latin America and the Caribbean. Women have acquired greater self-esteem and recognition of their rights as women and greater legitimacy in the public sphere. Such ideological changes are the best guarantee that these women will resist any attempt to reestablish the old order and will continue to press for their rights.

CONCLUSION

Clearly the changes in gender role among Latin American and Caribbean women in the postwar period have promoted greater gender consciousness. Women have become increasingly important members of the labor force and contributors to the household economy; they have organized social movements for human rights and social welfare; and they are trying to voice their demands in labor unions and political parties. Women's demands posed less of a threat as long as they were confined to domestic issues such as the provision of public services or the rising cost of living and did not directly attack male interests in more established power structures such as labor unions or political parties. As they move away from these domestic issues into more strategic gender interests that attempt to restructure the sexual division of labor, they will undoubtedly encounter greater resistance. Yet only through a more egalitarian sexual division of labor and the full incorporation of women into the public sphere will Latin American and Caribbean women be able to translate their gender consciousness into further gains in gender equality.

The obstacles to gender equality in Latin America and the Caribbean are both ideological and structural. I have argued, based on my own research, that women have been more successful in challenging their subordination in the home than at work or in politics. Working women have a greater role in decisionmaking, and many no longer look to their husband as the sole head of household or economic provider. At the same time, women face severe disadvantages in the labor market as unions, the state, and political parties continue to regard them as supplementary workers and neglect their needs. Therefore, the greatest resistance to gender equality in Latin America and the Caribbean appears to lie at the levels of the workplace and the state rather than the home.

This is an interesting reversal of one prominent trend in feminist theory, which maintains that the family "is the central site of the oppression of women" (Barrett 1980: 211). It is true that women's domestic responsibilities limit their possibilities of participation in paid employment and even in social movements. But women's concern for their families is also what propels many of them to seek ways of adding to the household income and to struggle for human rights and economic justice. Thus, the family is a contradictory institution for women, serving as a source both of subordination and of legitimacy for their entrance into the public sphere. Women also find gratification and social identity in their domestic role, which may explain why working-class women reject feminist attacks on the family. Working-class women in Latin America and the Caribbean want to establish more egalitarian relationships in the family while retaining it as a source of emotional and material support.

The structural constraints to further advances in women's equality in Latin America and the Caribbean lie principally in the economic and political forces now endangering the entire region. The economic crisis has increased the importance of women's contribution to the household, but it also has placed a heavy burden on women to meet the rising cost of living, cuts in government services, and high levels of unemployment. In many countries in the region, the need to pay the foreign debt consumes half or more of government revenues and undermines the government's ability to stimulate economic growth or relieve poverty and income inequality. Under these circumstances, it is not surprising that most governments in the region have been largely unresponsive to women's demands, leading to disillusionment and in some cases to withdrawal.

However, although Latin American and Caribbean women may suffer setbacks, I doubt that they will retreat entirely into the private sphere. The growth of gender consciousness has given greater credibility and visibility to women's issues so that women's organizations now are recognized as a political force, although some may be coopted for partisan political ends. Genuine gender equality will not be achieved until women are integrated as equals into the power structure and can represent their own interests and not have them mediated by men. As Julieta Kirkwood (1986: 65) reminds us, the issue is not simply one of women's incorporation into a male-defined world but is one of transforming this world to do away with the hierarchies of class, gender, race, and ethnicity that so long have subordinated much of the Latin American population—men as well as women.

NOTES

This chapter was first presented in very preliminary form as part of a panel organized in honor of Dr. Charles Wagley, Professor Emeritus of Anthropology at the University of Florida, who received the Kalman Silvert award from the Latin American Studies Association in 1988 in acknowledgment of his distinguished service and scholarship in the field of Latin American studies. Dr. Wagley was a member of my thesis committee at Columbia University and has served as my mentor since those early days. This chapter is dedicated to him with enormous respect and gratitude. Dr. Wagley died in November 1991.

1. The Latin American and Caribbean region is marked by great ethnic diversity, resulting from the subjugation of indigenous Indian populations by Spanish, Portuguese, and other European colonists and the importation of African slaves, primarily into the Caribbean basin and Brazil. These oppressed Indian and black populations continue to be concentrated at the bottom of the socioeconomic ladder, and Indian groups are found primarily in the rural areas

of Bolivia, Peru, Ecuador, Guatemala, and Mexico. At the same time, because of extensive miscegenation between white European and other races, the rigid color bar found in the United States is replaced by a fluid color-class continuum with darker-skinned people at the lower end of the socioeconomic scale. Although Indian communities often are characterized by more egalitarian relationships between the sexes, women's high illiteracy rates, low educational levels, and lack of knowledge of Spanish or Portuguese have limited their access to the larger society and lowered the status of women in indigenous communities vis-à-vis men (ECLAC 1988c: 8).

2. Women in Argentina, Chile, and Uruguay already had fairly high educational levels and labor force participation rates prior to 1960, due to more developed forms of urbanization and industrialization that preceded the rest of the region as well as earlier support for female public education in these countries. Another factor in the level of development of these countries is the predominantly European nature of their populations compared to countries with large indigenous populations, in which the problems of educating these groups has been compounded by their lack of knowledge of Spanish or Portuguese. Educational and occupational gains made by women (and men) in Cuba are due largely to the conscious effort of the socialist revolutionary government, which took power in 1959.

3. The supplementary work status of women stems from a sexual division of labor in which women are assigned primary responsibility for reproductive tasks, whereas men are considered the primary wage earners.

4. In 1980, the percentage of women in the service sector, which includes a high proportion of domestic servants as well as white-collar workers, ranged between 45 and 55 percent of women in most Latin American and Caribbean countries (ECLAC 1988b: 3–10).

5. Export processing refers to the unskilled assembly-line work carried out largely by women in certain developing countries and results from the fragmentation of production brought on by increasing international competition. Because of its emphasis on export production, export processing is the reverse of import substitution, which was designed to build up industry to meet the country's domestic needs.

6. Middle- and upper-class women in Latin America and the Caribbean usually have domestic servants, but the only assistance poor women can draw on consists of female relatives living either with them or nearby or occasionally neighbors, who are not always willing or able to help. Only Cuba has a nationwide government program to provide child care centers for working mothers.

BIBLIOGRAPHY

Abreu, Alfonso, Manuel Cocco, Carlos Despradel, Eduardo Garcia Michel, and Arturo Peguero. 1989. *Las Zonas Francas Industriales en la República Dominicana: El Exito de una Política Economica.* Sto. Domingo: Centro Internacional para el Desarollo Económico.

Alvarez, Sonia. 1989. "Women's Movements and Gender Politics in the Brazilian Transition." In *The Women's Movement in Latin America: Feminism and the Transition to Democracy,* Jane Jaquette, ed. Winchester, Mass.: Unwin and Hyman, 18–71.

Arizpe, Lourdes. 1975. *Indígenas en la Ciudad de Mexico. El caso de las Marías.* Mexico City: Ed. Sep. Setentas 182.

――――. 1981. "The Comparative Advantage of Women's Disadvantages." In *Signs* 7, no. 2 (Winter 1981): 453–473. Special issue edited by H. Safa and E. Leacock.

――――. 1982. "Relay Migration and the Social Reproduction of the Peasantry." In *Toward a Political Economy of Urbanization in Third World Countries,* Helen Safa, ed. New Delhi, India: Oxford University Press, 19–46.

Barrett, Michele. 1980. *Women's Oppression Today.* London: Verso Editions.

Bernería, Lourdes, and Martha Roldán. 1987. *The Crossroads of Class and Gender.* Chicago: University of Chicago Press.

Blondet, Cecilia. 1989. "Women's Organizations and Politics in a Time of Crisis." Paper presented at a workshop at the Helen Kellogg Institute for International Studies, University of Notre Dame, Notre Dame, Indiana.

Bunster, Ximena, and Elsa Chaney. 1985. *Sellers and Servants: Working Women in Lima, Peru.* New York: Praeger.

Caldeira, Teresa. 1987. "Mujeres, Cotaneidad y Política." In *Ciudadanía e Identidad: Las Mujeres en los Movimientos Sociales Latinoamericanos,* E. Jelin, ed. Geneva: United Nations Research Institute for Social Development, 75–128.

Chaney, Elsa, and Mary García-Castro. 1989. *Muchachas No More: Household Workers in Latin America and the Caribbean.* Philadelphia: Temple University Press.

Cornia, Giovanni A. 1987a. "Economic Decline and Human Welfare in the First Half of the 1980s." In *Adjustment with a Human Face,* Giovanni A. Cornia, G. R. Jolly, and F. Stewart, eds. New York: Clarendon Press, 11–47.

―――. 1987b. "Adjustment at the Household Level: Potentials and Limitations of Survival Strategies." In *Adjustment with a Human Face,* Giovanni A. Cornia, G. R. Jolly, and F. Stewart, eds. New York: Clarendon Press, 90–104.

Cornia, Giovanni A., and F. Stewart. 1987. "Country Experience with Adjustment." In *Adjustment with a Human Face,* Giovanni A. Cornia, G. R. Jolly, and F. Stewart, ed. New York: Clarendon Press, 105–130.

Cornia, Giovanni A., G. R. Jolly, and F. Steward, eds. 1987. *Adjustment with a Human Face.* New York: Clarendon Press.

Deere, Carmen Diana, and Magdalena Leon, eds. 1987. *Rural Women and State Policy: Feminist Perspectives on Latin American Agricultural Development.* Boulder: Westview Press.

Duarte, Isis. 1988. "Crisis, Familia y Participación Laboral de la Mujer en la República Dominicana." Paper presented at the Center for Latin American Studies Annual Conference, University of Florida, Gainesville.

Economic Commission for Latin America and the Caribbean (ECLAC). 1988a. *Latin American and Caribbean Women: Between Change and Crisis,* LC/L.464 (CRM. 4/2). Santiago, Chile: ECLAC.

―――. 1988b. *Women, Work, and Crisis.* LC/L.458 (CRM. 4/6). Santiago, Chile: ECLAC.

―――. 1988c. *Women as a Social Protagonist in the 1980s.* LC/L.470 (CRM. 4/8). Santiago, Chile: ECLAC.

―――. 1988d. *Women in the Inter-Island Trade in Agricultural Produce in the Eastern Caribbean.* L. 465 (CRM. 4/9). Santiago, Chile: ECLAC.

―――. 1988e. *Women and Demographic Change: Statistics and Indicators.* LC/L.473 (CRM. 4/11). Santiago, Chile: ECLAC.

Feijoo, María del Carmen, and Monica Gogna. 1987. "Las Mujeres en la Transícion a la Democracia." In *Ciudadanía e Identidad: Las Mujeres en los Movimientos Sociales Latinoamericanos,* E. Jelin, ed. Geneva: UNRISD, 129–188.

Gonzalez de la Rocha, Mercedes. 1988. "Economic Crisis, Domestic Reorganization, and Women's Work in Guadalajara, Mexico." *Bulletin of Latin American Research* 7, no. 2: 207–223.

Humphrey, John. 1987. *Gender and Work in the Third World.* London: Tavistock Publications.

Jaquette, Jane. 1989. "Women and the New Democratic Politics." In *The Women's Movement in Latin America: Feminism and the Transition to Democracy,* Jane Jaquette, ed. Winchester, Mass.: Unwin and Hyman, 1–17.

Jelin, Elizabeth. 1987. "Introduction." In *Ciudadanía e Identidad: Las Mujeres en los Movimientos Sociales Latinoamericanos,* E. Jelin, ed. Geneva: UNRISD, 1–18.

Joekes, Susan. 1987. "Employment in Industrial Free Zones in the Dominican Republic: A Report with Recommendations for Improved Worker Services." Washington, D.C.: International Center for Research on Women. Prepared for U.S. AID–Dominican Republic.

Kirkwood, Julieta. 1986. *Ser Política en Chile: Las Feministas y los Partidos*. Santiago: Facultad Latinoamericana de Ciencias Sociales.

Molyneux, Maxine. 1986. "Mobilization Without Emancipation? Women's Interests, State, and Revolution." In *Transition and Development: Problems of Third World Socialism*, R. Fagen, C. D. Deere, and J. L. Corragio, eds. New York: Monthly Review Press, 280–302.

Portes, Alejandro. 1983. "The Informal Sector: Definition, Controversy, and Relation to National Development." *Review* 7, no. 1: 151–174.

Ramirez, Nelson, Isis Duarte, and Carmen Gomez. 1986. *Población y Salud en República Dominicana*. Sto. Domingo: Instituto de Estudios de Población y Desarollo, Boletin 16.

Roldán, Martha. 1985. "Industrial Outworking, Struggles for the Reproduction of Working-Class Families and Gender Subordination." In *Beyond Employment: Household, Gender, and Subsistence*. New York: Basil Blackwell, 248–285.

Safa, Helen I. 1985. "Female Employment and the Social Reproduction of the Puerto Rican Working Class." In *Women and Change in Latin America*, J. Nash and H. Safa, eds. South Hadley, Mass.: Bergin and Garvey Publishers, 84–105.

———. 1987. "Urbanization, the Informal Economy, and State Policy in Latin America." In *The Capitalist City: Global Restructuring and Community Politics*, M. P. Smith and J. Feagin, eds. New York: Basil Blackwell, 252–272.

———. 1990. "Women and Industrialization in the Caribbean." In *Women, Employment, and the Family in the International Division of Labor*, S. Stichter and J. Parpart, eds. London: Macmillan.

Souza Lobo, Elizabeth (forthcoming). "Brazilian Social Movements, Feminism, and Women Workers' Struggle in the São Paulo Trade Unions." In *Strength in Diversity: Anthropological Perspectives on Women's Collective Action*, Constance Sutton, ed.

Standing, Guy. 1989. "Global Feminization Through Flexible Labor." *World Development* 17, no. 7 (July): 1,077–1,096.

Stolcke, Verena. 1984. "The Exploitation of Family Morality: Labor Systems and Family Structure on São Paulo Coffee Plantations, 1850–1979." In *Kinship, Ideology, and Practice in Latin America*. Chapel Hill: University of North Carolina Press, 264–296.

———. 1988. *Coffee Planters, Workers, and Wives: Class Conflict and Gender Relations on São Paulo Plantations, 1850–1980*. New York: St. Martin's Press.

5

Women, Employment, and Social Change in the Middle East and North Africa

VALENTINE M. MOGHADAM

Throughout the contemporary world, class and gender are the fundamental "fault lines" (Papanek 1985)—or major divisions among people—in society. The intersection of class and gender means that there is no unitary, undifferentiated category; no abstract, universal Woman but rather, "women immersed in systems of social class relations" (Jelin 1982). Education and employment often reflect and indeed perpetuate these divisions. Occupations and professions are largely class phenomena for both men and women, but they exhibit a pronounced gender hierarchy as well. There is considerable sex-typing within the labor market, and around the world certain occupations are typically male or female (Hartmann and Reskin 1986), even though at times in the development cycle or during periods of social change, class structures and gender relations may be altered. For example, in the United States, the legal profession—once the bastion of male authority—has opened its ranks to women. In the former Soviet Union, the medical profession and the scientific community were heavily female, as were certain production-related activities normally considered "men's work" around the world. Such changes in gender relations and in the structure of employment may come about as a result of development processes, social activism, or state action.

CLASS, GENDER, AND THE STATE
IN THE MIDDLE EAST

In the Middle East and North Africa, class, gender, and the state are the principal determinants of women's work and women's lives. In late-developing states, the role of political elites is central; and this suggests that government policy toward women strongly influences female access to the modern sector, as Susan Marshall (1984) and Mounira Charrad (1980) have found for North Africa. Thus, beyond the fundamental social determinants of class and gender, impacting factors are the nature and policies of the state and the type and level of economic development. And what of cultural-ideological norms, generally emphasized in the case of Muslim countries? In the Middle East, the cultural-ideological realm of social life indeed plays a critical role in shaping the parameters of women's activities. It is important, however, to specify its nature and role and its relation to other social structures.

The theoretical framework that informs this chapter assumes that in societies everywhere, cultural institutions and practices, economic processes, and political structures are interactive and relatively autonomous. Each social formation is located within and subject to the influences of a national class structure, a regional context, and a global system of states and markets. In some societies, notably the industrialized West, economic relations and structures tend to predominate, playing a stronger role in the workings of policy and in the reproduction of the society as a whole. In other societies and at other times, cultural or ideological matters may override other considerations. In part because modernization is fairly recent in the Middle East and partly because of earlier colonial encounters with the West, culture (cultural defensiveness, cultural self-definition) tends to play a stronger role in Middle Eastern societies. At the heart of culture lie concepts of male and female, womanhood, masculinity, and the family—gender. Cultural identity generally and gender specifically have become increasingly politicized in the Middle East, a region that is undergoing the long and arduous transition to modernity. When women are regarded as the custodians of cultural values and traditions in the face of real or perceived external challenges, we can expect women's roles to be more privatized than public and their reproductive functions in particular to be fetishized.

The gender configurations that draw heavily on religion and cultural norms to govern women's employment patterns and women's lives in the Middle East are not unique to the Muslim countries of the region but also are present in the Jewish state of Israel. Women cannot initiate divorce, and rabbinical judges are reluctant to grant women divorces. As in Saudi Arabia, Israeli women cannot hold public prayer services. The sexual division of labor in the home and in the society is shaped largely by the Halacha, or Jewish law, and by customary practices that continue to discriminate against women (Aloni 1984). Marital relations and the marriage contract in Israel, governed by Jewish law, determine that the husband should pay for his wife's maintenance, whereas she should provide household services. "The structure of the arrangement is such that the woman is sheltered from the outside world by her husband and in return she adequately runs the home. The obligations one has toward the other are not equal but rather based on clear gender differentiation" (Lahav 1977: 199).

Even so, gender is not fixed and unchanging in the Middle East (and neither is culture) because internal regional differentiation exists in gender codes, as measured by differences in women's legal status, educational levels, fertility trends, and employment patterns. For example, sex segregation in public is the norm and the law in Saudi Arabia but not in Syria, Iraq, or Morocco

(Ingrams 1988). Following the Iranian Revolution, the new authorities prohibited abortion and contraception and lowered the age of consent to thirteen for girls. But in Tunisia contraceptive use is widespread, and the average age of marriage is twenty-four (Weeks 1988: 26). In Afghanistan, female illiteracy may be the highest among Muslim countries, but important steps were taken between 1978 and 1985 to expand educational facilities and income-generating activities for women (Moghadam 1992). Women's status and employment opportunities are dissimilar in such countries as Turkey, Saudi Arabia, Iran, South Yemen, and Algeria, as we will see presently. Variations across the region and changes within a society are linked to wider changes such as the expansion of the state, incorporation within and responses to the world market system, socialist reform, and stages in the development cycle.

The countries of the Middle East and North Africa differ in their social composition, economic structures, and the nature of their political regimes. Some of the countries have sizable Christian populations (e.g., Egypt, Syria, Iraq); others are ethnically diverse (Iran, Afghanistan); some have had strong working-class movements and trade unions (Egypt, Tunisia, Iran, Turkey). In almost all countries, a sizable section of the middle classes has received Western-style education. Politically, the state types range from theocratic monarchism (Saudi Arabia) to secular republicanism (Turkey). Middle East regimes have been characterized as "authoritarian-Socialist" (Algeria, Syria, Iraq), "radical Islamist" (Iran, Libya), "patriarchal-conservative" (Saudi Arabia, Morocco), and "authoritarian-privatizing" (Turkey, Tunisia, Egypt).

Economically, the countries of the region can be divided into the following groups: (1) oil economies poor in other resources, including very small populations (United Arab Emirates [UAE], Saudi Arabia, Oman, Qatar, Kuwait, Libya); (2) mixed oil economies (Tunisia, Algeria, Syria, Iraq, Iran, Egypt); and (3) non-oil economies (Israel, Turkey, Jordan, Morocco, Sudan, North Yemen, South Yemen). The countries are further divided into the city-states (such as Qatar and the UAE), the "desert states" (for example, Libya and Saudi Arabia), and the "normal states," which have a more diversified structure and whose resources include oil, agricultural land, and large populations (e.g., Turkey, Egypt, Iran, Syria). Some of these countries are rich in capital and import labor (e.g., Libya, Saudi Arabia, Kuwait), whereas others are poor in capital or are middle-income countries that export labor (Algeria, Egypt, Tunisia, Turkey, Yemen). Consequently, industrialization patterns and the pace of socioeconomic changes tend to differ among these various types. The structure of the labor market and the characteristics of the labor force, including the female labor force, also are varied.

Table 5.1 illustrates some economic characteristics of Middle Eastern countries as well as juridical features relevant to women. A key factor shared by all countries except Tunisia and Turkey is the absence of a comprehensive civil code. Most of the countries of the Middle East and North Africa are governed in varying degrees by Islamic canon law, the Sharia. (Similarly, Israeli law is based on the Halacha.) Like the laws and traditions of the other world religions, Islam does not prescribe gender equality and equal treatment

TABLE 5.1 Some Characteristics of Middle Eastern and North African Countries, 1989

Country	Income Level High	Income Level Medium	Income Level Low	Oil Exporter	Labor Exporter	Highly Indebted	Signatory of CEDAW[a]	Comprehensive Civil Code
Afghanistan[b]			X					
Algeria		X		X	X	X		
Bahrain	X		X					
Egypt		X		X	X	X	X	
Iran[b]		X		X				
Iraq		X		X	X		X	
Israel[b c]		X						
Jordan		X			X			
Kuwait	X		X					
Lebanon					X			
Libya	X		X			X		
Morocco		X			X	X		
Oman	X		X	X				
Qatar	X		X					
Saudi Arabia	X		X					
Sudan			X		X	X		
Syria		X			X			
Tunisia		X			X	X	X	X
Turkey[b]		X			X	X	X	X
United Arab Emirates	X		X					
N. Yemen[d]		X			X			
S. Yemen[d]			X		X	X	X	

[a] Convention on the Elimination of All Forms of Discrimination Against Women, adopted by the UN General Assembly in 1979.
[b] Non-Arab countries.
[c] Non-Muslim country.
[d] North and South Yemen were unified in 1991.

Sources: International Labour Office, World Labour Report 1984 (Geneva: ILO, 1984); World Bank, World Development Report 1990 (New York: Oxford University Press, 1990); United Nations Department of Public Information, Information Bulletin (on CEDAW) (New York: UN DPI, September 1989).

before the law. As a result, state law, limited industrialization, and cultural attitudes combine to keep women in a situation of economic dependency and limited labor force participation.

The discussion that follows is concerned with the links among development, social change, and women's work in the modernizing countries of the Middle East and North Africa. It explores and assesses women's employment opportunities and the specific characteristics of the paid female labor force in the formal sector. This chapter does not examine housework, the informal sector, or agricultural production—all areas in which gender is an organizing principle of labor use and women are both active and productive, albeit invisible in national census profiles and "manpower" surveys, and unrewarded by capital, by the state, and often by male kin. Rather, the focus is on the gains made by women in the formal labor market and their access to remunerative work in the modern sector, a necessary (but not sufficient) condition of women's empowerment.

WOMEN AND DEVELOPMENT: THE THIRTY-YEAR RECORD

Beginning in the 1960s, state expansion, economic development, oil wealth, and increased integration within the world system have combined to create educational and employment opportunities favorable to women in the Middle East. For about ten years after the oil price increases of the early 1970s, a massive investment program by the oil-producing countries affected the structure of the labor force, not only within the relevant countries but throughout the region as a result of labor migration. Since then, the urban areas have seen an expansion of the female labor force as women have occupied paid positions in factories and offices as workers, administrators, and professionals. Feminist concerns and women's movements also emerged, and by 1980, most Middle Eastern countries had women's organizations dealing with issues of literacy, education, employment, the law, and so on. These social changes have had a positive effect in reducing traditional sex segregation and female seclusion and in producing a generation of middle-class women who are not dependent on family or marriage for survival and status.

But the overall impact in terms of altering and improving women's work and women's lives has been limited. Moreover, social tensions and difficulties have emerged from the economic strategies pursued (excessive reliance on oil revenues, high military expenditures) and the political mechanisms deployed (authoritarian rule). By 1980 the heady days of the 1970s, when the Organization of Petroleum Exporting Countries (OPEC) was a major international economic actor, were over. High population growth rates coupled with strong rural-urban migration have concentrated larger numbers of the unemployed in major urban areas. In the 1980s, countries of the Middle East and especially North Africa experienced low or negative economic growth rates, declining state revenues, and high levels of indebtedness to foreign creditors. In some cases (Egypt, Morocco, Algeria), debts have become enormous in relation to the country's economic capacities; Turkey was at one point on the World Bank's list of "severely indebted middle-income countries." The most active Arab borrowers from the World Bank—Algeria, Egypt, Jordan, Morocco, Syria, Tunisia—have had to impose austerities on their populations as a result of World Bank and International Monetary Fund (IMF) structural adjustment policy packages, and several have experienced "IMF riots." Women's livelihood has been adversely affected by the debt and the inflationary-recessionary cycles that have been plaguing the region and indeed the entire Third World (Commonwealth Secretariat 1989; South Commission 1990). The austerities required by debt servicing and structural adjustment, social disparities, and political repression have tended to delegitimize Western-style systems and revive questions of cultural identity. In this context, Islamist movements are renewing calls for greater control over female mobility. These movements are especially strong in Algeria, Tunisia, Egypt, and Turkey. In Iran, Islamists came to power in 1979. The extent and strength of Islamist movements vary across the region. In general they do not call for total female domesticity. But insofar as cultural concerns take precedence over economic concerns, the question of women's autonomy and mobility, including active participation in the paid labor force, will remain a controversial one.

In Lebanon, Afghanistan, Iran, and Iraq, and for the Palestinians in Israel and the West Bank, civil war and political conflict have introduced new variables into the equation, with distinct effects on the labor market and the economy generally and on women's work and lives specifically. Civil conflict does not usually produce conditions conducive to development or to women's enhanced access to resources. In a situation of low employment and high fertility, women's social position is stagnating, if not regressing.

The concept of "integrating women in development" has come under attack by Western and Third World feminist researchers. They argue that women have indeed been integrated into development projects—much to their disadvantage as they have become the latest group of exploited workers, a source of cheap and expendable labor (Fuentes and Ehrenreich 1983; Elson and Pearson 1981). It also has been argued that capitalist development has reduced the economic status of women everywhere, resulting in marginalization and impoverishment (Ward 1984; Sen and Grown 1987). It is true that the term *development* obscures the relations of exploitation, unequal distribution of wealth, and other disparities (not to mention environmental degradation) that ensue. But it is also true that within a national economy framework, there is room to improve working women's lot: Sex-segregated occupational distribution can be challenged and altered, as can gender-based wage differentials, inadequate support structures for working mothers, unfair labor legislation pertaining to women, and so on. Moreover, although the proletarianization of women entails labor control (as it does for men), wage work also provides prospects for women's autonomy—a not-insignificant consideration in patriarchal contexts.

Whether modernization and paid employment have resulted in an increase or a diminution of women's economic status continues to be a matter of debate for the Middle East as for other regions of the Third World. Some have argued that in nomadic communities, men's work and women's work are complementary and that modernization reduces, marginalizes, and devalues women's work. Women of rural backgrounds, it is argued, suffered a decline in status; they lost the productive role they traditionally played in the preindustrial economy as the goods they produced were replaced by imported or locally produced factory goods (Rassam 1984). Fatima Mernissi's research, however, suggests a link between the deterioration of women's position and their preexisting dependence on men. Her interviews with Moroccan women working in various craft industries such as weaving textiles and rugs indicate how dependent women are on men as intermediaries, a situation that only increases their precarious economic position with capitalist expansion (Mernissi 1978, 1988).

Research by Turkish and Iranian women scholars suggests the importance of cultural-ideological factors in shaping women's work and status, the salience of precapitalist patriarchal relations, and the complex and contradictory nature of the relationship between development and women's status (Kandiyoti 1977, 1984, 1988; Berik 1985, 1987; Isvan-Hayat 1986; Afshar 1985; Moghadam 1988a, 1991). Deniz Kandiyoti's research comparing the status of Turkish women in nomadic tribes, peasant villages, rural towns, and cities reveals that the influence of the patrilineal extended household—in which the father dominates younger men and all women and there is a hierarchy by age among the women—is pervasive in all sectors but is less so in the towns and cities because of neolocal residence and the diminished importance of elders.

It is true that compared to peasant and nomadic women, urban women play a sharply reduced role in the productive process, even though they are more likely to head their own households. But peasant and nomadic women do not receive recognition for their own labor, not even for their offspring because these belong to the patrilineal extended family. In many parts of rural Turkey, women traditionally have been called the "enemy of the spoon," referring to the fact that they will share the food on the table without contributing economically to the household (Berik 1985). Gunseli Berik's study of carpet weavers in rural Central Anatolia reveals that the labor power of the female weavers and the wages that accrue to them are controlled by male kin (Berik 1985, 1987). This pattern also has been found for Iran (Afshar 1985) and Afghanistan (Moghadam 1992). Thus, because of the existence of "archaic and patriarchal family structures," "we cannot speak of a simple decline in women's status with the transition to an urban wage labor economy. Their diminished role in production may be offset by other factors, which are, however, increasingly specific to certain class sectors" (Abadan-Unat 1981: 127; Kandiyoti 1977).

Development therefore must be seen to have had historically a differential impact on people's lives, particularly on those of women. Its effects have been positive as well as negative depending on region, culture, and class. The structure of preindustrial relations and women's preexisting positions in their communities provides important clues as to the impact of modernization on women's status. The mobility and autonomy women enjoyed in the Andes and parts of sub-Saharan Africa prior to colonialism and modernization stand in contrast to the situation of women in the belt of "classic patriarchy" (Kandiyoti 1988): North Africa, the Muslim Middle East (including Turkey and Iran), and South and East Asia (Pakistan, Afghanistan, India, and China). In this region, patriarchal family structures remain strong in rural areas where women, although unveiled, are controlled (Keddie 1989). It is in this sense that integrating women into development remains a relevant and legitimate objective. The material bases of classic patriarchy crumble under the impact of capital penetration, infrastructural development, and women's education and employment.

WOMEN AND DEVELOPMENT: INTERNATIONAL ECONOMIC FACTORS AND STATE POLICIES

International Economic Factors

In this section I consider the impact of global economic factors, national development, and state policies—especially during the 1960s and 1970s—on women's status and employment. In the 1960s and 1970s, the Middle East was a participant in a global process variously called the internationalization of capital (Palloix 1977), the new (or changing) international division of labor (Frobel, Heinrichs, and Kreye 1980; Warren 1980; Southall 1988),and global Fordism (Lipietz 1982). In this regard, the transnational corporations (TNCs) were significant, as were national development plans and domestic industrialization projects. Since that period, there has been both an increase in recorded urban female labor force participation, especially among working mothers in the age group 25–44, and greater unemployment and underemployment. Although all regions saw a rise in the rates of labor force participation, the largest increase was reported for the Middle East at 53 percent (ICRW 1980:9).

Significant developments that influenced these trends were the changing structure of world labor markets involving massive rural and international migration; the growth of the service and industrial sectors; the decline of the labor force in agriculture; the relocation of labor-intensive industries; and the spread of new technologies, changing the future of work. During the 1970s, then, the trends included the following: regional and global decline in agriculture for both men and women; increase in the service sector; and a shift toward industrial employment, especially in the developing countries—many of which had embarked on rapid industrialization as a key factor in their development. These trends were all present in the Middle East and North Africa, with variations across the region.

In the 1960s, most of the large Middle East countries such as Iran, Egypt, Turkey, and Algeria embarked on import-substitution industrialization (rather than the development of manufacturing for export), in which machinery was imported to run local industries producing consumer goods. This was associated with an economic system characterized by central planning and a large public sector. Whatever the economic shortcomings of this approach (Mabro 1988), it opened up some employment opportunities for women, mainly in the civil service (as a result of the expansion of the state apparatus) but also in state-run factories or industrial plants in the private sector that were receiving state support. There was also some foreign investment through the TNCs.

The TNCs created employment opportunities for many women throughout the Third World, leading to the globalization of female labor (Joekes 1987). An important feature of the global restructuring of employment that affects women workers has been the relocation of labor-intensive industries from industrially developed to developing countries in search of cheap labor— mostly young, unmarried, and inexperienced women to engage in industrial work (ILO-INSTRAW 1985: 21). Textiles and clothing were the first industries relocated, followed by food processing, electronics, and in some cases pharmaceutical products. In this process, various forms of subcontracting arrangements were made to relocate production, or subsidiaries were set up with foreign or partly local capital. This TNC relocation has affected women primarily in Mexico and Southeast Asia, but Morocco, Tunisia, and Turkey also were affected. Free-production zones were established in Bahrain, Jordan, Lebanon, Syria, Democratic Yemen, Egypt, and Tunisia (Frobel et al. 1980). In Iran, a world market factory—commencing operations in 1974 with U.S. and West German capital investment—produced shoes, leather goods, textiles, and garments (Frobel et al. 1980: Appendix, Table III-17/18). In Tunisia, 40 percent of all employed women worked in the industrial sector; in Morocco this figure was nearly 30 percent (ILO-INSTRAW 1985).

For the oil-producing countries of the Middle East, increased oil revenues and foreign exchange facilitated changes in the structure of the economy. The increase in the activities of capital was followed by increased male employment and an increase in the labor force involved in industry and services. These changes also affected women, who were increasingly brought into the labor force. Massive interregional migration of men from the labor surplus countries of Jordan, Egypt, Lebanon, Syria, and North Yemen to better-paying jobs in the oil-rich states of the region (such as Libya, Saudi Arabia, Kuwait, and the UAE) also affected female employment patterns. Among other things, the working-age population remaining in the rural areas came to be dominated by women (Chamie 1985b:3). Some of the labor-receiving countries experienced a dramatic rise in female labor force participation; this was true for Bahrain and Kuwait, although not for Libya and Saudi Arabia. The female activity rate in Bahrain reached 11.1 percent in 1981, whereas in Kuwait the economically active female population doubled between 1970 and 1980. By 1980 women's employment represented 18.8 percent of total salaried employment (ILO 1985c). In a 1982 special economic report by the World Bank on the People's Democratic Republic of Yemen (the PDRY, or the former South Yemen), women's employment was estimated at more than 20 percent. Here, too, between 1976 and 1984 the number of women working in the public and mixed sectors together doubled. The migratory trend created labor shortages in agriculture and in the labor markets of the sending countries (Azzam, Abu Nasr, and Lorfing 1985). The agricultural sector thus became dependent on its female resources. Male outmigration also increased the phenomenon of female-headed households.

Concomitantly, new job vacancies were created in the service and industrial sectors that were filled by women. For the relatively well-educated women, services (teaching, health, and welfare) were and remain the main areas of possibility, whereas in the more developed Middle Eastern countries (such as Turkey and Egypt), women's participation increased in commercial and industrial undertakings and in public administration. During the period of rapid growth, some governments tended to provide generous benefits to working women. In Iraq, the ruling Baath Party encouraged a wide range of employment for women, who by the late 1970s comprised 30 percent of the country's medical doctors and pharmacists, 33 percent of its teachers and university lecturers, 33 percent of the staffs of government departments, 26 percent of workers in industry, and 45 percent of those on farms. Maternity leave was comparatively generous, and the jobs of pregnant women were protected (a practice adopted from socialist countries). In Turkey as well, a woman on maternity leave was given the right to return to the job she held before childbirth. Employment protection also existed in Iran; labor legislation enacted before the Revolution and retained for most of the 1980s provided women with twelve weeks of maternity leave (ILO 1985a:16).

The degree of occupational choice that women had within the structure of employment was linked to, among other factors, the type of industrialization the country was undergoing as well as the attendant expansion of the state structures and the public and private sectors. In some places, development and state expansion afforded women a range of work opportunities in the professional labor market that was wider than that in the most industrialized societies of the West. This was particularly striking in Turkey, where during the 1970s the female share of teaching, banking, and the medical profession reached one-third and where one in five practicing lawyers was female (Kazgan 1981). This pattern occurs in other Third World countries such as Mexico, Argentina, and India. Cross-national studies indicate that in societies undergoing capitalist development, there is a curvilinear relationship between the level of industrial and economic development and the range of options open to women in professional careers. At intermediate levels, there are higher proportions of women in professional schools and in the professional labor market than at either extreme. In such countries, law, medicine, dentistry, and even engineering constitute a "cluster" of occupations that appear as women's options (Safilios-Rothschild 1971).

Ayse Oncu (1981) offers a provocative alternative explanation for this phenomenon: that a kind of quota system operates for the upper class and limits the social mobility of the lower classes. She suggests that under conditions of rapid expansion, the elite recruitment patterns into the most prestigious and highly remunerated professions are maintained by the admission of women from the upper reaches of the social hierarchy (Oncu 1981: 189).

In developing countries, female employment increased significantly during the 1970s; especially high increases occurred in Syria and Tunisia, where the female labor increase topped that of men (ILO-INSTRAW 1985: 35). Female unemployment also increased at the same time. The formal economy could not absorb all the entrants to the labor force, and the urban population in developing countries had been growing rapidly due to natural population growth and high in-migration rates. Thus, the period also saw unemployment, the expansion of the urban informal sector, and the rising phenomenon of female heads of households resulting from male migration, separation, divorce, and widowhood. In 1980 the female share of unemployment was generally higher than the share of employment (ILO-INSTRAW 1985: 36). For example, the female share of unemployment in Syria was 16 percent; in Tunisia, it was 18 percent. Moreover, low wages tended to enlarge the informal sector and to push women into it, although except for Egypt little is known about Middle Eastern women's informal-sector activities.

By 1980, therefore, the global trends in female employment included the proletarianization of women, and their sectoral distribution in services and industry; the globalization of female labor through TNCs and female labor migration; the feminization of poverty; and the interrelated phenomena of high unemployment rates, growth of the urban informal sector, and the proliferation of female-headed households. All of these trends were present in varying degrees in the Middle East and North Africa. Variations in the region are best explained by examining state policy.

The Significance of State Policy

The process of incorporation of women in the labor market also was mediated by the state, which in Third World countries is an active economic agent and a major actor in its own right. The state can act as a facilitator or an impediment in the integration of female citizens in economic (and political) life. Legal changes and state-sponsored education in particular have affected women's work opportunities. Indeed, the work potential of Middle Eastern women has increased with education. Literacy rates are still low in comparison to Latin America and East Asia, and a serious gender disparity remains in educational attainment; but state-financed education has produced a generation of women who actively seek employment. The positive relationship between female education and nonagricultural employment is marked throughout the Middle East. Census data reveal that each educational level is reflected in a corresponding increase in the level of women's nonagricultural employment and in lower fertility (Chamie 1985b; Moghadam 1991). Women's employment and education are obviously linked: Education is assumed to have increased the aspirations of women in certain sectors of society for higher income and better standards of living (Azzam, Abu Nasr, and Lorfing 1985: 11; Mernissi 1987: xxvii). Moreover, it has weakened the restrictive barriers of traditions and increased the propensity of women to join the labor force.

During the decade of the 1980s, however, women faced restrictions on their mobility deriving from both economic problems and the rise of Islamist movements. I now survey a few cases to show the extent to which the depth and scope of the socioeconomic changes of the 1960s and 1970s and in particular the vicissitudes of women's status in the past thirty years have been determined largely by the nature of the state and the political will of the ruling elites.

Turkey provides a nearly unique example (the other being Tunisia) of a country that replaced the Islamic personal status laws with a civil law code regulating personal and family relations and equalizing the duties and responsibilities of the sexes. The Turkish state has frequently been authoritarian, but it has been consistently secular. A consequence has been the expansion of professional opportunities for women in law (Abadan-Unat 1978: 303). But during the 1980s, there was a slight shift in state orientation. The social-democratic years of the 1970s were halted by a military coup in 1980. Since 1983, around seven hundred Koranic schools have been established throughout the country, and their graduates have raised calls for Islamization. Prime Minister Turgut Ozal, the architect of a privatization and structural adjustment program, is also the most openly Islamic Turkish leader in modern times.

In Tunisia, government policy after independence prioritized women's emancipation and integration in development, and the constitution and civil code reflected and reinforced that position. In the constitution, all citizens are ensured the same rights and obligations as well as equality before the law. Polygamy and unilateral divorce were forbidden, although in matters of inheritance men and women still were not equal. A law in 1960 gave the minority of women who are members of the social insurance service (mainly those employed in industry, handicrafts, and services, with the exception of housework) the right to pregnancy leave six weeks before and six weeks after delivery. During this period, 50 percent of monthly wages were to be paid (SIDA 1974). In the 1980s, the distribution of the female labor force was more balanced in Tunisia than in many other countries: 26 percent in agriculture, 48 percent in manufacturing, 21 percent in services. Women's participation in formal politics matched the trends in employment. In 1981 there were seven female deputies in Parliament; in 1983 there were 50,000 female members of the ruling social-democratic Neo-Destour Party and 57,000 members of the National Union of Tunisian Women; and in 1985 492 women were voted municipal councillors throughout the country (United Nations Fund for Population Activities/Ministère du Plan 1984). Yet, economic problems have encouraged Islamist forces and threatened women's gains. In May 1989, Islamic tendencies competed openly in Tunisia's parliamentary elections, winning 14 percent of the total vote and 30 percent in Tunis and other cities and beating the main secular opposition party—the Movement of Democratic Socialists—into third place (*The Economist*, July 8, 1989: 48). Unlike his predecessor, the staunchly secular Habib Bourguiba, current president Ben Ali has built more mosques and restored Koranic universities.

By contrast, state managers in other cases remain wedded to the ideology of domesticity and refrain from encouraging female participation in the paid labor force. Examples are North Yemen, Saudi Arabia, and Algeria. In North Yemen, the 1975 census and manpower survey listed only 9 percent of all Yemeni women as participants in the urban modern-sector labor force. These women are generally young unmarried women in their late teens or early twenties or widowed or divorced women. Interestingly, in Yemen's case female factory workers actually exceeded female government employees (even though both categories represent a fraction of the total labor force in these areas); female production workers tend to be older, illiterate, and of low socioeconomic status, and they are often migrants to the cities (Myntti 1985). In government offices, women employees are veiled. Barriers to female employment include the importation of foreign labor to compensate for male out-migration (rather than training domestic female labor), inadequate access to education, and "culturally defined attitudes and practices . . . lack of child care facilities, and the legal code, the Sharia" (Myntti 1985: 48). In 1983 only 2 percent of North Yemen women were literate, and the total fertility rate was 6.8. Fertility rates are high throughout the Gulf states, ranging from 5.9 in the United Arab Emirates to 7.5 in Kuwait (Azzam and Moujabber 1985: 69).

A review of government policy in Saudi Arabia and Algeria reveals that state personnel have designed policy not only to promote economic growth and development but also to reproduce traditional familial relations. In Saudi Arabia women's place is in the home, and their lives are more circumscribed than in any other Middle Eastern country. Five percent of Saudi women work outside the home, mainly in the teaching and health sectors. Saudi culture—devotion to Islam, extended-family values, the segregated status of females, and the al-Saud monarchic hegemony—is being formulated in an increasingly deliberate fashion, constituting a new political culture that acts as a screen to ensure that technological and human progress remains within acceptable bounds (Gallagher and Searle 1985). For example, to minimize sensitivities concerning male physicians and female patients, a substantial number of Saudi female physicians are being trained to treat female patients. In the wake of the Gulf crisis following Iraq's invasion of Kuwait in August 1990, Saudi authorities have called for wider participation of women in the labor force "in the area of human services and medical services within the context of fully preserving Islamic and social values" (Ibrahim 1990: A1).

Throughout the 1960s and 1970s, the Algerian state promoted industrialization in tandem with the preservation of the close-knit family union. By the 1980s, as a result of a galloping birth rate, nearly three-quarters of its population was under age thirty, and many were unemployed. According to the 1987 census, the employed population numbered 3.7 million men and a mere 365,000 women—out of a total population of 13 million over age fifteen. The female share of the employed population is 8.8 percent. Yet, this represents a steady increase in female employment since 1966.

In the early 1980s, the Algerian government began to make concessions to the growing number of Islamists in the National Assembly. A Family Code was drafted that alarmed many women and provoked protest demonstrations. The final bill, passed in 1984, gives women the legal right to work but renders them economic dependents of men (Knauss 1987; Jansen 1987). In the midst of a privatization effort, faced with high rates of unemployment (around 22 percent), a heavy debt-servicing burden, and other assorted economic ills, Algerian policymakers were unwilling to risk legislation that could potentially aggravate the situation and thus conceded to the Islamists in the National Assembly. In the parliamentary elections of June 1990, the Islamist Party won the most seats, a situation North African feminists feel is bound to adversely affect women's existing fragile and limited rights (Baffoun 1990).

The result of the Algerian state's cultural conservatism is that women's participation in state and other social agencies is quite low compared with male participation. For example, women comprise only 11 percent of the employees of ministries, 34 percent of schoolteachers, 24 percent of higher education instructors, and 36 percent of public health workers. It follows that the majority of employed Algerian women are health workers (44.5 percent) and teachers (38 percent) (Nouredine 1991). Yet, Algerian women are more likely to work in the government sector than in the private sector. Indeed, 86 percent of employed Algerian women are engaged in the public sector versus 14 percent in the private sector. For Algerian men, the respective rates are 55 percent and 45 percent. Indeed, Saadi Nouredine concludes that "de facon globale le secteur public a été plus favorable à l'emploi féminin que le secteur privé" [in general, the public sector has been more favorable to female employment than has the private sector] (Nouredine 1991: 95).

Government-sector employment—limited though it is—is important for Iranian women as well. In Iran women who are waged and salaried are found primarily in the public sector, where they enjoy insurance, pensions, and other benefits, whereas in the private sector they are likely to be low-paid carpet weavers or be characterized as "unpaid family" (Moghadam 1991). Thus, formal or modern-sector employment, and especially opportunities within the civil service, is an advantage for Middle Eastern women.

In Jordan, one finds an overall low crude participation rate (19.6 percent in 1984 for both men and women), due partly to a very high rate of population growth (about 3.8 percent annually) and a large under-fifteen population, high out-migration, and low female economic activity. During the 1970s, the state encouraged education and indeed made education compulsory for nine years. There consequently has been an impressive increase in female education: By 1984–1985, girls accounted for around 48 percent of the total school enrollment (Hijab 1988: 96). The area of women's employment, however, has been less impressive. In 1979 the percentage of economically active women in the total labor force was only about 4 percent, whereas the female share of employees was only 9 percent. As in Yemen, out-migration of Jordanian male labor did not result in an increasing number of women being brought into the wage labor market; rather, their activities in the informal sector and as unpaid family workers increased. Labor shortages due to migration led to labor importation, mainly of Egyptians, at all levels of skills, rather than to the training of women in marketable skills to meet the shortages (Mujahid 1985).

Jordan's five-year plan (1980–1985) sought to further integrate women into the development process and predicted an increase in the total number of women in the working-age bracket, excluding agricultural workers, to nearly 14 percent (National Planning Council 1981). But by 1984 the crude female participation rate was only 4.8 percent. Nearly half of all women in the modern sector are in education, and textile workers represent about 30 percent of Jordan's female labor force. In an untoward economic situation characterized by a large external debt and high male unemployment, there has in fact been an implicit government policy to discourage female employment (Hijab 1988: 114). In the first parliamentary elections since 1967, which were held in November 1989, thirty-four of eighty seats were won by members of the Muslim Brotherhood and like-minded Islamists. This political development also will likely minimize efforts to integrate women into public life.

In some cases, a regime's search for political legitimacy, a larger labor force, or an expanded social base have led it to construct health, educational, and welfare services conducive to greater work participation by women and to encourage female activity in the public sphere. Examples are the Iraqi Baathists during the 1960s and 1970s, the Pahlavi state in Iran in the same period, and Tunisia under former president Bourguiba. In Egypt since Nasser's time, many women have entered previously male strongholds—universities, the administration, professions, industry, the business world, politics. But the economic crisis in Egypt as well as rapid demographic growth limit formal employment opportunities for women. Thus, the vast majority of Egyptian women are engaged in the informal sector as street vendors and hawkers, selling food and other wares, working at home as seamstresses, and generally engaged in a myriad of small-scale income-generating activities.

"Socialist" ideology sometimes has motivated state support for female emancipation, including education and employment. An example is the People's Democratic Republic of Yemen (PDRY, or South Yemen). Legal reform in the 1970s, modeled after that of other socialist states, expressly targeted the "traditional" or "feudal" family as "incompatible with the principles and programme of the National Democratic Revolution . . . because its old relationships prevent it from playing a positive role in the building up of society" (Molyneux 1985: 155–156). Left-wing radicals were responsible for the 1970 constitution, which explicitly included women as part of the "working people" and "productive forces" who had both the right and the obligation to work (Molyneux 1985: 159). The PDRY state consequently went further than any other Middle Eastern regime in legislating gender equality and mandating women's active involvement in the construction of the new order. Another example is Afghanistan. When socialists came to power in Kabul in 1978, they also attempted to implement a wide-ranging and radical program for women's emancipation, combining land reform with marriage reform and compulsory education (Moghadam 1992).

Although the above examples are intended to underscore the centrality of state action in the determination of women's legal status and employment opportunities, it also should be understood that state capacity is subject to such internal and external constraints as economic resources, political legitimacy, the weight of cultural values and institutions, regional trade, capital and labor flows, world market prices and global power politics. In the case of South Yemen, poor resource endowments have stymied government policy to emancipate and integrate women. (It should be noted that the two Yemens merged in 1990.) In the case of Afghanistan, the political elite was unable to implement its radical program for land reform and women's rights in the face of massive internal opposition from rural and tribal groups as well as external intervention. By the late 1980s, women's emancipation was put on the back burner in favor of "national reconciliation" and an end to hostilities. Another, less obvious example is Iran, whose new Islamic state in 1979 abrogated many of the liberal codes instituted by the previous state. Among other things, the new authorities adopted a pronatalist stance that deemed women, especially young mothers, inappropriate for full-time work. However, by the mid-1980s, a number of factors converged to modify and liberalize the Islamist state's position on women, education, and work. These factors included the expansion of the state apparatus, the dearth of male labor in a war situation, and women's resistance to their second-class citizenship (Moghadam 1988a, 1991). Thus, although state policy and national development plans have been among the principal determinants in shaping women's opportunities and expectations, other factors such as labor shortage, the high cost of living, and educational attainment influence the overall rate of women's participation in the work force, whereas resource endowments and political stability or instability also structure the limits and opportunities.

The active role of the state in national development has meant that for many women it is no longer a male guardian—father or husband—who is the provider, but the state. As Mernissi (1984: 448–449) remarks, "The North African woman of today usually dreams of having a steady, wage-paying job with social security and health and retirement benefits, at a State institution; these women don't look to a man any longer for their survival, but to the State. While perhaps not ideal, this is nevertheless a breakthrough, an erosion of tradition. It also partly explains the Moroccan women's active participation in the urbanization process: They are leaving rural areas in numbers equaling men's migrations, for a 'better life' in the cities—and in European cities, as well."

INDUSTRIALIZATION AND FEMALE EMPLOYMENT

Proletarianization of Female Labor

If industrialization in parts of the Third World "has been as much female led as export led" (Joekes 1987: 81), this is less pertinent to the Middle East. For one thing, a widespread Middle Eastern attitude is that factory work is not suitable for women. To be sure, in nearly all the large countries women are engaged in light manufacturing—clothing, woven goods, shoes, food processing, confectionaries. But modern-sector industrial work remains limited for both men and women. In part because of import-substitution policies and partly because of excess reliance on oil wealth, industry in the Middle

East has failed to make progress comparable to that achieved in India, Brazil, Hong Kong, or Singapore. Middle Eastern countries with large shares of manufacturing in their merchandise exports are Israel with 80 percent and Turkey with 57 percent (Mabro 1988: 695). Other Middle Eastern countries do not usually come near the top fifty in world manufacturing production. This has implications for patterns of female employment. Lower levels of industrialization and manufacturing for export mean less female proletarianization and activity in the productive sectors, including trade unionism.

In some cases, much of what purports to be industrial activity for women is in fact of a rural and traditional type, such as carpet weaving. An example is Iran. In the 1970s, Iran was sometimes included in the varying lists of newly industrializing countries (NICs), and the development literature noted a significant increase not only in male but in female participation in industry. One International Labour Organization (ILO) study cites the increase in female labor force participation in Iran in the same category as that of Hong Kong, Japan, and Singapore (ILO 1985a: 64). By 1976, industry's share of the total labor force was about one-third. According to ILO data, around 33 percent of the economically active female population in 1976 was engaged in industrial work. However, what this statistic masked was the dualistic nature of Iranian industry and the polarization of the industrial labor force (both male and female) between workers in small and traditional workshops and workers in large and modern factories (Moghadam 1987). Close examination of census data reveals that most female industrial workers were actually rural women involved in traditional manufacturing (carpets, handicrafts, textiles, and the like). A far smaller proportion was in the larger urban factories. The proportion of "female employers/own-account workers" was not as high in Iran as elsewhere (in Iran in 1976 it was 6.8 percent), but two-thirds of the women in this category were in manufacturing (ILO-INSTRAW 1985: 49). And a far larger percentage of women in "industrial/manufacturing" activities made up the category "unpaid family workers." This may explain the near absence of female participation in the factory councils that emerged from the strike committees in industrial plants during the Iranian Revolution (Moghadam 1988b).

Turkey's proximity to Europe and its greater participation in the international division of labor have drawn more women into world market activities. Agriculture, light manufacturing industry (tobacco, textiles-apparel, food-beverages, packaging of chemicals), and certain subdivisions of service industries are typically "feminine" occupations. Despite this and notwithstanding the large numbers of female professionals, Turkish women occupy a relatively unimportant place in the urban labor force. In the late 1970s the female share of the urban labor force was about 11 percent (Kazgan 1981: 136). In 1985 fully 69 percent of the economically active female population of 5.5 million was in agriculture and only 7 percent in industry. In Israel, the most industrialized economy in the region, the role of women in industrial work also is negligible.

In the cities of the Middle East, therefore, most women are marginalized from the formal-sector productive process and are concentrated in community, social, and personal services. The percentage of women, although low in the labor force as a whole (the female share of the paid labor force in Morocco in 1982 was 17.6 percent), is disproportionately high when one looks at the services sector in comparison to industry in general and manufacturing in particular. High percentages of the economically active female population in community, social, and personal services (group nine of the branches of industry in standard classifications) are found in Kuwait (88 percent) and Israel (48 percent). Tunisia and Morocco provide a contrast, however. In Tunisia, fully 48 percent of the female labor force is in manufacturing. In Morocco, nearly half of the economically active women in the urban areas are engaged in textile work, although much of this is home work (Centre d'Etudes et de Recherches Démographiques, Ministère du Plan 1989: 103–104).

Characteristics of the Female Labor Force

In 1975 the percentage of economically active females among females of working ages in Muslim countries (which would include those of Africa, South Asia, and Southeast Asia as well as the Middle East) was less than half of that in non-Muslim countries (Mujahid 1985: 114). By the 1980s, the female share of the labor force was still lower in Middle Eastern countries than elsewhere (8.8 percent in Algeria in 1987, 9 percent in Iran in 1986, 13.8 percent in Syria in 1984). In 1985 regional female labor force participation rates were as follows: Africa 23 percent; Latin America 15 percent; Asia (including the Middle East) 28 percent; the Middle East separately 11.4 percent (ILO-INSTRAW 1985: 18–19). In 1980 the ratio of women to men in the labor force was lowest in the Middle East (29 percent) and highest in Eastern Europe and the Soviet Union, where the ratio was 90 percent (Sivard 1985: 13). Figure 5.1 illustrates the regional disparities in 1980.

It should be noted that countries count their female labor force differently. When agricultural women are not counted, skewed figures may result, such as a disproportionately high recorded percentage of the female labor force in the social professions. Yet, some researchers report that because of the continuing importance of values such as family honor and modesty, women's participation in nonagricultural or paid labor carries a social stigma, and gainful employment is not perceived as part of their role (Azzam, Abu Nasr, and Lorfing 1985: 6; Mujahid 1985: 128). At present only Israel, Turkey, and Morocco come close to other Asian countries with their 30 to 40 percent female share of the total labor force (see Table 5.2 below).

The influence of cultural norms on female participation also is reflected in the occupational preferences of female workers. The most significant consideration appears to be the very low preference of females in Muslim countries for becoming "sales workers"—an occupation in which the likelihood of indiscriminate contact with outsiders is highest (Mujahid 1985: 115). This may be an extension of a long-standing pattern in which the merchant class has been typically male and the traditional urban markets—bazaars and souks— have been the province of men. It is also a function of socialization. In their recent study of sex role socialization in Iranian textbooks, Patricia Higgins

FIGURE 5.1   Women as a Percent of Men in the Paid Labor Force by
Region, 1980 (Ages 15-64)

Source: Ruth Leger Sivard, Women ... A World Survey (Washington, D.C.: World
Priorities, 1985), 13.

and Pirouz Shoar-Ghaffari (1989) note that in both pre- and postrevolutionary
textbooks, in nearly half of the lessons in which women were portrayed
working, they were doing housework; and in both eras three-quarters of the
lessons portraying women at work outside the home showed them in professional positions (almost always teaching). The remainder portrayed women in
agricultural work; no lessons in either set of texts portrayed women in blue-
collar, clerical, or sales and service positions. Throughout the Middle East, the
large numbers of women who choose teaching young children as a profession
view it as a natural extension of their mother role and therefore see this kind
of employment as socially very acceptable (Chamie 1985a: 77).

In the highly stratified societies of the Middle East and North Africa, social
class location in addition to state action and the level and pace of economic
development act on and modify gender relations and women's social positions.
Although state-sponsored education has resulted in a certain amount of
upward social mobility and has increased the numbers of women willing and
able to fill the administrative and welfare jobs in the ever-expanding state
systems as well as in the private sector, women's access to resources—
including education—is determined by their class location. The fact that a
large percentage of urban employed women in the Middle East are found in
the services sector or in professional occupations can be understood by
examining their social class background. As in other Third World countries

where social disparities are great, upper- and upper-middle-class urban women can exercise a greater number of choices (certainly vis-à-vis lower-middle-class, working-class, urban poor, or peasant women) and thus become much more "emancipated." In 1971 Constantina Safilios-Rothschild wrote that professional and marital roles become compatible because of the availability of cheap domestic labor and because of the extended family network. In 1990 this was still true for wealthy women, although except in Morocco, middle-class women in Middle Eastern countries were less likely to be able to afford domestic help and more likely to rely on a mother or mother-in-law. Although at the level of ideology and policy some states (such as Egypt) are committed to women's participation in industrial production, the system extracts the labor of women in economic need without giving them the social services to coordinate their productive roles in the family and the workplace (Badran 1982: 80).

As with their roles in production and in work generally, class also shapes women's choices and practices in reproduction. Fertility patterns are largely a class phenomenon. Educated middle-class and upper-class women in the professions tend to have fewer children, as the World Fertility Survey found for Egypt, Syria, Sudan, Morocco, Tunisia, Turkey, and Yemen. For example, although on average the desired number of children in Egypt is four and the mean number of children ever born to illiterate mothers is 4.4, it drops to 2.1 for women with secondary school educations. The mean number of children ever born to university-educated women is 1.8 (*World Fertility Survey* no. 42: *The Egyptian Survey*, November 1983). In general, Muslim societies are characterized by higher-than-average fertility and rapid rates of population growth (Weeks 1988: 12, 46), but this needs to be understood not only in terms of cultural prescriptions but also as a function of stage of development and as being variable by class.

ILO and census data reveal that since the 1960s, there has been a steady increase in women's labor force participation in nearly all Middle Eastern countries except Iran. During the 1980s, economic activity rates of women ranged from a low of 4.8 percent in Jordan, 6.8 in Syria, and 7 percent in Algeria to highs of 18 percent in Kuwait, 22 percent in Turkey, and 27 percent in Israel (ILO-INSTRAW 1988: 13). As mentioned above, there are high levels of male unemployment in Jordan, Egypt, and Iran as well as in Algeria, Tunisia, and Morocco. Table 5.2 provides data on some characteristics of the economically active population for a number of countries in the region.

In relation to Latin America, Southeast Asia, and the advanced industrialized countries, female activity rates in all age groups are quite low. Moreover, in general female labor force participation tends to be concentrated in the age groups 15–29; it is even lower in the older age groups. The exceptions are Turkey and Israel, where female activity rates are the highest in the region (over 45 percent) and are fairly consistent across the age groups. They are followed by Tunisia, which has a 30 percent activity rate for women in the age group 15–34. Kuwait and Qatar also report fairly high activity rates (37 percent) for women ages 25–49; these are professional women who in fact comprise the female labor force in those countries.

TABLE 5.2 Characteristics of the Economically Active Population, Various
Countries, 1980s

Country Year	Total Population	Total Economically Active Population	Percent Female	Total Salaried	Percent Female
Algeria					
1983	20,192,000	3,632,594	6.8	n.a.[a]	n.a.
1987	23,037,916	5,341,102	9.2	4,137,736	8.8
Bahrain					
1987	278,481	73,972	19.3	n.a.	n.a.
Egypt					
1984	45,231,000	14,311,300	21.4	6,376,800	14
Iran					
1986	49,400,000	12,820,291	10	5,327,885	9.4
Iraq					
1977	12,000,477	3,133,939	17.3	1,864,701	7.9
1983	14,700,000	n.a.	n.a.	n.a.	n.a.
Israel					
1987	4,365,200	1,494,100	39.0	1,110,800	41.5
Kuwait					
1985	1,697,301	670,385	19.7	619,722	20.8
Morocco					
1982	20,449,551	5,999,260	19.6	2,429,919	17.6
1986	24,000,000	14,000,000	35.0	n.a.	n.a.
Qatar					
1986	369,079	201,182	9.4	196,488	9.6
Sudan					
1973	14,113,590	3,473,278	19.9	905,942	7.4
Syria					
1984	9,870,800	2,356,000	13.8	1,216,781[b]	12.4[b]
Tunisia					
1984	6,975,450	2,137,210	21.2	1,173,630	14.3
Turkey					
1985	50,958,614	21,579,996	35.4	6,978,181	15.3
United Arab Emirates					
1980	1,042,099	559,960	5.0	518,969	5.2

[a] n.a. = not available.
[b] data for 1983.

Sources: Compiled by the author from the following: CERED, *Femmes et Condition Feminine au Maroc* (Rabat 1989); Office National des Statistiques, *Recensement Général de la Population et de l'Habitat 1987* (Algiers 1989); ILO, *Yearbook of Labour Statistics, 1986, 1987,* and *1988,* Tables 1 and 2A; ILO, *Yearbook of Labour Statistics, Retrospective 1945–89* (Geneva: International Labour Office, 1989), Table 2A; World Bank, *World Development Report* (Washington, D.C.: World Bank, 1985, 1990).

During the 1980s the regional average female share of the economically active population began to reach 20 percent, with somewhat higher shares in Israel, Turkey, and Morocco. Other countries with large populations (for example, Iran) do not count women in agriculture and therefore report a very small economically active female population or female share of the labor force. In terms of employment status, and as seen in Table 5.2, the female share of the total salaried population is generally under 20 percent—from lows of 5.2 percent in the United Arab Emirates and 7.4 percent in the Sudan to 20.8 percent for Kuwait and a high of 41.5 percent for Israel.

As seen in Table 5.3, the percentage of the economically active female population (EAP) that receives a wage or salary is high in Kuwait (97.7 percent) and Israel (79.7 percent), average in Syria (48 percent) and Egypt (42.3 percent), and low in Turkey (14 percent). In Iran's case, because the 1986 census counted so few women, the proportion of the female EAP appears high (51.6 percent). In Turkey, the female share of the salaried labor force is a mere 14 percent. Nearly 80 percent of the female labor force was classified "unpaid family workers" in 1980. These women are mostly in agriculture. In some cases, women in agriculture are not enumerated, but large percentages of female agricultural workers are found in Turkey, Egypt, and Syria.

Table 5.4 illustrates the distribution of the female economically active population in branches of industry, and Table 5.5 shows the occupational distribution of the female EAP. As can be seen in Table 5.4, the distribution in Algeria, Egypt, Israel, Kuwait, and Syria is skewed in favor of Group 9 of the major industry branches—community, social, and personal services. Turkey's female EAP is concentrated in agriculture. Tunisia's female labor force is more evenly distributed, and in a departure from the Middle Eastern norm, more women are in industry than in agriculture or services. The high incidence of women workers in the professional, technical, and related workers group in most countries may be the outcome of occupational stereotyping prevalent in the region, where women cluster around specific jobs such as teaching and health care. It also may be a function of the class distribution of income and work participation, whereby women from elite families are most likely to be those who are employed, as suggested earlier by Oncu (1981).

In terms of occupational distribution, there appears to be a very low preference of females in Muslim countries to become sales workers or even service workers. G.B.S. Mujahid (1985: 115) explains this in terms of cultural norms because these are occupations in which the likelihood of indiscriminate contact with outsiders is highest. This also may be an extension of a longstanding pattern in which the merchant class has been typically female, and the traditional urban markets—bazaars and souks—have been the province of men. It is, moreover, a function of socialization. School textbooks, for example, hardly ever depict women in blue-collar, clerical, or sales or service positions.

Table 5.5 shows the concentration of women in professional occupations, although large percentages of the female labor force also are found in agriculture (Egypt, Morocco, Syria, Turkey) and in production (Morocco). There is a marked disinclination for women to enter sales or even clerical occupations

TABLE 5.3 Distribution of Economically Active Women by Status of Employment in Selected Countries (in percent), Various Years

Country Year	Employers and Own-Account Workers	Salaried Employees		Unpaid Family Workers	Not Classified by Status	Total[a]
Algeria						
1977	1.7	42.1		0.5	55.7	100
1987[b]						
Bahrain						
1981	0.9	88.6	(11.7)[c]	-	10.3	100
Egypt						
1983	17.0	42.3	(14.5)	30.0	10.5	100
Iran						
1976	10.2	39.3	(12.0)	32.4	17.9	100
1986[d]	19.6	51.6	(9.4)	21.5	7.0	100
Iraq						
1977	10.6	27.3	(7.9)	58.0	3.6	100
Israel						
1982	11.1	79.7	(40.0)	3.2	6.0	100
1986	11.0	78.5	(41.1)	2.3	7.9	100
Kuwait						
1985	0.2	97.7	(20.8)	-	2.0	100
Morocco						
1982	14.5	36.3	(18.0)	27.5	21.6	100
Syria						
1979	9.9	41.7	(12.0)	44.5	3.9	100
1981	11.4	60.9	(8.7)	22.2	4.0	100
1983	9.8	48.0	(12.4)	36.9	4.7	100
Tunisia						
1984	27.2	38.7	(14.3)	20.5	13.4	100
Turkey						
1985	4.7	14.0	(15.3)	79.2	2.0	100
United Arab Emirates						
1980	0.8	97.5	(5.2)	-	1.5	100

[a] Rounded to 100 percent in some cases.

[b] Algeria's 1987 census (p.6) lists a female economically active population of 492,442. Of that figure, 74 percent are employed (occupées), 13 percent are unemployed, and 13 percent are partly employed housewives (Femmes au foyer partiellement occupées).

[c] This column refers to the female share of total employees, in percent.

[d] The 1986 census (indeed, all previous censuses) seriously undercounts the female economically active population. Out of a total female population of 24 million, of whom perhaps 12 million may be presumed to be of working age, only 1.4 million are counted; of that number, 987,000 are classified as "employed," which consists of salaried and unsalaried workers.

Sources: ILO, *Yearbook of Labour Statistics* (Geneva: ILO, 1981, 1985, 1986, 1987), Table 2A; Azzam, Abu Nasr, and Lorfing, 1985; ILO, 1985a; ILO, *Yearbook of Labour Statistics, Retrospective, 1945-89* (Geneva: ILO, 1989), Table 2A; Office National des Statistiques, *Recensement Général de la Population et de l'Habitat 1987* (Algiers 1989); *National Census of Population and Housing,* November 1986 (Islamic Republic of Iran, 1986).

TABLE 5.4   Distribution of Female Economically Active Population in Branches of Industry, Selected Countries (in percent), 1980s

Country and Year	Group 1	Group 2	Group 3	Group 4	Group 5	Group 6	Group 7	Group 8	Group 9	NAD[a]	Total Number
			Industry Branches								
Algeria 1985	3.6		11.9		2.7	2.7	3.0	75.7			326,000
Egypt 1984	41.2	0.003	8.6	0.3	0.6	6.8	1.1	13.7	23.8	4.7	2,354,600
Israel 1983	2.7		14.0	0.3	0.9	10.6	2.9	11.3	48.2	8.6	556,495
Kuwait 1983	0.08	0.25	0.96	0.05	0.89	2.2	1.5	2.2	89.3	1.5	132,128
Syria 1984	44.6	0.3	10.7	0.03	1.2	2.9	1.5	1.2	30.0	6.7	327,200
Tunisia 1984	22.1	0.4	40.6	1.1[b]	0.7	2.3	-	4.6	13.0	14.5	433,630
Turkey 1985	69.5	0.07	7.0	0.01	0.08	1.5	0.4	1.4	7.4	11.4	5,543,862

Group 1 - Agriculture, hunting, forestry and fishing.
Group 2 - Mining and quarrying.
Group 3 - Manufacturing.
Group 4 - Electricity, gas, and water.
Group 5 - Construction.
Group 6 - Wholesale-retail trade, restaurants, and hotels.
Group 7 - Transport, storage, and communication.
Group 8 - Financing, insurance, real estate, and business services.
Group 9 - Community, social, and personal services.

[a]NAD – not adequately defined, unemployed persons not previously employed, and/or unemployed persons previously employed.
[b]This includes groups 4 and 7.

Source: ILO, Yearbook of Labour Statistics 1988 (Geneva: ILO, 1988), Table 2A, pp. 50-131.

TABLE 5.5   Distribution of Female Labor Force by Occupation, Major Groups (in percent), 1980s

Country and Year	Group 1	Group 2	Group 3	Group 4	Group 5	Group 6	Group 7-9	Not Classified and Unemployed
Egypt								
1984	17.6	1.8	12.9	5.5	2.7	41.3	6.5	11.3
Israel								
1983	28.9	1.7	27.1	5.3	14.9	1.6	8.9	10.2
Kuwait								
1985	27.2	0.2	14.3	0.75	53.7	0.04	0.37	1.5
Morocco								
1982	6.6	5.4		1.4	13.7	32.5	33.2	6.8
Syria								
1984	25.9	0.9	7.9	1.2	2.4	43.7	10.3	6.7
Turkey								
1985	5.5	0.1	4.5	0.9	1.6	69.0	6.9	10.8

Group 1   - Professional, technical, and related workers.
Group 2   - Administrative and managerial workers.
Group 3   - Clerical and related workers.
Group 4   - Sales workers.
Group 5   - Service workers.
Group 6   - Agricultural, animal husbandry and forestry workers, fishermen and hunters.
Group 7-9 - Production/related workers, transport equipment operators, and labourers.

Sources: ILO, *Yearbook of Labour Statistics,* 1987, Table 2B, 118–181; 1988, Table 2B, 132-202; ILO, *Yearbook of Labour Statistics, Retrospective 1945–1989* (Geneva: International Labour Office, 1989), Table 2B, 420-735.

except in Israel. And all countries have few females in administrative and managerial occupations.

CONCLUSION

This chapter has schematically surveyed women's work and women's lives over the past three decades in the modernizing countries of the Middle East and North Africa. An essential point has been to underscore the diversity of women's positions within the region and to link women's status and work opportunities to their class location, state policies, and the broad cultural parameters. Many studies on the Middle East and commentaries by Islamists themselves tend to understate the heterogeneity of the region; they project a uniform culture and exaggerate its importance, elevating *culture* or *religion* to the status of a single explanatory variable. In this chapter the view of culture and religion as fixed, uniform, and predominant in the Middle East is rejected; rather, my position is that there is an interactive relationship of economic processes, political dynamics, and cultural practices. Only through such an approach can variations within the region and changes over time be understood and explained.

On the other hand, there continues to exist an exceedingly large population of underutilized labor—that is, women. To be sure, gains have been made since the 1960s, and more women have joined the salaried labor force. But female labor force participation is still low in relation to that of other regions of the world and in relation to male labor force participation. A convergence of economic, political, and cultural developments accounts for the lack of significant improvement in women's status in recent years. In popular accounts and in scholarly works, much has been made of the rise of Islamist movements, but little has been noted of the economic crisis facing the region. This crisis resulted in part from the drop in real prices of primary commodities, including oil, throughout the 1980s (until the Iraqi invasion of Kuwait in August 1990 raised the price of oil again). According to the United Nations, debt as a percentage of GNP for the Middle East and North Africa in 1989 rose to 70 percent; during the 1980s, the region's debt increased from $4.4 billion to $118.8 billion (UN DPI 1989). In Israel the serious economic plight has been alleviated by massive U.S. aid. But elsewhere, tough economic reforms along with poverty, unemployment, and debt servicing have led to a spate of popular protests and "IMF riots" in Algeria, Jordan, Tunisia, and Turkey. It is in this context of social and economic crisis that Islamist movements have gained ascendancy in the region, placing enormous political and ideological pressures on women.

But these movements also have their contenders. Expanding education and employment have created a generation of Middle Eastern women who do not need marriage and the family for survival and status. These are the women who are taking strong positions against Islamist movements (e.g., antifundamentalist women in North Africa, Iranian women in exile) and who are likely to be found at the forefront of movements for progressive social change in their countries.

BIBLIOGRAPHY

Abadan-Unat, Nermin. "The Modernization of Turkish Women." *Middle East Journal* 32 (1978).
―――. "Introduction: Labour Force Participation." In *Women in Turkish Society*, Nermin Abadan-Unat, ed. Leiden: E. J. Brill, 1981, 127–129.
Afshar, Haleh. "The Position of Women in an Iranian Village." *Women, Work, and Ideology in the Third World*, Haleh Afshar, ed. London: Tavistock, 1985.
Aloni, Shulamit. "Up the Down Escalator." In *Sisterhood Is Global*, Robin Morgan, ed. New York: Anchor Books, 1984, 360–364.
Azzam, H., and C. Moujabber. "Women and Development in the Gulf States." In *Women, Employment, and Development in the Arab World*, J. Abu Nasr, N. Khoury, and H. Azzam, eds. The Hague: Mouton/ILO, 1985, 59–72.
Azzam, H., J. Abu Nasr, and I. Lorfing. "An Overview of Arab Women in Population, Employment, and Economic Development." In *Women, Employment, and Development in the Arab World*, J. Abu Nasr, N. Khoury, and H. Azzam, eds. The Hague: Mouton/ILO, 1985, 5–38.
Badran, Margot. "Women and Production in the Middle East and North Africa." *Trends in History* 2, no. 3 (1982): 59–88.
Baffoun, Alya. "Feminism and Fundamentalism: The Tunisian and Algerian Cases." Paper prepared for the Roundtable on Identity Politics and Women, United Nations University–World Institute for Development Economics Research, Helsinki, October 8–19, 1990.

Berik, Gunseli. "From 'Enemy of the Spoon' to 'Factory': Women's Labor in the Carpet Weaving Industry in Rural Turkey." Paper presented at Middle East Studies Association annual meetings, New Orleans, November 22–26, 1985.

———. *Women Carpet Weavers in Rural Turkey: Patterns of Employment, Earnings, and Status.* Geneva: ILO, Women, Work, and Development Series no. 15, 1987.

Centre d'Etudes et de Recherche Démographiques. *Femmes et Condition Feminine au Maroc.* Rabat: Direction de la Statistique, 1989.

Chamie, M. "Labour Force Participation of Lebanese Women." In *Women, Employment, and Development in the Arab World,* J. Abu Nasr, N. Khoury, and H. Azzam, eds. The Hague: Mouton/ILO, 1985a, 73–104.

———. *Women of the World: Near East and North Africa.* Washington, D.C.: U.S. Department of Commerce and Agency for International Development, 1985b.

Charrad, Mounira. *Women and the State: A Comparative Study of Politics, Law, and the Family in Tunisia, Algeria, and Morocco.* Ph.D. dissertation, Harvard University, Department of Sociology, 1980.

Commonwealth Secretariat. *Engendering Adjustment for the 1990s.* London: Commonwealth Secretariat, 1989.

Elson, Diane, and Ruth Pearson. "The Subordination of Women and the Internationalization of Factory Production." In *Of Marriage and the Market: Women's Subordination in International Perspective,* K. Young, C. Wolkowitz, and R. McCullough, eds. London: CSE Books, 1981, 144–166.

Frobel, F., J. Heinrichs, and O. Kreye. *The New International Division of Labour.* Cambridge: Cambridge University Press, 1980.

Fuentes, Annette, and Barbara Ehrenreich. *Women in the Global Factory.* Boston: South End Press, 1983.

Gallagher, Eugene B., and C. Maureen Searle. "Health Services and the Political Culture of Saudi Arabia." *Social Science Medical* 21, no. 3 (1985): 808–814.

Hartmann, Heidi, and Barbara Reskin. *Women's Work, Men's Work: Sex Segregation on the Job.* Washington, D.C.: National Academy Press, 1986.

Higgins, Patricia, and Pirouz Shoar-Ghaffari. "Sex Role Socialization in Iranian Textbooks." Mimeo, Department of Anthropology, SUNY-Plattsburgh, 1989.

Hijab, Nadia. *Womanpower: The Arab Debate on Women and Work.* Cambridge: Cambridge University Press, 1988.

Ibrahim, Youssef M. "Saudis, Aroused by Iraqi Threat, Take Steps to Mobilize Population." *New York Times,* September 5, 1990, A1.

Ingrams, Doreen. "The Position of Women in Middle Eastern Arab Society." In *The Middle East,* Michael Adams, ed. New York: Facts on File, 1988, 808–814.

International Center for Research on Women (ICRW). *Keeping Women Out: A Structural Analysis of Women's Employment in Developing Countries.* Washington, D.C.: ICRW/AID, 1980.

International Labour Organization (ILO). *World Labor Report 1984.* Geneva: ILO, 1984.

———. *ILO and Working Women 1980–1985.* Geneva: ILO, 1985a.

———. *The State of the World's Women.* Geneva: ILO, 1985b.

———. *Growth and Adjustment in Asia: Issues of Employment, Productivity, Migration, and Women Workers.* Report of the Director-General. Tenth Asian Regional Conference, Jakarta, December 1985c.

———. *Yearbook of Labour Statistics, Retrospective 1945–1989.* Geneva: ILO, 1989.

———. *Yearbook of Labour Statistics.* Geneva: ILO, various years.

International Labour Office and United Nations Training and Research Institute for the Advancement of Women (ILO-INSTRAW). *Women in Economic Activity: A Global Statistical Survey 1950–2000.* Geneva and Santo Domingo: ILO and INSTRAW, 1985.

Islamic Republic of Iran. *National Census of Population and Housing 1986*. Tehran: Central Statistical Office, Plan and Budget Organization, 1986.

Isvan-Hayat, Nilufar. "Rural Household Production and the Sexual Division of Labor: A Research Framework." Paper presented at the Middle East Studies Association annual meetings, Boston, November 20–23, 1986.

Jansen, Willy. "God Will Pay in Heaven: Women and Wages in Algeria." Paper presented at the Middle East Studies Association annual meetings, Baltimore, November 1987.

Jelin, Elizabeth. "Women and the Urban Labor Market." In *Women's Roles and Population Trends in the Third World*, R. Anker, M. Buvinic, and N. Youssef, eds. London: Croom Helm/ILO, 1982.

Joekes, Susan. *Women in the World Economy: An INSTRAW Study*. New York: Oxford University Press, 1987.

Kandiyoti, Deniz. "Sex Roles and Social Change: A Comparative Appraisal of Turkey's Women." In *Women and National Development*, the Wellesley Editorial Committee, ed. Chicago: University of Chicago Press, 1977.

_____. "Rural Transformation in Turkey and Its Implications for Women's Status." In UNESCO, *Women on the Move: Contemporary Changes in Family and Society*. Paris: UNESCO, 1984, 17–29.

_____. "Bargaining with Patriarchy." *Gender and Society* 2, no. 3 (September 1988): 274–289.

Kazgan, Gulten. "Labour Participation, Occupational Distribution, Educational Attainment, and the Socio-Economic Status of Women in the Turkish Economy." In *Women in Turkish Society*, N. Abadan-Unat, ed. Leiden: E. J. Brill, 1981, 131–159.

Keddie, Nikki R. "The Past and Present of Women in the Muslim World." In *Journal of World History* 1, no. 1 (1989).

Knauss, Peter. *The Persistence of Patriarchy: Class, Gender, and Ideology in Twentieth-Century Algeria*. New York: Praeger, 1987.

Lahav, Pnina. "Raising the Status of Women Through the Law: The Case of Israel." In *Women and National Development*, the Wellesley Editorial Committee, ed. Chicago: University of Chicago Press, 1977.

Lipietz, Alain. "Toward Global Fordism?" *New Left Review* 132 (March-April 1982): 33–47.

Mabro, Robert. "Industrialization." In *The Middle East*, Michael Adams, ed. New York: Facts on File, 1988, 687–696.

Marshall, Susan. "Politics and Female Status in North Africa: A Reconsideration of Development Theory." *Economic Development and Cultural Change* (1984): 499–524.

Mernissi, Fatima. "The Degrading Effects of Capitalism on Female Labour." *Peuples Méditerranéens/Mediterranean People* 6 (January-March 1978).

_____. "The Merchant's Daughter and the Son of the Sultan." In *Sisterhood is Global*, Robin Morgan, ed. New York: Anchor Books, 1984, 447–453.

_____. *Beyond the Veil: Male-Female Dynamics in Modern Muslim Society*. Rev. Ed. Bloomington: Indiana University Press, 1987.

_____. *Doing Daily Battle: Interviews with Moroccan Women*, trans. Mary Jo Lakeland. London: The Woman's Press, 1988.

Moghadam, Valentine M. "Industrial Development, Culture, and Working Class Politics: A Case Study of Tabriz Industrial Workers in the Iranian Revolution." *International Sociology* 2, no. 2 (June 1987).

_____. "Women, Work, and Ideology in the Islamic Republic." *International Journal of Middle East Studies* 20 (May 1988a).

_____. "Industrial Policy and Labour's Response: The Case of the Workers' Councils in Iran." In *Trade Unionism and the New Industrialisation of the Third World*, Roger Southall, ed. Ottowa and London: University of Ottawa and Zed Press, 1988b.

———. "The Reproduction of Gender Inequality in Islamic Societies: The Case of Iran in the 1980s." *World Development* 19, no. 10 (October 1991): 1,135–1,349.

———. "Revolution, Islam, and Women: Sexual Politics in Iran and Afghanistan." In *Nationalisms and Sexualities*, A. Parker, M. Russo, D. Sommer, and P. Yaeger, eds. New York and London: Routledge, 1992, 424–446.

Molyneux, Maxine. "Legal Reform and Socialist Revolution in Democratic Yemen: Women and the Family." *International Journal of the Sociology of Law* 13 (1985): 155–159.

Mujahid, G.B.S. "Female Labour Force Participation in Jordan." In *Women, Employment, and Development in the Arab World*, J. Abu Nasr, N. Khoury, and H. Azzam, eds. The Hague: Mouton/ILO, 1985, 103–130.

Myntti, Cynthia. "Women, Work, Population, and Development in the Yemen Arab Republic." In *Women, Employment, and Development in the Arab World*, J. Abu Nasr, N. Khoury, and H. Azzam, eds. The Hague: Mouton/ILO, 1985, 39–58.

National Planning Council, Hashemite Kingdom of Jordan. *Five Year Plan for Economic and Social Development 1980–1985*. Jordan: NPC, 1981.

Nouredine, Saadi. *La Femme et La Loi en Algérie* [Women and the Law in Algeria]. Casablanca: Editions Le Fennec and Tokyo: United Nations University, 1991.

Office National des Statistiques. *Recensement Général de la Population et de l'Habitat 1987: Données Synthétiques*. Algiers: ONS, 1989.

Oncu, Ayse. "Turkish Women in the Professions: Why So Many?" In *Women in Turkish Society*, Nermin Abadan-Unat, ed. Leiden: E. J. Brill, 1981, 181–193.

Palloix, Christian. *L'internationalisation du Capital*. Paris: Maspero, 1977.

Papanek, Hanna. "Gender and Class in Education-Employment Linkages." *Comparative Education Review* 29, no. 3 (1985): 317–346.

Rassam, Amal. "Introduction. Arab Women: The Status of Research and the Status of Women." In *Social Science Research and Women in the Arab World*. London and Paris: Francis Pinter and UNESCO, 1984, 1–13.

Safilios-Rothschild, Constantina. "A Cross-Cultural Examination of Women's Marital, Educational, and Occupational Options." In *Women and Achievement*, M.T.S. Mednick, et al., eds. New York: John Wiley and Sons, 1971.

Sen, Gita, and Caren Grown. *Development, Crises, and Alternative Visions: Third World Women's Perspectives*. New York: Monthly Review Press, 1987.

SIDA (Swedish International Development Authority). *Women in Developing Countries: Case Studies of Six Countries*. Stockholm: SIDA Research Division, 1974.

Sivard, Ruth Leger. *Women . . . A World Survey*. Washington, D.C.: World Priorities, 1985.

South Commission. *The Challenge to the South: The Report of the South Commission*. Oxford: Oxford University Press, 1990.

Southall, Roger, ed. *Trade Unions and the New Industrialization of the Third World*. Ottawa and London: University of Ottawa and Zed Press, 1988.

UNFPA et la Ministère du Plan. *La Femme et La Famille Tunisienne à Travers Les Chiffres*. Tunis: United Nations Fund for Population Activities and the Ministry of Planning, 1984.

United Nations, Department of Public Information (UN DPI). *Economic Development: The Debt Crisis*. New York: United Nations, September 1989.

———. *Information Bulletin: The Convention on the Elimination of All Forms of Discrimination Against Women* [Information on CEDAW]. New York: United Nations, September 1989.

Ward, Kathryn. *Women in the World System: Its Impact on Status and Fertility*. New York: Praeger, 1984.

Warren, Bill. *Imperialism: Pioneer of Capitalism*. London: Verso, 1980.

Weeks, John R. "The Demography of Islamic Nations." *Population Bulletin* 43, no. 4 (December 1988).

World Bank. *World Development Report 1985.* New York: Oxford University Press for the World Bank, 1985.

———. *World Development Report 1988.* New York: Oxford University Press for the World Bank, 1988.

———. *World Development Report 1990.* New York: Oxford University Press for the World Bank, 1990.

PART THREE
Socialist Economies in Transition

The state has had a powerful effect on the lives of women in the former Soviet Union and East European countries. Communist ideology helped to shape state policies that directly encouraged paid work and provided support services for working mothers. But sex segregation still persists in the occupations of women and men as well as in women's heavier double burden of home work and paid work. Now that democratic revolutions have transformed many of these Communist governments, there is potential for change in women's roles toward somewhat lower levels of labor force participation and possibly a movement toward more part-time work and in-and-out attachment to the paid labor market, although the need for women's family income remains strong.

Political scientist Sharon L. Wolchik, in her chapter on women and work in Central and Eastern Europe, documents the strains that developed in women's roles under Communist rule. During the Communist period, economic policies put a premium on the mobilization of all available labor reserves. Wage policies made it difficult for families to live on one income. The result was very high labor force participation of women and their entry into previously male occupations. Gender inequalities, however, persisted in incomes and attainment of the highest positions. Now that political transformation is underway throughout the region, women have a greater opportunity to organize and articulate their interests. One likely direction for the future is a reduction in the current high levels of women's labor force participation.

Gail W. Lapidus, also a political scientist, spells out women's position in the former Soviet economy both at work and in the family. The USSR historically sought to devise policies that would simultaneously guarantee women equal treatment with men as workers and citizens and special protection as mothers. The results are mixed. Despite rising educational attainments and entry into a number of nontraditional scientific and professional occupations, Soviet women have tended to be concentrated in occupations of low rank and low pay. Occupational choices have been further profoundly influenced by continuing identification of authority with men. The sexual division of labor that has persisted within the family has resulted not only in public discussion of women's double burden but in growing alarm over rising divorce rates, declining birth rates, and other evidence of serious strain. Current policy debates reveal sharply diverging recommendations for dealing with the interaction of women's work and family roles. Gorbachev's political and economic reforms not only broadened the debate and increased its frankness, they also contributed to an economic and political crisis that has overshadowed all other issues and placed economic survival at the top of women's agenda.

As Eastern and Central Europe and the former USSR move toward democratic forms of government and a Western-style economy, several future developments in the work and lives of women appear likely. Greater ideological diversity will allow women to opt out of the work force if they are economically able. Counterbalancing this trend will be a continuing economic crisis that will make it necessary for women to continue working just to make ends meet. As to the course of job segregation, child care programs, or other specific trends, it is still anybody's guess how past socialist experience and new democratic ideas will be combined to shape the future lives of women and respond to their needs.

6

Women and Work in Communist and Post-Communist Central and Eastern Europe

SHARON L. WOLCHIK

Women's economic activities in Central and Eastern Europe reflect the impact of policies toward women adopted during more than forty years of Communist rule. As a result of the dramatic political and economic changes of 1989 and 1990, many policies regarding women's economic and other roles are currently being reconsidered. Political leaders and many women are reassessing the consequences of the uneven pattern of change in gender roles that occurred as the result of the policies of Communist governments.

The end of the Communist Party's monopoly of political power and the elimination of censorship have created new opportunities for women and men to express their opinions and articulate political views and policy preferences. As in a host of other areas, the new freedom of expression has been reflected in challenges to previous expectations regarding women's roles and women's issues. Women's economic roles are also being influenced by economic reforms that are altering the structure of employment opportunities, incentives, and wage systems as well as changing the organization of economic life in fundamental ways.

WOMEN'S WORK AND FAMILY ROLES
DURING THE COMMUNIST PERIOD

This chapter examines some of the implications of these changes for women's employment. In the first section, I focus on the changes that occurred in women's work and family lives during the Communist period. In the second section, I discuss the impact of current political and economic changes on women's work and gender roles.

Women's Economic Roles

Women's economic activities and other aspects of gender relations in Central and Eastern Europe were influenced profoundly by four decades of Communist rule (Wolchik 1978, 1979, 1981b, 1989). The political structures and values associated with Communist states as well as the strategy for political change, economic development, and social transformation adopted led to a distinctive pattern of change in women's roles. Women's status and gender relations also were conditioned by social and religious traditions, level of development, and political history (Wolchik 1985; Freeze 1985; Garver 1985; Bohachevsky-Chomiak 1985; Reed 1985).

However, no single underlying variable (such as economic development) appeared to account for variations in women's employment, access to education, or political power. In fact, differences among women according to living standards, general educational levels, and degree of urbanization were not as great as one would anticipate, given the continued disparity in levels of economic development within the region. Rather, the pattern of change in gender roles and gender inequalities was similar throughout the region (see Wolchik 1981c).

Communist policies toward women and the consequences of other policies adopted during the Communist period led to an increase in women's educational access and to women's large-scale entry into employment outside the home. Women's roles in the exercise of political power and in the home changed far less (Jancar 1978: 57–72; Wolchik 1981c: 448–465, and 1989; Kulcsar 1985 [Hungary]; Meznarić 1985 [Yugoslavia]; Siemieňska 1985 [Poland]; Shaffer 1981 [German Democratic Republic]; Wolchik 1979: 596–602, 1981b: 139–142 [Czechoslovakia]; Lapidus 1978: 232–284 [Soviet Union]).

Levels of women's employment outside the home have generally been higher in the more developed northern countries in the region (the former German Democratic Republic [GDR], Czechoslovakia, Poland, and Hungary) than in the Balkans. An exception is Bulgaria, where women's employment is among the highest in the region although the level of economic development is relatively low. Educational levels of women as well as men also have generally been higher in the northern countries, although women's percentages among all students and gender differences in educational levels do not vary consistently by development levels.

Women's very high level of employment outside the home, even in the prime childbearing ages, was a striking characteristic of the Central and East European states during the Communist period. As Table 6.1 illustrates, employment levels tended to be highest in those states that were more developed at the outset of the Communist period as well as in the more developed regions within countries. The somewhat lower levels of employment of women in Yugoslavia reflect the country's early move to a market socialist system.

The widespread entry of women into the labor force reflected in part the regime's commitment to the principle of women's equality. However, it also reflected the labor-intensive strategy of economic development and the rapid industrialization that were central to the Soviet model of economic develop-

TABLE 6.1 Women as a Proportion of the Socialized Sector of the Labor Force, 1950-1988

Year	Albania	Bulgaria	Czechoslovakia	GDR	Hungary	Poland	Romania	Yugoslavia
1950		27.4[a]	38.4	38.4		33.0[b]		23.2[c]
1960	25.1	33.5	42.8	44.3	32.5	32.8	27.1	27.0
1970	38.7	41.0	46.7	47.7	40.6	40.0	30.1	31.0
1980		47.1	45.4	51.0	45.7[d]	44.5		35.5
1988		49.5[e]	46.0	50.3	46.0[e]	46.8		38.3[e]

[a]1951. [b]1955. [c]1952. [d]1985. [e]1986.

Sources: Wolchik 1981c: 452-453; Federální Statistický úřad, 1982: 205, 1989: 194, 197; Staatliche Zentralverwaltung 1989: 115-116; Głowny urząd statystyczny 1989: 63; Savezni Zavod 1987: 136-137; Tsentralno Statistichesko Upravlenie 1987: 113; Hungarian Central Statistical Office 1987: 68-69. See Wolchik 1981c for a discussion of some of the problems involved in cross-country comparisons of women's labor force participation. Use of information on the socialized sector eliminates many of these problems, which arise particularly in the treatment of unpaid auxiliary family workers, many of whom are found in the private sector.

ment and the political and social transformation adopted by the Communist governments set up after World War II. Thus, elite efforts to encourage women to enter the labor force to help their homelands were accompanied by wage scales that virtually required two incomes per family to maintain a decent standard of living.

The high levels of women's employment characteristic of most Central and East European states also reflected the typical Communist policy of full employment and the lack of accurate mechanisms to measure labor costs. Demographic policies, including easy access to abortion, also facilitated the influx of women into the labor force (see David and McIntyre 1981; Heitlinger 1987).

The relatively low levels of women's employment outside the home in Yugoslavia illustrate the impact of both economic and demographic policies. In contrast to the other states in the region, in which central planning and control of the economy persisted throughout much of the Communist period, in Yugoslavia responsibility for economic decisionmaking soon passed to the republic level. Individual enterprises also were given far greater autonomy and responsibility than was the case in other states in the region. Hiring and other decisions that had an impact on the composition of the labor force thus rested not with central economic and political officials as elsewhere but with managers and directors of individual enterprises. Such decisions also were determined by considerations of profitability to a larger degree than in the other Communist states. In this situation, in which there was less pressure on women from governmental authorities to enter the labor force or on enterprise-level officials to hire women, traditional attitudes concerning women's economic roles were not challenged to the same degree as elsewhere. Moreover, the unemployment that accompanied Yugoslavia's move to market socialism was felt disproportionately by women workers and further influenced women's labor force participation.

Despite the influx of women into paid employment, considerable inequality persisted in the earnings and roles of men and women at work (Heitlinger 1979: 153–157, 1985; Jancar 1978: 25–32; Shaffer 1981: 71–83; Wolchik 1979, 1981b, 1981c; Kulcsar 1985; Meznarić 1985; Volgyes 1985; Woodward 1985; Mieczkowski 1985; McIntyre 1985). Women continued to earn from 20 to 30 percent less than men (Heitlinger 1979: 153–155; Jancar 1978: 25–28; Wolchik 1978: chapter 4, 1981c: 453–457). These persistent differences in men's and women's earnings in large part reflected continuing occupational segregation by gender. Thus, although women's representation among those working in technical areas increased in all countries during the Communist period, women continued to be concentrated in low-priority areas of the economy that had lower-than-average wages (Connor 1979: 239–243).

Women's wages and occupations also reflected the different educations men and women received. Although the educational levels of women improved in all of the Central and East European countries during the Communist period, there were marked differences in the educational specializations men and women chose or were encouraged to enter. At the secondary level, girls were far more likely to enter general secondary education than technical fields; they also comprised almost the entire student population in secondary teacher training institutes. The concentration of women students in general secondary education and the relatively large number of students who did not continue their education beyond the secondary level had a direct impact on the labor force. Many women entered the labor force directly after secondary school without the specialized skills they might have gained in vocational programs and thus became unskilled or semiskilled workers. In higher education, women tended to enter fields that traditionally had been seen as appropriate for women such as education, the arts and humanities, and medicine (which became feminized during the Communist period in most of these countries).

Thus, although far larger numbers of women entered technical education than previously, men and women continued to enter the labor force with markedly different skills. Throughout the Communist period, average wages were lower in those branches of the economy such as education, the service sector, retail trade, medicine, and light industry (where women were concentrated) than in higher-priority areas such as mining and heavy industry (where there was a higher concentration of men) (Wolchik 1978: chapter 2; Connor 1979: chapter 6; Jancar 1978: 13–19; Heitlinger 1979: 149–153). Men's incomes also were relatively higher than women's because of the tendency for women to be assigned to the lower end of skill and wage categories of an occupation, the willingness of women to accept positions for which they were overqualified in order to be nearer to their homes, and outright discrimination against women.

In addition, gender-related wage differentials resulted from the fact that few women held leading economic positions. Large numbers of women held leading positions in education and medicine where women predominated, but even in these fields women were less likely than men to be chosen for or to accept leadership positions (Siemieńska 1985: 314–315; Kulcsar 1985; Wolchik 1978: chapter 2; Jancar 1978: 28–32; Meznaríc 1985; Heitlinger 1979: 158–165; Kurti 1989; Olujíc 1989).

Thus, although paid employment outside the home had become an accepted part of the lives of many women in Central and Eastern Europe during the Communist period, many barriers to equal achievement by women remained. These inequalities can be traced to a number of factors, including the relationship between the public and private lives of women and public policies adopted by Communist leaders.

Family Lives

The increased educational access and participation in paid employment outside the home that characterized women's lives during the Communist period were not accompanied by any significant changes in gender roles within the home. There were a number of important changes in the family. The size of families decreased, particularly in urban areas, and the role of the extended family also diminished. Constitutional guarantees of equality in the areas of inheritance, divorce, and child custody coupled with other legal measures and the effects of modernization also reduced many of the most flagrantly abusive practices toward women in the family, including bride price, arranged marriages, and similar practices. These measures were particularly important in countries such as Albania and the southern parts of Yugoslavia, where patriarchal traditions and the influence of the clan or the extended family were strong in the pre-Communist period (Denich 1974; Kolsti 1985). The impact of legal changes and of women's new economic opportunities in this area also was evident in the increase in the number of divorces initiated by women. Survey research conducted in Czechoslovakia, Poland, Hungary, the former GDR, and Yugoslavia also indicates that, especially in urban areas, many couples had developed relationships characterized by greater respect and a more equal sharing of power than in the past (Wolchik 1978; Jancar 1978: 63–65; Heitlinger 1979: 144–146; Shaffer 1981: 144–148; Cole and Nydon 1989; Denich 1989).

However, traditional attitudes toward gender roles in the family continued to hold sway, particularly in rural areas. Evident in the ritualized laments of rural Romanian women that were associated with marriage, which mourn a young girl's loss of freedom and happiness and warn of the drudgery and hard work to come (Kligman 1985), such attitudes also were reflected in literature in certain areas of the Balkans (see Kolsti 1985 for a discussion about Albania). Although the prevailing attitudes toward women's roles in the family were not as overtly patriarchal in the more developed countries in the region or in the more developed areas of the Balkan countries, the results of social science research conducted in Poland, Hungary, Czechoslovakia, and Bulgaria in the Communist period document the survival of a tendency to see the male as head of the household and to expect that women would continue to defer to their husbands in decisionmaking (Siemieňska 1985; Woodward 1985; and Wolchik 1978: chapter 5).

Despite the lip service given to the notion of equality within the family, the actual division of labor within the home changed very little. Although urban, better-educated, professional men were more likely to spend more time on household tasks and child care than rural, less-educated, working-class men, women continued to bear the brunt of the responsibility for running the home and caring for children in all socioeconomic groups (Siemieňska 1985 [Poland]; Woodward 1985 [Yugoslavia]; Kulscar 1985; Volgyes 1985; and Volgyes and Volgyes 1977 [Hungary]; Scott 1974; Heitlinger 1979; Wolchik 1979, 1981b, 1978: chapters 6–7 [Czechoslovakia]; Shaffer 1981 [GDR]; Jancar 1978: chapter 4; Wolchik 1978: chapter 5).

Although many Central and East European men as well as women identified change in family roles as critical if women were to achieve equality, support for equality often remained at the level of theory (Bártová 1984; Bauerová 1974; Siemieňska 1985). During the Communist period, then, despite women's increased participation in activities previously considered appropriate only for men, there was little movement of men into areas of life previously considered women's preserves. The continued identification of women with the domestic sphere, and the expectation on the part of many women as well as men that women would continue to define themselves primarily in terms of their roles in the home had predictably negative results for women's achievement in the areas of work and public life (Jancar 1978: 88–105; Wolchik 1981c: 457–462, 1979: 456–467, 1981a).

Part of the explanation for the striking lack of change in this respect lies in the failure of Communist Party leaders, who controlled access to the policy-making process, to recruit women leaders. But the persistence of a traditional division of labor and gender roles within the home also contributed to these patterns by reducing the supply of women available for recruitment (Wolchik 1981a: 255–257, 1981c: 465–467).

Public Policies and Elite Priorities

The negative impact of the persistence of a traditional division of labor within the home on women's possibilities outside the home reflected and was exacerbated by elite policies toward women and elite priorities in other areas. In the early Communist period, Communist activists and leaders discussed the need to enact public policies to help women deal with the conflict between their domestic and work roles. However, as Stalinist systems were consolidated across the region, discussion of problematic aspects of women's situation ceased. Political leaders also did little in terms of committing public resources to ease women's burdens that the chosen strategy of economic development created. The emphasis on heavy industry led to the neglect of light industry and services and created shortages of consumer goods. The frequent shortages of the basic necessities of life that ensued because of uneven patterns of investment and poor economic performance resulting from central planning also complicated the task of running a household for most women. Certain options such as flextime or part-time work available to women in the West were not available to most Central and East European women ("Women's Employment" 1990: 25). The dominant image of the ideal socialist woman during this period, evident in the mass media as well as in the more specialized women's press, was that of an outstanding worker who also was politically active. Political leaders stressed the improvements socialism had brought to women; the conflicts between the image and reality were largely ignored (Scott 1974: chapters 9–10; Heitlinger 1979: 68–76, 162–165; Wolchik 1978: chapters 6–7, 1989: 55-57, 1981b: 125–127).

The consequences of this approach to women's issues began to be evident in the early 1960s. One of the most important of these was the decline in the birthrate. Once the connection among women's stressful situation, high levels of employment of women in the childbearing years, and the drop in the birthrate became evident, political leaders changed their approach to women's issues to some degree. This change was most noticeable in Hungary, Romania, Czechoslovakia, and the former GDR, in which the birthrate fell most quickly and most precipitously. However, it also was evident by the late 1970s in Bulgaria, the northern regions of Yugoslavia, and Poland—a country in which demographic trends followed a wave-like rather than a steadily declining pattern. The image of the ideal socialist woman was then enlarged to recognize the contribution women make to society by having and raising children, and a number of measures were adopted to help women deal with their multiple roles. In large part, however, these policies were determined by the desire of political leaders to increase the birthrate and to encourage young couples to have more children.

These policies—coupled with restrictions on abortion in Bulgaria, Czechoslovakia, Hungary, and Romania—include low-interest loans for young couples who had several children, increased children's allowances, subsidized supplies of baby clothes and goods, extensions of maternity leaves, and mothers' allowances. Paid maternity leave and mothers' allowances, which allowed women with more than one child to remain at home until their children reached the age of three, were very popular. Most women used paid maternity leave, and many—particularly those with few skills in poorly paid jobs—welcomed the possibility of earning a modest income while staying at home (David and McIntyre 1981; Heitlinger 1976: 123–135; Wolchik 1981c).

Albania, which was the least developed of the European Communist countries and continued to have the highest birthrate in Europe, was the glaring exception to this trend. Here the emphasis on the need for women to join the labor force and to be active outside the confines of the family continued throughout the 1970s and 1980s. Although it was articulated most forcefully in the 1970s as a way to break the power of the clans in the context of Albania's cultural revolution, the official view of women as workers first and foremost continued to color public discussions until the early 1990s. With the changes that have occurred in Albania since Ramiz Alia responded to mass efforts at emigration and to popular protests by allowing more open debate and criticism (Binder 1991), Albanian women activists have begun to challenge the earlier orientation as well as the previous regime's disapproval of such things as wearing cosmetics.

The impact of the pronatalist measures adopted in much of the rest of the region was paradoxical for women. On the one hand, the possibility of leaving the labor force with a guaranteed return to a similar position and continued, if reduced, earnings during the period when child-rearing demands were greatest appealed to many young women. On the other hand, these policies were problematic from the perspective of gender equality because they reinforced the notion, already prevalent among many groups, that work was a secondary concern for women, who defined themselves primarily in terms of their domestic, maternal roles. Women's retreat from the labor force for a period of three to six years had predictable consequences for their career advancement, particularly because measures to keep women from losing their qualifications while on leave were not implemented to any extent. Women's withdrawal from the labor force also reinforced the traditional division of labor within the home. Additional problems arose when women returned to the labor force. Although their situation was considered to be better than that of women in the United States and in many non-Communist European countries in that they were entitled to positions equivalent to those held prior to maternity leave, they had to face not only the reality of continued conflict between the home and work but the negative workplace attitudes created by the new emphasis on women's maternal roles.

The conflict Central and East European women experienced between the demands of home and work as well as continued gender inequality within the workplace during the Communist period led many women and men to reject the goal of women's equality. These attitudes were reinforced by the fact that women's paid employment as well as other aspects of gender equality were not chosen as goals by women themselves but were imposed from above on populations that in many respects were unwilling.

The appropriation by the state of the goal of gender equality and the impact of living for approximately forty years with the negative effects of work-home conflict and the uneven pattern of gender role change led many people to reject the goal of gender equality altogether. Others supported certain aspects of role change but held fast to traditional values and behaviors in other areas of life (Wolchik 1989: 61–65; Siemieňska 1985: 314–322).

Dissatisfaction with the impact of the uneven pattern of change in women's roles on women and on the family was clearly evident in social science research conducted during the Communist period. Although less frequently articulated in the mass circulation media, such attitudes also came to the fore during periods of political liberalization or crisis. In the period of theoretical renewal and rethinking that led to the 1968 political reforms in Czechoslovakia, for example, many people criticized what were perceived to be excessively high levels of women's employment. Proponents of economic reform frequently questioned the wisdom, from an economic perspective, of employing mothers of very small children; and educators and psychologists raised questions about the impact of extended public day care on the physical and psychological development of infants (Scott 1974: 123–133; Wolchik 1978). Leaders of the newly re-created women's organization also took issue with the earlier emphasis on women's economic roles and called for a differentiated approach to the needs of women (Scott 1974: 123–133; Wolchik 1978).

In Poland, activists and leaders of Solidarity criticized the focus on women's employment and called instead for measures to help women strengthen the family and fulfill their domestic roles more easily. A few former dissidents in Czechoslovakia, including some of those associated with Charter 77, affirmed women's right to paid employment, but most paid little attention to women's situations. Others, including the former dissident Czech writer Eva Kantůrková, called on women not to buy into the officially promulgated model of career and work but rather to devote themselves to developing their feminine characteristics. Kantůrková also urged women to join the community of the excluded—independent, dissident activists (Siemieňska 1986: 32–33; Jancar 1985: 177–181).

Views such as these were reinforced by the impact of the economic and political crises that characterized the 1970s and 1980s in most of these countries. Preoccupied with pressing economic issues and facing the potential disruption of political succession, Central and East European leaders paid little attention to reducing remaining gender inequalities in the workplace or elsewhere. Economic crises also diverted the attention of the population from these issues and, by increasing the importance of the family as an economic as well as a psychological unit, reinforced traditional conceptions of family and gender roles (Siemieńska 1986: 26–33; Wolchik 1989: 62–64). During this period, then, there was a coincidence of views between the regime, which emphasized women's maternal roles for demographic and economic reasons, and many groups in the population, who longed for earlier forms of family organization and behavior. In a pattern common to many other societies, focus on the broader social, political, and economic crises that existed throughout Central and Eastern Europe in the late Communist period led leaders and most citizens to give women's issues very low priority.

Impact of Perestroika and Glasnost

The impact of perestroika and glasnost in Central and Eastern Europe after Mikhail Gorbachev came to power in the Soviet Union intensified these tendencies. In contrast to the impact of political change in earlier periods, the changes in the political climate that occurred in several of these countries after the mid-1980s did not lead to a widespread debate over gender roles and women's employment. During earlier periods of political liberalization in Poland, Hungary, and Czechoslovakia, experts and some leaders of the women's organizations had challenged the emphasis on women's employment more openly. Debates that had been confined to specialized journals concerning the wisdom of employment of women with small children and the impact of extended day-care on children's psychological development spread to the broader-circulation periodicals (Scott 1974: chapter 6; Heitlinger 1979: 68–76; Wolchik 1979: 596–602).

By the mid-1980s, many of the positions these critics had advocated had been incorporated into official policies. In most of the East and Central European countries (except for Romania and Albania), it had been possible for some time to raise and discuss problematic aspects of women's situation at work and elsewhere. Thus, the impact of the policies associated with Gorbachev had limited effect on women's work roles. In discussions of economic reform, economists and other experts continued to debate the impact of proposed changes on levels of employment of various groups in the population, including women. Sociologists and other experts continued to report research findings documenting the double burden of women. But most citizens, including those most active in alternative or dissident organizations, focused on what were thought to be broader public issues.

Prior to 1989, feminist thought and activity were most institutionalized in Yugoslavia. There, several groups of young, professional women in the major cities in the northern republics of Slovenia and Croatia were able to discuss feminist issues and promote feminist research, in some cases within the framework of existing professional associations. Although they faced fewer institutional constraints, the number of feminist organizations remained small, and their links to other groups of women and influence on policymakers were weak (Jancar 1986). The acute political and economic crises Yugoslavia experienced in the late 1980s and early 1990s, and the ethnic conflicts and civil wars in 1991–1992 that have effectively broken up the Yugoslav federation have overshadowed all other public issues. Efforts to foster cooperation among feminists across ethnic lines have also been casualties of the war.

The loosening of the limits on debate and the de facto tolerance of independent organizations evident in Poland and Hungary in the late Communist period led to the formation of a number of small, independent women's groups in those countries. From the information available concerning the activities of these organizations, their emphases appear to have varied widely. Certain groups focused on issues related to women's equality, whereas others sought to create better conditions under which women could fulfill their maternal roles. A small number of groups and activists openly defined themselves as feminist and drew inspiration from Western feminist writings. Others eschewed both the term and the value of Western experience. The more open political conditions that prevailed in these countries in the late Communist period also led to more open discussion of several aspects of sexuality, including such previously taboo subjects as homosexuality and violence against women (Wolchik 1990).

Feminist trends also were discernible in the former GDR prior to the fall of the Communist system in that country and the unification of Germany in 1990. Such trends were first evident in the works of a number of women writers in the 1970s; literary works that contained critiques of policies that created hardship for women continued to be published throughout the rest of the Communist period and at times found their way into specialized professional publications (Rosenberg 1985). Although many rejected Western feminism, activists did articulate many of the grievances women experienced prior to the end of Communist rule.

In the former GDR as in much of the rest of the region, however, until the fall of the Communist system the penalties for organizing independent groups remained very heavy. In these countries, public debate over issues related to women's situation and gender roles remained confined to less-controversial topics. More controversial debate occurred primarily among elites and rarely reached the mass media.

WOMEN, WORK, AND GENDER ROLES IN THE POST-COMMUNIST PERIOD

The fall of Communist governments throughout much of the region in 1989 had a number of important implications for women's work and discussion of gender roles. The end of the Communist Party's monopoly of power, the elimination of censorship, and the creation or re-creation of multiparty, democratic political systems in many of these countries have enlarged the avenues available to all citizens to participate in politics. They also have vastly expanded the freedom of expression and the ability of interested citizens to articulate views relevant to policymaking. The end of the party's control of the process of political recruitment has allowed new leaders to emerge who do not adhere to Marxist-Leninist ideology. It is now possible for women as well as other citizens in all of these countries to form autonomous groups to define and advocate their own interests. As a result, the political framework for discussion of gender roles has changed dramatically.

Women's issues are not presently seen as top priority concerns by most people. Rather, just as the economic and political crises that existed in each of these countries were seen as more pressing concerns in the late Communist period, so the challenges of creating democratic political systems and functioning market economies are now given precedence. However, debates concerning women's roles are one of the many subthemes that have surfaced in a new way in the new political and economic context. As is the case with many other problems and issues that could not be discussed openly during the Communist period, past conflicts created by the one-sided pattern of gender role change are now under review in all of these countries.

As in earlier periods of political liberalization, many men and women are challenging the previous emphasis on women's employment. The reemphasis on women's maternal roles that formed the basis of the elites' approach to women's issues in all of these countries (with the exception of Albania) since the late 1960s or early 1970s has become the dominant tendency in discussions of gender issues. In contrast to earlier discussions, however, which were limited by the need to adhere to the values embodied in Marxism-Leninism, the recent critiques are more radical and the solutions proposed more far-reaching. Women activists in Albania also have begun to challenge the regime's policies toward women, including the one-sided emphasis on women's economic roles.

To some extent, public attitudes in this as in many other areas of life are presently characterized by a reaction to earlier patterns of behavior and values imposed from above. The experience of living with the results of the one-sided pattern of change in women's roles, which the Communist leaderships depicted as equality, helped further to discredit the idea of gender equality. As a result, many groups in each of the countries now want to see lower levels of women's employment. Regarding the previous patterns as mistaken, they call for a reduction in the numbers of women in the work force and emphasize the need for women to be able to choose to be employed or to stay at home with their children. Part of a more general rejection of the values imposed by the Communist regimes, these attitudes are reflected in the discussions of public figures and in the mass media. They also are evident in the activities and goals of many of the new, independent women's groups that have formed since the end of the Communist systems.

Candidates in the multiparty elections that took place in most of these countries in 1989 and 1990, for example, devoted little attention to issues related to women's situation. The attitudes expressed in a televised debate just prior to the June 1990 elections in Czechoslovakia appear to be typical of the discussion that did occur. Asked their opinions on whether women should work, representatives of all of the political parties agreed that a way should be found for women to care for their small children at home. A representative of one party went so far as to argue that women with children under the age of ten should be required to remain out of the labor force (Czechoslovak television 1990). Similar attitudes toward women's roles were articulated by Lech Walesa, now president of Poland, in the context of his 1990 presidential election campaign.

Many of the independent women's groups that have formed in the Central and East European countries since the end of 1989 also have supported a reevaluation of women's roles. The Czech Mothers, for example—a group of young, highly educated, urban women at home with small children—define the task of their organization as strengthening the family and helping women to fulfill their maternal and family roles. Another group—the Society of Czech Women—which began in Prague and now has branches throughout many cities in the Czech lands, defines its tasks in similar terms, as does a new, independent newspaper for women, *Nora* (Jasková 1990: 6; Panková 1990: 1). In a clear reaction to the past, representatives of these groups deny that they are feminists and emphasize the need to recognize women's distinctive features and interests (Wolchik 1990, 1991).

The consensus that previous levels of women's employment were too high also appears to be shared by many professionals, including several who have conducted research on women's roles in the past. Arguing that the rest of the world can learn from the mistakes of the Communist experience, they concur with the call made by leaders of the women's groups for public policies that make it possible for women to devote themselves to their families for longer periods than are currently possible (Bártová 1990; jul 1990; "Ženy rokovaly" 1990; Burešová 1990).

The increased activities of the churches and the ability of church officials and lay activists to play a role in public policy debates, now that the state does not restrict the activities of religious organizations or penalize those who openly acknowledge their faith, reinforce these views. The activists of several of the new women's groups in Czechoslovakia and Hungary, for example, are practicing Catholics who held to their religious beliefs and took part in a subculture of Catholic activists even during the Communist period. Catholic officials in Czechoslovakia and Poland have called for a return to traditional family values. In addition to calling for measures to allow women to devote their attention to their children and families, church officials and activists have also advocated measures to restrict access to abortion.

The impact of these attitudes concerning women's roles also has been reflected in other public policy areas that affect women's employment levels. Public officials in the Ministries of Health and Labor and Social Affairs in several of these countries have begun to review labor legislation as well as demographic policies. In Czechoslovakia, for example, parents with only one child as well as women who have never been employed are now eligible to receive paid allowances to remain at home to care for small children; these benefits may be used by fathers or mothers. A further extension of unpaid maternity leave is currently under consideration. Similar policies are being discussed in Poland and Hungary (Kroupová 1990; ha 1990: 2).

Economic factors also favor a reduction of the levels of women's labor force participation in much of the region. In countries such as Poland, Czechoslovakia, Hungary, and the former GDR, economic reforms designed to introduce market economies will reduce the underemployment (employment of people in positions that do not correspond to their qualifications or to real economic need) that characterized centrally planned economies during the Communist period and make the price of labor a critical factor in production decisions. Market-oriented reforms also will lead—at least in the short term—to increased unemployment of women as unprofitable enterprises close. Yugoslavia's experience with market socialism indicates that women are more likely to be fired or laid off than male workers as market considerations become more important (Meznaríc 1985: 216–219; Woodward 1985: 244–246). Similar patterns are emerging elsewhere in the region. Sixty-three percent of the unemployed in Bulgaria in June 1990 were women ("Record Low Birth Rate" 1990: 10). In recent years women also have been overrepresented among the unemployed in relation to their proportion of the labor force in Poland and Czechoslovakia. In the new economic and political conditions, it is also likely that enterprise managers will be able to act more openly on the reservations many appear to have concerning the profitability of employing women with small children.

In sum, we are likely to see a decline in levels of women's employment in the near future throughout Central and Eastern Europe. It is also unlikely that there will be concerted action by either political leaders or women activists to remedy the remaining inequalities in the workplace given the current economic and political climate (Wolchik 1991).

However, a number of factors will limit the extent to which women leave the labor force. Despite the turn toward a more traditional gender role orientation, there are political forces and activists who continue to support the goal of women's equality in each of these countries. The official women's organizations that dominated discussions of women's issues during the Communist period continue to exist, although they have lost the vast majority of their members. Their leaders remain committed to the principle of equality and stress that a way must be found for women to both maintain their economic independence and fulfill their maternal roles (ep 1990: 2; dap 1990: 5). However, given the association of these organizations with the old regime and the degree to which their old leaders—most of whom have been replaced—have become objects of ridicule in the public eye, their efficacy as women's advocates is severely limited. Thus, other groups may be better able to advance policies to further women's equality. Activists and leaders of the old, official women's organizations and some specialists whose work centered on women's issues attempted to form a party of women in the course of the election campaign in Czechoslovakia, for example, but did not succeed. A small group devoted to promoting women's equality did form part of a coalition, but it did not win enough votes to seat any deputies ("Strana žen" 1990: 2; "Hovoříme: 1990: 4). The Independent Women's Union in the former GDR also did poorly in the 1990 elections (Fricke and Schmidtke 1990: 44).

Women professionals in a variety of fields are less likely than women with few skills and small children to support the return-to-the-home movement. Some of these women as well as several of the few women elected to office in the new governments openly call for greater attention to gender inequalities (Brendlová 1990: 28; Radke 1990: 36–42; Burešová 1990; Nováček 1990: 3). Many of these women share the view that greater attention should be given to women's maternal roles. However, many also point to the need to increase women's political activism and representation among political leaders (see Šiklová 1990; Navarová 1990).

Although they eschew the feminist label, some of the more traditional of the new, independent women's groups may eventually emerge as defenders of women's right to work. In Czechoslovakia, for example, the Czech Mothers, in addition to attempting to strengthen women's family roles, also organize lectures on public topics ranging from the impact of the ecological crisis on the food supply to how to start a small business. Other women's groups, by creating space for women to meet and discuss various aspects of their lives, also may give rise to feminist consciousness in the future. More extended experience with staying out of the labor force coupled with continued experience with barriers to advancement and other forms of inequality when women return to work after a leave also may increase women's willingness to challenge the current orientation. In several countries—most notably Poland, Hungary, and parts of Yugoslavia—there are also small feminist groups that explicitly support women's equality and employment. These groups, which have links to Western feminists and consist primarily of well-educated, urban professional women, may gain supporters now that they can organize openly and propagate their ideas freely. Members of these groups are likely to use their new political freedoms to promote policies that would benefit women who work, such as flextime and part-time employment, as well as to question persistent inequalities in other areas. Feminist activists also have protested efforts, which were successful in the Polish case, to curtail women's right to abortion (Kolarová 1990: 10). Women now also have the opportunity to use the independent trade unions, political parties, and other political organizations that have developed in the post-Communist period to press for attention to their interests.

Important as the attitudes toward women's roles and changes in the political climate are, the most critical influences on women's work roles will come from economic trends and policies. Policies designed to reintroduce the market will have a major impact on women's work opportunities. Currently, economic reforms are creating two somewhat conflicting pressures on women. On the one hand, the reforms and resulting unemployment provide support for those who view current levels of women's employment as too high. At the same time, the economic dislocations the reforms are producing increase the need for women to contribute to their families' incomes. The serious economic disruptions introduced by the transition to market economies, efforts to redirect trade, the collapse of the CMEA trading network, and the breakup of the Soviet Union will reduce the public resources that can be diverted to support women's retreat from the labor force. In the current economic climate, it is unlikely, for example, that wages will be increased to such an extent that most households will be able to maintain a satisfactory standard of living with one income. Instead, economic reforms are depressing the standard of living temporarily and thus making women's economic contribution more essential.

Increases in the costs of many of the necessities of life that were previously subsidized by the state—such as food, fuel, housing, child care, and medical care—and the threat of unemployment also have increased the economic pressure on families to have two wage earners. Given the economic difficulties these governments face, public policies clearly will not be able to compensate for lost income sufficiently to allow women to remain at home for greatly extended periods of time. Many of these countries are already reducing expenditures on social services, including public child care. The cost of such services also has increased. In Czechoslovakia, for example, fees for nurseries increased 36.5 percent and those for kindergartens 86.3 percent in the third quarter of 1990 (min, 1990: 2; Mayer 1990: 33–35 [GDR]). Thus, as the move to re-create market economies continues in Central and Eastern Europe, many women will continue to enter and remain in the labor force as they did in the Communist period, due at least in part to economic necessity.

Survey research conducted in Bulgaria, Czechoslovakia, Hungary, Poland, Romania, Yugoslavia, and the former GDR during the Communist period found that many groups of women had ambivalent attitudes toward their employment. Although the large majority of women indicated that they worked primarily for economic reasons, many also indicated that they would continue working even if their husband's income were sufficient to allow them to remain at home. Many, particularly professional women with higher educations, reported high levels of satisfaction with their jobs (Siemieňska 1985: 312–314; Shaffer 1981: 67–68; Jancar 1978: 181–184; Scott 1974: 117–121; Wolchik 1978. Some groups of women thus may be expected to remain in the labor force for noneconomic reasons.

The move to a market economy now under way has created new choices and pressures for those women who decide to enter the labor force. Women will be able to begin their own businesses as well as work for private and state enterprises. Women's economic opportunities also will be influenced by the structural changes that are occurring as market economies are reintroduced. The end of state subsidies for unprofitable enterprises and the reorientation of the economies away from the emphasis on heavy industry toward the service sector will lead to the elimination of substantial numbers of positions for unskilled workers in industry. The need to take labor costs into account and show a profit also will lead to a streamlining of the retail and service sectors in which women presently predominate. Thus, not only the amount of employment but also the structure of women's employment is likely to change in the near future.

Women also are likely to face increased pressures to improve their performance at work. Private employers in particular may demand more from their employees than was customary during the Communist period, when the well-known saying "we pretend to work, and they pretend to pay us" largely reflected reality. Joint ventures with a substantial foreign interest may take the lead in this respect. But newly reorganized state enterprises as well as enterprises that have been privatized with domestic capital also will have to give some attention to profitability and thus will expect more from their employees. Women as well as men in leading positions will face the need to develop the new managerial skills needed in a market economy.

CONCLUSION

Women's work roles in Central and Eastern Europe today continue to reflect the legacy of the Communist period, when policies toward women and broader economic and political imperatives led to high levels of women's employment but persistent gender inequality in the workplace. Challenges to this pattern have emerged at both the mass and the elite level since the fall of Communist systems in the region. However, in this area as in many others, there are a number of barriers to rapid change—either in the direction of a large-scale return of women to the home or of a concerted effort to promote gender equality.

In the near future, most women will continue to work outside of as well as in the home. They thus will experience the impact of the radical changes in the organization of economic life in both sectors. In both of these areas, new issues will join those of the past. As a result of the backlash against the earlier uneven pattern of changes in women's roles, relatively few groups are raising political issues concerning the impact of the economic transformation on women or on the remaining inequalities in women's work. However, the new opportunities for political debate and participation that are available in these countries now mean that women have far greater opportunities than they did previously for attempting to resolve problems related to gender inequality. As economic reforms continue and as more women and men have first-hand experience with the operation of market economies, discussion of women's work and other roles likely will focus on many of the same issues that are important in Western Europe and the United States. These issues include inequalities in income, occupational segregation, the lack of women in leading positions, the difficulties in combining work and family roles, and the need for change in men's roles within the family. In the short run, however, such discussions also will be influenced in important ways by the multitude of economic as well as political issues involved in the process of transition now underway in all of these countries.

BIBLIOGRAPHY

Bártová, Eva. "Společenská a politická aktivita v reflexi veřejného mínění.: *Sociologický časopis* 20, no. 4 (1984): 358–375.
_____ . Interview. Institute of Sociology, Prague, March 1990.
Bauerová, Jaroslava. *Zamestnaná žena a rodina*. Prague: Práce, 1974.

Binder, David. "Albania: Land of Talking Men and Toiling Women." *New York Times,* April 23, 1991, A4.

Bohachevsky-Chomiak, Martha. "Ukrainian Feminism in Interwar Poland." In *Women, State, and Party in Eastern Europe,* Sharon L. Wolchik and Alfred G. Meyer, eds. Durham, N.C.: Duke University Press, 1985, 82–97.

Brendlová, Eva. ". . . Like a Successful Night Out with the Guys: Trying to Answer the Question, Where Did the Women Stay?" *Narodna obroda,* July 7, 1990, 3. Reported in "Women Not Represented in New Slovak Government." Joint Public Research Service–East European Report 90-112, August 2, 1990, 28.

Burešová, Dagmar. Interview. "V parlamentě piskat nebudu." *Rudé právo,* July 7, 1990, 1.

Cole, John W., and Judith A. Nydon. "Class, Gender, and Fertility: Contradictions of Social Life in Contemporary Romania." *East European Quarterly* 23, no. 4 (Winter 1989): 469–476.

Connor, Walter D. *Soclialism, Politics, and Equality: Hierarchy and Change in Eastern Europe and the USSR.* New York: Columbia University Press, 1979.

Czechoslovak television. Televised debate among parties, June 1990 parliamentary elections, June 5 1990.

dap. "Služba žen pro ženy." *Zeměděské noviny,* September 9, 1990, 5.

David, Henry P., and Robert J. McIntyre. *Reproductive Behavior: Central and Eastern European Experience.* New York: Springer Publishing Co., 1981.

Denich, Bette. "Sex and Power in the Balkans." In *Woman, Culture, and Society,* Michelle Zimbalist Rosaldo and Louise Lamphere, eds. Stanford, Calif.: Stanford University Press, 1974, 242–262.

――――. "Paradoxes of Gender and Policy in Eastern Europe: A Discussant's Comments." *East European Quarterly* 23, no. 4 (Winter 1989): 499–506.

ep. "Ženske organisace dnes." *Rudé právo,* July 7, 1990, 2.

Federální statistický úřad; Český statistický úřad; Slovenský statistický úřad. *Statistická ročenka Československé Socialistické Republiky.* Prague: Státní nakladatelství politické literatury, 1982, 1989.

Freeze, Karen J. "Medical Education for Women in Austria: A Study in the Politics of the Czech Women's Movement in the 1980s." In *Women, State, and Party in Eastern Europe,* Sharon L. Wolchik and Alfred G. Meyer, eds. Durham, N.C.: Duke University Press, 1985, 51–63.

Fricke and Schmidtke. "Independent Women's Association Advocates Social Charter." *Neues Deutschland,* February 19, 1990, 1. Reported in "Independent Women's Association Established." FBIS-EEU-90-038, February 26, 1990, 44.

Garver, Bruce M. "Women in the First Czechoslovak Republic." In *Women, State, and Party in Eastern Europe,* Sharon L. Wolchik and Alfred G. Meyer, eds., Durham, N.C.: Duke University Press, 1985, 64–81.

Głowny urzad statystyczny. *Rocznik statystyczny.* Warsaw: Głowny urzad statystyczny, 1989.

ha. "Ne mateřský, ale rodičovský příspevek." *Hospodářské noviny,* September 21, 1990, 2.

Heitlinger, Alena. "Pro-Natalist Population Policies in Czechoslovakia." *Population Studies* 30 (1976): 123–135.

――――. *Women and State Socialism: Sex Inequality in the Soviet Union and Czechoslovakia.* Montreal: McGill–Queen's University Press, 1979.

――――. "Passage to Motherhood: Personal and Social Management of Reproduction in Czechoslovakia in the 1980s." In *Women, State, and Party in Eastern Europe,* Sharon L. Wolchik and Alfred G. Meyer, eds. Durham, N.C.: Duke University Press, 1985, 286–300.

――――. *Reproduction, Medicine, and the Socialist State.* Houndmills, England: Macmillan, 1987.

"Hovoříme s představitelkámi politické strany žen a matek v ČSFR." *Rudé právo,* July 30, 1990, 4.

Hungarian Central Statistical Office. *Statistical Yearbook.* Budapest: Statistical Publishing House, 1987.

Jancar, Barbara Wolfe. *Women Under Communism.* Baltimore: Johns Hopkins University Press, 1978.

_____. "Women in the Opposition in Poland and Czechoslovakia in the 1970s." In *Women, State, and Party in Eastern Europe,* Sharon L. Wolchik and Alfred G. Meyer, eds. Durham, N.C.: Duke University Press, 1985, 168–185.

_____. "The New Feminism in Yugoslavia." In *Yugoslavia in the 1980s,* Pedro Ramet, ed. Boulder: Westview Press, 1986, 201–223.

Jasková, Kamilla. "Rozhovor mezi plenkámi." *Rudé právo,* April 6, 1990, 6.

jul. "Kolotoc bez legrace." *Mladá fronta,* April 5, 1990, 4.

Kligman, Gail. "The Rites of Women: Oral Poetry, Ideology, and the Socialization of Peasant Women in Contemporary Romania." In *Women, State, and Party in Eastern Europe,* Sharon L. Wolchik and Alfred G. Meyer, eds. Durham, N.C.: Duke University Press, 1985, 323–343.

Kolarová, Jana. "Zabijení dětí nebo opravněný lekarský zakrok." *Forum,* June 27, 1990, 10.

Kolsti, John. "From Courtyard to Cabinet: The Political Emergence of Albanian Women." In *Women, State, and Party in Eastern Europe,* Sharon L. Wolchik and Alfred G. Meyer, eds. Durham, N.C.: Duke University Press, 1985, 138–151.

Kroupová, Alena. "Komu, kdy, jaký mateřský příspevek." *Hospodářské noviny* 13, June 6, 1990, 1–2.

Kulcsar, Rozsa. "The Socioeconomic Conditions of Women in Hungary." In *Women, State, and Party in Eastern Europe,* Sharon L. Wolchik and Alfred G. Meyer, eds. Durham, N.C.: Duke University Press, 1985, 195–213.

Kurti, Laszlo. "Red Csepel: Working Youth in a Socialist Firm." *Eastern European Quarterly* 23, no. 4 (Winter 1989): 445–468.

Lapidus, Gail W. *Women in Soviet Society: Equality, Development, and Social Change.* Berkeley: University of California Press, 1978.

Mayer, Susanne. "At the End of Playtime: The Cutback of Nursery Schools and Day Care Centers for Socialism's Children Has Begun." *Die Zeit,* May 4, 1990, 100. Reported in "Child Care Cutbacks, Social Dislocation Viewed." Joint Publication Research Service–East European Report 90-089, June 21, 1990, 33–35.

McIntyre, Robert J. "Demographic Policy and Sexual Equality: Value Conflict and Policy Appraisal in Hungary and Romania." In *Women, State, and Party in Eastern Europe,* Sharon L. Wolchik and Alfred G. Meyer, eds. Durham, N.C.: Duke University Press, 1985, 270–285.

Meznaríc, Silva. "Theory and Reality: The Status of Employed Women in Yugoslavia." In *Women, State, and Party in Eastern Europe,* Sharon L. Wolchik and Alfred G. Meyer, eds. Durham, N.C.: Duke University Press, 1985, 214–220.

Mieczkowski, Bogdan. "Social Services for Women and Child Care Facilities in Eastern Europe." In *Women, State, and Party in Eastern Europe,* Sharon L. Wolchik and Alfred G. Meyer, eds. Durham, N.C.: Duke University Press, 1985, 257–269.

min. "Moja penazenka spl'asla." *Verejnost,* November 13, 1990, 2.

Navorová, Hana. "Impact of Economic and Political Changes in Czechoslovakia for Women." Unpublished manuscript, 1990.

Nováček, Petr. "Postradám alty a soprany." *Zemědělské noviny,* July 17, 1990, 3.

Olujíc, Maria B. "Economic and Demographic Change in Contemporary Yugoslavia: Persistence of Traditional Gender Ideology." *East European Quarterly* 23, no. 4 (Winter 1989): 477–485.

Panková, M. "Spojuje nas nejen vira." *Lidová demokracie*, March 19, 1990, 1.

Radke, Heidrun. "Scientific-Technological Progress and Women's Personality Development." *Wirtschaftswissenschaft* 1 (January 1990): 68–80. Reported in "S&T Developments Enhance Women's Employment Status." JPRS-EER-90-028, March 7, 1990, 36–42.

"Record Low Birth Rate, High Death Rate Reported." Sofia BTA 1558 GMT, August 24, 1990. Reported in FBIS-EEU-90-166, August 27, 1990, 10.

Reed, Mary E. "Peasant Women of Croatia in the Interwar Years." In *Women, State, and Party in Eastern Europe*, Sharon L. Wolchik and Alfred G. Meyer, eds. Durham, N.C.: Duke University Press, 1985, 98–112.

Rosenberg, Dorothy. "The Emancipation of Women in Fact and Fiction: Changing Roles in GDR Society and Literature." In *Women, State, and Party in Eastern Europe*, Sharon L. Wolchik and Alfred G. Meyer, eds. Durham, N.C.: Duke University Press, 1985, 344–361.

Savezni zavod za statistiku. *Statisticki godisnjak Yugoslavije*. Belgrade: Savezni zavod za statistiku, 1987.

Scott, Hilda. *Does Socialism Liberate Women?* Boston: Beacon Press, 1974.

Shaffer, Harry G. *Women in the Two Germanies: A Comparative Study of a Socialist and a Non-Socialist Society*. New York: Pergamon Press, 1981.

Siemieňska, Renata. "Women, Work, and Gender Equality in Poland: Reality and Its Social Perception." In *Women, State, and Party in Eastern Europe*, Sharon L. Wolchik and Alfred G. Meyer, eds. Durham, N.C.: Duke University Press, 1985, 305–322.

――――. "Women and Social Movements in Poland." *Women and Politics* 6, no. 4 (Winter 1986): 5–36.

Šiklová, Jiřina. "Are Women in Middle and Eastern Europe Conservative?" Unpublished manuscript, 1990.

Staatliche Zentralverwaltung fur Statistik. *Statistiches Jahrbuch der Deutschen Demokratischen Republic*. Berlin: Staatsverlag der DDR, 1989.

"Strana žen." *Mladá fronta*, April 9, 1990, 2.

Tsentralno statistichesko upravlenie. *Statisticheski Godishnik na Narodna Republika B'lgariia*. Sofia. Komitet po edinna sistema za sotsialna informatsiia, 1987.

Volyges, Ivan. "Blue-Collar Working Women and Poverty in Hungary." In *Women, State, and Party in Eastern Europe*, Sharon L. Wolchik and Alfred G. Meyer, eds. Durham, N.C.: Duke University Press, 1985, 221–233.

Volgyes, Ivan, and Nancy Volgyes. *The Liberated Female: Life, Work, and Sex in Socialist Hungary*. Boulder: Westview Press, 1977.

Wolchik, Sharon L. "Politics, Ideology, and Equality: The Status of Women in Eastern Europe." Unpublished Ph.D. dissertation, University of Michigan, Political Science Department, 1978.

――――. "The Status of Women in a Socialist Order: Czechoslovakia, 1948–1978." *Slavic Review* 38, no. 4 (December 1979): 583–603.

――――. "Eastern Europe." In *The Politics of the Second Electorate: Women and Public Participation*, Jane Lovenduski and Jill Hills, eds. London: Routledge and Kegan Paul, 1981, 252–277.

――――. "Elite Strategy Toward Women in Czechoslovakia: Liberation or Mobilization?" *Studies in Comparative Communism* 14, nos. 2–3 (Summer-Autumn 1981b): 123–142.

――――. "Ideology and Equality: The Status of Women in Eastern and Western Europe." *Comparative Political Studies* 13, no. 4 (January 1981c): 445–476.

――――. "The Pre-Communist Legacy, Economic Development, Social Transformation, and Women's Roles in Eastern Europe." In *Women, State and Party in Eastern Europe*, Sharon L. Wolchik and Alfred G. Meyer, eds. Durham, N.C.: Duke University Press, 1985, 31–43.

_____ . "Women and the State in Eastern Europe and the Soviet Union." In *Women, the State, and Development*, Sue Ellen M. Charlton, Jana Everett, and Kathleen Staudt, eds. Albany: State University of New York Press, 1989, 44–65.

_____ . "Women and the Collapse of Communism in Central and Eastern Europe." Paper presented at the World Congress of Slavic Studies, Harrogate, England, July 1990.

_____ . "Women's Issues in Czechoslovakia." In *Women and Politics Worldwide*, Barbara Nelson, ed. New Haven: Yale University Press, 1991.

"Women's Employment and Income in the GDR." Wochenbericht-D1W, May 10, 1990. Reported in JPRS-EER-90-104, July 13, 1990, 25.

Woodward, Susan L. "The Rights of Women: Ideology, Policy, and Social Change in Yugoslavia." In *Women, State, and Party in Eastern Europe*, Sharon L. Wolchik and Alfred G. Meyer, eds. Durham, N.C.: Duke University Press, 1985, 234–256.

"Ženy rokovaly." *Zemědělské noviny*, September 28, 1990, 2.

7

The Interaction of Women's Work and Family Roles in the Former USSR

GAIL W. LAPIDUS

In the industrial societies of Europe and United States as in the developing countries of the Third World, the relationship between changes in women's economic roles and changes in the structure and functions of the family has attracted growing attention from social scientists and policymakers alike. It is increasingly recognized that the scope and patterns of female employment critically influence key features of economic and social behavior and, more important, of fertility.

For policy analysts concerned with Third World issues, these linkages present an opportunity rather than a problem: They hold out the prospect that development strategies that enhance the educational and employment opportunities of women will not only increase national income but also may contribute significantly to population control. In Europe and the United States, by contrast, these linkages are a source of concern. Rising levels of female labor force participation have been accompanied by rising divorce rates and declining birthrates, provoking widespread anxiety that the institution of the family is threatened by current trends. An array of economic and social programs is undergoing reevaluation with a view to the impact of these programs on family stability and family size, and long-standing debates over what constitutes "equal protection" of workers who are also women have been reignited.

Because of its special relevance to all these concerns, the Soviet experience from 1917 to its dissolution in 1991 deserves the close attention of social

I would like to thank Sage Publications for permission to use materials originally published in, "Women and Family Roles in the USSR," in Ann H. Stromberg, Barbara A. Gutek, and Laurie Larwood, *Women and Work Vol. 3*. Newbury Park, Calif.: Sage Publications, 1988, 87–121.

scientists and policy analysts. Extensive reliance on female labor was a central feature of Soviet economic development for several decades, with important consequences for virtually every aspect of economic and social life. In the early 1990s, the Soviet Union claimed the highest female labor force participation rates of any industrial society; women constituted 51 percent of all workers and employees. At the same time, rising divorce rates and sharply declining birthrates made the single-child family the norm in the urban European part of the country, whereas large families remained widespread in the Muslim regions of Soviet Central Asia. Indeed, important regional and ethnic variations linked to sociocultural as well as economic differences made the Soviet Union a fascinating universe for comparative study.

But the Soviet experience is important above all because the effort to develop policies that simultaneously guaranteed women equal treatment as citizens and workers and special treatment as mothers had distinctive consequences for women's work and family roles, even though Soviet statements acknowledge that this dual goal was not actually attained (*Programme* 1986). Moreover, new departures in economic and social policy involving marketization and privatization are likely to have major consequences for women, as recent developments in Eastern Europe demonstrate. For all these reasons, a close examination of the Soviet experience is especially pertinent today.

Until the late 1960s, Soviet writings interpreted high rates of female employment as unambiguous evidence that socialism and sexual equality went hand in hand and that Soviet policy had created optimal conditions for the harmonious combination of women's work and family roles. In the 1970s and 1980s, a growing array of studies by Soviet scholars as well as numerous Soviet novels and films began to document the conflicting demands of women's dual roles, the constraints these demands placed on occupational mobility, and their harmful effects on the health of women workers and the well-being of their families (Dogle 1977; Gruzdeva and Chertikhina 1983; Kotliar and Turchaninova 1975; Mikhailiuk 1970; Novikova 1985; Sakharova 1973; Shishkan 1976). A succession of scholarly conferences, union trade meetings, and Communist Party gatherings devoted to problems of female labor and *byt* (everyday life) yielded an abundance of often-conflicting diagnoses, recommendations, and goals (Buckley 1986; Kharchev and Golod 1971; "Povyshat' Politicheskuiu Proizvodstvennuiu" 1975; Solov'ev, Lazauskas, and Iankova 1970). There is growing Soviet recognition of the fact that economic objectives pursued without regard to their social consequences not only risk failure but also threaten to exacerbate what are already perceived to be acute social problems. Consequently, significant changes in the training and utilization of female labor depend on and are likely to elicit further changes in a broad array of social institutions, especially the family. Family and population policies in turn will directly affect the future size and quality of the Soviet labor force.

In this chapter, I first sketch a profile of the Soviet female labor force and its place in the national economy. The next three sections examine the interaction of female work and family roles and the major sources of strain between them. A fifth section explores the variety of Soviet responses to the dilemma raised by this interdependence and their possible implications for broader economic and social policies, and a concluding section focuses on the impact of Mikhail Gorbachev's political and economic restructuring on women's roles. By treating the work and family roles of Soviet women as not merely the outcome of personal characteristics and preferences but as behavior that was shaped by a specific structural context, this study also points to the distinctive way in which the Soviet pattern of development joined family and economic systems, and it illuminates several of its most salient and problematic consequences.

HISTORICAL LEGACY

The role of women in the Soviet labor force was shaped by a distinctive set of assumptions and historical developments that influenced Soviet policy until late 1991. Central to the Soviet approach—as it was to Marxist and Leninist theory—was the conviction that women's entry into social production held the key to the creation of a genuinely socialist society. The family, by contrast, was initially seen as the antithesis of the factory, the embodiment of tradition and backwardness—as Nikoda Bukharin put it, the "most conservative stronghold of the old regime" (Geiger 1968: 52).

In the view of the revolutionary Bolsheviks, it was necessary to deprive the family of its economic base and to redirect its energies and loyalties from private to public domains, replacing its most important educational and social functions with publicly provided services. The nationalization of industry and the collectivization of agriculture would divest the family of its economic power; the expansion of public education and institutional child care would diminish its influence over the socialization of children; and the creation of public laundries and dining rooms would complete the shift of family functions to the wider society and thus free women for participation in the labor force. The economic independence of women was seen as the guarantee that women would enter both work and family roles on an equal basis with men.

Maternity was transformed into a social function. Early Soviet policies therefore recognized the potential contribution of women to both production and reproduction and attempted to provide conditions for the simultaneous performance of both. The Soviet approach sought women's equality through a shift of functions from the private to the public domain rather than, as in contemporary feminist strategy, through a redefinition of male and female roles.

Stalinist priorities, however, precluded any major shift of family functions to the larger society. On the contrary, the family's importance for social stability, economic performance, and population growth received increasing official recognition. Simultaneously, Stalin's industrialization strategy, with its strong emphasis on heavy industry, limited the development of consumer industries and services, which compelled the household to provide itself with a wide range of goods and services that are normally shifted outside the household in the course of economic development. The underdevelopment of social services meant that rising female employment outside the household would supplement rather than replace female labor within it.

Soviet norms and institutions thus ultimately rested on the premise that women but not men had dual roles. On the one hand, female employment was encouraged by measures that accorded women equal rights with men, expanded their educational opportunities and professional training, and shifted some of the additional costs of female labor from the individual enterprise to the larger society. At the same time, the growth of female industrial employment was exceptionally dependent on special arrangements to accommodate the continuing heavy burden of family responsibilities. The effort to make female occupational roles permeable to family needs created especially sharp differences in the conditions of male and female labor. The result was a distinctive pattern of linkages between the family and the occupational system that had fundamentally differentiated consequences for women and men.

FEMALE LABOR AND THE SOVIET ECONOMY

Although from the start Soviet policy rested on an ideological commitment to the full participation of women in social production, it was the inauguration of rapid industrialization under the first five-year plan in 1928 that transformed a politically desired objective into a pressing economic need. Rapid economic expansion combined with the effects of civil war, collectivization, purges, deportations, and ultimately World War II created a rising demand for industrial labor at the same time that falling real income and a growing deficit of males brought forth an increased supply of female labor. In 1946 there were only fifty-nine men for every one hundred women in the 35–59 age group. Large numbers of women had to become self-supporting. Political deportations and wartime losses transformed wives and widows into heads of households; in addition, the scarcity of men left a large proportion of Soviet women with no opportunity to marry. Female-headed households made up almost 30 percent of the total number of households in 1959.

The gradual return to demographic normality in the postwar period combined with the steady improvement of living standards might have been expected to diminish the pressures for high levels of female employment. Yet between 1960 and the early 1970s, an additional 25 million women were added to the Soviet labor force, raising their numbers to about 51 percent of the total. Over 85 percent of working-age women are now either employed or studying full time; their average length of employment increased from 28.7 to 33.5 years between 1960 and 1970; the average number of nonworking years dropped from 12.3 to 3.6 in that same period (Kotliar and Turchaninova 1975: 106–107). The only major untapped reserves of female labor in the USSR in late 1991 were found in the Central Asian and Transcaucasian republics, where female participation rates outside agriculture—especially among the local nationalities—remained extremely low (Ubaidullaeva 1987). (Numbers and percentages of female workers from 1922 to 1985 are given in Table 7.1.)

TABLE 7.1 Average Number and Percent of Female Workers and Employees in the Soviet Union, 1922–1985

Year	Total Number of Workers and Employees (in thousands)	Number of Female Workers and Employees (in thousands)	Women as Percent of Total
1922	6,200	1,560	25
1926	9,900	2,265	23
1928	11,400	2,795	24
1940	33,900	13,190	39
1945	28,600	15,920	56
1950	40,400	19,180	47
1955	50,300	23,040	46
1960	62,000	29,250	47
1965	76,900	37,680	49
1970	90,200	45,800	51
1976	104,235	53,632	51
1980	112,480	57,700	51
1985	116,829	59,669	51

Note: Women constituted 55 percent of the total population in 1959 and 63.4 percent of the age cohort 35 and over; by 1985, the figure had dropped to 53 percent.

Sources: TsSU SSSR 1972: 345, 348; 1975: 28–29; 1977: 470; 1979: 278–279; 1980: 387–388, 391; 1981: 160; 1985: 409; Zhenshchiny v SSSR 1980: 70; Zhenshchiny v SSSR 1986: 53.

The continuing climb in female participation rates in recent years is partly the result of explicit official policies that seek to compensate for a growing labor shortage by drawing housewives into the workplace. High female participation rates also reflect continuing economic pressures. Soviet wage scales and pensions were not designed to support a family on the income of a single breadwinner. The average monthly wage, for example, was less than two-thirds of what is required to support a family of four at even the officially recognized level of "material well-being." Opinion surveys of women factory workers clearly demonstrated that economic need is the major determinant of female employment and that family income and female labor force participation are inversely related (Kharchev and Golod 1971: 38–69; Osipov and Shchepan'skii 1969: 444, 456).

The fact that participation rates continued to rise despite the economic improvements of the 1960s and 1970s, however, suggests that other forces also were at work. "Economic need" is relative; as rising aspirations outrun rising incomes, a second income may still appear essential. Moreover, rising wages increase the opportunity cost of not being employed, encouraging women to prefer employment to either larger families or more leisure. This factor becomes even more significant as educational attainments rise because in the Soviet Union as elsewhere, education and professionalism tended to strengthen labor force attachment.

Soviet ideology reinforced these economic pressures by emphasizing the intrinsic value of work as well as its contribution to economic independence, social status, and personal satisfaction. The role of "mere housewife" was sharply devalued in Soviet society. As Soviet surveys indicated, relatively few women would have withdrawn from the labor force even if it had become economically feasible (Iankova 1975: 43; Mikhailiuk 1970: 24; Pimenova 1966: 36–39). However, had the opportunities for part-time work expanded significantly, substantial numbers of women would likely have availed themselves of that opportunity.

The large scale of female participation in Soviet economic life, however, did not obliterate many features that in the USSR as elsewhere, distinguished male and female employment. Indeed, the sharpest line of differentiation among Soviet workers in 1991 was that of sex. In the occupational structure as in the family, sex remained a significant basis for the allocation of social roles, with the result that male and female workers differed in the distribution of income, skill, status, power, and even time.

Patterns of Female Employment

Despite the massive scope of female participation in the Soviet labor force, here as in the West, women tended to predominate in economic sectors and occupations that rank low in status and pay and were underrepresented in the more prestigious professions and in managerial positions. In industry as in the economy as a whole, women were heavily concentrated in a relatively small number of areas and were significantly underrepresented in others. Women constituted over 80 percent of food and textile workers and over 90 percent of garment workers but less than 30 percent of the workers in coal, lumber, electric power, and mineral extraction in the early 1990s.

Moreover, in industrial employment as in the professions, women were concentrated at lower levels of the occupational pyramid. Although Soviet data are scarce, they clearly indicate that even as women began to enter the middle and upper ranks of industry, they continued to predominate in low-level, unmechanized, and unskilled jobs. Thus, in a typical industrial city studied in one Soviet survey, approximately 4 percent of the women workers were highly skilled, 30 percent were of average skill, and 66 percent were low skilled, compared with 31 percent, 50 percent, and 19 percent, respectively, for men (Sonin 1973: 362–363). Within individual enterprises, a similar pattern prevailed. In a group of machine-building enterprises studied by another Soviet research team, almost 95 percent of the women workers but only 5 percent of the men occupied the three lowest skill classifications. No women were found in the highest classification (Kotliar and Turchaninova 1975: 67–68). Although it often is assumed that technological progress will bring greater equality, increasing mechanization frequently widens the gap between men and women workers. The massive influx of older and less-educated women into industry in the 1960s, for example, resulted in an increase in their share of unskilled, manual jobs. Newly mechanized and automated work went primarily to males.

Women have been better represented among technical specialists than among skilled workers in industry, and they have occupied a particularly prominent place in teaching and medicine, although even here the proportion of women declines at higher levels of the pyramid. Women still have been largely absent from positions of managerial authority. To be sure, the proportion of women among enterprise directors, for example, rose from a mere 1 percent in 1956 to 9 percent in 1975 and to 11 percent in 1985, but females definitely did not move into management to the extent that their training, experience, and proportion of the relevant age cohort warranted.

Women workers also have manifested lower levels of sociopolitical participation than their male counterparts. At every level of education and occupational attainment, women workers were far less likely than men to become Communist Party members. As a result of recent political reforms, including democratization and competitive elections, their representation in legislative bodies actually diminished. Women have been virtually absent from the Soviet political elite. Since 1918 the proportion of women in the Central Committee of the Communist Party never exceeded 5 percent. Only two women were ever members of the Politburo, and only one was named to Gorbachev's Presidential Council.

The limited occupational mobility of women in industry is compounded by their lower enrollment rate in programs to improve their professional qualifications. Only one-third of the women workers in a Soviet study expressed a desire to upgrade their skills compared with over one-half of the men, and the women were less confident that their efforts would be suitably rewarded (Kotliar and Turchaninova 1975: 76–84). According to the findings of other studies, young women workers raised their qualifications at the same rate as their male counterparts when their situations were identical; but from ages twenty-one to twenty-five, when family responsibilities fall increasingly on their shoulders, their participation diminished (Bliakhman, Zdravomyslov, and Shkaratan 1965: 66; Gruzdeva and Chertikhina 1975: 97). Family responsibilities also limit women's occupational mobility. Soviet studies of labor turnover in Novosibirsk indicated that women left their jobs half as often as men because of dissatisfaction with the job content or pay and that 59 percent of women who changed jobs took a step down in occupational status (Antosenkov and Kupriianova 1977: 48–50, 77; Kotliar et al. 1982: 200; Reznik 1982: 111). Extensive Soviet reliance on combining full-time work with study was particularly disadvantageous to women with families; the enrollment of women in evening programs virtually ceased with the birth of a child.

The Earnings Gap

The uneven distribution of women across economic sectors and occupations combined with their underrepresentation in positions of high skill and responsibility resulted in a considerable gap between male and female and earnings. The 1989 publication of the first Soviet figures on distribution of wages by age and sex shown in Table 7.2 largely confirmed earlier Western estimates that average full-time female earnings were 65 percent to 75 percent of males' (SSSR v Tsifrakh v godu 1989: 71–72; Lapidus 1982: xxi–xxvii; Ofer and Vinokur 1981).

TABLE 7.2   Distribution of Soviet Full-Time Workers and Employees in Various Age Groups by Wage Levels, March 1989 (percent in each earnings interval)

Rubles Earned	Years of Age				
per Month – Men	16–24	25–29	30–39	40–49	50+
Under 80	4.1	1.4	0.8	0.8	2.4
80–90	4.5	2.1	1.3	1.2	2.9
91–100	4.9	2.2	1.3	1.2	2.3
101–120	10.0	5.7	3.7	3.3	5.6
121–140	9.5	6.8	4.5	4.1	6.1
141–160	12.5	10.1	7.1	6.4	8.5
161–180	11.3	10.7	8.9	8.2	10.9
181–200	10.2	10.5	10.0	10.0	10.1
201–220	6.4	8.0	8.2	8.1	7.6
221–250	8.3	11.2	12.7	13.3	11.5
251–300	8.5	12.4	15.7	16.6	13.4
301–350	4.2	6.9	9.2	10.0	7.8
351–400	2.4	4.4	5.9	6.1	4.3
Over 400	3.2	7.6	10.7	10.7	6.6

Rubles Earned	Years of Age				
per Month – Women	16–24	25–29	30–39	40–49	50+
Under 80	6.7	3.5	2.6	2.9	6.3
80–90	13.9	8.5	5.8	5.4	9.1
91–100	9.5	6.9	4.8	4.2	5.7
101–120	18.9	15.3	11.5	10.2	12.2
121–140	14.1	14.5	12.1	10.0	10.5
141–160	12.3	14.1	13.2	11.9	11.2
161–180	7.7	10.6	11.5	11.4	10.8
181–200	5.6	7.6	9.5	9.6	8.1
201–220	3.4	5.0	6.6	7.1	5.9
221–250	3.4	5.5	7.8	9.0	7.1
251–300	2.7	4.7	7.4	9.2	6.9
301–350	1.0	1.9	3.4	4.2	3.1
351–400	0.4	0.9	1.7	2.2	1.5
Over 400	0.4	1.0	2.1	2.7	1.6

Note: A recomputation of these data by Alexeev and Gaddy (1991) demonstrates that female wages ranged from 68–75 percent of those of males.

Source: SSSR v tsifrakh v 1989 godu: 71-72.

The wage disparity is even more surprising in view of official assertions that women were guaranteed equal pay for equal work and in light of the fact that the educational attainment of much of the female industrial labor force actually exceeds that of males. Also female labor force participation was more continuous in the USSR than in the West, and virtually all employed women worked full time.

The explanation of the wage gap is to be found in certain features of Soviet economic organization and policy, not only in the distinctive characteristics of the female labor force. First, economic sectors and industrial branches with high wage levels and greater wage differentials—such as heavy industry and construction—are those in which women are underrepresented; those that have a high concentration of female employees—light industry and the services—are those in which lower wage levels and narrower differentials prevail. In construction, where women constituted 28 percent of the labor force in 1985, monthly earnings averaged 236.6 rubles; in public health and physical culture, where females made up 84 percent of the work force, earnings averaged 132.8 rubles.

Also contributing to the earnings gap is the fact that blue-collar occupations are more highly rewarded than most white-collar occupations, even when white-collar employees have higher levels of educational attainment. For example, in 1985 the average wage of industrial workers was 211.7 rubles a month and 164.6 rubles for white-collar personnel in industry (TsSU SSSR 1986: 397). A detailed portrait of the social structure of a group of Leningrad machine-building enterprises revealed that the occupational categories with the highest proportion of women were at the bottom of the scale in income but in the middle range in educational level; unskilled manual workers had lower educational levels but received higher incomes (Shkaratan 1967: 36). Thus, the large-scale movement of women into white-collar and professional occupations in the USSR, including teaching and medicine, was associated with a sharp decline in their average status and pay relative to skilled blue-collar employment. Moreover, work considered especially difficult or dangerous is particularly lucrative but often is forbidden to women.

Soviet sources often attributed the earnings gap to differences in the qualifications and productivity of male and female workers, but the evidence suggests that this explanation is not sufficient. Although Soviet law required that equal work receive equal pay, in practice there was no mechanism to ensure that women were placed in positions commensurate with their training and skills. Women thus were frequently overqualified for the jobs they held. A study of industrial enterprises in Taganrog reached the startling conclusion that 40 percent of all female workers with higher or secondary specialized education occupied low-skill industrial positions compared to 6 percent of comparable males; only 10 percent of these highly educated women, compared to 46 percent of their male counterparts, occupied high-skill positions. Most striking of all was the fact that distribution of the male labor force as a whole, without respect to education, was more favorable than the distribution of this highly educated female contingent (Gruzdeva 1975: 94; Zdravomyslov, Rozhin, and Iadov 1967). Because women confront a narrower range of choices in the job market and attach more weight to a job's compatibility with domestic responsibilities than to its content, and because the jobs most readily available to women are those in which lower wages prevail, lower earnings are not exclusively a result of lower qualifications or productivity.

Finally, the possibility of direct wage discrimination cannot be completely ruled out. A Western analysis of unpublished Soviet wage data in the 1970s concluded that only one-fourth of an average male-female wage differential of 40 rubles per month could be attributed to the combined effects of sex differences in education, age, economic sector, and skill level or responsibility (Swafford 1978: 661–665).

Clearly, then, equality of economic opportunity for women has not followed automatically from higher levels of educational attainment and labor force participation. In the USSR as in the United States, men have derived greater benefits from educational and occupational attainments, even when women's work experience and levels of current labor force participation have been comparable.

It often has been argued—in the Soviet Union as in the West—that these patterns reflect not discrimination but fundamental differences in the occupational preferences and valuations of men's and women's economic contributions. Soviet studies have made it abundantly clear that from early childhood through adolescence and on into adulthood, boys and girls diverge in their educational and occupational choices. Fewer adult women express an interest in a career as opposed to a job, and in choosing a job, women attach more weight to convenience than to content. Yet these individual choices are made within a socially structured context of opportunities and costs.

Three features of the Soviet system must be singled out for their role in shaping women's preferences and choices. First, despite the fact that Soviet women entered many scientific and technical fields, sexual stereotyping of occupations was not eliminated; in fact, it was explicitly sustained by official attitudes and policies. Measures that restricted the hiring of women for jobs considered unsuitable or harmful to females, that limited their employment in heavy or dangerous work, and that encouraged their entry into suitably "female" occupations served to channel and not merely to protect female labor. Although the rationale for particular classifications has been questioned, the distinction in principle between "men's work" and "women's work"— based on biological and psychological stereotypes—remained unchallenged. Soviet labor economists routinely wrote of the need to create working conditions that corresponded to the "anatomical-physiological peculiarities of the female organism and likewise to the moral-ethical temperament of women." They assumed that "the psycho-physiological make-up of women permits them to carry out certain kinds of work more successfully than men, such as work demanding assiduity, attention, accuracy, and precision" (Kotliar and Shlemin 1974: 222; Manevich 1971: 168). It is consistent with these assumptions, therefore, that each of the 1,100 occupations for which training was offered at Soviet technical-vocational institutions was explicitly designated for males, for females, or for both sexes and that only 714 of the occupations were accessible to women.

Second, female occupational choices are profoundly influenced by the continuing identification of authority with men. As many Soviet sources have testified, women who pursue demanding careers encounter subtle but widespread prejudices, which impede their professional mobility and limit their accession to positions of responsibility. As two prominent male scholars argued in 1983, "The increase in the number of women with scholarly degrees accounts for the decrease in the number of those who really develop science. . . . The 'rebellious' spirit, the predisposition to search for new, non-traditional methods in science are more typical among men than women" (Sokolov and

Reimers 1983: 77). According to other Soviet studies, women were widely—though erroneously—believed to have less initiative and creativity than men and to be less suited for managerial positions (Pavlova 1971). Even among highly educated scientific workers, men *and* women expressed a strong preference for placing males in supervisory roles (Shubkin and Kochetov 1968). After a comprehensive discussion of the recruitment and training of industrial executives in the pages of a leading Soviet journal, it took a letter from an irate female reader to point out that "for some reason it seems taken for granted that an executive is a man" (*Literaturnaia Gazeta* 1976: 10).

This problem did not go unrecognized. Complaints that insufficient attention was paid to recruiting women for responsible positions occurred with monotonous regularity in official pronouncements. At one meeting of a provincial Communist Party committee, the underrepresentation of women in positions of authority was explicitly attributed to the presence of "a certain psychological barrier: On the one hand, a number of leaders fear to entrust women with responsible positions, and on the other, women themselves demonstrate timidity, doubting their strength and refusing under various pretexts a transfer to leadership positions" ("Povyshat' Politicheskuiu Proizvodstvennuiu" 1975: 44).

Dubious about the utility of further exhortation and impatient with the slow pace of change, one labor specialist proposed a more radical solution: the adoption of sexual quotas, with the number of women in managerial positions to be proportional to the number of women working under their jurisdiction (Tolkunova 1967: 103). Gorbachev called for the promotion of more women to positions of authority and named a veteran trade union official to the party Secretariat. But the overall proportion of women in key political positions did not change significantly following his accession to power.

A third social determinant of the pattern of female employment is the official treatment of household and family responsibilities, culturally and in legislation, as primarily and properly the domain of women. Thus, the fundamental assumption of Soviet economic and family policy—that women and women only have dual roles—effectively assigned women a distinctive position in both the occupational and the family systems and had important consequences for their behavior in both domains.

FEMALE WORKERS AND THE FAMILY

Just as family roles affect the scope and pattern of female employment, so does women's work affect many aspects of family life, including patterns of marriage and divorce, fertility, and the family division of labor. Soviet scholars share the view of Western sociologists that education, occupational status, income, and social participation are resources that directly influence family authority; and they contend that by reducing gender disparities in these areas, socialism guaranteed the independence of women in marriage, enhanced their power within the family, and produced a more egalitarian pattern of family life.

Recent patterns of marriage and divorce in the USSR offered some support for this view. The combination of early marriage, a relatively high marriage rate, a large male-female age difference at the time of marriage, and a low rate of divorce characteristic of many traditional agricultural societies is usually interpreted as an indicator of women's limited productive status and opportunities compared with the value attached to their reproductive role. This pattern still predominates in the largely agricultural and Muslim regions of what was Soviet Central Asia. By contrast, access to education, employment, and independent income—typical of the more developed, European regions of the former USSR—tended to enhance a woman's freedom to enter or leave marriage by reducing the relative value of the resources gained through marriage. Thus, the proportion of married women was considerably lower in the Russian Republic than in Uzbekistan, the mean age of marriage was higher, the age disparity between spouses was considerably smaller, and the rate of divorce was substantially higher.

Nevertheless, a considerable disparity in economic resources and prospects between males and females persisted in even the most developed regions of the USSR and may have increased with the rising number of female-headed households (Chuiko 1975: 145; Kharchev 1964: 212).

Female employment also affects family structure through its influence on childbearing. An inverse relationship between female employment and fertility was first established in the 1930s; more recent studies show that although the gap has narrowed, nonworking women have 20 to 25 percent more children than do their working counterparts, and the latter have 2.5 times as many abortions (Strumilin 1964: 140; Musatov 1967: 321; Nemchenko 1973: 35–36; Shlindman and Zvidrin'sh 1973: 74). This difference helps to account for the inverse correlation of urbanization with birthrates. Urban women both desire and expect to have fewer children than rural women, and women in large cities expect to bear fewer children than their counterparts in small cities; the figures reach an alarming low of 1.69 in Moscow and 1.55 in Leningrad (Belova 1975: 109, 129; Borisov 1976: 72–77; Sysenko 1974: 36–40).

Birthrates also vary with educational attainment, occupational status, and professional skill. White-collar mothers have far fewer children than workers, and workers have fewer than collective farmers. Among workers, family size is inversely related to skill level. The highest proportion of third, fourth, and fifth children is found among unskilled workers and those with low qualifications; relatively few large families are found among workers with high qualifications or with engineering and technical skills (Sysenko 1974: 37, 40; Belova 1975: 146).

In seeking to reverse these trends, Soviet scholars and planners noted with interest that most women have fewer children than they appear to want. This gap has led some to conclude that specific obstacles—limited financial resources, poor housing, and crowded preschool facilities—are responsible for low urban birthrates and that measures to alleviate these problems would have a positive effect on fertility. But Soviet investigations of the relationship between income and fertility yielded contradictory results; subjective perceptions of family needs play a crucial mediating role. Moreover, the effects of education on reproductive motivations and behavior are difficult to disentangle from those of income. Not surprisingly, efforts in the 1970s to strengthen the family and reverse the declining birthrate had disappointing results.

The tendency for increased female education, employment, and level of professional qualification to be associated with lower rates of marriage, later marriage, high rates of divorce, and declining family size and for stable family patterns and high birthrates to be found among the least "liberated" Soviet women provoked an understandable concern. As the prominent Soviet sociologist, the late A. G. Kharchev (1972: 58) noted ruefully, "Life shows that improved conditions and equal rights for both sexes do not automatically strengthen the institution of marriage."

Numerous Soviet writings have argued that women's entry into the work force resulted in greater female authority within the family, greater male participation in housework, and a more egalitarian pattern of family decision making. Yet this pattern is not fully corroborated by a voluminous body of Soviet time-budget investigations. Although men and women devoted roughly equal time to paid employment and physiological needs, working women spent on average twenty-eight hours per week on housework compared with about twelve hours per week for men; men enjoyed 50 percent more leisure time than women.

Within the family, a sharply defined sexual division of labor persists. A first category of activities, such as gardening and repairs, is predominantly male; a second, including shopping and cleaning house, is predominantly female although shared to some degree by males; a third group of activities, including cooking and laundry, is performed almost exclusively by women. In short, nearly 75 percent of domestic duties fall to women; the remainder are shared with husbands and other family members (Iankova 1970a: 43; Slesarev and Iankova, 1969: 430–431).

Several conclusions can be drawn from the findings of time-budget studies (Lapidus 1979: 256–258). First, male-female differences in the allocation of time are apparent, even among single students living in dormitories. Second, this basic male-female differential increases with marriage: The share of housework performed by husbands does not offset the additional time spent by wives. Third, there is a positive relationship between female employment outside the home and male help within. Fourth, the male-female differential is sharply increased with the birth of a first child. Finally, educational level seems to have an important effect on the allocation of time to domestic chores but not necessarily on the participation of males in these chores. A study of time use among workers with higher or specialized secondary education found that although the total amount of time devoted to housework was lower, the male-female differential was actually larger than that found in worker families with lower educational qualifications (Gruzdeva 1975: 9). Even high female educational attainments failed to obliterate sharp sex-role differences: The five most prevalent daily activities of women with specialized education differed far more from those of comparable males than from the activities of women with only four grades of schooling.

The effects of socioeconomic or occupational status are even more difficult to extract from the Soviet data. As with education, the evidence suggests that the male-female division of labor does not necessarily become more equal at higher levels of the social hierarchy. At every level of the occupational ladder, the total working time of employed women exceeds that of males. Contrary to the assertions of several Soviet scholars, the reduction in women's housework and increase in leisure time was not so much a result of greater male help as it was of the availability of household appliances and services that higher income brings (Trufanov 1973: 106).

The time males devoted to housework varied with the demands of their work roles and with their jobs and educational levels. Blue-collar males actually devoted more time to housework than their white-collar counterparts. The latter—particularly those engaged in demanding careers—devoted more time to work, study, and social participation and less time to household chores than any other category.

In light of these patterns, it is unrealistic to assume that further economic development would bring a dramatic decline in women's household responsibilities or a sharp increase in leisure time. As a distinguished Soviet sociologist has argued, women do not simply shed their former duties as development occurs; they acquire new ones. Higher standards of housekeeping and child rearing may prevail, and the breakup of extended families means that tasks once shared by two generations of women now fall exclusively on one (Iankova 1970a; 1970b).

Nor would reductions in female working time automatically yield the increase in leisure many Soviet writers anticipated. The shift from a six-day to a five-day workweek in 1967 yielded a comparatively greater increase in male leisure than in female leisure time, as did a more recent experiment with shortening the workday of women factory workers (Gordon and Rimashevskaia 1972: 24, 62–79; Porokhniuk and Shepeleva 1975: 102–108; Pimenova 1974: 131). In both cases, men gained more leisure, but women devoted more of the released time to child care and domestic responsibilities than to study, social participation, or leisure pursuits.

Women's educational efforts virtually cease with the birth of a child, but family responsibilities have little effect on the ability of male workers to continue their studies. As two Soviet authors explicitly recognize, men combine employment with study by limiting the time they devote to family chores at the expense of other members of the household who, in effect, subsidize these educational pursuits (Gordon and Klopov 1972: 200–201). By freeing males from routine household and child care chores, women workers advance the occupational mobility of males at the cost of their own.

INTERDEPENDENCE OF WORK AND FAMILY ROLES

This profile of the female labor force has pointed to the ways in which the interaction of women's work and family roles contributes to a sharp differentiation between the activities of male and female workers. For men and women alike, work and family roles are inversely related and tend to compete with each other for time and energy. In the case of women, however, family roles are assigned primacy and define the nature and rhythms of female employment. Soviet women's family responsibilities have intruded into the workplace—and have been accommodated by it—to a degree unusual in contemporary industrial societies. Provisions for pregnancy leaves, for leave to care for sick children, for nursing infants during work hours, and for exemptions of pregnant women and mothers from heavy work, overtime, or travel have been predicated on the view that child rearing and other "exclusively female" family responsibilities take a certain priority that work arrangements must accommodate. Women were explicitly encouraged to view work from the perspective of their roles as wives and mothers.

This limited insulation of female work roles from family roles has resulted in characteristic patterns of female behavior. Women workers have been less demanding than their male counterparts, as is generally true of workers whose mobility is blocked and whose work satisfaction depends less on the content of their jobs than on working conditions. Under these circumstances, it is understandable that married women have been seriously underrepresented in enterprise activities requiring additional commitments of time and energy and in volunteer movements and public affairs generally.

The opposite has been the case for males. An extensive network of evening and correspondence courses attended overwhelmingly by males, the numerous assignments requiring travel away from home, and the proliferation of party meetings and sociopolitical obligations in which males predominate have all been predicated on the assumption that they constitute legitimate claims on males' time and energy even at the expense of family responsibilities. As A. G. Kharchev (1972: 60–61) put it, the fact that "men often think about production work at home, [whereas] women frequently think about domestic concerns at work" reflects a fundamental difference in the structure of male and female work and family roles. The boundaries between occupational and family systems are permeable, but in opposite directions for men and women.

Male and female roles, like work and family roles, also are interdependent and mutually reinforcing (Pleck 1977: 417–427). Women are integrated into the labor force in segregated and subordinate roles. Horizontal occupational differentiation and vertical stratification by sex effectively shield male roles from competition from women and limit the situations in which females exercise authority over males. Norms that classify occupations as especially suitable for women or that give women authority primarily when it is exercised over other women create a dual labor market that helps to insulate male jobs from the effects of rising levels of female employment and that preserves male predominance in positions of responsibility and leadership. This pattern is as characteristic of the political arena as it is of the economy.

A parallel pattern is found within the family itself. Norms that sustain a sexual division of labor by defining housework and child care as preeminently "women's work" also serve to insulate the male from pressures for increased participation in domestic work as women take on paid employment. The effect is to create a domestic counterpart to the dual labor market—one part of the labor supply does not take on certain types of work even when there is a surplus of workers, whereas the other part is overburdened and leaves needed work undone. At best, men help with housework and child care; no fundamental redefinition of male roles is involved.

The effects of this sexual division of labor both on the job and at home have not been totally benign. As the massive participation of women in full-time paid employment eroded the traditional rationale for a sexual division of labor within the family, it increased the level of conflict between men and women over the division of domestic tasks. These rising resentments, Soviet analysts argue, contributed to alcoholism and high divorce rates and became a potential source of disenchantment with the institution of the family.

A second source of strain has been the high degree of tension between female work and family roles, resulting in the deliberate limitation of family size. Taking a benign view of this trend, one Soviet writer noted:

> The current decline in the birth rate . . . will contribute to the manpower shortage—but it also . . . can be viewed . . . as a spontaneous response by women to their excessive work load and lack of equality with men—a response that consists of eliminating the single factor over which they have the greatest control. The falling birthrate is an . . . indispensable lever that women can use in their effort to achieve full equality with men (Riurikov 1977: 119).

For the Brezhnev leadership, these were alarming trends. By impinging on a wide range of economic, political, and military concerns, they compelled fundamental reconsideration of the entire spectrum of policies involving female work and family roles.

POLICY DILEMMAS AND OPTIONS

The irreplaceable contribution of women to both production and reproduction presented the Brezhnev leadership with a classic policy dilemma of two mutually contradictory processes. By opening a new range of educational and professional options for women, Soviet development encouraged them to acquire new skills, values, orientations, and aspirations that competed with their traditional domestic roles. At the same time, the high value attached to the family, the critical social roles assigned to it, and the large investments of time and energy needed to sustain it seriously constrained women's occupational commitments and achievements.

The resulting "contradictions," in the language of Soviet analysts, between the occupational and family roles of working women had an extremely high economic, demographic, and social cost. These contradictions adversely affected women's health and welfare as well as their opportunities for professional and personal development; they "engender tensions and conflicts in internal family relations, lead to a weakening of control over the conduct of children and a deterioration of their upbringing, and finally, [they are] one of the basic causes of the declining birthrate" (Kharchev 1970: 19; Shishkan 1976: 38).

These tensions, it was feared, were likely to be increased rather than diminished by economic, demographic, and technological trends. Thus, it was with a heightened sense of urgency that the Brezhnev leadership began to confront the complex issues surrounding female labor and its social requisites and consequences. Enlisting the aid of social scientists as well as of several newly created legislative and administrative bodies, the administration launched a serious and sustained quest for a strategy that would encourage a more effective use of scarce labor resources without further compromising family stability and that also would reverse the declining birthrate in the developed regions of the USSR.

A first group of proposed measures was aimed at redistributing female labor resources by removing women from employment in unsafe and unhealthy conditions—transferring them from low-skilled, nonmechanized, and heavy labor to more skilled and suitable jobs—and achieving a demographically more balanced regional labor market by providing a better mix of "men's" and "women's" work. A number of critics also urged that skills of women workers be upgraded and given higher priority and increased incentives and that, following the example of the German Democratic Republic, vocational programs be adapted to the schedules and responsibilities of working mothers (Kostakov 1976: 101–160; Kotliar and Shlemin 1974: 110–119; Sergeeva 1976: 37–46).

A second group of proposals focused on improving the working conditions of women. Despite the elaborate provisions of protective labor legislation, complaints abounded that existing regulations were inadequate and their requirements widely violated, even in industries such as textiles that were considered especially suited to women. Some experts urged that existing protective legislation be tightened and that an effort be made to reduce night work, overtime, and inconvenient work shifts for women.

Some analysts even advocated reducing the "intensity" of female labor by introducing differentiated work norms. Insisting that women's contributions to the domestic economy and to childbearing constitute socially useful labor not paid for by society, these writers urged that women be assigned reduced work norms and even a shortened working day without loss of pay (Iankova 1975: 44–46; Iuk 1975: 122; Sakharova 1973). By refusing to exclude women's domestic responsibilities from the definition of work, and by arguing that working mothers have a right to be compensated for the double shift they perform, the advocates of such measures were not only insisting that socially useful labor be properly rewarded; they also were placing the blame for current shortcomings on the shoulders of policymakers.

A third group of recommendations sought to improve the supply of consumer goods and everyday services to reduce the strain of women's dual roles. A number of studies argued that investments in refrigerators, public laundries, or rapid transit would generate savings of time that would more than compensate for initial investments. Calls for the more rapid expansion of preschool facilities were coupled with reminders that the lack of such facilities contributes to underemployment of women, high rates of turnover, and lowered productivity. Moreover, the slow pace of progress in "revolutionizing everyday life" encouraged a number of writers to press for greater reliance on private and cooperative arrangements. They called for parent nurseries in housing developments, economic unions of families to share the burdens of shopping and repairs, and even the creation of bureaus to provide nannies and governesses for child care.

Taken together, these three groups of recommendations amounted to an agenda for slow but incremental reform to reduce the conflict between "men's" and "women's" work. They rested on the assumption that a combination of technological progress and socioeconomic reform sponsored by a benevolent party leadership would obviate the need for more far-reaching changes in the structure of family or work.

Some Soviet experts, however, argued that the problem would in fact require a more controversial set of choices. One option that had vocal advocates was an all-out effort to elevate the social status and material rewards associated with reproduction, even if this resulted in a decline in female labor force participation. Alarmed by low birthrates, a number of prominent Soviet scholars urged that a comprehensive population policy receive highest priority (Urlanis 1974: 283). They called for measures to enhance fertility potential, to alter social values in favor of larger families, to increase the economic incentives for larger families, and to modify the pension system to reward child rearing as well as production.

The central and most controversial aspect of this pronatalist position was its desire to transform maternity into professional, paid social labor. Financial subsidies, tailored not to the direct costs of children but to the opportunity cost of female labor, would be offered to induce new mothers to withdraw from the labor force for periods of up to three years; a sliding scale of benefits tied to wage levels would ensure a more equal distribution of births among different social strata. The costs of such a program, its advocates argued, would be offset by its long-term contribution to the labor supply and by the more immediate savings generated by a cutback in public nurseries. Viewing high maternal employment as a temporary necessary evil, the advocates argued that at the present stage of economic development, Soviet society could afford and would greatly benefit from a shift toward family upbringing of young children.

Measures such as these could widen the options of many women, but they also have potentially far-reaching economic and social costs. Relatively long interruptions in female labor force participation could result in deterioration or obsolescence of skills and pose substantial problems of retraining and reentry. Moreover, the lower return on investments in women's education might adversely affect their educational opportunities and increase the reluctance of employers to hire or train them for skilled and responsible positions. By assigning primacy to female family and reproductive functions while reducing the scope and centrality of female employment, increasing the permeability of female work roles to family responsibilities, and forestalling a more equal division of family responsibilities, this approach—in the view of its critics—represented an unacceptable step backward. It would have re-created a division of labor based on sex.

A radically different set of policy options was derived from the premise that the more effective use of female labor, not stimulation of fertility, was the overriding priority. Arguing that work is of critical importance to women's personal development as well as to the economy and that economic progress and national power depend on the quality of the labor force rather than on its size, proponents urged the further expansion of women's economic role in terms of greater equality with men—along with a reduction in the household burdens that inhibit such expansion.

One commentator (Berezovskaia 1975: 12) insisted that assignment to positions of responsibility rather than "protection" should receive priority. Recognizing that women's double burden reduces their ability to raise their skill levels, to master more complex jobs, and to undertake more responsible duties, this approach called for a more equal sharing of family responsibilities (Iurkevich 1970: 192). But even the most outspoken Soviet feminists emphasized the biological and psychological differences between men and women and attached high value to women's family and maternal roles. Unlike some of their Western counterparts, they did not embrace the notion of transcending gender in the allocation of social roles.

Emphasizing that new attitudes are a precondition for new patterns of behavior and refusing to treat them as a purely private and personal matter, a number of writers called for a more systematic intervention by the state, the party, and public organizations to inculcate egalitarian values. Even the postrevolutionary Women's Department (Zenotdel) was held up as a model by one labor economist, who explicitly deplored its premature abolition by Stalin (Sonin 1973: 378–379).

Some within this group advocated that the more immediate problems faced by working mothers with young children would be better alleviated by an expansion of part-time work rather than by extended maternity leaves (Martirosian 1976: 54–61; Novitskii and Babkina 1973: 133–140; Shishkan 1971: 42–47). By making it possible for more women to enter the labor force and to maintain some continuity of employment without sacrificing the time available for child rearing and family chores, part-time employment would meet the needs of many women workers without incurring the extremely high costs of the more radical pronatalist program.

Clearly, instituting part-time work on a large scale would raise a host of problems (Moses 1983). It is far more feasible in routine white-collar and service occupations than in highly skilled technical positions or supervisory jobs. In industry, it would require the creation of special sectors and assembly lines that would segregate part-time workers from the full-time labor force. In all likelihood, it would increase the concentration of women in low-skilled and poorly remunerated jobs. In addition, if recent experiments with shortened workdays are any indication, it also would be likely to forestall a more equal division of household responsibilities. Recent small-scale experiments with an alternative of flextime, therefore, are especially promising because of their potential for avoiding an intensification of the sexual division of labor.

Even if the Brezhnev leadership was relatively slow in coming to an awareness of these economic and demographic issues, they gradually came to occupy an important place on the political agenda. In effect, specific measures introduced under Brezhnev sought to strike a balance between a labor-extensive strategy and a labor-intensive strategy. On the one hand, these measures encouraged high female participation rates by raising minimum wages, expanding the child care network, modifying the pension system, and exploring the possibilities for the expansion of part-time work. At the same time, concern over declining birthrates was evident in the family allowance program introduced in 1974, which extended maternity leave benefits to *kolkhoz* (collective farm) women, liberalized sick leave for parents of young children, and expanded partially paid maternity leave to a full year. In this as in other areas, however, the Brezhnev leadership failed to act with the vigor and decisiveness necessary to address the problem adequately.

IMPACT OF GORBACHEV'S POLICIES
ON WOMEN'S ROLES

The accession of Mikhail Gorbachev to the Soviet leadership and the inauguration of what became an increasingly far-reaching program of reforms had dramatic, although largely unintended, consequences for women's roles. On the one hand, the political changes associated with glasnost and democratization eliminated many of the taboos that had long constrained the discussion of gender issues and created unprecedented opportunities for social and political activism around a broad range of causes. At the same time, the mounting economic crisis precipitated by the leadership's erratic economic policies drove sheer economic survival to the top of women's agendas. As rampant inflation and the breakdown of the consumer sector produced growing hardship and increasing social unrest, "hunting and gathering" absorbed an increasing share of time and attention.

None of this was anticipated in the first months or even years of the Gorbachev era. To the extent that he had any new approach to women's issues in mind, its direction remained unclear and indeed contradictory. Some of his early initiatives gave women's issues higher visibility, including his energetic advocacy of the promotion of more women in political life and his appointment of Aleksandra Biryokova to the party's powerful Secretariat; his role in the creation of a national women's organization intended to link the Soviet Women's Committee to a broad nationwide network of local women's councils; and his emphasis on the need for new attention to be given to social and family policy. The prominent role and unprecedented visibility of his wife Raisa, however controversial, also altered the ethos of secrecy and male domination traditionally surrounding the general-secretary.

Gorbachev's early economic policies appeared to signal more ominous implications for women. The effort to promote more rapid economic growth and increased technological innovation by stimulating greater competition within the workplace carried with it the prospect of massive dismissals of redundant workers and growing wage differentiation. Coupled with Gorbachev's call for an expansion of the service sector, these prospects suggested the likelihood of a long-term shift in female labor force participation from industrial to service employment (Kostakov 1986). Had the Soviet leadership moved forward with a decisive economic program aimed at marketization and privatization, Soviet women would have confronted some of the problems of their counterparts in Poland, East Germany, and elsewhere in Eastern Europe. In the Soviet case, however, it was the economic dislocation resulting from the absence of decisive reform that had devastating consequences for women. Under these circumstances it may appear cavalier to focus on the implications of Gorbachev's political reforms for Soviet women. However, it may be that the most positive and enduring legacy of Gorbachev's leadership will be the intellectual, political, and spiritual liberation his reforms unleashed.

The impact of glasnost on discussion of women's issues was particularly dramatic. Not only did this discussion radically broaden in its scope, frankness, and forms of discourse, but a series of issues that were previously taboo—including prostitution, rape, contraception, and homosexuality—became legitimate topics of analysis and debate. Just as terms such as *command-administrative system* and *totalitarianism* were incorporated into political discourse, concepts such as *patriarchy* or *muzhkratiia* (male-dominated bureaucracy) increasingly became staples of feminist discourse.

In addition to the process of democratization, which unleashed an unprecedented wave of sociopolitical activism across the Soviet landscape, the past few years also encouraged the emergence of a variety of new forms of feminist organization and mobilization (Buckley 1990). Some are small-scale and relatively informal women's groups devoted largely to consciousness-raising and to the study and dissemination of feminist literature, often Western in origin. Others—such as the clubs of women journalists, writers, or scholars—are based on professional ties, often within a single city, and devoted to improving the status and conditions of women in a given field. A third type is represented by the creation of women's sections within larger organizations or political movements not specifically concerned with women's issues; the women's group of Sajudis, the Lithuanian Popular Front, or the loose organization of women deputies to the Supreme Soviet are examples of this genre. Finally, more explicit political action groups emerged, some—such as the Soviet Women's Committee—long part of the establishment but now adapting to new conditions, and others—such as the organizations of soldiers' mothers calling for changes in military practices—spontaneous efforts to deal with new issues.

Political activism among Soviet women was given further impetus not only by the new opportunities created by a more open and competitive political milieu but by the decline in female representation in national and republic legislative bodies as a result of electoral reform. Although the dismantling of the old quota system, which guaranteed a certain proportion of seats to women as well as to members of other social categories, resulted in a reduction of the proportion of female deputies—from 33 percent to 16 percent at the all-Union level—those who gained political prominence were more likely to be genuine political actors rather than mere tokens.

All these trends have had a significant impact on patterns of discourse about women's roles. Although many of the approaches characteristic of the 1960s and 1970s continued into the Gorbachev era, a novel element appeared in the 1980s. Changes in the status and roles of women were no longer seen as exclusively the outcome of state policies; they began to be viewed as the outcome of women's own capacity for political organization (Woodruff 1991).

The collapse of the USSR and the emergence of fifteen new states from its former territories open a new chapter in the evolution of women's roles in this region. It will no longer be possible to discuss policy and its outcomes in these broad terms; policies toward women and changes in women's position will be functions of the increasingly diverse political, economic, and cultural orientations of these new nations as they struggle to escape from and deal with the legacy of Communist rule.

BIBLIOGRAPHY

Alexeev, Michael V., and Clifford G. Gaddy. February 1991. "Trends in Wage and Income Distribution Under Gorbachev." Berkeley-Duke Occasional Papers on the Second Economy in the USSR, Paper no. 25, 28–29.

Antosenkov, E. G., and Z. V. Kupriianova. 1977. *Tendentsii v Tekuchesti Rabochikh Kadrov.* Novosibirsk: Nauka.

Belova, V. A. 1975. *Chislo Detei v sem'e.* Moscow: Statistika.

Berezovskaia, S. June 25, 1975. "Prestizh—Zabota Nasha Obshchaia." *Literaturnaia Gazeta,* 12.

Bliakhman, L. S., A. G. Zdravomyslov, and O. I. Shkaratan. 1965. *Dvizhenie Rabochei sily na Promyshlennykh Predpriiatiiakh.* Moscow: Ekonomika.

Borisov, V. A. 1976. *Perspektivy Rozhdaemosti.* Moscow: Statistika.

Buckley, M., ed. 1986. *Soviet Social Scientists Talking: An Official Debate About Women.* London: Macmillan.

_____. July 16–19, 1990. "Gender and Reform." Paper presented at Workshop on Perestroika in Historical Perspective, King's College, Cambridge, England.

Chuiko, L. V. 1975. *Braki i Razvody.* Moscow: Statistika.

Dogle, N. V. 1977. *Usloviia Zhizni i Zdorov'e Tekstil'schchits.* Moscow: Meditsina.

Geiger, K. 1968. *The Family in Soviet Russia.* Cambridge, Mass.: Harvard University Press.

Gordon, L. A., and E. V. Klopov. 1972. *Chelovek Posle Raboty.* Moscow: Nauka.

Gordon, L. A., and N. M. Rimashevskaia. 1972. *Piatidnevnaia Rabochaia Nedelia i Svobodnoe Vremia Trudiashchikhsia.* Moscow: Mysl'.

Gruzdeva, E. B. 1975. "Osobennosti Obraza Zhizni 'Intelligentnykh Rabochikh.'" *Rabochii Klass i Sovremennyi mir* 2, 91–99.

Gruzdeva, E. B., and E. S. Chertikhina. 1975. "Zhenshchiny v Obshchestvennom Proizvodstve Razvitogo Sotsializma." *Rabochii Klass i Sovremennyi mir* 6, 133–147.

_____. 1983. *Trud i byt Sovetskikh Zhenshchin.* Moscow: Politizdat.

Iankova, Z. A. 1970a. "O Bytovykh Roliakh Rabotaiushchei Zhenshchiny." In N. Solov'ev, I. Lazauskas, and Z. A. Iankova, eds., *Problemy byta, Braka i sem'i.* Vil'nius: Mintis, 42–49.

———. 1970b. "O Semeino-Bytovykh Roliakh Rabotaiushchei Zhenshchiny." *Sotsial'nye Issledovaniia* 4, 76–87.

———. 1975. "Razvitie Lichnosti Zhenshchiny v Sovetskom Obshchestve." *Sotsiologicheskie Issledovaniia* 4, 42–51.

Iuk, Z. M. 1975. *Trud Zhenshchiny i sem'ia.* Minsk: Belarus'.

Iurkevich, N. G. 1970. *Sovetskaia sem'ia; Funktsii i Usloviia Stabil'nosti.* Minsk: Belorusskii gosudarstvennii universitet.

Kharchev, A. G. 1964. *Brak i sem'ia v SSSR.* Moscow: Mysl'.

———. 1970. "Byt i sem'ia." In N. Solov'ev, I. Lazauskas, and Z. A. Iankova, eds., *Problemy byta, Braka i sem'i.* Vil'nius: Mintis, 9–22.

———. 1972. *Zhurnalist,* 11.

Kharchev, A. G., ed. 1977. *Izmenenie Polozheniia Zhenshchiny i sem'ia.* Moscow: Nauka.

Kharchev, A. G., and S. I. Golod. 1971. *Professional'naia Rabota Zhenshchin i sem'ia.* Leningrad: Nauka.

Kostakov, V. G. 1976. *Trudovye Resursy Patiletki.* Moscow: Politizdat.

———. 1986. "Chelovek i Progress." *Sovietskaia Kultyra,* February 1, 3.

Kotliar, A. E., and A. Shlemin. 1974. "Problemy Ratsional'noi Zaniatosti Zhenshchin." *Sotsialisticheskii trud* 7, 110–119.

Kotliar, A. E., and S. I. Turchaninova. 1975. *Zaniatost' Zhenshchin v Proizvodstve.* Moscow: Statistika.

Kotliar, A. E., et al. 1982. *Dvizhenie Rabochii sily v Krupnom Gorode.* Moscow: Finansy i statistika.

Lapidus, G. W., 1979. "The Female Industrial Labor Force: Dilemmas, Reassessments, Options." In A. Kahan and B. Ruble, eds., *Industrial Labor in the USSR.* New York: Pergamon.

———, ed. 1982. *Women, Work, and Family in the USSR.* Armonk, New York: M. E. Sharpe.

Literaturnaia Gazeta. September 15, 1976. Letter to the editor.

Manevich, E. L., ed. 1971. *Osnovnye Problemy Ratsional'nogo Ispol'zovaniia Trudovykh Resursov v SSSR.* Moscow: Nauka.

Martirosian, E. R. 1976. "Pravovoe Regulirovanie Nepolnogo Rabochego Vremeni." *Sovetskoe Gosudarstvo i Pravo* 10, 54–61.

Miklhailiuk, V. B. 1970. *Ispol'zovanie Zhenskogo Truda v Narodnom Khoziaistve.* Moscow: Ekonomika.

Moses, J. 1983. *The Politics of Women and Work in the Soviet Union and the United States.* Berkeley, Calif.: Institute of International Studies.

Musatov, I. M. 1967. *Sotsial'nye Problemy Trudovykh Resursov v SSSR.* Moscow: Mysl'.

Nemchenko, V. 1973. "Mezhotraslevoe Dvizhenie Trudovykh Resursov." In D. E. Valentei, ed., *Narodonaselenie.* Moscow: Statistika.

Novikova, E. E. 1985. *Zhenshchina v Razvitom Sotsialisticheskom Obshchesive.* Moscow: Mysl'.

Novitskii, A., and M. Babkina. 1973. "Nepolnoe Rabochee Vremia i Zaniatost' Naseleniia." *Voprosy Ekonomiki* 7, 133–140.

Ofer, G., and A. Vinokur. 1981. "Earnings Differentials by Sex in the Soviet Union: A First Look." In S. Rosefielde, ed., *Economic Welfare and the Economics of Soviet Socialism.* Cambridge: Cambridge University Press, 127–162.

Osipov, G. V., and I. Shchepan'skii, eds. 1969. *Sotsial'nye Problemy Truda i Proizvodstva.* Moscow: Mysl', 416–438.

Pavlova, M. September 22, 1971. "Kar'era Ireny." *Liternaturnaia Gazeta,* 13.

Pimenova, A. L. 1966. "Sem'ia i Perspektivy Razvitiia Obshchestvennogo Truda Zhenshchin pri Sotsializme." *Nauchnye Doklady Vysshei Shkoly: Filosofskie Nauki* 3, 35–45.

Pimenova, V. N. 1974. *Svobodnoe Vremia v Sotsialisticheskom Obshchestve.* Moscow: Nauka.

Pleck, J. H. 1977. "The Work-Family Role System." *Social Problems* 4, 417–427.

Porokhniuk, E. V., and M. S. Shepeleva. 1975. "O Sovmeshchenii Proizvodstvennykh i Semeinykh Funktsii Zhenshchin-Rabotnits." *Sotsiologicheskie Issledovaniia* 4, 102–108.

"Povyshat' Politicheskuiu Proizvodstvennuiu Aktivnost' Zhenshchin: S Plenuma Ivanskogo Obkoma KPSS." 1975. *Partiinaia Shizn'* 16, 39–45.

Programme of the Communist Party of the Soviet Union. 1986. Moscow: Novosti.

Reznik, S. D. 1982. *Trudovye Resursy v. Stroitel'stve.* Moscow: Stroiizdat.

Riurikov, I. B. 1977. "Ieti i Obshchestvo." *Voprosy Filosofii* 4, 111–121.

Sakharova, N. A. 1973. *Optimal'nye Vozmozhnosti Ispol'zovaniia Zhenskogo Truda v Sfrere Obshchestvennogo Proizvodstva.* Kiev: Vishcha shkola.

Sergeeva, G. P. 1976. "O Professional'noi Strukture Rabotaiushchikh Zhenshchin." *Planovoe Khoziaistvo* 11, 37–46.

Shishkan, N. M. 1971. "Nepolnyi Rabochii den' dlia Zhenshchin v Usloviiakh Sotsializma." *Nauchnye Doklady Vysshei Shkoly: Ekonomicheskie Nauki* 8, 42–47.

———. 1976. *Trud Zhenshchin v Usloviiakh Razvitogo Sotsializma.* Kishinev: Shtiinsta.

Shkaratan, O. I. 1967. "Sotsial'naia Struktura Sovetskogo Rabochego Klassa." *Voprosy Filosofii* 1, 28–39.

Shlindman, S., and P. Zvidrin'sh. 1973. *Izuchenie Rozhdaremosti.* Moscow: Statistika.

Shubkin, V. N., and G. M. Kochetov. 1968. "Rukovoditel', Kollega, Podchinennyi." *Sotsial'nye Issledovaniia* 2, 143–155.

Slesarev, G. A., and Z. A. Iankova. 1969. "Zhenshchina na Promyshlennom Predpriiatii i v sem'e." In G. V. Osipov and I. Shchepan'skii, eds., *Sotsial'nye Problemy Truda i Proizvodstva.* Moscow: Mysl', 439–456.

Sokolov, B., and I. Reimers. 1983. "Effektivnye Formi Upravleniia Nauka." *EKO* 9, 72–87.

Solov'ev, N., I. Lazauskas, and Z. A., Iankova, eds. 1970. *Problemy byta, Braka i sem'i.* Vil'nius: Mintis.

Sonin, M. I. 1973. "Aktual'nye Sotsial'no-Ekonomicheskie Problemy Zaniatosti Zhenshchin." In A. Z. Maikov, ed., *Problemy Ratsional'nogo Ispol'zovaniia Trudovykh Resurov.* Moscow: Ekonomika, 352–379.

Strumilin, S. G. 1964. *Izbrannye Proizvedeniia. Vols. 3: Problemy Ekonomiki: Truda.* Moscow. Nauka.

Swafford, M. 1978. "Sex Differences in Soviet Earnings." *American Sociological Review* 5, 657–673.

Sysenko, V. 1974. "Differentsiatsiia Rozhdaemosti v Krupnom Gorode." In D. I. Valentei, ed., *Demograficheskii Analiz Rozhdaemosti.* Moscow: Statistika.

Tolkunova, V. N. 1967. *Pravo Zhenshchin na Trud i ego Garantii.* Moscow: Iuridicheskaia Literatura.

"Trud i Byt Zhenshchin." 1978. *EKO,* 3.

Trufanov, I. P. 1973. *Problemy byta Gorodskogo Naseleniia SSSR.* Leningrad: Leningradskii Gosudarstvennyi Universitet.

Tsentral'noe Statisticheskoe Upravlenie pri Sovete Ministrove SSSR (TsSU SSSR). 1972. *Narodnoe Khoziaistvo SSSR: 1922–1972.* Moscow: Statistika.

———. 1975. *Zhenshchiny v SSSR.* Moscow: Statistika.

———. 1977. *Narodnoe Khoziaistvo SSSR 60 let.* Moscow: Statistika.

———. 1979. *SSSR v Tsifrakh v 1978 godu: Kratkii Statisticheskii Sbornik.* Moscow: Statistika.

———. 1980. *Narodnoe Khoziaistvo SSSR v 1979 godu.* Moscow: Statistika.

———. 1981. *SSSR v Tsifrakh v 1980 godu: Kratkii Statisticheskii Sbornik.* Moscow: Finansy i Statistika.

———. 1985. *Narodnoe Khoziaistvo SSSR v 1984 q.* Moscow: Finansy i Statistika.

———. 1986. *Narodnoe Khoziaistvo SSSR v 1985 q.* Moscow: Finansy i Statistika.

Ubaidullaeva, R. 1987. *Selskaia Zhizn.* March 24, 2.

Urlanis, B. 1974. *Problemy Dinamiki Naseleniia SSSR.* Moscow: Nauka.

Woodruff, D. 1991. "The 'Woman Question' and the State Question: Current Soviet Debates." Unpublished manuscript, Department of Political Science, University of California, Berkeley.

Zdravomyslov, A. G., V. P. Rozhin, and V. A. Iadov, eds. 1967. *Chelovek i ego Rabota.* Moscow: Mysl'.

Zhenshchiny v SSSR. 1980. *Vestnik Statistiki* 1, 69–79.

———. 1986. *Vestnik Statistiki* 1, 51–67.

PART FOUR
Industrial Economies

The five chapters on Germany, Great Britain, Japan, the Nordic countries, and the United States all show how industrialization has profoundly changed women's labor force participation and altered the life patterns of women. In recent years this change has become more self-conscious, and each of these nations has adopted explicit social policies to support gender equality and women's advance in the paid labor force.

But there is considerable variation among the countries. At one end of the continuum, the Nordic countries have the most advanced and most generous provisions for supporting women's paid work along with parenthood and family life. At the other end of the continuum, Great Britain and especially Japan reveal great ambivalence about support for gender equality or women's advances in education and the labor force. The picture in the two Germanies and in the United States falls somewhere between these two extremes.

Economist Hedwig Rudolph wrote her chapter in the midst of the reunification of the two Germanies. In the western Federal Republic of Germany (FRG), women gained access to the labor market by accepting a high degree of sex segregation by both occupation and rank. Despite their increased investments in education, West German women are still far from getting rewards comparable to those of their male peers. In the eastern German Democratic Republic (GDR), forty years of affirmative action policies have somewhat mitigated the effects of sex inequality in occupations and pay, but gender inequality persists nonetheless. Social policies to support families have focused exclusively on working mothers. In the wake of reunification, there is considerable uncertainty about where women's employment is headed. One possibility is that there will be both a quantitative and a qualitative rollback in gains already made.

British Labour Party official Emma MacLennan examines trends in women's employment in Great Britain and the ways in which public policies have affected women's choices in the labor market. During the 1980s government policy resisted and reduced public support for working women. But today skill shortages and demographic trends are creating a pressing demand for women workers. A debate now rages over whether, without government intervention, the market will be able to provide the support working women need and whether women with young children should be encouraged to work at all.

The resolution of this debate will determine the choices available to British women in the future.

In their chapter on the place of women in Japanese society, Ann Cordilia—a sociologist—and Kazuko Ohta—a historian—note Japanese women's long history of productive contribution to unpaid agricultural and family-based work. Women's current position in the paid labor market, however, is markedly subordinate compared to other countries at similar levels of development. Except through access to their husbands' salaries, women do not share in the Japanese "economic miracle." Young educated women are especially dissatisfied with their future prospects given the nature of the Japanese employment system, which accepts them easily for entry-level positions but makes promotion and retention difficult. In the face of these obstacles, Cordilia and Ohta report on how college women think about their future roles and come to terms with the difficulties of combining work and family.

The chapter on the Nordic countries by sociologist Elina Haavio-Mannila and social psychologist Kaisa Kauppinen covers women's work in Denmark, Finland, Iceland, Norway, and Sweden. These countries are unusual in their commitment to equal political rights for women and legal protection against sex discrimination. Women in these Nordic countries make up a higher proportion of local and national elected officials than anywhere else in the world. A very high proportion of married women and mothers is also in the paid labor force, and high-quality public day care and paid parental leave are part of the infrastructure. There is still strong occupational sex segregation in the labor market, however. If the expansion of the social welfare state continues and an even higher proportion of the gross national product is devoted to social security expenditure, the gap between men's and women's incomes is likely to narrow further. Economic problems at home and disruption in Europe arouse concern about the survival power of the welfare system.

Psychologist Joseph H. Pleck, in his chapter on work-family policies in the United States, focuses on the origins and development of social policies that have accompanied the rapid expansion of women's economic roles. Since the 1960s, three policies have received attention from research and advocacy groups as vehicles for helping working women and their children. Beginning in the 1970s, the debate over child care was concerned with what types of care were best and the effects of child care not only on children but on mothers' employment. The 1990 Act for Better Child Care represented the growing legitimacy of both mothers' employment and child care outside the home. A second type of policy, the development of part-time and flexible work schedules, is receiving new attention as part of a broader corporate emphasis on "flexibility" in staffing and scheduling. Flexibility is both criticized and supported as an aid to meeting combined pressures of work and family responsibilities. The third policy, parental leave, also has gained growing acceptance as pregnancy has been covered by state and federal disability programs and collective bargaining agreements. Current proposed national legislation advocates temporary medical leave and child care leave for parents of newborns and young children. At present, however, such provisions have been enacted only at the state level.

These chapters on women's changing roles in industrial countries suggest that women's rising labor force participation will not be reversed but is a trend woven into the very fabric of modern society. So long as gender inequity continues in occupational distribution and pay, there will be two major strategies to combat it. The first is equal rights legislation that prohibits all forms of sex discrimination. The second is family policy that helps women share their traditional family and parenting roles not only with men but with the larger community.

8

Women's Labor Market Experience in the Two Germanies

HEDWIG RUDOLPH

Fundamental national concerns were at the center stage of political discussion in Germany in 1990. The historical event of the decade—the process of political unification of the two Germanies—dominated the debate. The necessary transformation from a centrally planned to a market economy in the former German Democratic Republic (GDR) is bound to produce massive shocks in the labor market, the effects of which will not be restricted to the eastern part of the country.

There is abundant evidence in history that women are more vulnerable on average than men to labor market crises. Surprisingly, the employment situation of women and their prospects are only marginal issues in the discussion to date.

This portrait of female gainful employment in the Federal Republic of Germany (FRG) combines two perspectives: first, a review of past changes—how they occurred and where they have been frustrated—and second, likely future changes in the face of the unification of the two Germanys in fall 1990 after forty years of separate (although in many respects not unrelated) political and economic development.

The future common label for the economy of Germany will be that of social market economy, and it is feared that the legal and institutional structures of the FRG will simply be transferred to the GDR, regardless of difficulties of adjustment. The fact that the new permeability creates new conditions on both sides of the still-existing border appears to receive little attention. Presumptions about the future of female employment in Germany from the point of view of the FRG must consider the historical development that took place in the GDR.

The analysis of both parts of the country pays special attention to the question of whether and to what extent the increasing labor force participation of women has been accompanied by decreasing occupational segregation by sex. My thesis is that women's integration into paid work has been paralleled by a process of horizontal and vertical fragmentation of the employment structures in both countries, notwithstanding their different political ideologies. The concluding argument of the chapter is that the coincidence of the political unification of the two Germanys and the process toward the development of an internal European market accentuates the need for active policies in favor of women. The spectrum of problems includes the lack of availability of skilled jobs in the service sector (especially part-time jobs), the lack of adequate child care facilities, and above all, the absence of strong legislation for affirmative action.

EMPLOYMENT OF WOMEN

More Working Women, More Working Mothers

Among the most striking developments in the labor market is the growing absorption of women into gainful employment. Their numbers have increased considerably since 1960. In 1988, 55 percent of all women between ages 15 and 65 were in the labor market, a percentage that is low by some international standards. One reason may be that women began their increase in labor market participation in 1965 from a *very* low level. Also, as I explain later, account must be taken of the fact that there are institutional barriers to the employment of mothers, such as few child care facilities. On the other hand, participation rates in younger age categories (20–44 years) are much closer to the rates observed in other countries. Over time, as these younger women become the senior members of the female labor market, the current relatively low participation rates may rise to the levels of women's work participation in other countries.

Overall, as shown in Figure 8.1, the participation rates of men are considerably higher than those of women. The difference in these participation rates is largely accounted for by the lower rates of married women. The rates for single women follow a pattern similar to that of their male peers, although at a slightly lower level. Married women, and especially mothers, have the lowest work rates of any group, although they had the highest growth rates in labor force participation between 1961 and 1980. In this period, the rate of employment for women with one child rose from 37.2 to 47.3 percent; for women with two children the respective figures were 31.7 and 37.4 percent (Gottschall 1989: 18). Christian Brinkmann and Gerhard Engelbrech (1989: 538 ff.) provide empirical evidence that women increasingly engage in or want to engage in paid work. In lower-status occupations, "push factors" (economic needs) dominate, whereas "pull factors" (professional interests) operate among women with higher family incomes.

Employment rates of women according to age (see Figure 8.1) show that the activity of married women determines the curve for all women. Between ages 20 and 34, participation decreases from over 60 percent to 55 percent; it then rises slightly for women ages 35–45. The biggest change in labor market

FIGURE 8.1   Activity Rates According to Age, April 1988

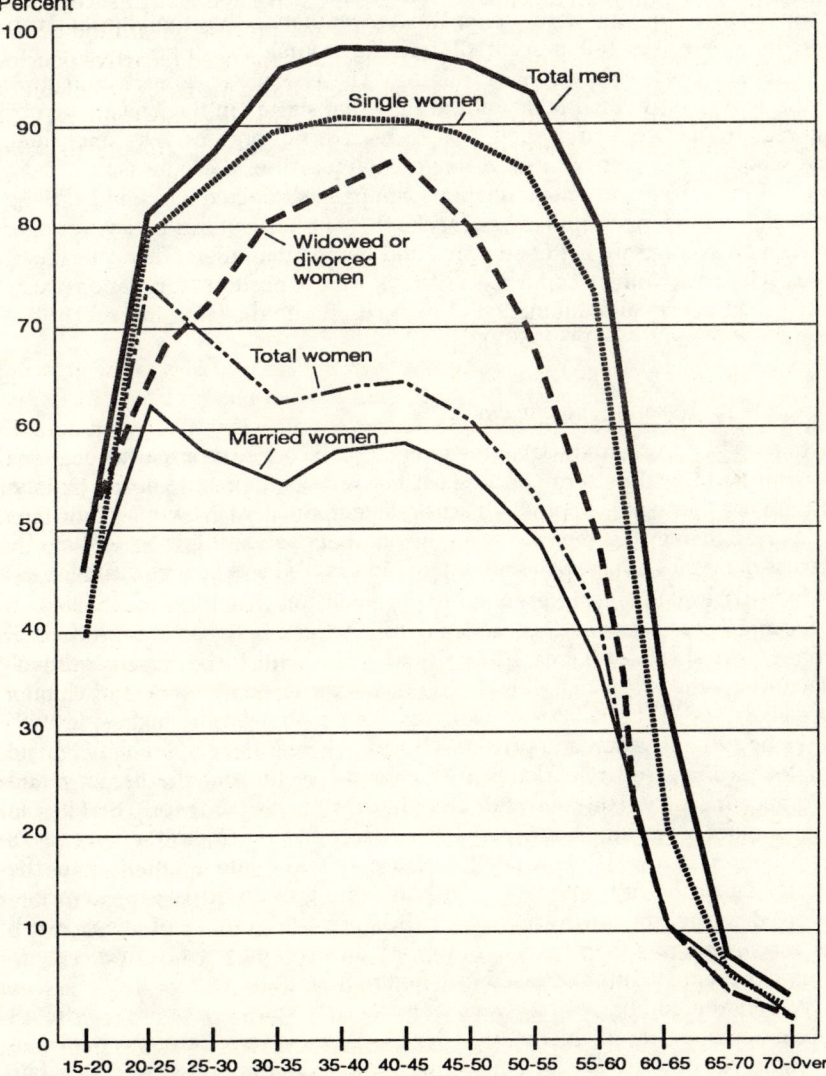

Source: Statistisches Bundesamt, ed., 1990; *Stand und Entwicklung der Erwerbståtigkeit 1988*; Fachserie 1, Reihe 4.4.1 (Stuttgart: Metzler-Poeschel), 32.

activity between 1965 and 1985 took place in the middle-age group (35–49 years). Two reasons stand out. This postwar generation of women profited both from economic prosperity (*Wirthschaftswunder*) and from an expanding supply of places for vocational training in the "dual system"—the German training system of long tradition and strong reputation that combines instruction in enterprises (60 percent of training hours) and training in public vocational schools (40 percent of training). These women also took advantage of the active educational policy of the state that started in the 1960s whereby the regional network of schools was increased, tuition fees were abolished, and school books were delivered free of charge. All of these measures had a parallel in widespread public relations campaigns targeted at parents ("Send your child for a longer time to better schools"). Because of this policy, younger women on average are better educated and trained than their older colleagues. Thus, German women confirm the thesis that a positive correlation exists between educational attainment and integration into the labor market (Brinkmann and Engelbrech 1989: 537).

Structure of Women's Employment

In the FRG, women's progressive integration into the labor market does not confirm traditional patterns of the past but reflects the restructuring process of the West German economy. I discuss the employment growth according to industries, then give some figures on the occupational distribution, and finally discuss the issues of occupational segregation as well as earnings differentials.

Industries. Women represented 40.9 percent of all persons employed in 1988, an increase from 38.2 percent a decade earlier. Between 1960 and 1985, women's employment increased in all industries with the exception of manufacturing—the sector that, however, remains the largest employer of women (see Figure 8.2). The *number* of working women showed the highest growth in public administration and private services, whereas the *proportion* of female employees increased remarkably in the public sector and the banking and insurance industry. The *volume* or amount of women's paid work, that is, the total number of working hours per year—a more accurate indicator of women's contribution to the labor market because it takes into account both the shortening of the full-time work week and the growth of part-time work—followed a slightly downward trend. Because the volume of men's work declined even more than did that of women during the period, women's share of employment slightly increased (see Figure 8.3).

Within the public sector, women were not equally represented in all departments and at all hierarchical levels. Women were rare exceptions in positions of authority and power except in the educational system and public health services. The vast majority fill the lower ranks of clerical jobs. Jobs in the public sector are privileged by a lower probability of unemployment and more liberal regulations for access to part-time work, even for positions of higher status. Some even provide temporary unpaid leave for family reasons (Langkau-Hermann 1985: 18). On the other hand, clerical jobs in the public sector often are threatened by the risk of deskilling and even of unemployment,

FIGURE 8.2 Female Employment in Various Sectors, 1960-1985

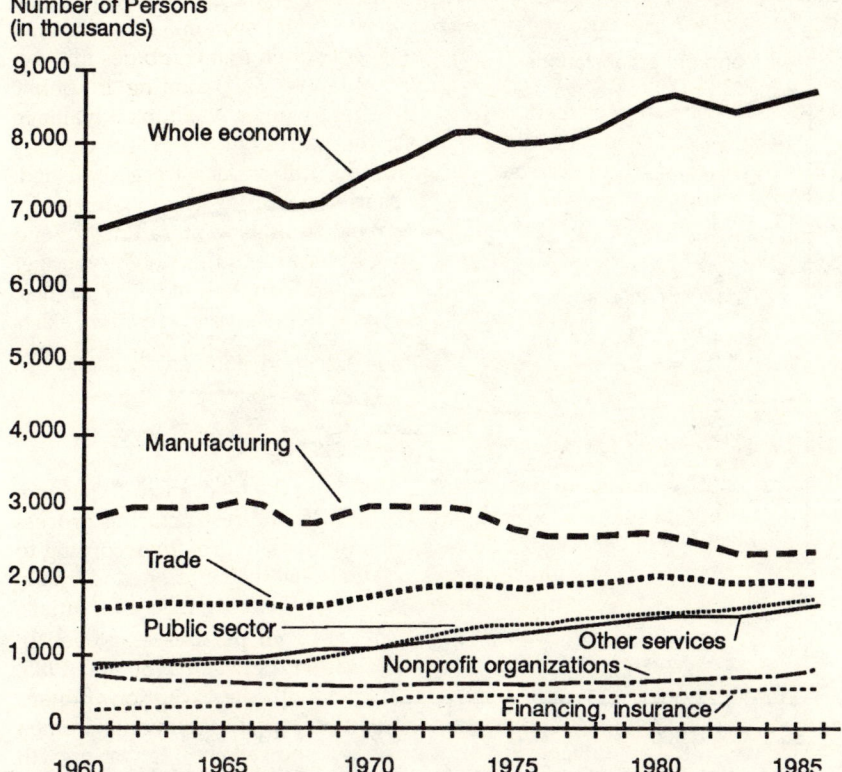

Source: Frank Stille. "Bestands und Entwicklungsdaten zur Struktur des Arbeitsmarktes Unter Besonderer Berücksichtigung von Frauenarbeitsplätzen" (Report to the Federal Ministry of Youth, Family, Women, and Health). (Berlin: Deutsches Institut für Wirtschaftsforschung, 1988).

twin perils that also confront clerical workers employed in private industry (Rudolph 1986a). The extremely biased representation of women within the hierarchy of employees in the public sector points to systematic discrimination and challenges the claim that public authorities are the forerunners in campaigns for equal opportunity.

Occupations. Women have been employed as manual workers since the early days of industrialization (Willms 1983), but after World War II the focus of their activity changed to reflect the restructuring of West German industry. Women's main fields of activity have moved from textile and clothing industries (where they still represent 50 and 80 percent of jobholders, respectively) to the electrical industry, a major industry group in Germany today. A number of female workers who have passed vocational training examinations as

FIGURE 8.3   Female Employment (percent of total volume)[a]

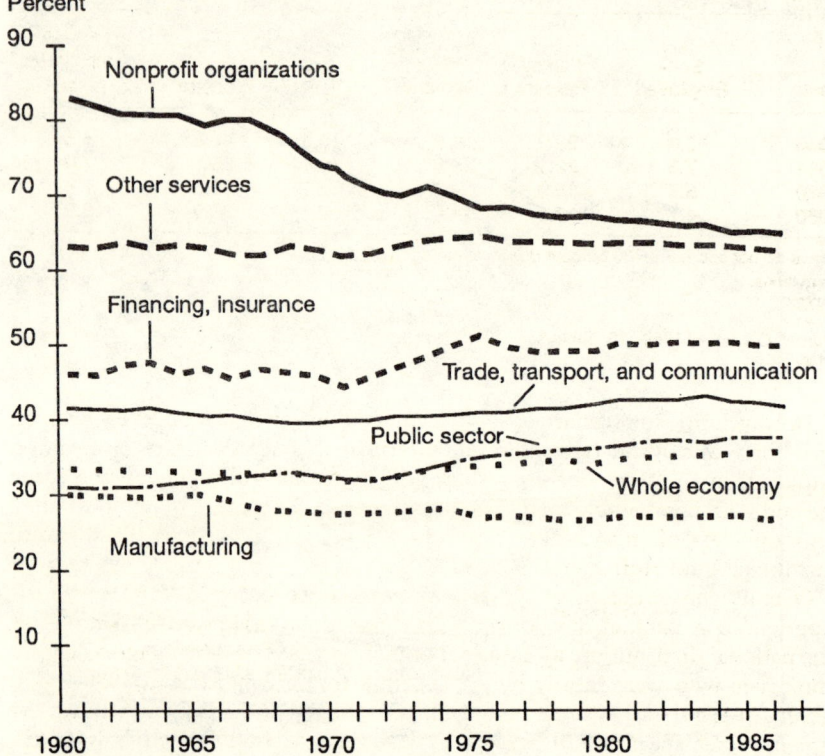

[a]Volume equals the number of gainfully employed persons times the number of working days per year.

Source: Stille (1988).

hairdressers, saleswomen, or doctor's assistants are employed in unskilled jobs, such as those in assembly lines of the electrical industry (Bednarz-Braun 1983). Women's blue-collar work without question is classified as unskilled in labor market analysis. In fact, some economic scenarios have interpreted a decline in the proportion of female workers as an indicator of an improving skill structure of the labor force (e.g., Albrecht and Schmid 1985).

In addition to blue-collar unskilled labor, women occupy an increasing number of clerical jobs in all branches, jobs that have increased in number with the growth of administrative tasks. Since the early 1970s, women have entered skilled clerical jobs (Gottschall 1989: 17) and have participated in large numbers in the expanding services and in jobs in public welfare (Willms 1983: 107 ff.). In fact, Uwe Becker (1989) points to a parallel between the level of women's employment and the percentage of the service sector in total employment.

TABLE 8.1   Employment of Women by Occupation as Percent of Female Work Force, 1950-1980[a]

Year	Self-Employed	Family Helpers	Civil Servants	Clerks	Workers	Female Employees (total)[b]
1950	7.6	32.0	1.2	19.0	40.2	4.5
1961	7.3	22.1	1.5	32.8	36.1	7.0
1970	5.7[c]	15.9	2.4	35.2	36.2	7.8
1980	4.7	7.5	4.0	52.7	30.9	8.9

[a]Rows do not add up to 100 percent due to rounding.
[b]In millions.
[c]1973.

Source: Gottschall 1989: 16, Table 1.

However, in white-collar occupations at medium-qualification levels, women aged forty and older (who did not interrupt their careers) are more often employed in ordinary positions than are their male colleagues of the same age and with comparable qualifications (15 versus 9 percent). In addition, they are found less often in higher positions (14 versus 21 percent) (Brinkmann, Engelbrech, and Hofbauer 1988: 732).

Overall, the doubling of the female work force between 1950 and 1980 experienced a parallel development of three remarkable transformations in occupational distribution, as Table 8.1 demonstrates. The percentage of female employees who were family helpers shrunk from 32 percent in 1950 to 7.5 percent in 1980. In that same period, the proportion of clerical workers almost tripled, increasing from 19 percent to 52.7 percent. In 1980 clerical workers comprised more than half of all female employees. The category of female blue-collar workers lost its once dominant position and in 1980 contained less than one-third of all workers.

Occupational Segregation

How did the process of women's integration into paid work affect the central and knotty issue of occupational segregation? A thorough analysis on the basis of ten employment censuses taken between 1882 and 1982 substantiated the historical presence of labor market segregation according to sex (Willms-Herget 1985). Segregation is the combined result of the concentration of women in certain occupations and dissimilarity between women's and men's occupations.

Concentration. The proportion of women working in occupations in which male colleagues are the exception (less than 10 percent of workers) decreased from its peak of 22 percent in 1939 to 7 percent in 1982. Male domains remain, however. Over the entire period, the proportion of men working in occupations with less than 10 percent female colleagues never fell below 35 percent and reached 41 percent in 1982.

Dissimilarity. Despite these changes in concentration, the index of dissimilarity—which takes into account changes in the division of paid labor between men and women—has not changed. Today, as six decades ago, at least 58 percent of the female labor force would have to move from an occupation in which female employees are overrepresented to one with male dominance (and vice versa) in order to establish an equal distribution of sexes.

Index of Segregation. This index is the most complicated but also the most appropriate one concerning the development of segregation over time. The segregation index weights occupational dissimilarity (i.e., disproportional sexual distribution of the labor force in occupations) with the proportion of labor each occupation absorbs. Thus, changes in the division of manpower according to industries as an influence on segregation (and vice versa) can be isolated. Figures show that the overall index of segregation in FRG did not diminish between 1925 and 1982. If the occupational weights of 1925 are held constant, segregation would actually have increased. This means that the growth of the service industry has reduced sexual segregation because "new" occupations developing in the tertiary sector have been less sexually standardized than the "old" occupations in manufacturing. However, on average, sexual standardization became even more rigid as the expanding modern "female" occupations absorbed disproportionately large numbers of women.

Segregation and Training. The segregated structure of the labor force is roughly reflected in the vocational choices after graduation from school. During the 1980s there was much research, public discussion, and political activity concerning the narrow range of vocational options chosen by women (Rudolph 1986b). To a greater extent than their male peers women concentrate on a few "typically female" occupations (see Table 8.2). During recent years, the concentration of women in terms of vocational choices has gradually decreased; girls seem to adjust their vocational choices to the training opportunities offered them.

In 1978 the Federal Ministry of Education and Science started an experimental training scheme that involved 1,200 young women in about 200 cooperating firms; the women were trained for occupations such as mechanic, electrician, and joiner. This model program, which received much public attention, demonstrated that for women there are no insurmountable obstacles to participating in technical vocations. Yet the number of women in atypical training during the 1980s increased only slightly, especially in male-dominated occupational fields such as engineering crafts.

Criticism of these kinds of training schemes in political debate and from the scientific community did not concentrate as much on their ineffectiveness as on the lack of nontraditional labor market opportunities, both middle and long term. The claim is made that current training policy will only continue and reinforce the pattern of the past: Positions and occupations ceded to women will continue to be those that are no longer attractive to men (Willms-Herget 1985).

TABLE 8.2   Trainees in the Ten Most Popular Recognized Skills According to Numbers and Sex, 1987

Female Trainees

Skills	Number	Percent
Hairdresser	61,585	93.0
Office clerk	49,639	80.2
Saleswoman (entry level)	49,589	77.7
Saleswoman, foodstuffs	48,591	98.7
Industrial clerk	42,564	62.7
Doctor's assistant	35,035	99.9
Clerk, retail (second-level)	34,005	63.6
Dentist's assistant	29,670	99.9
Bank clerk	28,989	51.6
Clerk, wholesale and foreign trade	22,248	43.9
	401,915	(55 percent of all female trainees)

Male Trainees

Skills	Number	Percent
Motor vehicle mechanic	77,134	99.0
Electrician	48,332	99.1
Engineering fitter machinist	39,862	98.6
Painter and decorator	31,889	91.3
Joiner	31,674	91.5
Clerk, wholesale and foreign trade	28,475	56.1
Plumber	27,885	99.0
Bank clerk	27,205	48.4
Industrial clerk	25,304	37.3
Baker	24,684	85.4
	362,444	(36 percent of all male trainees)

Sources: Statistisches Bundesamt, ed., *Berufliche Bildung* 1987 (Stuttgart: Metzler–Poeschel, 1989) Fachserie 11, Reihe 3, 24ff.

Segregation and Income. The sexual segregation of labor markets is accompanied by distinct income differentials. In 1987 hourly earnings of women amounted on average to only 73.4 percent of what men received (Stille 1988: 29). The wage differentials are not due to open wage discrimination. Rather, their primary cause is the personnel planning of firms that allocate workers to work and training places. In this process, women are given the least favorable jobs regardless of their qualifications (Fiedler and Regenhard 1987: 182).

To summarize, the position of German women in the labor market definitely improved during the last decade. Their employment rate increased, although slowly, and more women are employed in the safer jobs of the civil service and in skilled jobs in general. However, they have only slowly gained access to higher-level positions. Occupational segregation persists, with accompanying wage differentials.

MODERN WORK SCHEDULES—
BETTER CHANCES FOR WOMEN?

About one-third of the enormous growth of economic productivity in West Germany between 1955 and 1989 was redistributed to the work force through various reductions in the standard hours of working time, which were instituted without any reduction in earnings. An alternative work schedule adjustment—part-time work—also increased during the period. The implementation of part-time work has resulted in reduced working hours and wage reductions. Although it offers the advantage of reducing the pressures of work, it also has a number of negative features.

The first period of tremendous growth in the amount of part-time work began in the early 1960s. At that time, enterprises—especially those in the retail trade—were eager to recruit housewives to compensate for the labor shortage (Eckart 1986). The offer of half-day jobs, preferably in the morning, was promoted as a chance for women to reconcile paid work with family duties.

The situation in the labor market has totally changed, and in recent years the growth of part-time work reflects the employers' strategy of encouraging maximum flexibility in working time to adapt to production needs (Duran et al. 1982). The growing number of part-time jobs almost exclusively go to women (93 percent). In 1988, 10 percent of the total labor force did not work full time; among working women, the proportion was 22.8 percent. During the 1980s almost two out of three new jobs for women were part time.

The typical part-time worker is a married woman between 35 and 54 years of age. Empirical evidence shows that one out of four women working part time has no children, and two out of three have none under age fifteen (Bielinski and Strümpel 1988: 21 ff.). Obviously, a considerable number of families, especially of the middle class, reach an adequate living standard with one income. In 1988 only 46 percent of married women without children were employed, 18.7 percent on a part-time basis. Part-time work provides some extra money without demanding too much of the time or energies women need for "their" home work.

The most popular argument in favor of part-time work is that it allows women to combine a career (although modest) with family duties. Part-time work solves the problem for mothers of how to combine paid and unpaid work, a critical issue because a number of men "tolerate" their wives' gainful employment only on the condition that the men are not burdened with part of the house work and care of the children. In the FRG these conditions have been extremely difficult to fulfill with a full-time job because child care facilities are rare—they are available for only 3 percent of children under age three. In addition, schools that run a full day are the exception. The school day typically ends before lunch or early in the afternoon. Therefore, for many women—not only single mothers but also the majority of women because life companions do not customarily share the household tasks—the double burden of meeting work and family demands is cumbersome. Only the younger and better-educated men are likely to participate in housework (Metz-Göckel and Müller 1985). Thus, many women have no alternative but to interrupt their careers when a child is born and to seek a part-time job when they reenter the labor market. Neither situation is without economic cost.

In 1985 one out of four women reported at least one break in their careers for family duties. However, both the number and the length of breaks have decreased during recent years, particularly among younger women. In 1986 one-third of all married women ages 40 to 50 had been out of employment for more than eight years; among 30- to 40-year-old women, the figure was only one-tenth (Brinkmann, Engelbrech, and Hofbauer 1988: 736). There are two reasons for this trend. First, women's qualifications are rising on average, resulting in a stronger career orientation. Second, women face incalculable risks in gaining reentry to the job market once they have left paid work.

Women who have interrupted their careers and who reenter the labor market, especially as part-time workers, often must accept job offers that do not measure up to their qualifications. In addition, they frequently face less attractive working conditions and remuneration than they enjoyed previously (Brinkmann and Engelbrech 1989: 545 ff.).

German labor law and collective bargaining agreements between employers and unions protect people in regular part-time jobs from open discrimination by including most part-time workers in public social security as well as employer-sponsored retirement plans. Yet part-time workers still are less well-off than their colleagues with full-time contracts. Part-time workers do not receive full fringe benefits; promotions as well as job security also are negatively affected (Büchtemann 1988). Moreover, part-time jobs cluster in specific low-wage sectors (for example, retail trade) and are found mostly in lower-status occupations.

However, the greatest growth in part-time work since 1975 has been in "marginal" part-time work. Such part-time jobs call for fewer hours (contracts below nineteen or even fifteen hours per week are exempt from social security contributions) and often have undefined weekly work schedules that also may be temporary. They reflect a strategy of firms to optimize their competitive position in the market. Women between ages 31 and 50 are especially overrepresented in marginal part-time jobs (Büchtemann and Schupp 1986: Table 8: 54). Because earnings in these jobs are insufficient to cover subsistence needs, they perpetuate a woman's financial dependence on the "head of the family." This is why such part-time work is sometimes called the modern-day version of helping family workers (Kurz-Scherf 1987).

Even marginal part-time jobs are not necessarily traps for women attempting to make a professional reentry. More than one out of three women successfully uses them as a bridge to more adequate employment (Büchtemann 1988). A majority of women, however, and many men as well—especially in their middle years—would prefer a work schedule of twenty to thirty-five hours per week, a part-time category that is rarely available (Brinkmann and Kohler 1989: 477).

The acceptance of unprotected, marginal part-time jobs has been promoted by the growth in unemployment since the early 1980s. For a number of women, the alternative to a bad job has been unemployment. In fact, women have had a higher risk of unemployment in times of labor market crisis. An analysis of unemployment figures for the years 1973 to 1983 shows that male unemployment increased and decreased along with business fluctuations. Female unemployment, however, was not characterized by this variability. It continued to increase even when the cyclical downturn abated (Grüning 1985: 66).

Traditionally, women have been overrepresented among the unemployed: In February 1990 their unemployment rate was 9.2 percent compared with 7.6 percent for men. The number of unemployed men showed a downward trend (shrinking by more than one-fourth) between 1985 and 1990, whereas the number of unemployed women remained virtually unchanged at around one million. Labor market experts estimate that nearly another one million women must be counted as a hidden reserve—that is, they would seek employment if labor market conditions did not discourage them (Brinkmann 1987). If we also take into account the enormous growth in female employment that occurred during the same period, we see the high degree of labor market pressure created by women who want to reenter the paid labor market. A positive change of attitude among women should be mentioned in this context. The high female unemployment rates indicate a change of attitude among women. They now defend their right to paid work by registering as unemployed instead of joining the hidden reserve as they used to do during the labor market crisis in the 1970s.

Not only is the unemployment rate higher for women than for men, but women are unemployed for longer periods than their male peers. Surprisingly, the rate of unemployment is not positively correlated with the age of unemployed women. The most severely affected groups are women under age 34 and those over 55 (Bundesanstalt 1989: 332). For women in their middle years, the fit between their own willingness to work for money and employers' willingness to hire them seems to be more balanced.

Fifty percent of unemployed women (and men) do not have vocational training or a professional certificate. Among older unemployed women, almost two-thirds are unskilled. Women are underrepresented in publicly financed programs providing further vocational training or retraining under the Labor Market Promotion Act, which focuses on unemployed persons and those threatened by unemployment. In 1987, however, women constituted one-third of the trainees; twenty-five years earlier they represented only one-fourth of trainees (Statistisches Bundesamt 1987: 108 ff.). The low participation rate of unemployed women in training courses does not primarily reflect a lack of motivation on their part but represents the combined effect of a lack of programs that fit their skill levels and modest efforts on the part of the labor administration to upgrade the skills of older women who have few or none.

As a consequence of low earnings, women's unemployment benefits on average amount to little more than half (54 percent) of the sum unemployed men receive. Four out of ten unemployed women (compared with three out of ten men) are not eligible for unemployment benefits (Statistisches Bundesamt 1987: 107 ff.). This is the case partly because women more often than men fail to meet eligibility requirements concerning the duration of former employment due to their "patchwork" careers. It is also true because one kind of benefit *(Arbeitslosenhilfe)* depends on a means test, which often disqualifies married women.

To summarize, women are more severely affected by unemployment than their male colleagues; their rate of unemployment is higher; they are out of jobs longer; and they receive lower, if any, benefits. In addition, women are less likely to participate in training programs that may improve their chances for reentry into the labor market. This supports the thesis that the structure of unemployment reflects that of the labor market, especially in the FRG where the unemployment insurance system is based on the individual contributions made during former paid work.

THE LABOR SITUATION IN THE
FORMER GERMAN DEMOCRATIC REPUBLIC

The situation of women in the labor market of the former German Democratic Republic (GDR) looks quite different from that in the FRG, at first glance at least. Their labor force participation rate, including both working women and women in vocational training, increased tremendously between 1950 and 1989—reaching more than 90 percent in the age groups between fifteen and sixty. Starting from 40 percent in 1950, women represented half of the nation's work force in 1989 (Radtke 1990: 68).

Political as well as economic "push and pull" factors help to explain women's work status (Rudolph et al. 1990). Legal, administrative, and financial measures were introduced—especially during the 1970s—to integrate women into the labor force in accordance with the right and obligation to work contained in the constitutional law of the GDR (Enders 1986: 27). These measures included special programs for vocational upgrading of women, equal pay legislation, suspension of provisions such as prohibition against women's working at night, and expansion of child care facilities. The dramatic fall of the birth rate between 1965 and 1975 was recognized as a warning signal of women's discontent with working and living conditions. The government reacted with a series of measures combining financial aid, institutional support, and reductions in working time for mothers, including a paid leave, of up to one year following the birth of a child (Enders 1986: 30 ff.).

Social policies aimed at a reconciliation of work and family could not dissuade women from working part time, however. In spite of moral persuasion and political pressure, the proportion of women working half time was only reduced from about 35 percent in 1970 (Helwig 1987: 89) to 26 percent in 1989 (Burkhardt and Zierke 1990: 36). More favorable working conditions for working mothers—shorter distances between home and workplace, a higher solidarity among female colleagues in similar situations, more convenient working hours—were reasons many women changed jobs when returning to work after their maternity leaves, even though the new jobs often did not fully use their qualifications (Enders 1986: 36).

With respect to women's incomes, there is some evidence that the GDR was no exception to the worldwide "iron law," which purports that industries with large proportions of women should have income levels below the overall average of all industries (Enders 1986: 33). In 1988 women in the GDR working full time had a net monthly income that was 76 percent that of their male colleagues (Ott et al. 1990: 7). Even so, the fact that male wages have been rather low has been a strong incentive for women to seek employment in order to create a better standard of living for the family (Friedrich-Ebert-Stiftung 1987: 12 ff.).

Due to the active educational and training policies in the GDR during the last decades, 87 percent of all working women had vocational or professional certificates. In the FRG, less than 40 percent have such certification. Four out of ten university graduates in the GDR were female (Radtke 1990: 68); in the FRG the proportion is less than one out of ten.

Notwithstanding this remarkable progress, gender equality was far from being realized. There is empirical evidence that employment patterns were sex-biased (Radtke 1990: 70 ff.). Although the occupational choices were not made freely but were politically directed according to labor market requirements, the variety of female occupations showed a rather traditional pattern. Women held more than half of the positions in some professions such as medicine, pharmacology, and teaching. Along with the "feminization" of these professions over the past several decades, their prestige decreased and the wage levels remained low. The proportion of women also diminished as the hierarchical level increased. In all sectors of the economy, women were underrepresented in middle management, and they were rare exceptions at the top level of management. These marked contradictions to the socialist ideal of equal participation only added to the double burden of women in the GDR who, as elsewhere, were responsible not only for paid work but for housework as well (Enders 1986: 33).

Let us look more closely at fields such as engineering and computer science, fields in which GDR women made the most spectacular progress. The proportion of women in technical education both at the level of craftsmen and at universities increased continually and reached about one-third. However, the proportion of women training for the technical crafts stagnated or even slightly decreased after the mid-1970s (Lemke 1988: 78). Engineering studies, on the other hand, seem to have become more attractive to women. More women were found in electronics and computer sciences than in mechanics at both the level of engineers and of skilled workers (Radtke 1990: 70).

These statistics indicate undisputable progress compared with the professional variety and qualification levels of women around 1970. In comparison to their male colleagues, the employment situation of GDR women was less favorable, however. Female workers were more likely than men to have low-paid, monotonous, and stressful jobs. Even skilled women were not allowed access to the most sophisticated modern machinery. It was argued that they lacked the required specific qualifications (Radtke 1990: 74 ff.). There is no information as to whether women refused further training to acquire these skills or whether this was a typical instance in which men ascended the job ladder through acquiring additional qualifications, keeping their superior positions by taking one step sideways and one upward (Cockburn 1985).

The GDR maintained an extremely high level of participation of women in the labor market for more than a generation. But women no longer seem willing to bear the double burden of both full-time employment and responsibility for most of the housework. The increasing demand for part-time work (Burkhardt and Zierke 1990: 36) and the high divorce rate (38 percent in 1987) can be interpreted as active coping strategies.

In the GDR, the political measures to transform gender equality from political ideals into practical life were almost exclusively geared to providing assistance for women as wives and mothers. Most men did not feel the need to change their patriarchal life-style (Enders 1986: 35). Only recently have feminist researchers pointed to the fact that demographic and family problems were commonly at the root of measures labeled *women's policy*. They asked for a reappraisal of the masculine self-concept as a precondition for gender relations that offer equal opportunities to women and men (Nickel 1990).

ONE GERMANY, ONE EUROPE: WOMEN'S PERSPECTIVES

The labor market participation of women steadily increased in the two Germanys since the end of World War II but at somewhat different rates. By 1990 nearly all women between ages 15 and 60 were in the labor force or in training in the GDR, whereas this was true for little more than half of the female population in the same age group in the FRG.

Women's employment had a number of parallel characteristics in East and West Germany. The distribution according to industries was similar, with strong and increasing emphasis on the tertiary sector, which includes finance, insurance and real estate, personal and recreational services, education, health, and public administration. Concerning occupations, in both regions the greatest numbers of women were found in clerical jobs, the fastest-growing segment of the labor market.

In spite of women's easier access to paid work, sex-specific labor market segregation persists both horizontally and vertically. The fact of gendered labor markets is more obvious in the FRG; but it was far from being abolished in the GDR, despite the multifaceted affirmative action programs that existed for decades. The survival of sex-specific labor markets can be taken as an indication that gender relations changed only gradually and only slightly in a more egalitarian direction in the GDR.

In both regions women have taken advantage of the active educational policies of the past decades. The number of women holding higher education certificates, both of a general and a vocational character, has increased more than that of their male peers. However, women have not been able to escape the fact that in terms of income, career perspectives, and job security, the labor market provides a lower return for the educational investment of women than for that of men.

The political and economic developments up to the summer of 1990 supported pessimistic expectations as to the "progressive" aspects of women's situation in the GDR. The radical political and economic transformation process will dramatically cut women's chances for self-sustained living. Moreover, the restructuring of industries entails the risk of narrowing the spectrum of jobs available for women.

The labor market prospects for German women after unification are uncertain. Some problem areas will presumably be aggravated, such as the mismatch of demand for and supply of service-sector jobs and for all types of part-time work. The question of child care will have to be approached from a fresh perspective with respect to both quality and quantity.

Guidelines for policies aimed at improving women's position in the labor market should take a broader range of occupations into account. Positive action with the aim of diminishing segregation, whether through the use of quotas or moral persuasion, should concentrate not on those occupations in which female employment rates are extremely low but on those that show an upward trend of employment. In addition, female occupations should be upgraded in social and economic value, a policy German unions are slowly beginning to seek.

The most important lesson German women have learned during the last decades is that they must insist on the formulation and implementation of active women's policies, not only of policies oriented toward the reproduction of families. The success of programs aimed at more equality in gender relations will depend largely on powerful legislation concerning affirmative action, which is still pending in the new unified Germany.

BIBLIOGRAPHY

Albrect, Christoph, and Günther Schmid. 1985. *"Beschäftigungsentwicklung und Qualifikationsstruktur in Berlin 1977–1983."* Discussion paper International Institute for Management–Labor Market Policy 85-4. Berlin: Wissenschaftszentrum Berlin.

Becker, Uwe. 1989. "Frauenerwerbstätigkeit—Eine Vergleichende Bestandsaufnahme." *Aus Politik und Zeitgeschichte* 28–29: 22–28.

Bednarz-Braun, Iris. 1983. *Arbeiterinnen in der Elektroindustrie.* München: Deutsches Jugendinstitut.

Bielinski, Harald, and Burkhard Strümpel. 1988. *Eingeschränkte Erwerbsarbeit bei Frauen und Männern.* Berlin: Edition Sigma.

Brinkmann, Christian. 1987. *Methodische und Inhaltliche Aspekte der Stillen Reserve.* Mitteilungen aus der Arbeitsmarkt- und Berufsforschung 4/1987. Nürnberg: Institut für Arbeitsmarkt- und Berufsforschung.

Brinkmann, Christian, and Gerhard Engelbrech. 1989. "Beschäftigungsprobleme der Frauen." In *Beschäftigungsprobleme Hochentwickelter Volkswirtschaften.* Schriften des Vereins für Socialpolitik. N.F. Bd. 178, 533–560.

Brinkmann, Christian, Gerhard Engelbrech, and Hans Hofbauer. 1988. "Berufsverläufe von Frauen." In Dieter Mertens, ed., *Konzepte der Arbeitsmakt- und Berufsforschung.* Beitrage aus der Arbeitsmarkt- und Berufsforschung 70. Nürnberg: Institut für Arbeitsmarkt- und Berufsforschung.

Brinkmann, Christian, and Hans Kohler. 1989. *Teilzeitarbeit und Arbeitsvolumen.* MittAB 4/ 1989. Nürnberg: Institut für Arbeitsmarkt- und Berufsforschung.

Büchtemann, Christoph, F. 1988. "The Socioeconomics of Individual Working Time Reduction: Empirical Evidence for the FRG." Paper prepared for the International Workshop on the Reduction of Working Time, Arnoldshain, FRG, March.

Büchtemann, Christoph F., and Jürgen Schupp. 1986. "Zur Sozioökonomie der Teilzeitbeschäftigung in der Bundesrepublik Deutschland: Analysen aus der Ersten Welle des Sozio-Ökonomischen Panel." Discussion paper IIM-LMP 86–15. Berlin: Wissenschaftszentrum Berlin.

Bundesanstalt für Arbeit, ed. 1989. *Amtliche Nachrichten 3.* Nürnberg.

Burkhardt, Manfred, and Irene Zierke. 1990. "Die Gestaltung der Lebenszeit und die Einführung Neuer Technologien." *Wirtschaftswissenschaft* 38, no. 1: 31–48.

Cockburn, Cynthia. 1985. *Machinery of Dominance: Women, Men, and Technical Know-How.* London: Pluto Press.

Duran, Marga, Margitta Klähn, Melanie Nassauer, Jenny Naumann, and Hedwig Rudolph. 1982. *Geteiltes Leid ist Halbes Leid—ein Binsenirrtum!* Berlin: Kleine.

Eckart, Christel. 1986. "Halbtags Durch das Wirtschaftswunder. Die Entwicklung der Teilzeitarbeit in den Sechziger Jahren." In Helgard Kramer, Christel Eckart, Ilka Riemann, and Karin Walser, *Grenzen der Frauenlohnarbeit. Frauenstrategien in Lohn- und Hausarbeit seit der Jahrhundertwende.* Frankfurt and New York: Campus, 183–249.

Enders, Ulrike. 1986. "Kinder, Küche, Kombinat—Frauen in der DDR." *Aus Politik und Zeitgeschichte* 6–7: 26–37.

Fiedler, Angela, and Ulla Regenhard. 1987. *Das Arbeitseinkommen der Frauen. Analysen zur Diskriminierung auf dem Arbeitsmarkt.* Berlin: Berlin Verlag Arno Spitz.

Friedrich-Ebert-Stiftung, ed. 1987. *Frauen in der DDR. Auf dem Weg zur Gleichberechtigung?* Bonn: Neue Gesellschaft.

Gottschall, Karin. 1989. "Frauen auf dem Bundesrepublikanischen Arbeitsmarkt: Integrationsprozesse mit Widersprüchen und Grenzen." In Ursula Müller and Hiltraud Schmidt-Waldherr, eds., *FrauenSozialKunde.* Bielefeld: AJZ, 11–41.

Grüning, Marlies. 1985. *Erwerbslosigkeit von Frauen. Eine Strukturanalyse der Arbeitslos Gemeldeten Frauen und Männer nach Krisenphasen von 1973 bis 1983.* Eschborn: Rationalisierungs-Kuratorium der Deutschen Wirtschaft.

Helwig, Gisela. 1987. *Frau und Familie. Bundesrepublik Deutschland—DDR.* Köln: Wissenschaft und Politik.

Kurz-Scherf, Ingrid. 1989. "Teilzeitarbeit: Individuelle Notlösung und/oder Vorbotin Einer Neuen Zeitordnung?—Plädoyer für die Entpatriarchalisierung der Herrschenden Zeit-Ordnung." In Ursula Müller and Hiltraud Schmidt-Waldherr, eds. *FrauenSozialKunde.* Bielefeld: AJZ, 42–57.

Langkau-Hermann, Monika. 1985. "Frauen in Führungspositionen im Öffentlichen Dienst." Bonn: unpublished paper.

Lemke, Christiane. 1988. "Ingenieurinnen in der DDR: Möglichkeiten und Grenzen Staatlicher Förderpolitik." In Doris Janshen and Hedwig Rudolph, eds., *Frauen Gestalten Technik.* Pfaffenweiler: Centaurus, 75–81.

Metz-Göckel, Sigrid, and Ursula Müller. 1985. *Der Mann. Brigitte-Untersuchung 1985.* Hamburg: Gruner und Jahr.

Nickel, Hildegard Maria. 1990. "Geschlechtertrennung Durch Arbeitsteilung." Paper prepared for the Congress of Sociology, East Berlin, January.

Ott, Notburga, Heidrun Radtke, Wera Thiel, and Gert Wagner. 1990. "Kindererziehung und Erwerbsarbeit. Marktwirtschaftliche Möglichkeiten Einer Erziehungsfreundlichen Erwerbsarbeit in Deutschland." DIW discussion paper no. 7. Berlin: Deutsches Institut für Wirtschaftsforschung.

Radtke, Heidrun. 1990. "Wissenschaftlich-Technischer Fortschritt und Persönlichkeitsentwicklung der Frau." *Wirtschaftswissenschaft* 38, no. 1: 68–80.

Rudolph, Hedwig. 1986a. "Frauenarbeit in der Technischen Produktion: Vom Tendenziellen Fall der Zumutbarkeitsgrenze." In Komitee für Grundrechte und Demokratie, ed., *Technik, Mensch und Menschenrecht.* Sensbachtal: Eigenverlag, 119–126.

———. 1986b. "Viel Bewegung—Wenig Fortschritt: Berufsbildungspolitik für Frauen." In Helga Thomas and Gert Elstermann, eds., *Bildung und Beruf.* Berlin, Heidelberg: Springer, 93–104.

Rudolph, Hedwig, Eileen Appelbaum, and Friederike Maier. 1990. "After German Unity: A Cloudier Outlook for Women." *Challenge* (November-December): 33–40.

Statistisches Bundesamt, ed. 1987. *Frauen in Familie, Beruf und Gesellschaft.* Mainz: Kohlhammer.

———. 1989. *Berufliche Bildung 1987.* Fachserie 11, Reihe 3. Stuttgart: Metzler-Poeschel.

———. 1990. *Stand und Entwicklung der Erwerbstätigkeit 1988.* Fachserie 1, Reihe 4.4.1. Stuttgart: Metzler-Poeschel.

Stille, Frank. 1988. "Bestands—und Entwicklungsdaten zur Struktur des Arbeitsmarktes Unter Besonderer Berücksichtigung von Frauenarbeitsplätzen" (Report to the Federal Ministry of Youth, Family, Women, and Health). Berlin: Deutsches Institut für Wirtschaftsforschung.

Willms, Angelika. 1983. "Segregation auf Dauer? Zur Entwicklung des Verhältnisses von Frauenarbeit und Männerarbeit in Deutschland 1882–1980." In Walter Müller, Angelika Willms, and Johann Handl, *Strukturwandel der Frauenarbeit 1880–1980.* Frankfurt/M., New York: Campus, 107–181.

Willms-Herget, Angelika. 1985. *Frauenarbeit. Zur Integration der Frauen in den Arbeitsmarkt.* Frankfurt/M., New York: Campus.

9

Politics, Progress, and Compromise: Women's Work and Lives in Great Britain

EMMA MacLENNAN

In Great Britain today there is much concern about the "demographic timebomb" due to strike by the turn of the century. The lower birth rate and deferred childbearing of the generations born after 1945 have caused a demographic trough in the British population. By the year 2000, the number of young workers is projected to fall by 1.1 million from the number in 1990 in a total labor force of around 28 million (Spence 1990).

Official projections are that women—particularly married women—will fill the breach. The labor force in the twenty-five to fifty-four age bracket is expected to increase by 1.9 million, more than enough to make up for the loss of younger workers. Ninety percent of the personnel in this projected increase will be women (Spence 1990).

If official projections are correct, the extent to which women will be the beneficiaries of these trends will depend on the framework of legal and social support for women at work and in the home. This chapter examines the position of women in Great Britain today and describes the trends in public policy that will shape women's lives in the future.

TRENDS IN WOMEN'S EMPLOYMENT

Since 1960 the pattern of women's employment in Great Britain has changed dramatically. There has been a continuing growth in the numbers and proportion of women in the employed labor force. There also has been an increase in economic activity among women, particularly married women working part time. A growing number of women have entered male occupational preserves, and progress has been made toward the goal of equal pay.

Despite this, women's inequality remains a feature of British employment. A new pattern is emerging in which some women have achieved higher skill and earnings levels, but the majority continue to do low-paid jobs. These trends have been shaped by public policy in a number of areas.

Women's share of employment in Britain has grown rapidly since World War II. In the first half of the twentieth century, the percentage of female employees in England and Wales grew by less than 1 percent. But from 1961 to 1981, the share of women among the employed labor force in Great Britain grew from 32.4 percent to 39 percent—an increase of over one-sixth in two decades (Office of Population Censuses and Surveys [OPCS] 1964, 1984). During the 1980s this surge gained pace, with the share of women's employment in 1987 reaching just under half (45.7 percent) of the employed population (OPCS 1990a). This increase in women's employment can mainly be accounted for by a growth in services. From 1961 to 1989, the number of jobs in public and private services grew by nearly 50 percent, from 10.6 million to 15.4 million. Sixty percent of these jobs were filled by women (Mitchell 1988; Department of Employment 1990). By 1989 more than 80 percent of all women's jobs occurred in the service sector.

The majority of women entering the labor market during these years were married. In 1911 less than 10 percent of married women were economically active. In 1973 this proportion had grown to over half (Equal Opportunities Commission [EOC] 1987), and by 1987 more than two-thirds (68 percent) of married women of working age were classed as economically active—just under the participation rate for unmarried women (74 percent) (OPCS 1990b).

Along with the increase in married women's employment, there has been an enormous growth in the importance of part-time work, particularly in the service sector. Between 1961 and 1981, the growth in women's part-time jobs outstripped the net rise in women's employment overall (1.53 million jobs compared with 1.51 million) (OPCS 1964, 1984). Some female jobs—most of them full time—were being lost in manufacturing. But many of these women were finding part-time service-sector jobs, and more and more jobs were being offered on a part-time basis. In 1990 around 45 percent of all employed women were part-time workers (OPCS 1990c).

The rising participation rate of married women in employment, the increase in part-time work, and the growth in services have all been interconnected. The expansion of the service sector created a demand for labor in traditional female occupations, and the married women who filled these jobs worked part time in order to meet family needs—both for additional income and to fit in with child care constraints. Despite the increase in women's labor force participation, these trends have not always meant greater equality for women workers, in either the jobs they do or the conditions of work they enjoy.

OCCUPATIONAL SEGREGATION AND WAGE DISCRIMINATION

Occupational Segregation

With the expansion in services, women's work in Great Britain has become more heavily concentrated in relatively few occupations. According to the most recent Labour Force Survey, 76 percent of all women in employment fall within just four occupational groupings: education, welfare, and health (14 percent; clerical and related (30 percent); selling (10 percent); and catering, cleaning, hairdressing, and other personal services (22 percent) (OPCS 1990c).

However, a minority of British women have made inroads into some of the most impenetrable male occupational preserves. For example, in 1960 there were no women in the British judiciary. By 1987, 42 of 985 British judges were women. In 1975 just 14 percent of general medical practitioners were women. By 1985, 21 percent were women, as were nearly half of all newly qualified doctors (EOC 1988b).

But although women are entering traditional male areas, they are rarely making it to the highest levels. Examples abound. A cabinet office report on the Civil Service found that in six government departments (including the Department of Employment), there were no female executives above grade 4 (Brindle 1988). A 1988 internal study by the Esso Company found that within six years, female recruits to the company were on average two grades behind their male contemporaries ("Women and Work" 1989).

Women still fall prey to the old-boy network, which has dominated the professions in Britain. This has consisted of ties made in public and private boys' schools such as Eton and Harrow and later in the universities. The public school bias that once was so rife is dying out, but university contacts remain potent. "Oxbridge" (Oxford and Cambridge) continues to dominate political life and the professions, and some companies recruit higher-level staff only from that source. For example, a recent Policy Studies Institute (PSI) report *Doctors and Their Careers* found that it was common practice for appointments to be made through personal contacts (Allen 1988).

Attitudes toward women, although much changed since the 1970s, also continue to act as a barrier to women's progress. A study by the Department of Management Sciences of Manchester University found that "Victorian" assumptions about the role and ability of women were widespread among employers. A common view was that women were unlikely to display the commitment necessary for a career. Women were thought to be unreliable in higher-level jobs and better suited to lower-paid, more mundane jobs often performed on a temporary basis (Collinson 1988).

The most significant barrier to women's promotion, however, is the conflict they face between the development of a career and their commitment to raising a family. The PSI study of the medical profession found that nearly half of female doctors said that having children and working unsocial hours had held them back (Allen 1988). A survey of one thousand British Telecom managers revealed that 60 percent of female managers felt that few women would rise to senior positions within the company without better provision to help them combine a career with domestic responsibilities ("BT Women" 1988).

Wage Discrimination

Women also remain behind men in the amount they earn. In April 1989, the gross weekly earnings of adult women working full time were just 67.6 percent of those of full-time male workers.

Part of the explanation lies in the different hours worked by men and women in Britain. Men work longer hours and work an average of four hours of overtime every week, earning premium rates of pay, compared with just one hour of overtime worked by women. But even taking the differences in hours and overtime payments into account, women's gross hourly earnings in 1989 still were just 76 percent of average hourly earnings for men (Department of Employment 1989a).

It is the segregation of women into lower-paid and under-valued "women's" jobs and their concentration in the lower grades within occupations that account for the continuing disparity between male and female earnings. The earnings gap between male and female workers is only rarely a result of women and men's being paid different rates for doing the same job. The Equal Pay Act discussed in the next section has largely done away with such overt discrimination in rates of pay.

The fact that so many women work part time is also a reason for women's low pay. In 1989 gross hourly earnings for part-time female workers were just 75 percent of those of full-time female workers (Department of Employment 1989b). Part-time workers are less well protected by employment legislation than full-time workers (see "Flexible Work" below) and are used as a disposable work force to fill in during times of peak demand. Part-time workers therefore are rarely on a promotion ladder and often do not qualify for length-of-service payments or other employee benefits.

Another reason for the low earnings of women working part time is the national insurance gap they fall into. On earnings of less than £52 a week, neither employees nor employers are required to pay national insurance contributions on the employee's earnings. For employers, this means a savings of 10.45 percent of the part-time worker's wage bill. But once earnings exceed £52, contributions are due on the entire amount. This acts as an incentive for employers to hold wages below the national insurance threshold, which has become an effective ceiling on the earnings of many women working part time. About a third of all part-time workers have earnings below the national insurance threshold. A person earning the average part-time hourly wage would breach this threshold after only thirteen hours of work.

The absence of a legal minimum wage in Britain provides further explanation as to why women's earnings are low. Women's work is concentrated in industries that are labor-intensive and dominated by small firms and in which trade unions have made little headway. Of the nearly 10 million workers in Britain who earn less than the Council of Europe's recommended "decency threshold" (68 percent of adult earnings), three-quarters are women. Increasingly, women have been calling for a national statutory minimum wage as a means of achieving greater equality in pay.

Some low-paid workers (around 2.5 million people, mainly women) are covered by industry-wide minimum pay rates set by the Wages Councils, statutory bodies that date from the turn of the century. However, underpayment is widespread and awareness of the legal minimum is low. In 1989, 29.9 percent of establishments visited by the Wages Inspectorate were illegally underpaying their staffs (House of Commons 1990a). Government policy has been to cut such wage protections. Since 1979 the Wages Inspectorate has been reduced by over one-third, leaving just one inspector per 35,000 employees. Other powers of the Wages Councils have been abolished or reduced and the councils are under threat of abolition, despite their potential importance for women's pay.

Sex-Discrimination Legislation

In the 1970s, two major acts were introduced in Parliament to outlaw discrimination at work. The Equal Pay Act of 1970 and the Sex Discrimination Act of 1975 have had a substantial impact on women's status at work. But unless they are amended to overcome weaknesses in the law, both may have reached the limits of their effectiveness.

The Equal Pay Act provided for equal pay for men and women employed by the same employer doing the same or essentially similar work. Its main impact was in forcing employers, particularly in the public sector, to integrate pay scales for men and women in the same or very similar jobs. There is no doubt that this act played an important role in the improvement of women's relative earnings during the 1970s. Women's gross hourly earnings rose from 62 percent of male earnings in 1970 to 71 percent of male earnings in 1979 (MacLennan and Fonda 1985). However, progress stagnated in the 1980s.

The main problem with the Equal Pay Act was that most women did not work alongside men doing the same work, or if they did (as with male nurses) the men were equally poorly paid. A special mini-census of women and employment in 1980 found that 57 percent of all women said that only women did the same sort of work they performed at their workplaces. A further 9 percent either worked alone or were the only people doing a particular type of work for their employer (Martin and Roberts 1984). Without a male comparator in the job, a claim for equal pay was impossible.

Under the Treaty of Rome, which established the European Community, directives agreed on by the Councils of Ministers and the European Parliament or judgments of the European Court have the effect of law in the member states of the European Community. Directives may be issued in order to remove obstacles to the creation of a European economic community "without frontiers," which includes a general power to act against sex discrimination among the member states. Increasingly, domestic courts in the member states are directly enforcing community law in their judgments, although as a last resort there is a right of recourse to the European Court, which was established as a final appeal court for European law.

Thus, in 1984 a ruling by the European Court forced the United Kingdom to amend the Equal Pay Act to include the principle of equal pay for work of equal value. This allows for claims to be made by a woman employed at work deemed to be of equal value to that of a man in terms of the demands it makes in such categories as effort, skill, or decisionmaking.

The equal value amendment revitalized the Equal Pay Act, stimulating a large number of new claims. But the amendment was poorly drafted, making it difficult to interpret and apply. Since its introduction, a series of test cases, although mostly resulting in victories for the claimants, have reached some contradictory interpretations of the law.

It was hoped that the Sex Discrimination Act of 1975 would improve women's prospects of gaining equal pay by breaking down job segregation and discrimination both in and outside of work. The act made it unlawful to discriminate, either directly or indirectly, on the grounds of sex or marital status. It provided for the establishment of the Equal Opportunities Commission to promote women's equality, monitor progress, and help enforce the law. As a result of the act, most forms of overt discrimination in job advertising and recruitment disappeared. In addition, test cases raised public awareness of the discrimination faced by women and broke down many symbolic social barriers they faced.

But the Sex Discrimination Act also is flawed in a number of ways that have limited its impact. Discrimination is extremely difficult to prove, and the burden of proof is on the complainant. There is no requirement under the act for employers or others to undertake positive-action programs. Hence, a 1989 survey found that only one-fifth of private-sector managers considered their companies to have a "coherent policy of commitment to equal opportunities" (Smith 1989). Section 6 of the act exempts all firms employing fewer than six persons, thus excluding substantial numbers of women from coverage. In 1986 nearly a fifth of all jobs in the United Kingdom were in firms employing five or fewer staff members (Bannock and Daly 1990).

The Equal Opportunities Commission, trade unions, and women's organizations have been calling for a further revision of the laws on equal pay and discrimination. They would like to see provision for class actions. At present, the success of one claimant does not set a precedent for other women, who must bring further cases to court. The huge delays before cases are heard by a tribunal—an average of fourteen months—are also a source of concern. The high costs involved mean few women initiate cases without the backing of a trade union or the commission itself. And for many women the Equal Pay Act remains useless, despite the equal value amendment, because no men are working in comparable jobs.

Due largely to the failings of the equal pay and sex discrimination legislation, more and more women are turning to European courts for a remedy in cases of unequal treatment. European Court rulings have been decisive in formulating legal precedent, whereas U.K. legislation has been weak: The United Kingdom has been in court over its equality legislation more often than any other European country. Judgments by the higher courts have applied European law directly when domestic legislation was lacking, thus plugging gaps in British law. A number of directives relating to equal treatment have forced changes on the British government. The European Community will likely continue to be a lever in the United Kingdom, bringing many of the improvements in domestic legislation that women have been demanding.

EDUCATION AND TRAINING

Career choices and opportunities often are determined at a very early age. In Britain girls and boys still tend to make different subject choices in secondary school. In 1985 over 90 percent of pupils studying cooking or domestic subjects were girls. Girls were overrepresented in languages and arts subjects and underrepresented in math, chemistry, computer sciences, physics, and technical drawing. Only around one-fifth of physics pupils, for example, were girls (EOC 1988b). One survey found that some schoolgirls thought women were not allowed to be doctors. Few were prepared to contemplate going into traditional "male" occupations (Weston 1988).

There is evidence that schools and career officers do not always give girls equal chances to learn nontraditional skills. A recent Equal Opportunities Commission study found stark examples of discrimination in girls' access to "male" skills, with girls continuing to be pushed toward needlework and home economics while boys were doing metalwork and woodwork. Single-sex schools (not uncommon in Britain) were the worst offenders; some of these simply did not offer facilities for girls or boys to learn nontraditional skills (EOC 1988a).

The new skills of information technology are an example of how schools may help to prevent girls from achieving in the same way as boys. In 1981, 22.5 percent of new computer science graduates were women. By 1988 this proportion had fallen to below 10 percent. According to a campaigning group run by women working in new technology, the Women into IT Campaign, the reason for this drop was a 1981 government decision that every school should offer training in the use of computers. Once computers were pushed into schools, math departments took over their use and ensured that boys were the main users (Large and Bradbury 1989).

Skills gained at school are particularly important in Great Britain, where 47 percent of all sixteen-year-olds remain in full-time education. Britain is unique among its main competitor nations in its high proportion of sixteen-year-old school dropouts, with 20 percent going into employment, 25 percent going into a training scheme for unemployed young people, and 8 percent simply unemployed. Of the 47 percent who remain in full-time education, only around two-thirds are actually in school (32 percent of all sixteen-year-olds). The rest (15 percent of all sixteen-year-olds) go on to further education colleges to gain specific vocational qualifications (Central Statistical Office 1988).

University or polytechnic degrees are rare among both women and men in Britain. In 1989 just 10 percent of men and 6 percent of women had degree qualifications. Nearly half of all men and women (50 percent of men and 43 percent of women) had secondary school qualifications only, whereas 29 percent of men and 36 percent of women had no formal qualifications (House of Commons 1990b).

Those with higher educational qualifications are likely to do better in the job market than others; women with fewer degrees do less well than men.

Equally important, however, is the type of course undertaken by male and female graduates. Among new first degree university graduates in 1987, 50 percent of men had engineering, medical, or science degrees compared with just over one-quarter of women. In contrast, less than a quarter of the men and nearly half of the women had social science or arts degrees. The same pattern applied to male and female graduates with polytechnic or college degrees and students in further vocational education. Not unexpectedly, these qualifications had an effect on the destination of graduates entering employment after finishing their degrees, with far more men going into professional and scientific jobs than women and more women working in lower-paid social welfare occupations (Tarsh 1989).

For those who leave full-time education, government-sponsored training schemes are the most frequent destination. The Youth Training Scheme (YTS) has been the main source of out-of-school training for young people of both sexes. It has been heavily criticized for sex-stereotyping and even for exaggerating the push into traditional fields of employment. Eighty percent of female YTS trainees work in clerical, retailing, and personal services compared with 75 percent of women in adult employment (Trades Union Congress 1987). A local study in one inner London borough found that 83 percent of female trainees in YTS in 1987 were learning clerical or child care skills, whereas 70 percent of young men were training for mechanical or other manual occupations (Ross 1987).

In Britain, education and training can be a route to higher-paid jobs in nontraditional skills. Some degree courses are opening to women far more than in previous years. But for the majority of young girls and women entering their first jobs, educational courses and training schemes continue to push toward traditional sectors of employment and lower "women's" wages. A greater emphasis is needed in career education on nontraditional skills for both girls and boys, and better enforcement of equal opportunities policies also is needed in schools to ensure that girls are not discouraged from acquiring a broader range of skills.

RECONCILING WORK AND HOME

Flexible Work

A major issue in Britain today is that of provision for flexible work to enable more married women to combine family commitments with paid employment. The government has placed the onus on employers to provide the support and inducements necessary to attract married women into the labor market, arguing that an alternative of universal state support for child care would be far too expensive (Patten 1990). But not all employers have welcomed this responsibility. The Confederation of British Industry has made it clear that government expectations that employers can accommodate the needs of working women without assistance from the state are unrealistic (Brindle 1990).

As the issue remains unresolved of who is to provide—and pay for—the support necessary to meet women's needs, the skills of British women remain an underutilized resource. Of the 6 million women in Britain who choose not to work for pay, one-third have educational qualifications in the form of secondary school achievement tests or higher qualifications that are being wasted while they are not in the labor market. Those who do reenter the work force after a period at home frequently do so at a lower skill level than that of their previous job (Elias and Main 1982). In Britain in the early 1990s, where 62 percent of the work force is described by the European Commission as unskilled—the highest proportion of any European country—the waste of women's skills is a national scandal. In the coming years, under pressure from demographic changes, Britain may face a skills crisis.

Industries that have relied on cheap female labor in the past are the most exposed. Britain's National Health Service is already beginning to face staffing crises due to adverse population trends, as evidenced by a 13 percent drop in recent years in the number of newly qualified nurses (NHS Training Authority 1989). Financial services, which rely heavily on female labor, also are beginning to feel the pitch, particularly as they are located primarily in southeast England where recruitment difficulties are greatest.

As a result of these pressures, industries such as financial services have taken the lead in attempting to accommodate the needs of working women. A number of clearing banks have introduced career break schemes for their staffs. These allow employees to leave work for a period yet to keep in touch with their skills with the guarantee of a job when they return (Industrial Relations Services 1989a).

More flexibility in working hours is also a growing trend. This includes a greater use of flextime, in which employees work a set number of hours per week at times that suit them. Opportunities for part-time work, previously almost exclusively limited to the lowest-paid clerical staff, are being extended to employees in higher grades. Job sharing, whereby one full-time post is split between two part-time workers, also has become more widespread.

As part-time work is extended to more senior-level staff, pressures also are growing for equal treatment for part-time workers. In the financial sector, where one in six employees works part time, a recent survey revealed that employers are approaching complete harmonization of pay and benefits for full- and part-time staff, with pro rata rights for part-time workers (Industrial Relations Services 1989b). Such "single-status" agreements were virtually non-existent only a few years ago.

A growing minority of employers also provide workplace nurseries and other child care subsidies for their staffs. Despite generous tax relief, workplace nursery provision remains rare. For most employers the cost is prohibitive. A cheaper and potentially more popular alternative is to provide child care "checks" or vouchers that can be redeemed toward the cost of a registered baby sitter or day nursery.

But although companies in some sectors have made strides toward meeting the needs of working women, they remain a minority. The majority have not faced up to the implications of demographic trends. One survey has estimated that fewer than 14 percent of British employers have addressed the needs of

mothers returning to work, despite nearly seven years of publicity warning of
the impending labor shortage (Rajan and Van Eupen 1990). Unless the labor
market begins to tighten very perceptibly, many employers are reluctant to
amend old practices.

The main concession by employers to the needs of working women continues to be the opportunity to work part time. Around 45 percent of all employed
women work part time. But opportunities for part-time work are rarely offered
in higher-paid, higher-skilled jobs. Instead, part-time workers are found in
jobs that are subject to peaks and troughs of demand (e.g., cashiers), in which
they form an easily disposable, fill-in work force. This is encouraged by the
fact that part-time workers have fewer employment rights than full-time
workers. Because of hours-of-work qualifications for entitlement (in most
cases requiring sixteen hours or more work a week), 48.4 percent of all women
working part time are not eligible for basic employment rights such as
protection against unfair dismissal and the right to maternity pay and leave
(House of Commons 1988).

Another cheap form of flexibility offered by employers is home work,
particularly in light manufacturing industries where an estimated 59,000 home
workers were employed in 1981 (National Homeworking Unit 1990). Home
workers are notoriously low paid, some earning as little as 50 pence an hour—
about the price of a loaf of bread. Women from all backgrounds do home
work but many of the lowest paid tend to be ethnic minorities, often non-
English speaking. The vast majority are mothers with young children. They
are effectively a hidden work force, often working long hours in unhealthy
conditions—surrounded by fabrics or using toxic glues in confined back rooms
in their homes, which are typically overcrowded and poorly heated. They are
virtually out of the reach of trade unions and the protection of the law.

There are also the new home workers operating from their "back-bedroom
offices" with the aid of a fax and a personal computer. Many of these are self-
employed professionals who, because of the nature of their jobs, have relatively
high earnings and good work conditions. But many others suffer from the
lack of employee status that persons doing similar work in the workplace
enjoy. Like traditional home workers, they are isolated and unorganized, and
they earn less than on-site staff doing the same jobs (Huws 1983).

Finally, there are the domestic workers. Many women reconcile the need
to earn an income with their role as mothers or as carers by doing domestic
work—working as baby sitters, taking in ironing, doing early-morning cleaning, or performing other jobs that enable them to be at home most of the day.
Increasing labor force participation of women also means that demand for
these workers is increasing. A growing division between rich and poor women
is predicted over the next decade as a result. Because the top third of wealthiest
households are two-earner couples, they rely on low-paid domestic labor to
enable them to maintain their incomes.

Care of Dependents

Apart from Portugal, the United Kingdom has less publicly funded child
care for children under five than any other country in the European Com-

munity, with only 2 percent of British toddlers in publicly financed child care (Moss 1988). Facilities for school-age children are even less common than for those under five. For parents of children ages six to fourteen, holiday play schemes provide places for only three children in one thousand. After-school or latchkey schemes have places for just two children per one thousand.

The need for a national child care policy was dismissed by former Prime Minister Margaret Thatcher in a 1990 interview on the BBC radio "Woman's Hour" program. Such a policy, she contended, could lead to a "whole generation of crèche children." She argued that women should stay at home with their children for the first three to four years and that nursery care is "no life for a child. . . . I don't think you can have a child in a nursery all day" (Thatcher 1990). This lack of support for child care is echoed by other government spokespersons.

In 1990 fewer than half the number of places in public nurseries exist in Britain than were found in 1945. The places that do exist are rationed under government guidelines to children in "special need," giving priority to children of single parents who have no option but to work. Increasingly, due to pressures of demand, rationing has narrowed selection down to children "at risk." In 1985 there were just nine public nursery facilities per one thousand children under age five (Cohen 1988). As a result, private nurseries have grown in popularity. Private or voluntary day nurseries now provide more day care facilities than do public nurseries (Greener 1989).

Decisions about public child care provision are left largely to the discretion of local authorities and local education authorities. Hence, levels of provision vary widely throughout Britain. Further, sharp cuts in the revenue support given to local authorities by the Treasury in the 1980s have meant that throughout Britain, day care and nursery care are increasingly in competition with other local services for scarce resources.

For most mothers, choices about child care are severely constrained by the scale and variety of local provisions and the cost of the different options open to them. Public nurseries are free or low cost but are only available to a tiny minority of women. The vast majority of mothers who work rely on the free labor of family members, particularly fathers and grandmothers, for all or part of their child care needs (Cohen 1988).

The rest—around one-third of all working women—pay for child care of one form or another. Many turn to baby sitters (usually women with their own children who look after other children in their own homes). Those who can afford it hire nannies or au pairs, who often live in with the family. Private child care arrangements such as these range in cost from around one-quarter to over 100 percent of average female full-time earnings. Cheaper forms of child care are most in demand.

For many women, the absence of choices concerning child care is a vicious circle. The lack of affordable, full-time care of acceptable quality means that they are forced into low-paid, part-time jobs. A 1979 survey found that nearly one-quarter of mothers who did not return to work following maternity leave gave the lack of affordable child care as the main reason (Cohen 1988). A more recent study estimated that nearly half a million British women do not work for pay or work substantially reduced hours because of lack of child care for preschool-aged children (Metcalf 1989).

But it is not only the care of children that limits the employment opportunities and life-styles of many women. A special census in 1985 found that one in seven adults was providing informal care for an elderly or disabled person and that one in five households included a care giver. Women were slightly more likely to be care givers than men (15 percent compared with 12 percent and also were more likely to carry the main responsibility for providing care (10 percent compared with 6 percent). But the major difference between male and female carers was the impact caring had on the economic activity of the carer. Women who worked part time or who were not employed were more likely to be care givers than women working full time, whereas care giving was unrelated to men's economic status (Green 1988).

Support for care givers in Britain is also poor. The census of carers found that two-thirds received no regular help from health or social services or voluntary groups (Green 1988). The need for support is growing as a result of demographic changes that will mean a nearly 50 percent increase during the next decade in the number of people over eighty-five (EOC 1989).

Government community care policies have flown in the face of this need, increasing pressures on families who already receive inadequate support for the care they provide. *Community care* has meant the phasing out and closure of large hospitals for the mentally ill and the handicapped with little to compensate by way of community-based services. Between 1970 and 1986, nearly 27,000 people left mental illness hospitals. The corresponding increase in day care places was 5,259 and in community homes and hostels it was 4,212 (House of Commons Social Services Committee 1985).

As with day care provision for children, one reason for the lack of support for community care has been the reduction in government revenue support for local authorities. As a result, finance for existing services has had to be met from increases in local taxation—a task made even more difficult as a result of the introduction of the unpopular flat-rate poll tax. Money to pay for new or growing needs was even more scarce. Although the poll tax is due to be abolished in April 1993, it has left a legacy of underfunding for support services for people caring for dependents.

TAXES AND WELFARE BENEFITS AS SOCIAL POLICY

Two areas of policy in Great Britain in which traditional assumptions about the role of women have been most transparent and that are causing the most intractable arguments are those of taxation and the system of welfare benefits.

Taxes

Until recently British income tax was based entirely on the family unit with the presumption of female dependency. Under the aggregation rule, the husband was responsible for filling in the couple's tax return, and their incomes were added together and taxed jointly. Single people and married women had their own personal tax allowance, but married men were given a higher married man's allowance. The rationale for having this special tax allowance was that married men should be assisted by public funds in their task of maintaining their wives.

Until the mid-1970s, similar allowances existed for children, but these were abolished in favor of a universal child benefit for each child that was paid directly to the mother—who in most families is the person who actually spends money on feeding, clothing, and keeping the children. It was generally recognized that a tax allowance given in the husband's pay packet was an inefficient way of targeting support for children. There was no guarantee that husbands would pass the money on, and a higher tax allowance for mothers would miss the target because many women do not pay taxes.

But although child tax allowances were restructured, there was no attempt to reform the subsidy for dependent wives despite the fact that some of these "dependents" were earning more than their husbands. Women were growing increasingly unhappy with the fact that their incomes were added to their husbands' and effectively taxed at his highest marginal rate of tax. They resented the lack of privacy in their financial affairs, which was the result of the aggregation rule. And many resented the privileged tax treatment given to their husbands purely because they were married and male.

As a result of these criticisms, in April 1990 a new system of independent taxation was introduced under which husbands and wives are taxed separately and their incomes are no longer aggregated. However, the notion of female dependency still underlies the new system. The married man's allowance has been replaced by a married couple's allowance of the same value, which is still paid to the husband in the first instance. Only if the husband's income is less than this allowance can any unused portion be transferred to his wife. In practice a married man still pays less tax than his wife, even if both earn the same amount.

The short-lived community charge (more commonly known as the poll tax) also discriminated against married women, although for different reasons. The poll tax was a flat-rate "head" tax introduced by the Conservative government in 1989–1990 to replace property taxes for financing local government. Due to its near-universal unpopularity, the poll tax is due to be replaced by a new system of property taxes in 1993. While it lasted, a married woman was legally required to pay the poll tax in full—even if she had no income of her own—as long as her husband's income was sufficient. In households where household income was not shared, this was a source of considerable grievance.

Welfare Benefits

The system of welfare benefits in Britain also discriminates fundamentally against married women. The postwar architects of the British welfare state designed a two-tier system of benefits for people in and out of work. The top tier, the system of national insurance benefits, consists of benefits for working people based on regular contributions from their weekly wage. These include benefits for unemployment, maternity leave, sickness, industrial injuries, and the basic retirement pension—all of which are paid without a means test. There is also a second-tier system of safety net benefits based not on contributions but on a test of low household income.

A large proportion of women are excluded from entitlement to national insurance benefits due to an inadequate contribution record. Because wives were generally expected to be dependents and therefore covered under dependency additions payable to married men (but not married women) with most national insurance benefits, until 1978 employed married women were not required to pay a full insurance contribution. This meant they had no entitlement to national insurance benefits in their own right. In 1990 around 1.4 million women in Britain continued to pay contributions at a reduced rate, having retained the right they had prior to 1978 to pay a reduced contribution. In addition, nearly half (45 percent) of all women working part time earned too little to pay contributions, which are only due on earnings above a certain threshold (£46 a week in 1990) (House of Commons 1988). Many other women are excluded from entitlement because their contribution record is irregular or patchy—often as a result of doing seasonal, temporary, or casual work.

Because of the household means test required for receipt of income-related benefits for those not covered by the national insurance system, many married women also fall outside this safety net. If her spouse is working, a married woman cannot fall back on means-tested support if she fails to qualify for national insurance benefits. When both members of a couple are out of work, benefits are normally paid to the husband on behalf of his family; a married woman has no independent entitlement.

Despite this, the majority of recipients of means-tested income maintenance benefits in Britain are women. They consist of female pensioners (who greatly outnumber men), single-parent families (nine out of ten of whom are headed by single mothers), young single women, and young widows. Because they are more likely than men to be low paid and less likely to have savings, a decent pension, or access to occupational benefits, women are more likely than men to be forced to turn to the state for support when they become unemployed, retired, widowed, or divorced.

The predominance of women among those dependent on means-tested welfare benefits in Britain is significant. The income provided by these benefits is less, relative to average earnings, than what was deemed to be a subsistence level of income by the National Assistance Board nearly fifty years ago. Benefits are held below a subsistence standard to satisfy the principle of less eligibility—building in work incentives by ensuring that benefits provide an uncomfortable standard of living. Because women are the primary recipients of these means-tested welfare payments, they form the majority of the poor in Britain.

Since 1980, therefore, women have suffered most from the Conservative government's antipathy to the welfare state. Although the overall expenditure on benefit payments has risen with rising unemployment, the value of most benefits has been cut and a variety of benefits have been abolished or restricted to narrowly defined minorities. There have been severe cuts in the value of the basic state pension. Benefits such as the maternity grant have been abolished, and rules for entitlement to maternity leave have been made more difficult for claimants. The structure of means-tested payments has been modified in ways that penalize the most needy claimants. The most important benefit for women, the child benefit, has been sharply reduced in value.

The attack on welfare dependency over the past decade has raised a deep conflict within conservative thinking in relation to the role of women in society. On the one hand, government social security policies have been aimed at forcing women, particularly those who are single parents, to take paid employment or suffer severe impoverishment. New availability-for-work tests have been introduced that require unemployed claimants to show that they would be available at once to take a full-time job if one were offered them. This includes being able to demonstrate that they can make immediate arrangements for the full-time care of any children or other dependents.

On the other hand, the government has resisted demands for state support for child care and other provisions to enable mothers to return to work after childbearing. Maternity rights and employment protections for women in work have been cut. Such policies have been part of the government's noninterventionist laissez-faire economic policy. But images of the traditional family also have been invoked, which suggest that support for working mothers would undermine family life.

State Support and the Labor Market

The demands of the labor market, in which married women are projected to take 90 percent of all new jobs over the next five years, have forced policymakers to reconsider the issue of female dependency. A debate now rages as to whether the tax or benefit system is the best way to provide financial support for working women and indeed, whether any such support should be part of the government's laissez-faire approach.

Tax reliefs are seen by some as the "acceptable" face of state support. Thus, the married couple's allowance has more than maintained its real value through successive Conservative budgets. In contrast, the child benefit has been reduced in value since 1987. A considerable lobby exists that favors a general tax allowance for the costs of child care; some government ministers are among its supporters. An equally strong lobby, primarily among the government's opposition, favors more direct government expenditure on child care and an improvement in the level of the child benefit.

For the moment these issues remain unresolved. Eventually, however, most people feel some concession toward meeting child care needs may emerge, at least in part because of the importance of the women's vote in future general elections.

CONCLUSION

Demographic trends are forcing women's issues to the center of political debate in Great Britain. The thrust of government policies has been to privatize public services, cut public expenditure, and rely on the market to meet demands without intervention from the state. This entire approach is now being challenged as a result of women's needs at a time when the labor market desperately needs women.

Without government intervention to improve women's employment rights, ensure equal opportunities in education and training, and provide the child care and social services needed by women caring for dependents, the majority of British women will not benefit from the increased demand for their labor. A minority of women, the "high flyers," will be assisted through improved company benefits and rising wages for women with rare skills. But most women will continue to reconcile work and family commitments with difficulty. They may pay dearly for expensive forms of private child care. They may accommodate school hours or cheaper part-time care by working part time. Or they may do home work or domestic work, joining a largely low-paid and low-status work force.

If, on the other hand, the political complexion of the government changes— either through a more caring face of conservatism or by a change in government—the outcome for women may be very different. Given the support that is needed for working women, the growing demand for women's labor could bring a substantial improvement in women's status. As employers and politicians realize the implications of society's needs, the coming decade may see more of women's needs answered.

BIBLIOGRAPHY

Allen, Isobel. *Doctors and Their Careers*. London: Policy Studies Institute, 1988.

Bannock, G., and M. Daly. "Size Distribution of U. K. Firms." *Department of Employment Gazette*. London: Her Majesty's Stationery Office, May 1990, 255–258.

Brindle, David. "Women Slow to Reach Top Civil Service Posts." *Financial Times*, February 25, 1988.

———. "Firms Cannot Afford Childcare." *The Guardian*, April 25, 1990.

"BT Women Suffer Widespread Inequality." *Financial Times*, June 28, 1988.

Central Statistical Office. *Social Trends 18*. London: Her Majesty's Stationery Office, 1988.

Cohen, Bronwen. *Caring for Children: Report for the European Commission's Childcare Network*. London: Commission of the European Communities, 1988.

Collinson, David. *Barriers to Fair Selection*. Manchester: Equal Opportunities Commission, 1988.

Department of Employment. *New Earnings Survey Part A*. London: Her Majesty's Stationery Office, 1989a.

———. *New Earnings Survey Part F*. London: Her Majesty's Stationery Office, 1989b.

———. *Employment Gazette*. London: Her Majesty's Stationery Office, April 1990, S11, Table 1.4.

Elias, P., and B. Main. *Women's Working Lives: Evidence from the National Training Survey*. Coventry: Institute for Employment Research, University of Warwick, 1982.

Equal Opportunities Commission. *Sixth Annual Report.* Manchester: Equal Opportunities Commission, 1987.

———. *Access to Craft Subjects in School Curricula and West Glamorgan Primary and Secondary Schools.* Manchester: Equal Opportunities Commission, 1988a.

———. *Women and Men in Britain 1987.* London: Her Majesty's Stationery Office, 1988b.

———. *Press Release.* January 11, 1989.

Green, Hazel. *Informal Careers: Special Report of the General Household Survey 1985.* London: Her Majesty's Stationery Office, 1988.

Greener, Kim. "Day Care of Children." House of Commons Library Research Note no. 443, April 5, 1989.

House of Commons Parliamentary Debates. *Official Report* 139, October 25, 1988, col. 183.

———. *Official Report* 169, March 14, 1990a, cols. 253–254.

———. *Official Report* 169, March 26, 1990b, cols. 71–72.

House of Commons Social Services Committee. *Community Care with Special Reference to Adult Mentally Ill and Handicapped People.* Second Report of the Committee, 1984–1985. London: Her Majesty's Stationery Office, 1985.

Huws, Ursula. *The New Homeworkers.* London: Low Pay Unit, 1983.

Industrial Relations Services. "Career Break Schemes." *IRS Employment Trends 431.* London: Industrial Relations Services, 1989a.

———. *Equal Opportunities Review No. 28.* London: Industrial Relations Services, 1989b.

Large, P., and N. Bradbury. "Skills Crisis in IT as Computers Go Male." *The Guardian,* February 17, 1989.

MacLennan, E., and N. Fonda. "Great Britain." In *Women Workers in Fifteen Countries,* Jenny Farley, ed. Ithaca, N.Y.: Cornell University Press, 1985, 90–111.

Martin, J., and C. Roberts. *Women and Employment: A Lifetime Perspective.* London: Her Majesty's Stationery Office, 1984.

Metcalf, Hilary. "The Under-Utilisation of Women in the Labour Market." *Institute for Manpower Studies Report No. 172.* Brighton: University of Sussex, 1989.

Mitchell, B. R. *British Historical Statistics.* Cambridge: Cambridge University Press, 1988.

Moss, Peter. *Childcare and Equality of Opportunity: Report to the European Commission.* London: Her Majesty's Stationery Office, April 1988.

National Health Service Training Authority. *Equal Opportunities: A Training and Resource Pack.* Bristol: NHS Training Authority, 1989.

National Homeworking Unit. *The National Homeworker.* Birmingham: National Homeworking Unit, Spring 1990.

Office of Population Censuses and Surveys. *Census of Employment 1961.* London: Her Majesty's Stationery Office, 1964.

———. *Census of Employment 1981.* London: Her Majesty's Stationery Office, 1984.

———. *Census of Employment 1987.* London: Her Majesty's Stationery Office, 1990a.

———. *General Household Survey 1987.* London: Her Majesty's Stationery Office, 1990b.

———. *Labour Force Survey 1987.* London: Her Majesty's Stationery Office, 1990c.

Patten, John, MP. House of Commons. *Hansard* 38, July 16, 1990, col. 757.

Rajan, A., and P. Van Eupen. "Good Practices in the Employment of Women Returners." *Institute for Manpower Studies Report No. 183.* Brighton: University of Sussex, 1990.

Ross, Karen. "Training for Equality." *New Society,* November 6, 1987.

Smith, Michael. "Commitment to Equal Pay Policies Lacking." *Financial Times,* January 17, 1989.

Spence, Alan. "Labour Force Outlook to 2001." *Department of Employment Gazette.* London: Her Majesty's Stationery Office, April 1990, 186–198.

Tarsh, Jason. "New Graduate Destinations." *Department of Employment Gazette.* London: Her Majesty's Stationery Office, November 1989, 585.

Thatcher, Margaret, MP. Interview. BBC Radio 4, May 17, 1990.

Trades Union Congress. *The Education and Training of Girls and Women.* London: TUC Publications Department, 1987.

Weston, Celia. "Sex Stereotypes Still Dominate Schoolgirls' Choice of Career." *The Guardian,* October 20, 1988.

"Women and Work." *The Guardian,* January 18, 1989.

10

Central in the Family and Marginal in the Work Force: Women's Place in Japanese Society

ANN CORDILIA

KAZUKO OHTA

When the position of Japanese women in the labor market is examined historically, it is clear that except for women of the highest class, most women in Japan have spent at least part of their lives participating in the productive economy. Yet it is also true that women have not usually derived independent economic power from their labor. Rather, their work, usually on the family farm or in the family business, has been a continuation of their subordinate role in the family.

Among contemporary Japanese women, some continuities with the historical past are evident. Japanese women participate in the economy at a high rate, yet they have not achieved the same degree of economic equality with men as women in other countries at similar levels of development. Young contemporary women expect to work for long periods of their lives but continue to view work as a secondary role for women that must accommodate the needs of husbands and children. Their work options are limited due to the cultural expectations about men's and women's roles, discrimination against women in the workplace, and work structures that conflict with women's family obligations.

This chapter reviews the work situation of women in Japan, examining its links with the past and suggesting possible directions for the future. We first present a historical overview of women's role in the economy and the social, cultural, and legal contexts of women's work. We then examine the contemporary work situation of women, the work status of women in relation to men, and the barriers to women's advancement. We report the findings of a research project that examines work attitudes and career plans of contemporary Japanese college women. Using these research findings, we suggest structural solutions to women's work problems and explore developments in Japan that will affect the future work situation of women.

HISTORICAL OVERVIEW OF WOMEN'S ROLE
IN THE JAPANESE WORK FORCE

In the preindustrial *samurai* households,[1] farm households, and small business households of Japan, all women's work was intimately linked to the family. Housework was considered women's domain and was an area in which women, especially older women, exercised control. The household might be large, consisting of extended family members and workers in the family business. The household budget and the direction of the numerous household activities were overseen by the "head woman," usually the wife of the male head of the family. Younger women—especially new daughters-in-law—had a very low status and often were treated like servants, even though with age they might assume a position of power within the household (Ackroyd 1959; Hane 1982: 79–83).

Housework, however, was not the principal job of most women. Only upper-class women from *samurai* families limited themselves to doing or directing housework. Almost all other women worked throughout their lives either on family farms or in family businesses. In fact, especially for young wives, this was often their main activity—leaving housework and child rearing primarily to the head woman or to be sandwiched in between the farm or business duties that were vital to the family's welfare (Lebra 1981b). Even though their contribution was of central importance to the success of the farm or business, it did not bring women independent control of financial resources. These resources were controlled by the head of the family, usually the senior male.

In some places in Japan, male inheritance was not firmly established, and the family farm or business was left to a daughter who exercised considerable control over economic resources. These arrangements favoring female inheritance were limited to farming and shopkeeping families. The traditional *samurai* family was patriarchal in which first-born males inherited the family property and women were severely restricted in their rights to obtain a divorce, own property, or undertake legal action of any kind (Pharr 1977). This subordinate status was extended to all classes of women by the Meiji Civil Code of 1898, after which date, in theory at least, a woman passed her life under the control of men—first her father, then her husband, and finally her eldest son (Ueno 1987; Lebra 1981a; Dore 1973: 91–120). Thus, during the Meiji restoration in the late nineteenth century, when modern industry began to develop in Japan and new forms of nonfamily labor in factories were introduced, labor practices were developed that assumed the legal subordination of women.

Although most women continued to work on family farms or in family businesses, many young unmarried women were recruited to work in the new factories of the Meiji era. The labor contract was drawn up between the employer and the young woman's parents, who received the bulk of her wages. The young women were treated like "daughters" by the companies: They lived in company dormitories, were heavily restricted in their activities, and had control over only a small part of the money they earned. Their employment was not viewed as a long-term self-supporting arrangement. Rather, factory work was seen as an interlude between completion of school and marriage. Women were generally expected to quit work in their early twenties to marry (Hane 1982: 172–204).

By the late 1930s, the proportion of farms and family businesses in the economy had declined, so fewer men and women were employed within the family based economy (Beasley 1974: 215–218). Increasing numbers of men became "salarymen," working for large corporations in settings separate from the home (Ueno 1987). More women also began to work outside the family farm or small business. Following the pattern begun in the Meiji factories, both working-class and middle-class women worked for wages before marriage and left employment at the time of marriage or childbirth. If they married a salaryman, they confined their work to housekeeping and child rearing.

Although they may have wanted their sons to remain on the family farm, many parents were happy to have their daughters marry a salaryman. The housewife role associated with *samurai* carried high status and freed women from the unrelenting physical labor required by the family farm or, to a lesser extent, by the family small business (Vogel 1963: 30–39).

The post–World War II period brought about radical changes in law, family, and educational structures. The 1947 constitution mandated complete legal equality for women, and the 1947 Labor Standards Law stated that women would be paid equal wages for equal work. In addition, various kinds of protective legislation eased the often oppressive working conditions of women. The effectiveness of the laws that sought to equalize wages for equal work was limited because women seldom did the same work as men. Traditional values limited the kinds of jobs to which women felt they could aspire. In addition, the laws did not change recruitment and personnel practices, which effectively barred women from equal access to jobs (Pharr 1977; Hayashi 1985).

In 1985 the Japanese Equal Employment Opportunity (EEO) Law was passed; this law "prohibits gender discrimination with respect to vocational training, fringe benefits, retirement, and dismissal" and encourages companies to "try to equalize opportunity with regard to recruitment, hiring, job assignment, and promotion" (Edwards 1988: 940). The EEO Law, although it is only a guideline and provides no penalties for companies that violate its provisions, is important because it is aimed at the structural conditions that limit women's access to good jobs. However, like the laws passed during the U.S. occupation following World War II, its passage was influenced by *gaiatsu*, or foreign pressure (Green 1989). The EEO Law was passed at the end of the United Nations Decade for Women, in part as a response to the U.N. call for an end to discrimination against women. Thus, as in the case of earlier laws affecting gender equality, the political commitment to effective enforcement of the law may have been lacking. In a survey of firms by the Ministry of Labor (Japan Institute of Labor 1989a), 80 percent of firms claimed they did not discriminate against women in recruitment and employment. Yet an inspection of newspaper employment ads reveals that sex is often specified as a qualification for particular jobs (Japan Institute of Labor 1989). In addition, such practices as requiring women to quit their jobs when they marry or bear a child are still common (Japan Institute of Labor 1988b).

Postwar changes in family structure also have influenced women's lives and work. Since the end of World War II, the extended family as a living unit has been giving way to the nuclear family, which in 1990 accounted for 60 percent of all Japanese families (Prime Minister's Office 1990: 5). In addition, the relative importance of family farms and small businesses in the economy has continued to decline. Although these developments have freed women to work outside the home, they also have separated young mothers from the older generation, which often had cared for children. This has made motherhood even more of a barrier to outside employment than was true in the past.

The drop in the total fertility rate from 4.11 in 1940 to 1.53 in 1990 (Japan Institute of Labor 1992) combined with the increase in women's longevity has changed the nature of women's life cycle. With a life expectancy of eighty-one years, women can expect to live forty-five years after their youngest child enters elementary school and twenty-eight years after their youngest child is married (Prime Minister's Office 1990: 3–4; Hirota n.d.). Thus, women have a long stretch of time in which the demands of motherhood diminish as a barrier to employment.

The divorce rate has remained quite low at 1.26 per 1,000 population compared with 4.8 per 1,000 in the United States, 3.2 in England, and 3.4 in the USSR (Prime Minister's Office 1990: 48). This combined with a high marriage rate means that most women can expect to live with a male primary breadwinner for most of their lives. Thus, women who need to support themselves either because they remain single or because they are single heads of households are less common in Japan than in other industrialized countries.

Perhaps the most striking change in postwar Japan has been its transformation from a defeated and impoverished nation into a dynamic and wealthy country. Japanese families have an increased discretionary income to spend, and one of the ways in which they have spent it is on their daughters' education. Ninety-five percent of girls (93 percent of boys) enter the educationally demanding senior high school, and 37 percent of females (36 percent of males) go on to higher education. Of these, 40 percent of females and 94 percent of males attend four-year universities, and 60 percent of females go to junior colleges (Prime Minister's Office 1990: 9–10). As a result, the educational level of Japanese women is one of the highest in the world.

CONTEMPORARY WORK SITUATION OF WOMEN

The extreme sexual division of labor in the salaryman family began to erode seriously in the 1960s and 1970s, when the number of women in the nonfamily work force increased strikingly (Ministry of Foreign Affairs 1987; Japan Institute of Labor 1986). This happened simultaneously with a decrease in the number of women who served as unpaid family enterprise workers on the family farm or in its small business. In 1960 employees, who comprised 41 percent of the female work force, were slightly outnumbered by family enterprise workers. By 1970, 55 percent of women workers were employees, whereas the percent of family workers had dropped to 31. By 1980 only 23 percent were family enterprise workers and 63 percent were employees (Fujii 1983; Japan Institute of Labor 1986). Because the number of family based workers declined and increasing numbers of fifteen to nineteen-year-olds chose to attend school rather than enter the work force, the overall labor force participation rate (including employees, the self-employed, and family enterprise workers) of both men and women fell slightly during this period. The women's rate went from 55 percent in 1960 to a low of 46 percent in 1975, then rose to 49 percent in 1988 (Japan Institute of Labor 1986; Prime Minister's Office 1990). This overall rate of labor force participation is comparable to that of women in other advanced industrialized countries. However, the pattern of employment is distinctive in that a large proportion of Japanese women—about 20 percent—are employed as unpaid family enterprise workers (Brinton 1989: 550–551).

The declining labor force participation of 15–19-year-old women was partly offset by the growing number of married women who joined the young unmarried women already working in large numbers in the nonfamily labor force. The percentage of married female employees increased from 39 percent in 1965 to 59 percent in 1987 (Ministry of Labor 1988). In 1980, 26 percent of married women were employed in the nonfamily labor force (Preston and Kono 1988: 279). Women's total labor force participation (including employees, self-employed women, and family enterprise workers) by age forms an "M curve" that has twin peaks at ages 20–24 and 40–49 and is lower between ages 25 and 34 when children are being raised (see Figure 10.1). This reflects the fact that many women work full time before marriage or childbirth, remain outside the labor force when their children are young, and later return to the labor force to help defray the costs of housing and children's education.

The growth of the part-time labor force is another significant development (Prime Minister's Office 1990: 52). Between 1960 and 1987, the number of part-time workers increased from 6.3 percent to 11.6 percent of the total labor force and from 8.9 percent to 23.1 percent of the female labor force (Ministry of Labor 1988). In 1990 females accounted for 72 percent of all part-time employees in nonagricultural industries (Prime Minister's Office 1990: 52). The vast majority of female part-time workers are housewives. Although married women comprise only 59 percent of all female employees, they make up 86 percent of female part-time workers. These workers are also older. Seventy-eight percent of female part-time workers are over thirty-five, compared with 60 percent of all female workers (Japan Institute of Labor 1986). Part-time workers are employed almost exclusively in wholesale and retail trade, in eating and drinking establishments, and in manufacturing. They tend to work for small enterprises. In 1982, 52 percent were in firms with less than thirty employees.

FIGURE 10.1 Women's Work Force Participation by Age, 1989

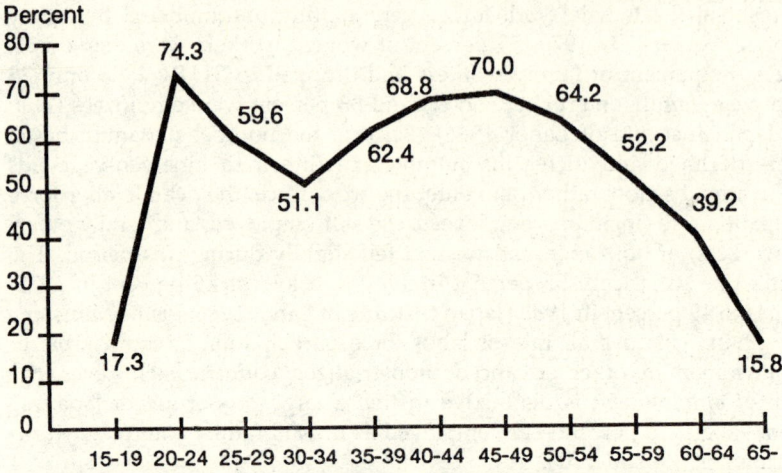

Source: Ministry of Labor, *Fujin rodo no jitsujo* (Facts on the Female Labor Force) (Tokyo: Ministry of Labor, 1990); Foreign Press Center, *Facts and Figures of Japan*, 1991.

Status of Women at Work

Although the overall work force participation of Japanese women is high, Japanese women are far from having equality in the types of work they do. Compared with men, they are underrepresented in management and the professions and overrepresented in clerical positions. Disproportionately few women are in career-track jobs in large companies, whereas disproportionately many are temporary workers, part-time workers, and workers in small companies.

Women are severely underrepresented in the professions, except for nursing, social work, and teaching. Even in teaching they are a minority, except at the kindergarten and elementary school levels. Only about 18 percent of senior high school teachers are women, and they most often teach girls' physical education and home economics. At the university level, only 9 percent of professors are women (Dorfman 1987: 15).

Women also are poorly represented in management positions in both the public and the private sectors. Compared with the United States, where 10 percent of males and 5 percent of females are classified as managers or officials of firms or government agencies, in Japan 7 percent of males and only 0.8 percent of females are so classified (Brinton 1988: 311).

Women managers in Japan are found most often in small and medium-sized corporations—that is, in companies with fewer than one thousand employees. Women who head companies most often come into their positions by succeeding their fathers or husbands in the family business (Green 1989:

24). Women run nearly 2.5 million nonagricultural businesses, the majority of which have fewer than five employees (Steinhoff and Tanaka 1988: 113). About 25,500 women serve as presidents of companies with five or more employees.

Women are poorly represented in management positions in the public sector. In the national government, only 0.7 percent of section chiefs (*kacho*) and only 0.8 percent of department heads (*bucho*) are women. Although this representation is small, it is about twice that of women managers in large corporations, where women are least able to attain managerial status (Steinhoff and Tanaka 1988: 112). Occasionally, women supervise groups of other women, but they are almost totally absent from the ranks of the generalist executives of large companies.

The most common occupations of women employees in Japan are clerical work and skilled and production-process work. Thirty-three percent of employed women are engaged in clerical work, accounting for 52 percent of all clerical workers. Twenty-one percent of employed women are in skilled and production-process work, representing 27 percent of all workers in this category (Japan Institute of Labor 1986; Prime Minister's Office 1990). Women hired to work for large companies are mainly clerical workers or blue-collar production-process workers. These female clerical workers often are relegated to the decorative role of "office flower" in which they function as *ochakumi*—that is, as tea servers and photocopiers. Some "office ladies" (OLs) do more challenging work such as translation, designing newsletters, or answering correspondence; even so, they are barred from promotion to managerial levels (Lo 1990; Rohlen 1979). Like female managers, female clerical and production-process workers are more likely to be found in the small and medium-sized manufacturing, retail, and service businesses, which pay less and offer fewer benefits than the large companies (Brinton 1989; Cook and Hayashi 1980).

Finally, Japanese women are disproportionately represented in the ranks of unpaid family enterprise workers. Twenty percent of Japanese women who work are family enterprise workers compared with 2.8 percent of Japanese men (Brinton 1989: 251).

These differences in the occupational distribution by sex translate into a large wage gap between men and women. The disparity between male and female wages in Japan is greater than that of other advanced industrial countries, although the gap has narrowed somewhat over the last two decades (see Table 10.1). In 1970 the hourly wage index for women was 56.1 percent that of men; in 1986 that index had only risen to 60.5 percent (Ministry of Labor 1988). This disparity in wages remains even when age and years of service are controlled (see Figure 10.2). Young male and female workers receive similar hourly pay, but whereas the wage curve for men rises steeply until age forty-five, the wage curve of female full-time workers flattens at about age thirty. Older female part-time workers experience no wage advantage over younger workers.

Part of the wage disparity between male and female full-time workers may be accounted for by the fact that many women leave work for a period of time

TABLE 10.1   Hourly Wage Index for Females, Nonagricultural Sector[a]

	1970	1980	1986
Australia	73.9	93.5	91.9
France	86.9	87.4	88.5
Denmark	72.4	84.5	82.3
Belgium	66.7	69.4	74.4
West Germany	69.2	72.4	73.1
United Kingdom	60.1	69.7	69.5
United States	62.3	63.4	68.2
Japan	56.1	58.9	60.5

[a]Male Wage Index = 100.

Source: Ministry of Labor, *Fujin rodo no jitsujo   (Facts on the Female Labor Force)* (Tokyo: Ministry of Labor, 1988).

to raise a family and thus accumulate fewer years of service than men. However, even when years of service are controlled, a consistent wage disparity that increases with longer service continues to exist (Figure 10.2). Beginning female part-time workers earn less than full-time workers and show very little increase in wages with years of service.

Barriers to Women's Advancement in the Japanese Employment System

Cultural and structural factors interweave to form a barrier to women's advancement at work. The traditional conception of the centrality of the family to women's role affects women's attitudes toward their own career plans and is at the root of many discriminatory attitudes and practices in the workplace. These attitudes and values interact with a work structure that even when it does not discriminate against women, is a barrier to their career advancement because it is designed to fit the lives of men and is in conflict with the lives of most wives and mothers. The two main structural barriers women face are the lifetime employment system and the demanding nature of better jobs in Japan.

Working on a career track in a large corporation is one of the most rewarding kinds of employment in terms of pay, prestige, and security. Large companies hire workers right out of school into both the white-collar and blue-collar career tracks. These employees become part of the lifetime employment system. The company invests heavily in their training, particularly for white-collar work. They have a high level of job security, receive generous benefits, and are eligible for promotions and pay raises largely on the basis of seniority (Crawcour 1978). The system is based on the premise that both the company and the employee make a long-term commitment to each other.

About 30 percent of newly graduated men and women are hired by large companies. Of these, 71 percent of the men but only 23 percent of the women enter the career track. The majority of women are hired for clerical positions, most of which require minimal training, do not include potential for promotion, and are not included in the lifetime employment system (Brinton 1989).

FIGURE 10.2   Wage System for Male and Female Full-Time and Part-Time Workers by Age and Years of Service

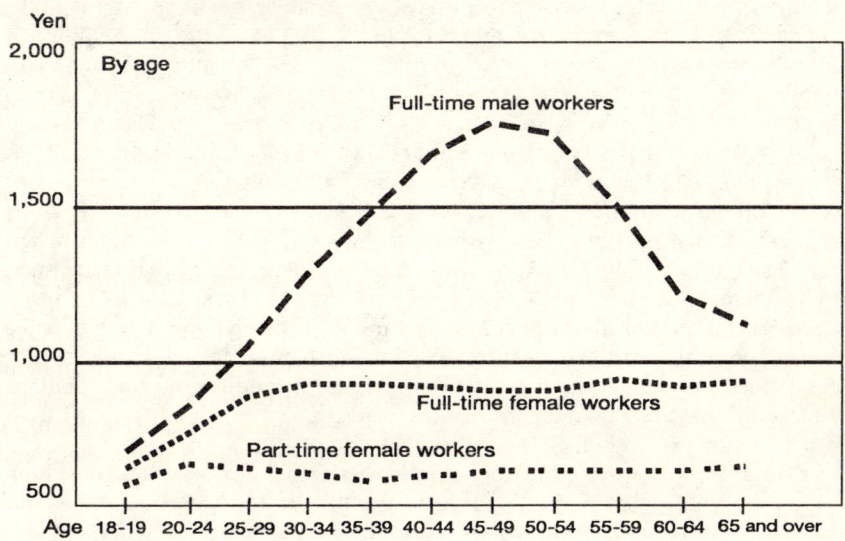

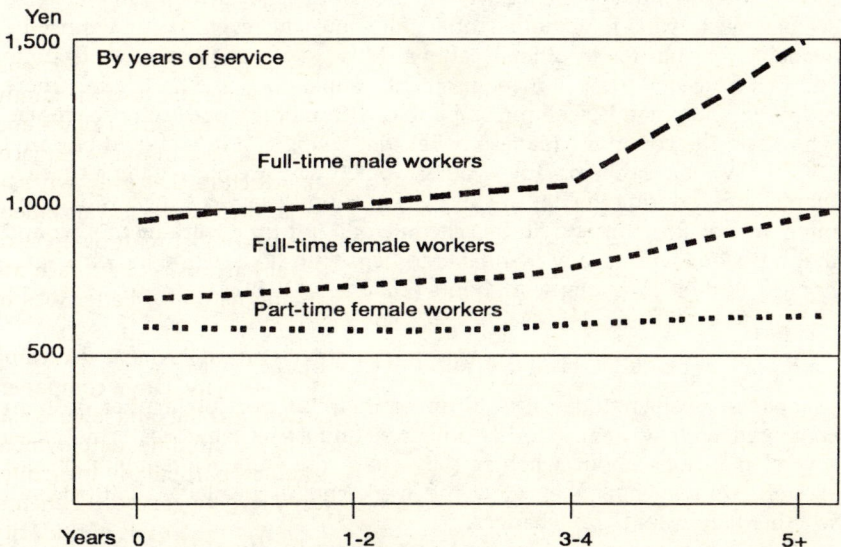

Note: Hourly wages for full-time workers were calculated by dividing monthly scheduled earnings by monthly scheduled actual working hours.

Source: Ministry of Labor, *Basic Statistics Survey on Wage Structure* (Tokyo: Ministry of Labor, 1987); Japan Labor Bulletin 28, no. 9 (1989).

The companies' justification for this is that women will quit in a few years to marry, and thus they will not work long enough to reimburse the company for the lengthy and expensive training it gives career-track employees (Takeuchi 1982). In fact, most women do expect to quit at marriage or childbirth to fulfill their family obligations (Lo 1990: 103; Japan Institute of Labor 1990; Bando 1986). But it also is true that many companies give women little choice. Even women who want to continue to work are pressured into what is termed "early retirement" (Lo 1990; Steinhoff and Tanaka 1988). The companies then replace the "retirees" with younger women at entry-level pay.

A work structure that is not designed to fit the work commitment rhythms of most women prevents these women from entering the career track when they leave school. The structure also makes it almost impossible for women to be hired on a career track when they reenter the work force following a child-rearing period. Because companies prefer to hire young new graduates for career-track positions, reentry women most often take jobs in smaller companies—often as part-time workers where regardless of their skill or education, they may be relegated to low-paid, insecure, menial work with no provision for promotion.

Even if women were more able to enter better-paid career-track jobs, they would be confronted with the incompatibility of the inflexible time and mobility requirements of these jobs with the heavy demands of wifehood and motherhood. White-collar employees in the national government and business sectors must work long hours, often late into the evening, and must be available for transfer to other locations. Most wives and mothers of young children consider these job requirements impossible to fulfill. Even more ordinary job demands seem incompatible with motherhood to those women who share the common Japanese belief that young children should be cared for only by their mothers. Other young women who are more willing to leave their children during the day are aware that support services such as day care often are not structured to fit the schedule of a full-time working mother and that husbands will usually be unable to help with housework and child care because of their own long work hours (Takahashi 1989).

THROUGH THE EYES OF COLLEGE WOMEN

Japanese women today are aware of their inferior job market position compared with women in other advanced industrial countries. This raises several questions about whether they share the same work ambitions as Western women, how they view the work choices available to them, and whether they want to see changes.

To examine these questions, I (Ann Cordilia) conducted a study of work attitudes and goals of Japanese female college students as part of a broader study of college life in Japan (Cordilia 1989a, 1989b). About 37 percent of Japanese women go to college. Like noncollege women, they tend to work before marriage; they are less likely to work when they have small children but are likely to return to the labor market as their children grow up (Edwards 1988; Japan Institute of Labor 1990).

Work attitudes of college students are interesting to study for several reasons. Because of the importance of a person's first job within the Japanese employment system, work plans upon graduation from college play a central role in shaping a person's career. As Mary Brinton (1988: 316) points out, "Low interfirm mobility, seniority-based wage and promotion systems, and firm-specific training in Japan combine to make an individual's first job crucial in terms of getting on a successful career track." College women also are interesting because they are in an anomolous position: They have high educational qualifications that fit them for careers, yet they will probably achieve only a marginal position in the work force.

Between 1988 and 1990 I interviewed thirty-five male and eighty female college and junior college students from twenty-one schools in eight cities in Japan. In the course of the study, I asked first-, second-, third-, and fourth-year women about their attitudes toward work and followed them through the job-hunting process in their senior year. I was particularly interested to learn about job opportunities available to them, the barriers that stood in their way, and how they attempted to come to terms with the available choices.

The Majority Response: Centrality of the Motherhood Role and Limited Career Aspirations

In the interviews I found distinct echoes of Susan Pharr's (1976) study of young women in the 1970s. Pharr categorized Japanese women as *neotraditionalists* who choose to focus their lives almost completely on the wife-mother role, *modern women* who view the domestic role as central but who want to be active in other spheres as well, and *radical egalitarians* who reject traditional sex roles. Like the women in Pharr's sample, the majority of the college students I interviewed are modern women who are committed to the centrality of the mother role in their own lives and yet also wish to have other roles, particularly in the work force.

College women sometimes recalled that in high school they had fantasies about pursuing an exciting career in addition to having a family. In most college settings, however, these ideas find little support. *Sempai* (older students and graduates), who have recently married or made some compromises in their own dreams, tell *kohai* (younger students) that it is unrealistic to think of combining career and motherhood. A university student described the changes in her thinking as follows.

> As a sophomore, I thought I wouldn't quit my job when I married, but now I am not so sure. My friends who have worked and are married tell me that I think in theories, not in reality. My male friends say I will be a good wife and wise mother (*ryosai kenbo*) and that I will change my mind about working. I still think I am right, but my friends know me well so they might be right also. . . . I think it is hard to work and be a *ryosai kenbo*, but if I try hard perhaps I can do both. But sometimes when one tries to do two important things, one ends up doing both badly, so I don't know (junior, city of Nagoya).

In college, career ambitions begin to seem somewhat unrealistic, whereas choosing motherhood and modifying career goals become marks of maturity. Students are increasingly convinced of the rewards of motherhood, the danger of jeopardizing their chances for a successful family through their career choice, and the loneliness and lesser social acceptance that accompany the single state. Most commonly, by the time female college students enter the job market, motherhood has become their central goal and any job they take must accommodate its demands.

Although a career is not the primary goal of most college women, they do not lack career ambition. They seldom want to do the same kinds of work as men because they realize the difficulty of combining a Japanese-style "man's job" with raising a family, but they want to do interesting work—work that will enable them to use their education. Early in the recruitment process, women become aware of some of the difficulties they will face in achieving this goal. They are confronted with the fact that companies do not take women candidates as seriously as men. Companies recruit men actively and early in the year, while waiting for women to apply. As one woman said, "As for men, companies approach them directly and ask them to come to the company, but for women, we have to search for the jobs ourselves. . . . Companies choose boys first, and after that they choose girls who have connections, and after that they choose girls with no connections" (University senior, city of Osaka). In addition, extraneous factors, such as whether the candidate has a connection with the company or whether she lives with her parents, have much more bearing on the success of a woman's candidacy than a man's.

Although all women operate under some handicap, the options open to individual women are closely related to the institution from which they graduate. Graduates of the most prestigious universities have the widest range of possibilities and the greatest likelihood of finding challenging work. Women from other universities are in a more ambiguous position. They are eligible to take the difficult exams for teaching and government posts, and they have some chance of finding challenging work within companies. Yet most compete with junior college graduates, whom the companies often prefer for routine jobs—ostensibly because they will work longer than the university graduates, who are two years older and likely to marry sooner. Although they may be hired more quickly, junior college graduates more often are limited to *ochakumi* positions.

Whatever their particular work options, a major problem faced by all job-hunting women is having to make crucial job decisions without enough experience to know their needs and desires or enough information about the job they will be entering. One manifestation of this problem confronts women who want to work in the career-track managerial jobs *(sogo shoku)* certain progressive companies—such as NEC, Fujitsu, and IBM Japan—set aside for women. These companies invest heavily in the training of a small number of female executives and give them the same work and promotions as men as well as the same long hours and types of transfers.

A few interviewees, all from leading universities, thought seriously about taking the examination to enter this track, but all had grave reservations about the wisdom of such a choice. At twenty-two, such a fast-track job seems exciting, but a twenty-two-year-old cannot predict how she will feel at twenty-five or so when she might want to marry and have a family. At that point, she may have difficulty finding a man who will accept a wife on the fast track and may simultaneously experience pressure not to quit her job because of the obligation she feels to the company for the large investment it has made in her training. Quitting would jeopardize the status of the other female executives and of future graduates of her university who might apply for jobs in the company.

According to one university senior,

The *sogo shoku* course is very difficult for university students. If they already have a prospect for marriage and they know the way of thinking of their [future] husband, it's OK. But many girls meet their husbands after they enter the company and many husbands want them to quit their jobs. . . . So to take the *sogo shoku* track is something of a risk, an adventure. A woman might find it hard to quit. The company spends a lot of money training her. The "OL" course is short. One or two years later, the "OL" earns money for the company. But the *sogo shoku* woman does not. The company lets only a few women in *sogo shoku*, so the damage is very great if one woman quits. Japanese women cannot resist the company, so they must meet a man who will agree to let them work. If I were in the *sogo shoku* course, I would feel that I had an obligation to the company and I could not quit. So to enter the course is a big decision (senior, city of Nagoya).

Given their uncertainty about how they will feel in a few years and the sense of the irrevocability of a decision to enter the fast track, most college women reject such a career. They simply do not know themselves or the world well enough to risk so momentous a decision at such an early age.

Lack of information about the type of work they will be assigned is another way in which women are handicapped in the job choices they must make. For example, a woman may hope to work on a "specialist" track that does not have the long hours or the mandatory transfers of the male career track but that trains her to do responsible work and may offer the possibility of promotion. Recruits, however, are not usually hired to fill a specific job. Rather, they enter the company after which they may be assigned to any number of different tasks. Women from the best universities may be assured by prospective employers that they will be assigned to a particular type of important work. But even graduates of good universities of the second rank often find it difficult to ascertain the kind of work they will be assigned to do, which is not revealed until they actually begin work. When asked whether she would be assigned to the same work as the men in her section, a newly hired university senior revealed her uncertainty.

I'm not sure. In most companies, we don't know what kind of position we are going to get. We will find out in April. There are more women in my section than men but most of the girls seem to be "OLs." I was asked in the interview, "Would you mind serving tea to co-workers." I said, "No." I had to give the "good girl" answer. . . . If a boy applied for this job, he would be given important work sooner than a girl. But I think girls can also do important work (senior, city of Nagoya).

Men are not told exactly what kind of work they will do either, but if they are hired on the executive track, they can predict that they will be rotated to learn a variety of jobs in the company. For women the situation is far more variable and making a prediction is more difficult.

Lack of information also hinders a woman's efforts to find a company in which she will not be required to "retire" in her twenties. Although most women say they will voluntarily quit at childbirth, they do not want to leave as early as some companies require, and they want to reserve the option to continue.

Schools, national and local governments, and some large well-known companies (such as Ricoh and Saison Group) do not make women quit as they grow older, but jobs in these organizations are few and difficult to obtain. Other big companies, such as Toyota or Brother, are widely known for their conservative policies. The policy of most big companies, although generally quite conservative, is not clearly spelled out because having an official "early retirement" policy violates the Equal Employment Opportunity Law. Yet college students have heard from *sempai* about the subtle pressures to which marriage-age women are subjected in order to induce them to quit. In the words of a university junior,

I don't know if it's legal or illegal, but many companies [require early retirement]. The boss does not directly tell a person to leave, but he creates a certain kind of atmosphere. He may give important work to a new young girl and not to the older woman. My friend says that if a lady does not get married and continues to work, the boss will introduce her to some boy. Her boss [did that to her. He said,] "How about this boy? I think this man is very suitable for you." Gradually my friend felt that she could not stay with that company, and she quit without any prospect of marriage. Originally, she was with a good company, but now she is with a small company. There are many cases like that (junior, city of Tokyo).

Students try to find out about retirement policies by asking company recruiters. A recruiter will usually state that his company permits women to continue working. If he adds that most women quit when they marry, the student can assume that this reflects company policy. Other recruiters give no such obvious cues. A newly hired university senior says,

In my company, there are some women in their thirties and forties, so I don't know if I will feel the pressure [to retire early]. In the interviews I asked, "Can I work after marriage?" All the companies say the same thing: "If you want, you can work." But I'm not sure. Do you understand *honne* [real feelings] and *tatemae* [the image presented to others]? Some companies really don't want us to quit our jobs, but other companies may want us to in reality, but they can't say this openly since there are laws against this. So they can't say, "Please quit after you marry and have children." But some companies do feel that way (senior, city of Kyoto).

Another difficult problem concerns the issue of returning to work after taking time off for child rearing. Given the difficulty of getting a good job at a later age, it is highly advantageous that a woman be permitted to return to her old company. Public schools, national and local governments, and some companies (such as Seibu and Ricoh) solve this dilemma by allowing employees to take lengthy childbirth leave. The problem is that either the competition to get these jobs is great or there is some handicap attached to them. For example, many married women will not work for department stores, which often are generous about childbirth leave but which require employees to work on Sunday—the traditional family day husbands spend with their wives and children.

If they cannot take childbirth leave, most interviewees plan to quit upon the birth of their child and to reenter the job market later. They acknowledge that they will probably be unable to compete for a job in the large prestigious companies that hire many new female graduates. Instead they will be relegated to smaller companies and even there, their opportunities will be limited. Some women say they will take any part-time employment, even working as a cashier in a supermarket. Others hope to develop a special qualification, such as computer or English translation skills, that might make them employable in a more flexible sector of the job market.

Because most good jobs in Japan must be entered soon after graduation from college, women are handicapped in taking advantage of even the limited career options available to them. Choices must be made between work and family. Because they have had little actual experience with work or motherhood, they have difficulty knowing what will be satisfying for them. Male students also are required to make early career decisions, but the choices for them are less conflicted and the paths more clearly laid out. In contrast, for women, pursuing work goals involves forging a new path, which is difficult to do without experience. The difficulty of getting accurate information from companies about the nature of jobs and employment practices only compounds the confusion.

Minority Response: Determination to Have a Career

A minority of women, about 10 percent of my sample, consider a career as at least equally important as a family and strongly desire to work at a career without interruption for the rest of their lives. When these women think through the issues they will have to face in order to pursue a career, they focus on the potential conflict between work and family. Some women plan to construct a family situation that will be compatible with a career, and others consider foregoing marriage and children for the sake of work.

Career-oriented college women often say that their ability to hold a job will be shaped by their family situation and that they must consciously plan their families in order to make a career possible. A career woman must choose a husband who will accept her job and be willing to contribute at least minimally to child care and housework. In addition, the husband must have the kind of career that will allow his wife to keep her job—that is, he cannot work excessively long hours or be required to transfer to another city. One college student stated that she was determined to marry a local government employee; she had not met him yet but had decided that that kind of job, with its shorter hours and stable location, would be compatible with a working wife. Other women plan for their mothers to care for their children—a very common pattern for working mothers—or hope to marry an eldest son and thus to live, according to custom, with the husband's family so that her mother-in-law can care for the children.

When women plan to enter fast-track careers such as the *sogo shoku* of a large corporation, their fears about the incompatibility of marriage and career are compounded. They share with the less career-oriented women the worry that they are making a somewhat irrevocable decision at a young age that may threaten their chances of having a family. Some respond by concluding that there is a basic incompatibility between marriage and family, so they decide to remain single. In doing this, they are following the lead of contemporary women in corporate management, about half of whom are single (Steinhoff and Tanaka 1988: 114–115). However, in Japan there is minimal cultural support for such a choice. These women fear that as they reach their mid-twenties, they will experience strong pressure to marry. They worry that they will be lonely in later life, and some are uncertain that they will be able to adhere to their resolve to remain single. Some point to models of single women teachers or friends who have good jobs and seem to live satisfactory lives; these models enable them to hope that they can do the same.

STRUCTURAL SOLUTIONS FOR THE WORK PROBLEMS OF JAPANESE WOMEN

In considering how to view Japanese women's work situation, it is tempting to apply the models of women's liberation with which we are most familiar. This may require that we disregard much of what Japanese women tell us and impute a kind of "false consciousness" to their perceptions of their situation. An alternative approach is to start with how the women themselves define their situation and what they say about their own work goals. Most Japanese college women say that they aspire to have both family and work, that their primary goal is motherhood, and that they want work that is compatible with the pursuit of their family goals. These ideas are not limited to college women but are expressed widely throughout the female population (Lo 1990: 103; *Asahi Shinbum* 1989: 14; Bando 1986). A minority of women (about 10 percent of my sample) rank career as central to their lives and intend to shape the rest of their lives to accommodate its requirements.

The Equal Employment Opportunity Law speaks mainly to the needs of this minority of women because its aim is to promote equal access for women to the male career world. By outlawing the early retirement policy and slightly increasing maternity leave benefits, it does address some issues of importance to the majority of women, but it fails to confront the most central issue for women attempting to combine work and family—the very nature of jobs in Japan. As long as career-track jobs are structured so that employees must work very long hours and be subject to mandatory transfers, they will be inappropriate for most wives and mothers regardless of maternity leave policy and availability of day care. As long as the lifetime employment system rewards an employee for choosing a company early in life and staying with it without any break in one's career, women will be seriously handicapped. This system fits with men's lives, which are organized around career, but is incompatible with the lives of women who have family responsibilities that compete with their career commitment.

How likely is it that labor practices will change to accommodate the needs of women? The present marginal condition of the female labor force has advantages for Japanese companies (Carney and O'Kelly 1987). "Office ladies" who work for a short period of time and part-time workers who have no job security provide a cushion of low-paid employees whose high attrition rates help companies adjust the size of their work forces during times of economic downturn. Thus, companies have a stake in resisting change in personnel practices that would allow women to be integrated in large numbers into the regular work force.

Nonetheless, there are promising areas of change for women in the more flexible segments of the economy. Specialist-track jobs, described as a compromise between noncareer jobs and *sogo shoku*, are being developed, especially in computer-related fields. These career-track jobs do not have the same promotion and pay as the regular executive positions. However, they are more flexible in their demands, require only forty hours of work per week, and do not require a willingness to transfer work locations. An increase in the number of such jobs would allow many more women to remain in the labor market. Job structures more suited to women's needs also are likely to develop in the service sector and in smaller companies, which find it difficult to attract qualified male employees. These areas are already somewhat more flexible in ways that benefit women. Most public schools, for example, do not limit themselves to hiring new graduates and are willing to employ "older" people in their late twenties or early thirties.

It is unquestionably true that women will continue to play a substantial role in the Japanese labor force. With a longer life span and fewer children, the average woman can expect to have thirty adult years in which she is not actively raising a family. At the same time, due to the low birthrate, there will be a smaller number of young men to fill jobs in companies and a rapidly growing nonworking older population for the country to support. These changes will increase the importance of women's contribution to the work force. The question is not whether women will continue to participate in the labor market; rather, it is whether women will continue to be ghettoized in low-paid, menial, and insecure work or whether work will be redesigned to allow women more access to responsible, secure, and well-paid jobs in one of the world's richest economies.

NOTES

1. *Samurai* refers to the military caste that was the highest-ranking caste in feudal Japan until it was stripped of its privileges in the late nineteenth century during the Meiji Restoration.

BIBLIOGRAPHY

Ackroyd, Joyce. "Women in Feudal Japan." *Transactions of Asiatic Society of Japan* 7 (1959): 31–68.

Asahi Shinbum Newspaper. "The Consciousness of Working Women in Japan." May 23, 1989, 14.

Bando, Mariko Sugahara. "When Women Change Jobs." *Japan Quarterly* 33, no. 2 (1986): 177–182.

Beasley, W. G. *The Modern History of Japan.* New York: Praeger, 1974.

Brinton, Mary. "The Social Institutional Bases of Gender Stratification: Japan as an Illustrative Case." *American Journal of Sociology* 94, no. 2 (1988): 300–334.

_____ . "Gender Stratification in Contemporary Urban Japan." *American Sociological Review* 54 (1989): 549–564.

Carney, Larry S., and Charlotte S. O'Kelly. "Women's Work and Women's Place in the Japanese Economic Miracle." Paper presented at the American Sociological Association Annual Meeting, Chicago, 1987.

Cook, Alice, and Hiroko Hayashi. *Working Women in Japan.* Ithaca, N.Y.: Cornell University Press, 1980.

Cordilia, Ann. "Hopes and Dreams: Career Aspirations Among College Women in Japan." Paper presented at the American Sociological Association Annual Meeting, San Francisco, 1989a.

_____ . "College: Its Relation to High School and Employment Requirements in Japan and the United States." *Nanzan Journal of American Studies* 11 (1989b): 10–22.

Crawcour, Sidney. "The Japanese Employment System." *Journal of Japanese Studies* 4, no. 2 (1978): 225–245.

Dore, R. P. *City Life in Japan.* Berkeley: University of California Press, 1973.

Dorfman, Cynthia, ed. *Japanese Education Today.* Washington, D.C.: U.S. Government Printing Office, 1987.

Edwards, Linda. "Equal Opportunity in Japan: A View from the West." *Industrial and Labor Relations Review* 41, no. 2 (1988): 240–250.

Foreign Press Center. *Facts and Figures of Japan.* Tokyo: Foreign Press Center, 1991, 56.

Fujii, Toshiko. "Women Workers Today." *Kodansha Encyclopedia of Japan.* Tokyo: Kodansha, 1983.

Green, Gretchen. "Women in Japan's Labor Force." *Journal of the ACCI* 10 (1989): 21–28, 92.

Hane, Mikiso. *Peasants, Rebels and Outcastes.* New York: Pantheon Books, 1982.

Hayashi, Hiroko. "Japan." In *Women Workers in Fifteen Countries*, Jennie Farley, ed. Ithaca, N.Y.: ILR Press, 1985, 57–67.

Hirota, Hisako. "Japanese Women Today." *Facts About Japan Series.* Tokyo: International Society for Educational Information, n.d.

Japan Institute of Labor. "Problems of Working Women." *Japanese Industrial Relations Series.* Tokyo: Japan Institute of Labor, 1986.

_____ . "Trends and Issues Regarding Working Women." *Japan Labor Bulletin* 27, no. 1 (1988a): 2.

_____ . "Violations of Equal Opportunity Law Most Clearly Observable in Retirement and Dismissal." *Japan Labor Bulletin* 27, no. 7 (1988b): 2.

_____ . "Survey on How Equal Employment Opportunity Law Has Taken Root." *Japan Labor Bulletin* 28, no. 8 (1989a): 2.

_____ . "Wage System for Female Part-Time Workers." *Japan Labor Bulletin* 28, no. 9 (1989b): 7.

_____ . "Attitudes of Working Women and Firms' Response." *Japan Labor Bulletin* 29, no. 6 (1990): 1–3.

_____ . "Changing Marriage and Family Structure: Women's Perspective." *Japan Labor Bulletin* 31, no. 1 (1992): 4–8.

Lebra, Joyce, Joy Paulsen, and Elizabeth Powers. "Evolution of the Feminine Ideal." In *Women in a Changing Japan*, Joyce Lebra, Joy Paulsen, and Elizabeth Power, eds. Stanford, Calif.: Stanford University Press, 1981a, 1–23.

_____ . "Women in Rural Japan." In *Women in a Changing Japan*, Joyce Lebra et al., eds. Stanford, Calif.: Stanford University Press, 1981b, 25–49.

Lo, Jeannie. *Office Ladies, Factory Women*. Armonk, N.Y.: M. E. Sharpe, 1990.

Ministry of Foreign Affairs. "Number of Female Salaried Workers in Japan Increases 35% in 10 Years." *Information Bulletin 1986–1987*. Tokyo: Public Information Bureau, 1987, 152–153.

Ministry of Labor. *Basic Statistics Survey on Wage Structure*. Tokyo: Ministry of Labor, 1987.

_____ . *Fujin Rodo No Jitsujo*. Tokyo: Ministry of Labor, 1988.

Pharr, Susan. "The Japanese Woman: Evolving Views of Life and Role in Japan." In *The Paradox of Progress*, Lewis Austin, ed. New Haven: Yale University Press, 1976, 301–327.

_____ . "Japan: Historical and Contemporary Perspectives." In *Women's Roles and Status in Eight Countries*, Janet Z. Giele and Audrey C. Smock, eds. New York: John Wiley and Sons, 1977, 219–255.

Preston, Samuel H., and Shigemi Kono. "Trends in Well-Being of Children and Elderly in Japan." In *The Vulnerable*, John L. Palmer, Timothy Smeeding, and Barbara Boyle Torrey, eds. Washington, D.C.: Urban Institute Press, 1988, 277–307.

Prime Minister's Office. *Japanese Women Today*. Tokyo: Prime Minister's Office, 1990.

Rohlen, Thomas. *For Harmony and Strength*. Berkeley: University of California Press, 1979.

Steinhoff, Patricia, and Kazuko Tanaka. "Women Managers in Japan." In *Women in Management Worldwide*, Nancy Adler and Dafna Izraeli, eds. Armonk, N.Y.: M. E. Sharpe, 1988, 103–121.

Takahashi, Michiko. "Working Mothers and Families." *Review of Japanese Culture and Society* 3, no. 1 (1989): 21–30.

Takeuchi, Hiroshi. "Working Women in Business Corporations." *Japan Quarterly* 29, no. 3 (1982): 319–323.

Ueno, Chizuko. "Genesis of the Urban Housewife." *Japan Quarterly* 34, no. 4 (1987): 130–142.

Vogel, Ezra. *Japan's New Middle Class*. Berkeley: University of California Press, 1963.

11

Women and the Welfare State in the Nordic Countries

ELINA HAAVIO-MANNILA
KAISA KAUPPINEN

According to the editors of *Nordic Democracy* (Allardt et al. 1981: 1), "The basic . . . reason for international interest in the Nordic countries is related to their roles as . . . balanced but vital, progressive but nonrevolutionary democratic social welfare societies." The Nordic welfare systems *have* improved the lives of women in Denmark, Finland, Iceland, Norway, and Sweden. Many of the demands women in other countries make for measures to increase equality and security are a reality in the Northern European countries. Nordic women also have attained a relatively good position in society. But many things still must change before women and men are equal in all spheres of life. U.S. sociologist Joan Acker, who worked for many years at the Swedish Center for Working Life, observed that the Swedish welfare system does not fundamentally disturb the existing male dominance and the underlying gender construction of work, trade unions, and political organizations (Acker 1989).

This chapter describes how women work and live in the Nordic welfare states. What are the antecedents of women's increasing participation in work? Can the effects of women's participation be seen at the macro level of societies—in their political systems, economic and social resources, or the early attainment of women's civil rights and political and social equality? What are the extent and influence of public social support by the welfare state and the informal help fathers give employed mothers? What is the nature of women's work: women's employment, patterns of sex segregation of work, and women's salaries in relation to men's? Finally we ask how women's work is related to the public social security system—the core element of the welfare state.

THE NORDIC WELFARE STATE

The essential elements of a welfare state—the term used widely to describe the social and political systems of the Nordic countries—are, according to

Stein Kuhnle (1981: 412), "governmental legislation which guarantees income maintenance and other kinds of support for individual citizens and families in case of occupational accidents or disease, old age, and unemployment." These original targets of social policy have been supplemented by various social programs, including family policies.

The welfare institutional model that is applicable to the Scandinavian countries promotes the principle that all citizens should be equally entitled to a decent standard of living and that full social citizenship rights and status should be guaranteed unconditionally. It aims at comprehensiveness, in contrast to residual social policy models such as that used in the United States, which aim to help only those in real need (Esping-Andersen and Korpi 1987; Allardt 1989: 40; Esping-Andersen 1990).

The Nordic countries have acquired their present democratic and parliamentary systems by different routes. However, the end result demonstrates many common features in the cultural, economic, and social experiences of women. One condition for this progressive development has been an openness to change, which has contributed to the transformation of originally conservative agricultural societies into advanced industrial welfare states (Allardt et al. 1981: 6–7).

National sovereignty and different economic and strategic conditions have set limits on the forms and content of Nordic cooperation and integration. During recent decades, Nordic cooperation has been supported by the expansion of Nordic public institutions, primarily the Nordic Council, for joint consultations between members of parliaments and governments in the Nordic countries. These bodies serve as platforms for joint investigations and exchanges of views and experiences as well as for organizing parallel solutions on a national basis. This situation has both been affected by and stimulated joint or parallel efforts in social and political research (Allardt et al. 1981: 7–8). The future will show whether European integration will greatly change this situation.

One effort to coordinate Nordic research on political sciences was the publication of a large comparative study of the role of women in shaping politics in the Nordic countries. The title of this project, *Unfinished Democracy* (Haavio-Mannila et al. 1985a), implied that political democracy in the Nordic countries still applies more to men than to women.

ANTECEDENTS OF WOMEN'S WORK

Demographic, Economic, and Cultural Features of Nordic Countries

As a background to our study of women's work and lives in the Nordic countries, a few demographic, economic, and cultural indicators of the quality of life in these countries are presented. At the end of the 1980s, there were nearly 23 million inhabitants in the Nordic countries. Of these, 8.4 million lived in Sweden, 5 million each in Denmark and Finland, 4 million in Norway, and 240,000 in Iceland. In the 1980s, the population growth rate—the average

TABLE 11.1   Demographic and Economic Position of the Nordic Countries, 1988

	Denmark	Finland	Iceland	Norway	Sweden
Population (in millions)	5.1	4.9	0.2	4.2	8.4
Population growth rate (in percent)	0.0	0.4	1.1	0.3	0.1
GNP per capita (in U.S. dollars)[a]	18,470	18,610	20,160	20,020	19,150
Economic growth rate (in percent)					
1980-1988	2.3	2.7	1.9	3.8	1.9
1986-1988	-0.5	4.1	2.6	2.4	2.3
Share of agriculture in GNP (in percent)	5	8	12	3	3
Total fertility[b]	1.5	2.6	2.1	1.8	1.9
Life expectancy					
Total	76	76	77	77	77
Women	78	79	80	80	80
Men	72	70	75	73	74

[a]GNP per capita in US$: Switzerland 27,260, Luxemburg 22,600, Japan 21,040, and the United States 19,780.

[b]The number of children a woman bears during her lifetime.

Sources: The World Bank Atlas 1989 (Washington, D.C.: World Bank, 1989); Nordic Statistical Secretariat, ed., Nordic Statistical Yearbook 1988, Vol. 27 (Stockholm: Nordic Council of Ministers and Nordic Statistical Secretariat, 1989).

annual percentage change in a country's population in these countries—was at most 0.4 percent except in Iceland, where it was 1.1 percent. (The absolute change in a year is the sum of births and immigrants minus the sum of deaths and emigrants.)

The population in the Nordic countries is ethnically homogeneous. Most Nordic countries have only a few thousand immigrants; in Sweden about one million immigrants and political refugees have arrived primarily since the end of the 1960s. The Scandinavian languages—Danish, Icelandic, Norwegian, and Swedish—closely resemble each other; Finnish is a different language, belonging to the Finno-Hungarian language group. Finland has a Swedish-speaking minority (6 percent), and the country is officially bilingual.

Measured by gross national product (GNP) per capita, the five Nordic countries were among the nine highest-ranking countries of the 184 countries included in the 1989 World Bank Atlas (Table 11.1). Only Switzerland, Luxemburg, and Japan had a higher GNP per capita than the Nordic countries. The GNP in the United States was almost as high as those in Iceland and Norway and a little higher than that in Sweden. The Nordic economies are growing moderately: In the 1980s, the average annual growth rate of the GNP per capita was 2–4 percent.

The low population growth rate is due to low total fertility rates—under 2.0 children. Accordingly, without substantial immigration the population will diminish in the future because there is not enough natural replacement to maintain the population in each country.

The affluence of the Nordic countries is reflected in the high average life expectancy at birth, which is about seventy-seven years. In each country women's life expectancy is six to nine years longer than that of men, which is common in all developed countries. In Finland the gender difference in life expectancy (nine years) is most pronounced.

The educational level of the Nordic inhabitants is high. There is practically no illiteracy, and the school enrollment rates of children between ages seven and fifteen are close to 100 percent.

Social Equality Between Women and Men

According to another international comparison conducted by the Population Crisis Committee (1988) and covering ninety-nine countries representing 92 percent of the world's female population, social equality between women and men in Finland and Sweden was the highest in the world; Denmark and Norway shared the next-highest ranking along with twenty other countries. (Iceland was not included in the study.) The following three variables were used to compare social equality of women and men in each country.

1. Political and legal equality indicators measured the degree to which women have legal protection against discrimination based on sex and the degree to which they can exercise political rights, including their representation in political decision making.
2. Economic equality measured the degree to which women can expect equal treatment with male coworkers in their workplaces and whether they are free in other ways to participate equally in economic life, including the right to own, manage, and inherit real property.
3. Equality in marriage and the family covers the right to enter freely into marriage, equal rights in divorce, and other issues involving family law.

The data used in the study suggested that only Finland and Sweden had made an unqualified commitment to equal political rights for women and to legal protection against sex discrimination. Despite this commitment, women still are underrepresented in political decision-making processes, as was indicated in Elina Haavio-Mannila's studies (Haavio-Mannila et al. (1985a) and more recently in that of Drude Dahlerup (1989). Also, economic equality as well as equality in marriage and family were ranked highest in the Nordic countries among nineteen Western industrial countries.

Road to Equal Opportunities for Women and Men

Table 11.2 shows some milestones along the road to equal opportunities in the Nordic countries. Political rights were achieved by Nordic women in the early 1900s. Finnish women got voting rights and became eligible for parlia-

TABLE 11.2   Some Milestones on the Road to Equal Opportunities in the
Nordic Countries

	Denmark	Finland	Iceland	Norway	Sweden
Women get voting rights and become eligible for election					
local	**1908**	1918	1909	1910	1919
parliamentary	1915	**1906**	1915	1913	1919
First woman in parliament	1918	**1907**	1922	1922	1921
First woman cabinet minister	**1924**	1926	1970	1945	1947
Women admitted to universities	1875	1901	1911	1884	**1873**
Women granted same eligibility as men for civil service	1921	1926	**1911**	1938	1925
Women granted right to ordination	1947	1988	**1911**	1952	1958
Equal pay for same position in civil service	**1919**	1962	1945	1959	1947
Equal pay for same position in industry/trade	1973	1962	1961	1961	**1960**
Act passed on equal opportunities at work	1978	—	**1973**	—	1980
Act passed on equal opportunities	—	1987	**1976**	1979	—
Contraceptive pill approved	Mid-1960s	**1961**	1966	1967	1964
Women entitled to decide on abortion	1973	**1970**[a]	1975[a]	1978	1975
Parents granted shared paternity/maternity leave for birth of child	1984	1978	1980	1978	**1974**
Right to six-hour work day for parents of small children	—	1988	—	—	**1979**

[a]Physician's certificate is needed, but in practice it is a mere formality.

Source: Österberg and Hedman (1989).

mentary elections in 1906; they were second in the world after New Zealand to receive the right to vote and were first in the world to be eligible for election. Women got political rights in local elections in Denmark, Iceland, and Norway between 1908 and 1910. The first women soon appeared in the Nordic parliaments, but it took some time before women first became cabinet ministers. In Denmark and Finland this occurred in the 1920s, in Norway and Sweden in the 1940s, and in Iceland in 1970 (Haavio-Mannila et al. 1985a).

In the late 1980s, about one-third of the parliamentary seats were held by women in the Nordic countries, except in Iceland where the proportion was one-fifth in 1987. In other countries, women's representation in the highest councils of government rarely exceeds 10 percent. The relatively high representation of women in the Nordic parliaments is partly related to the proportional voting system (Rule 1981; Darcy et al. 1987); it is partly related to the solidarity of women voters in support of candidates of their own gender. According to a Finnish study (Haavio-Mannila et al. 1985a), more than half of women voted for a female candidate in the 1984 Finnish parliamentary elections, whereas only one-tenth of the men did so. Support for women candidates was strongest among young well-educated women. Women candidates received the least backing from men with average educations and from farmers. It may be that men of medium- or lower-ranking positions are the most afraid of changes in the status quo if more women become politically active. Also, women politicians tend to initiate legislation regarding educational, social, and health care policies (Haavio-Mannila et al. 1985a).

Women were officially admitted to universities around the turn of the century, first in Sweden (1873) and last in Iceland (1911). Even before the formal admission of women to universities, however, some women had received academic degrees with special permission. For example, in Finland applications for permissions were numerous, and when the doors of the University of Helsinki were officially opened to women in 1901, 14 percent of the undergraduates were women (Eskola and Haavio-Mannila 1984: 4). The proportion of women in institutions of higher learning has risen steadily in all Nordic countries. At present, at least half of the university students are women, but they are concentrated in different areas than men. Women are in the majority in schools of education, public health and social work, and the humanities, whereas men constitute a majority in the technical and natural sciences. Even though women receive bachelor's and master's degrees at the same rate as men, the proportion of women receiving doctoral degrees is still lower, although it is steadily increasing. In Finland between 1966 and 1969, the proportion of doctoral degrees awarded to women was 9 percent. By 1976–1979, the proportion of women among new doctorates was 16 percent and in 1988 it was as high as 27 percent (Hurri 1989).

The contraceptive pill was officially approved as a birth control method in the 1960s (Table 11.2). In the 1970s, women in Denmark, Norway, and Sweden were entitled to decide on abortion without consultation with a physician. In Finland and Iceland, in 1990 a physician's certificate was still needed, even though Finland was the first country to grant the right to a legal abortion to every woman who wanted it. In practice, in most cases the physician's certificate is a pure formality. The right to abortion is granted during the first twelve weeks of pregnancy and during the first eighteen weeks in Sweden.

Even though abortion is free in the Nordic countries, abortion rates are low by international standards, and the number has been decreasing since the time women were entitled to decide. The youngest and the oldest women—those under twenty and over forty years of age—have the highest abortion rates per pregnancy. In 1986 the number of legal abortions per 1,000 live births was 363 in Denmark, 325 in Sweden, 295 in Norway, 219 in Finland, and 176 in Iceland (Nordic Council 1988: 29).

Sweden was the first Nordic country (1974) to guarantee the parents paid maternity-parental leave for the birth of a child. The last country to take this step was Denmark in 1984. By the end of the 1980s, men were showing a steadily although slowly growing interest in sharing the maternity-parental leave with their wives (see "Public Day Care" below).

Structural Change and Growth of the Public Sector

Compared with other Western industrial countries, the decline in agricultural population in the Nordic countries, particularly in Finland, took place relatively recently. In 1960 the proportion of the economically active population engaged in agriculture was 18 percent in Denmark, 35 percent in Finland, 23 percent in Iceland, 19 percent in Norway, and 14 percent in Sweden. By 1980 the figures had declined to 5–13 percent (Nordic Statistical Secretariat 1989: 49).

Similarly, the share of agriculture in the GNP has decreased in all Nordic countries to 3 percent in Norway and Sweden, 5 percent in Denmark, 8 percent in Finland, and 12 percent in Iceland in 1988 (Table 11.1). Also, in the 1970s the proportion of all workers who were industrial workers started to diminish. In 1980 only 20 to 28 percent of the economically active population in the Nordic countries was working in mining, manufacturing, and electricity; in 1960 the proportions varied between 23 and 35 percent. Only the proportions of people working in construction, commerce, and transport remained roughly the same between 1960 and 1980.

The most marked structural change has been the rapid growth in the numbers of people, particularly women, employed in the service sector. In 1980, 58 percent of Danish and 53 percent of Swedish economically active women were employed in the service sector; the proportion was 40 percent of Finnish women and 45 percent of Norwegian women. Among men, the percentages were much lower, varying between 14 and 26 percent (Nordic Statistical Secretariat 1989: 49). Most of the increase in that proportion has taken place in the public sector. Municipalities especially have increased their social, health, cultural, and educational services, which are financed mostly through taxes.

A large number of Nordic women do care giving and nursing as paid workers. Earlier they performed such services as unpaid work in the role of a mother, daughter, aunt, or grandmother. This work includes caring for children, the handicapped, the sick, and the elderly—people who cannot take care of themselves. Paid care-giving work is carried on largely in day care centers, old people's homes, hospitals, and similar institutions. But it also includes assistance provided in home settings such as home-based nursing services for the elderly (Waerness 1989: 222).

The importance of the public sector as an employer of women can be seen in the fact that more than 50 percent of all employed women in Denmark and Sweden and almost 40 percent in Finland were working within the public sector in 1985 (there are no comparable data for Iceland and Norway). The lower percentage for Finland is due to the fact that the public sector in that country employs a smaller proportion of all employees than is the case in Denmark and Sweden. Calculated another way, in the mid-1980s two-thirds of all public employees in Denmark, Finland, and Sweden were women, whereas two-thirds of all private-sector employees were men (Nordic Council 1988: 86).

Women receive a fair share of public health and other municipally provided assistance; they use more health and social services than men; and they more often receive care for the elderly. Public child care makes it possible for both parents, but especially for women, to work outside the home, even though public child care should not be seen as a special service for women. It is the right and the duty of both parents to care for their children. In practice, however, the availability of high-quality public child care has helped women to work outside the home.

Public Day Care as Part of the Nordic Infrastructure

In the Nordic countries, children under age one most often are cared for at home by their own parents, who are financially supported by the comprehensive maternity-parental leave system. Parental leave is designed differently in each Nordic country. It is longest in Sweden (fifteen months, with plans to expand it to eighteen months) and next longest in Finland (twelve months). In Finland the compensation for the lost income is 80 percent, and in Sweden it is 90 percent. In Iceland, Denmark, and Norway, the paid leave is considerably shorter—lasting from four to six months. In Norway, after the paid leave, one of the parents may take an additional six-month leave without pay with the guarantee of being able to return to his or her former job (Kauppinen and Haavio-Mannila forthcoming).

Starting in 1990, a new child care arrangement was provided for working parents in Finland. After the twelve-month paid maternity-parental leave, parents may choose between two alternatives: Either parents can stay at home until the child is three years old (with monetary compensation and job guarantees), or communities must arrange child care while the parents work outside the home.

In 1990 more than one-third of Finnish children six and under were cared for by parents who had chosen this form of child care arrangement or who were on maternity-parental leave. About half of the children were in municipal day care centers or approved family day care homes (39 percent in full-time care and 10 percent in part-time care). The rest (14 percent) were in private day care centers or their care was ensured by other private arrangements. Even before the new home care arrangement, employed Finnish parents could stay away from work with a job guarantee until the child was three years old. This child care arrangement could be used by either the mother or the father but not by both simultaneously. According to a survey conducted in 1989, this arrangement was used by 46 percent of women who had been gainfully employed before their maternity leave, by 35 percent of all women, and by 0.6 percent of men. The average length of the stay at home was 11.8 months

TABLE 11.3 Proportion of Children in Municipal Daycare by Age Group in the Nordic Countries, 1987 (Finland 1990) (in percent)

	Denmark	Finland	Iceland	Norway	Sweden
Two years and under					
Daycare center	18	13	13	7	18
Family daycare arrangement	27	16	14	1	13
Three to six years					
Daycare center	56	41	50	48	39
Family daycare arrangement	9	29	5	1	21

Sources: Nordic Statistical Secretariat (1989), 320-321; unpublished data provided by the Finnish Board of Social Affairs.

for mothers and 7.5 months for fathers. Only 15 percent of parents (mostly mothers) took the leave until the child was three years of age (Säntti 1990).

Both Finland and Sweden have legislation allowing parents to shorten their daily working hours: In Finland, this policy applies until the child is four years old (and during the child's first school term), and in Sweden it extends until the child is ten to twelve years of age. In 1989, 8 percent of the Finnish mothers who had this right actually shortened their daily working hours from eight hours to six. One reason for the low participation may be the relatively low monthly compensation for the lost income, which in 1989 was about 400 Finnish marks ($120) per month.

In 1987 roughly one-third of children age two and under received public municipal day care outside the home, either in a day care center or a family day care arrangement. The percentages varied considerably by country: Denmark, 45 percent; Finland, 29 percent (1990); Iceland, 27 percent; Norway, 8 percent; and Sweden, 31 percent (Table 11.3).

Between 1975 and 1987, the increase in the availability of municipal child care for children three to six years of age in the five Nordic countries was great. In 1987, 60 percent of children in this age group in Sweden and 65 percent in Denmark and in 1990, 70 percent in Finland had a place at a municipal child care center or alternatively in a family day home. In Iceland and Norway, where family day care is less common than in the other Nordic countries, about half of the children attended public day care centers, but a large proportion were on a part-time basis (Österberg and Hedman 1989: 15–16). This is the case because women often work part time in these countries.

Strengthening the Role of the Father

A unique aspect of the Nordic maternity-parental leave is that the leave is usually paid and can be divided between the two parents. In Finland the father can take leave for the last seven months of the twelve-month maternity-parental leave, but the mother is requested to use the first five months of the leave. The father has a right to an additional six to twelve "daddy days" in connection with the child's birth. The maternity-parental leave is similar in Norway in that the mother is expected to use the first six weeks of the thirty-five week-long leave. The daddy days, however, which are compensated at 80 percent of salary for Finnish fathers, are not compensated for Norwegian fathers. Thus, there are no statistics on how many fathers in Norway use the daddy days. Starting in 1991, Finnish fathers could take six extra daddy days, which they could use flexibly during the twelve-month leave period.

In Sweden parents can divide the maternity-parental leave between themselves for the entire period of the fifteen-month leave. In Denmark the maternity leave is eighteen weeks long, during which the father can use two weeks as paternity leave immediately after the child's birth. After the maternity leave is over, the parents can divide the ten-week-long parental leave between themselves. Thus, only in Sweden does the term *parental leave* refer to the entire fifteen-month period, even if in practice it is primarily the mother who uses the parental leave benefits. In Denmark, Finland, and Norway, as in Sweden, fathers are entitled to daddy days in connection with the child's birth.

The number of fathers participating in parental leave steadily increased during the 1980s in all Nordic countries including Finland as can be seen below (Lindroos 1986 and 1990 personal communication).

Year	Father Taking Paid Leave as a Percentage of All Fathers Eligible for Compensation of Lost Income (Finland)
1978	12.4
1980	13.1
1982	18.2
1984	24.0
1986	30.5
1988	35.8
1989	34.0

The majority of fathers receiving compensation used the daddy days, taking twelve days on average. Only a small minority (3 percent) of fathers took more time immediately following the birth of the child (Bergman 1989). The men most eager to participate in parental leave generally have high academic educations and work in upper-white-collar technical, scientific, humanistic, and artistic occupations. The other group of fathers who are eagerly participating in the parental leave are students (Lindroos 1986). One reason for the growth in fathers' participation may be the ideology that encourages men to share in the child care activities. Also, monetary compensation facilitates their participation because the compensation is about 80 percent of the father's lost salary.

In Sweden in 1985, 85 percent of the eligible fathers used the daddy days for an average of eight days. In the early 1990s, it is reported that the daddy days are being used by practically every eligible father and have become a normal practice (Lundén and Näsman 1989; personal communication, Lisbeth Näsman 1990). Fathers' participation in the fifteen-month leave program has slowly increased since the program's inception in 1974; only 2 percent of the fathers took the leave in 1975 compared with 27 percent in 1985 (Haas 1987). In Denmark in 1985, 45 percent and in 1988, 50 percent of the fathers used parental leave benefits. As in other countries, only a small minority of Danish fathers (5 percent) used more than the daddy day leave benefits—seven to ten weeks on average. The men most eager to use the benefits were those whose education was in teaching and social work.

The eagerness of men to participate in parental leave is in accord with women's wishes. According to our own analysis of Finnish data from a representative 1988 interview study of women ages eighteen to sixty-four, 39 percent (546) agreed completely with the statement: "In my opinion, at least two weeks' of paternity leave should be made mandatory for men." An additional 20 percent of the women agreed with this statement to some degree (Lonka et al. 1989).

One of the ideas behind shared maternity-parental leave is that it becomes less likely that employers will discriminate against women on the basis of long maternity leaves. The reform also has far-reaching psychological and sociological implications because equal parenting is seen as beneficial for the child's psychological development and well-being (Kauppinen and Haavio-Mannila forthcoming). When both parents share child care responsibilities, children have multiple role models and learn the varied styles of interaction that mothers and fathers have to offer (Haas 1987). Fathers who have taken parental leave usually express favorable feelings about it and report close and warm relations with their children (Kauppinen-Toropainen et al. 1984: 203).

According to a survey of Finnish men conducted in 1989, of the 301 men who had young children, 26 percent had taken the daddy days. The results showed that there is great interest in parental leave among Finnish men: 62 percent of the 503 men in the survey would like to use the daddy days, and 46 percent would be willing to take some additional days off to participate in the parental leave. Some of the fathers showed interest in sharing the new home care arrangement with their wives. Ten percent of the men with young children were willing to arrange child care at home by taking turns with their wives (Kiviranta et al. 1990).

The same 1989 survey showed that one out of four fathers had stayed at home to care for a sick child. In Finland a parent can stay at home for three to four days with full pay to care for a child with an acute illness—ear infection, flu, bronchitis. Finland has no annual upper limit for days of absence from work due to a child's illness; in Sweden the upper limit per year is sixty days. In 1985 in Sweden, men used 44 percent of the days used by parents in caring for sick children. In Finland during a six-month period in 1986, 34 percent of women and 14 percent of men were absent from work in order to care for a sick child (Nordic Council 1988: 102).

TABLE 11.4 Working Women's Employment in the Nordic Countries, 1986

	Denmark	Finland	Iceland	Norway	Sweden
Proportion of employed women, age 20 to retirement[a]	71	74	74	72	81
Proportion of women age 20 to retirement in full-time employment[a]	42	62	43	32	46

[a]In Finland, Iceland, and Sweden, the retirement age is 65 years; in Denmark and Norway it is 67.

Source: Nordic Council (1988): 73-74.

NATURE OF WOMEN'S WORK

Rate and Type of Employment

Women's gainful employment in all Nordic countries increased rapidly during the last two decades. In 1970, 52 percent of Danish, 64 percent of Finnish, and 59 percent of Swedish women from age twenty to retirement (about sixty-five years) were gainfully employed. In 1986 the proportions were 71 percent in Denmark, 72 percent in Norway, 74 percent in Finland and Iceland, and 81 percent in Sweden (Table 11.4). Gender differences in employment rates were small in Finland and Sweden, whereas in Iceland, Norway, and Denmark the proportion of employed women was considerably lower than that of men (Nordic Council 1988: 74, 78). Women made up 48 percent of the employed population in Finland and Sweden, 46 percent in Denmark, and 44 percent in Norway in 1987 (Nordic Statistical Secretariat 1989: 82–83).

Women work part time more often than men. In 1986 one-third of the women in Denmark, Iceland, Norway, and Sweden had a part-time job—that is, less than thirty-five hours a week—whereas in Finland the proportion was only 12 percent. As a consequence, the contribution of Finnish women to the national economy is greater than in the other Nordic countries (Nordic Statistical Secretariat 1989: 81). During the 1980s, unemployment rates have been very low in the Nordic countries—between 2 and 6 percent. In Denmark and Norway, women had slightly higher unemployment rates than men, whereas in Finland and Sweden the opposite has been true. In the 1990s, however, unemployment in Finland has risen to more than 10 percent. This is seen as a societal catastrophe that may threaten the social benefits that are the essence of the welfare state.

Sex Segregation of Work

Horizontal Sex Segregation. The influx of women into the labor market has not changed the extent of sex segregation at work. In the 1980s, 49 percent of all employed women in Finland, 53 percent in Norway, and 29 percent in

TABLE 11.5 Percent of All Gainfully Employed Women and Men Who Work in Totally Segregated, Heavily Segregated, and Balanced Occupations in the Nordic Countries

Sex Composition of Occupation	Denmark 1981		Finland 1986		Norway 1986		Sweden 1980	
	Women	Men	Women	Men	Women	Men	Women	Men
Totally segregated female-dominated occupations: 90-100 percent women	29	1	49	2	53	3	29	1
Heavily segregated female-dominated occupations: 60-90 percent women	36	7	26	8	32	11	50	13
Balanced occupations: 40-60 percent women	15	10	10	10	6	6	7	6
Heavily segregated male-dominated occupations: 10-40 percent women	18	43	13	35	8	30	11	33
Totally segregated male-dominated occupations: 0-10 percent women	2	39	2	45	1	50	3	47
Total	100	100	100	100	100	100	100	100
Number (in thousands)	1,140	1,167	787	1,804	1,485	1,264	891	2,208

Source: Nordic Council (1988): 82.

Denmark and Sweden worked in totally female-dominated occupations in which 90 to 100 percent of the workers were women. Very few men or women worked in occupations that were dominated by the opposite sex. The proportion of men in female-dominated occupations (60 to 90 percent women) varied from 7 percent in Denmark to 13 percent in Sweden, and the proportion of women in male-dominated occupations varied from 8 percent in Norway to 18 percent in Denmark (Table 11.5).

Among the Nordic countries, the Danish labor market was slightly less segregated by sex. In 1981, 36 percent of all the employed Danish population worked in totally sex-segregated occupations in which 90 to 100 percent of the people were of the same sex. The corresponding proportion was 41 percent in Sweden (1980), 49 percent in Finland (1986), and 53 percent in Norway (1986) (Nordic Council 1988: 82). The situation in Denmark is due to the relatively high proportion of women (35 percent) working in either balanced or male-dominated occupations.

In the early 1980s, half of all gainfully employed men and women in Denmark, Finland, Norway, and Sweden worked in twenty major occupations (Nordic Council 1988: 80–81). The proportions of women in sixteen of these occupations among the four Nordic countries are compared in Table 11.6.

In all countries, eight of the sixteen major occupations were female-dominated (office, catering, retail sales, cleaning, nursing, auxiliary nursing,

TABLE 11. 6 Percent and Numbers of Women in Sixteen Major Occupations in the Nordic Countries

Occupation	Denmark 1981		Finland 1986		Norway 1986		Sweden 1980[a]	
	%	N (thousands)	%	N (thousands)	%	N (thousands)	%	N (thousands)
Office or clerical staff	84	246	93	163	78	106	87	281
Catering staff	96	103	_[b]	_[b]	_[b]	_[b]	_[b]	_[b]
Retail sales staff	65	93	71	117	78	120	78	153
Cleaners	92	76	96	80	95	82	90	130
Nursing aides, junior nurses, clinic assistants	86	86	94	32	96	52	94	181
Daycare givers	92	46	100	36[c]	_[b]	_[b]	97	77
Home helpers	_[b]	_[b]	_[b]	_[b]	100	27	98	58
Registered nurses	96	51	95	42	90	41	95	56
Teachers	55	81[d]	_[b]	_[b]	63	60	78	64
Specialist teachers	_[b]	_[b]	65	50	52	25	53	50
Farmers	5	101	40	170	14	59	32	129
Transport workers, motor vehicle drivers	6	83	4	78	2	45	6	108
Machine repair technicians	0	44	0	46	0	39	8	120
Construction workers	1	48	2	44[e]	0	49	1	60
Company managers or senior executives	5	31	15	40	8	74	_[b]	_[b]
Engineers	3	38[f]	8	33	10	49[g]	5	55

[a] Or later data.
[b] Not one of twenty major occupations.
[c] Family daycare givers.
[d] Excluding secondary school teachers.
[e] Excluding timber work.
[f] Including architects.
[g] Construction engineers and technicians.

Sources: Figures received from Nordic Statistical Secretariat (1989) and Nordic Council (1988): 80-81.

day care, and home help staff). Two were balanced occupations (two different levels of teaching) and six were male-dominated (farming, transport workers, machine repair technicians, construction workers, managers, and engineers). Men's and women's work in the Nordic countries is traditionally segregated according to gender roles; women usually work in care-giving work, whereas men work in occupations related to material production and transportation or management.

Surveys of urban populations in Norway in 1983 and in Finland in 1981 showed that sex segregation of task performance at the workplace level was somewhat less pronounced in Norway than in Finland. Thirty percent of Norwegian women and 40 percent of Finnish women were engaged in work only with members of their own gender group (Haavio-Mannila 1989a: 126). The inter-country difference was smaller for men; in Norway 38 percent of men and in Finland 42 percent of men worked in totally sex-segregated workplaces.

Even though sex segregation by task performance was considerable, men and women had numerous daily contacts with each other. As an example, in Finland only 4 percent of women and 9 percent of men were working in exclusively male-dominated workplaces (Kauppinen-Toropainen et al. 1988: 19).

Women usually profit when they break occupational gender barriers. In Finland this benefit was more apparent for high-status while-collar women (engineers, architects, and the like) than for blue-collar women (bus drivers, welders, and similar jobs). The salary level of high-status women in male-dominated jobs was significantly higher and their work was more autonomous, more challenging, and less rigidly controlled than that of women who worked in comparable female-dominated jobs. However, women in typical "men's" jobs were more likely to work in a competitive and disharmonious working environment than those working in typical "women's" jobs. Also, more often than men in similar-gender nontraditional work roles, nontraditional women complained about sexual harassment and other forms of unwanted sexual attention (Kauppinen-Toropainen et al. 1988: Kauppinen et al. 1989).

Vertical Sex Segregation. Whereas horizontal segregation refers to different kinds of work at the same hierarchical level, vertical sex segregation means that men and women occupy different hierarchical positions. Table 11.7 shows that in Finland (and in other Nordic countries as well), women's hierarchical positions are lower than those of men. In Finland in 1985, women seldom held authoritative positions regardless of their socioeconomic status. This was especially true for the jobs representing lower socioeconomic job categories in which women were in the majority but represented a clear minority in leading positions. Similarly, in the upper socioeconomic category, women seldom occupied leading positions, and women were in a minority in research and planning (Partinen et al. 1989).

There are several negative consequences of such extensive sex segregation in the workplace. First, at the individual level, sex segregation may hinder individual self-fulfillment for both men and women. Second, it has proved difficult to attract men to female-concentrated occupations and workplaces because they have a strong female label. Third, at the ideological level, sex segregation strengthens sexual stereotypes; men are seen as technically minded and object-oriented, whereas women are regarded as nurturant and people-oriented. Finally, vertical sex segregation strengthens the notion that men are dominant by nature and apt to seek leading positions, whereas women are seen as submissive and willing to assume subordinate work roles (Kauppinen-Toropainen 1987).

Salaries and Wages

Pay equity between women and men in the Nordic countries has not been achieved. In the 1970s, attempts at a so-called wage solidarity policy were

TABLE 11.7 Percent of Women in Hierarchically Different Socioeconomic Positions in Finland, 1985

Socioeconomic Position	Percent of Women		N (thousands)
Total employed work force	48		2,228
Employers (total)	34		61
Farmers		38	12
Other employers		33	49
Self employed (total)	37		231
Farmers		38	152
Others		36	79
Upper socioeconomic (total)	40		296
Leading position		17	61
Research, planning		25	68
Teaching		61	72
Other		50	95
Lower socioeconomic (total)	71		747
Leading position		26	144
Independent work position		79	268
Routine-type work		91	122
Other		81	213
Blue-collar position (total)	35		919
Farm and forest		26	46
Manufacturing		24	410
Other production		39	173
Distribution and services		50	290
Other	40		17

Source: Partinen et al. (1989): 5; based on census data.

made in collective bargaining between employers' and workers' organizations. The goal was to achieve equal pay for equal work, regardless of the branch of the economy in which the work occurred, and to achieve wage equality among various kinds of jobs within a given branch of the economy. In the collective negotiations between employers and trade unions, an effort was made particularly to increase the wages of low-wage groups, including women. Special "equality," or women's supplements, for female-dominated fields of work is one of the major issues in income policy negotiations of trade unions with employers and the state in Finland. Job evaluations and pay equity based on this issue have been proposed to adjust inequities.

In general, Nordic women have lower salaries and wages than men. In 1984 in Finland, women's yearly earnings in full-time work were 72 percent of men's earnings. In Sweden women who were employed full time in 1981 earned about 80 percent of men's annual earnings (Gustafsson and Lantz 1985). The difference in wages between the sexes has not changed since the early 1980s, except in the manufacturing sector. In 1986 women in the manufacturing sector earned on average 93 percent of men's wages in Iceland, 90 percent in Sweden, 85 percent in Denmark and Norway, and 77 percent in Finland. In general, the lowest wages were found in industries in which women were in the majority—that is, textiles, clothing, and leather (Nordic Council 1988: 91–92).

Differences in the salaries of male and female white-collar employees in industry are greater than among blue-collar workers. One reason for this is that women and men occupy hierarchically different positions in the organizations (Table 11.7). This does not explain all of the salary differences between women and men, however. Neither do differences in education, age, or working hours sufficiently explain differences between women's and men's salaries. A gender residual remains that does not disappear when one adds new variables into explanatory models of salary disparity (Allén et al. 1992).

In Sweden, S. Gustafsson and P. Lantz (1985) studied the reasons for the wage gap between men and women in the manufacturing industry. They found that the wage differential was best explained (in a regression analysis) by men's and women's different work qualities and hierarchical positions and by women's younger age and lesser work experience. But a gender residual favoring men remained.

Lower salaries for women than for men are found in the public sector in the Nordic countries as well, even when differences in occupation and job titles are taken into account. However, in general, the gender gap is smaller here than in the private sector.

Women's salaries in gender-nontraditional occupations are higher than women's salaries on average; consequently, the wage gap is less pronounced. According to our studies of 4,502 employed men and women in Finland in 1984, upper-white-collar women working full time in male-dominated occupations earned 95 percent of their male counterparts' salaries; for the lower-status white-collar and for blue-collar women, the figure was 80 percent. (On average, women's salaries were 74 percent of men's salaries.) Our conclusion was that women got material benefits from working in gender nontraditional occupations and workplaces. For men, the effects of sex segregation pointed in the opposite direction: With increasing sex integration of work, men's monthly pay was lower compared with that of men in comparable male-dominated occupations (Kauppinen-Toropainen et al. 1988; Kauppinen et al. 1989).

Household Work

Throughout the Nordic countries, men spend more time on paid work than women, whereas women spend more time than men on unpaid work in the home. The difference is smallest in Finland because women rarely work part time (Table 11.4). Although women still carry the main responsibility for household work, the proportion of married or cohabiting women who take care of the daily household chores alone is diminishing. According to several Finnish interview studies, men's participation in household chores has systematically increased since 1966.

However, the increase in men's participation in household work has not kept up with the changes in women's many roles outside the home. This can be seen in time-use studies. In Finland, women's share of all household work was 67 percent in 1979 and 64 percent in 1987 (Niemi and Pääkkönen 1989); in the United States, it was 67 percent in 1987 (Robinson 1988). Household work in both studies included routine daily household chores (cooking, cleaning, laundry, and similar tasks) as well as maintenance, gardening, child care, and shopping.

Women's dissatisfaction with their husbands' participation in household work has increased steadily since the 1960s. In Helsinki in 1966, 48 percent of wives were "very satisfied" with the amount of domestic work done by their husbands (Haavio-Mannila 1967). In 1982 and 1988, the proportion of very satisfied women was only 34 percent, and one-fifth of the wives were very dissatisfied.

The most equal sharing of household tasks took place in families whose income level was high and in which the husband was young (twenty-five to thirty-four years of age), according to a study of Finnish men (Kiviranta et al. 1990). Other Finnish surveys (Haavio-Mannila 1980; Haavio-Mannila et al. 1984; Niemi and Pääkkönen 1989) also have shown that middle-class husbands participate more in household work than those in the working class or in farming. It seems likely that higher-status groups will be pioneers in a social change toward shared housework in the family in the same way they have been in other spheres of life.

The relative education, status, and income of the spouses also have an effect on the division of housework; the partner with a lower status does more housework to compensate for her or his inferior economic or social status contribution to the family (data from the surveys of Finnish women in 1988—Lonka et al. 1989; Finnish men in 1989—Kiviranta et al. 1990; Niemi and Pääkkönen 1989; Haavio-Mannila 1967, 1980, 1989b; Haavio-Mannila et al. 1984). Survey data on Finnish women and men in 1988 and 1989 showed that in about one-fifth of the families, the wife had a higher salary than her husband; one-third had equal salaries. There was more sharing in these families than in families in which the salary difference favored the husband (Kauppinen and Haavio-Mannila forthcoming).

WOMEN AND THE WELFARE STATE

The Nordic countries have a long tradition of a close relationship between the state and the civil society. Thus, there is a positive linkage between women and the state (Skard and Haavio-Mannila 1984). State social policies have increasingly intervened in the family sphere and performed functions traditionally belonging to the family, thereby changing the position of women considerably (Haavio-Mannila et al. 1985b: 69).

Scandinavian political culture expresses a benign view of the state as an instrument of popular will. The state is used to control the private forces of market and family, which are regarded as the major source of social and economic inequality. Scandinavian feminists act in accordance with their own political culture in turning to the state, even in those instances in which they wish to build alternative institutions (Hernes 1987, 1988).

The rise of welfare capitalism is characterized by the vigorous growth of state activities. One measure of this is the ratio of public expenditure to gross national product. Public expenditure constitutes the dispensation by the state (including local government) according to economic resources it has acquired from firms and households. The public expenditure–GNP ratio increased rapidly in all developed countries between 1960 and 1980. In the Nordic countries the ratio has been higher in Sweden, Denmark, and Norway than in Iceland and Finland (Kosonen 1985: 109–110).

Public expenditure growth is seen in many countries as a source of economic crisis, and expenditure cuts have been proposed as a cure. In the Nordic countries there have not been substantial cuts in social expenditure, and it is likely that the resources presently committed to public services will not diminish. The proportion of gross national product attributable to taxes and contributions to social security (health, industrial safety, unemployment, old age, invalidity, families and children, social assistance, and the like) has continued to increase in most Nordic countries. Only in Denmark has it been decreasing starting in 1982. In 1986 the ratio of social security expenditure to the gross national product was highest in Sweden (33.7 percent) followed by Denmark (26.4 percent), Finland (25.5 percent), Norway (22.6 percent), and Iceland (14.5 percent in 1984) (Nordic Statistical Secretariat 1989: 318).

At the macro level of societies, there is an association between women's economic equality with men and the expansion of the social welfare state— that is, the proportion social expenditures are of the GNP. Figure 11.1 shows that the higher the proportion social security expenditure is of GNP, the more equal the incomes of men and women in a country.

Women's economic equality with men can be seen as both a cause and a consequence of the welfare state (Waerness 1989). According to our comparison of the five Nordic countries, the more income women receive from their work (having other than earned income is rare in Scandinavia), the greater the need for public services for children, the handicapped, the sick, and the elderly. On the other hand, the better the employment possibilities for women in the public and private sectors, the more women are inclined to work for pay and the higher are their incomes in comparison with those of men.

Most Nordic women provide for their own economic survival because the family is no longer the primary means of provision for women. As was shown above, the responsibility for care—both within the household and in the welfare state—belongs to women. According to Joan Acker, in the Nordic welfare state a silent sexual contract exists, according to which women have a right to paid work and personal independence (that is, independence from being economically supported by a man) so long as they simultaneously agree to continually accept (1) human caring responsibilities in both the public and private spheres, (2) a subordinate position in the power structure, and (3) lower female salaries that indicate their secondary position in the labor market (Acker 1989; Julkunen and Rantalaiho 1989: 23). This silent sexual contract makes it possible for women to do whatever they want, but only so long as they remain subordinate to the men with whom they interact and have relationships (Haavind 1985).

FIGURE 11.1   Women's Economic Equality and the Welfare State

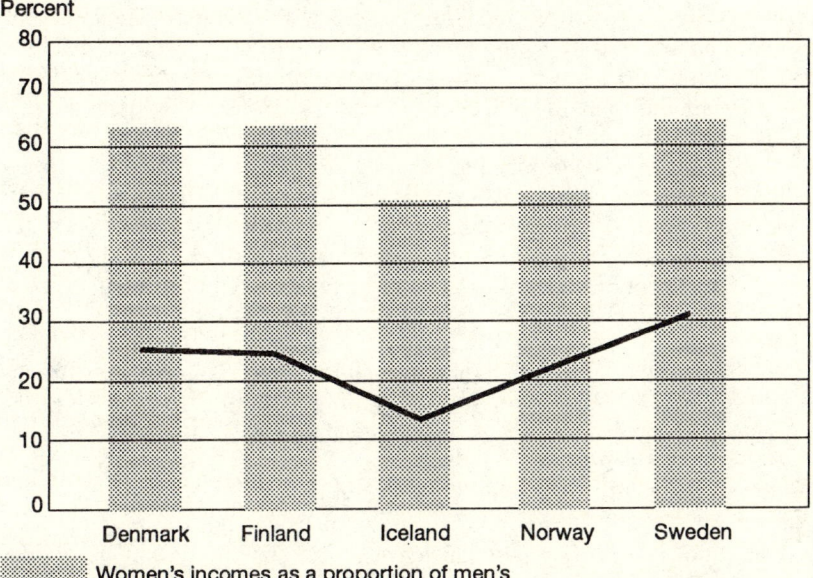

Percent

Women's incomes as a proportion of men's

Social security expenditure as a proportion of gross domestic product

Source: Nordic Statistical Secretariat (1989), 264, 318.

CONCLUSION

Equality between the sexes is both a myth and a reality in the Nordic welfare states. The silent system of gender valuation nevertheless gives women less value than men even in these countries, which according to international comparisons of gender equality rank highest in the world.

The data on ninety-nine countries used in a study by the Population Crisis Committee (1988) suggest that in the Nordic countries, commitment to equal political rights for women and to legal protection against sex discrimination is considerable. Women still are underrepresented in political decision making; but in comparison with other countries in the world, their proportion in local and national representative bodies is high. Also, economic equality between the sexes is the world's highest in the Northern European countries, even though women have not attained unqualified economic equality. The third aspect of equality between men and women, equality in marriage and the family, also was ranked highest in the Nordic countries.

An examination of some milestones along the road to equal opportunities in the Nordic countries shows that the development of citizenship and legal and social rights has taken place at approximately the same pace in all the Nordic countries. None of the five countries has been consistently ahead of the others; some reforms were adopted earlier in one country and others in another.

The Nordic social policy model aims at comprehensiveness, in contrast to means-tested social policy programs, which aim to help only those in real need. It promotes the principle that all citizens should be equally entitled to a decent standard of living and that full social citizenship rights and status should be guaranteed unconditionally. Much of women's paid work in the modern society consists of serving, helping, and caring for others (Waerness, 1989: 217). In the Nordic countries, paid care-giving work takes place mostly in the public sector; it is particularly in the municipalities that social and health services and primary education are provided. For example, in Finland in 1985, 73 percent of the municipal labor force consisted of women, whereas only 44 percent of the civil servants and 42 percent of the employees in the private sector were women.

The paid work of married women and mothers throughout their working-age life span is officially recognized as normal in the Nordic countries. Consequences for families are taken into consideration in public policymaking. For example, public day care provided by professionally trained care givers is part of the infrastructure of the Nordic countries. In addition, mothers and fathers are financially supported by a comprehensive and paid parental leave system. Unique to Nordic parental leave is the fact that it can be divided between the two parents. The number of fathers receiving paternity payments increased during the 1980s in all Nordic countries. Recent attitude surveys in Finland indicate that a growing proportion of fathers is willing to take advantage of the daddy days or even a longer period of paid leave in order to care for their children. Shared parental leave makes it more difficult for employers to discriminate against women on the basis of long leaves. Equal parenting is also seen as beneficial for the children's psychological development and well-being.

The influx of women into the labor force, however, has not changed the extent of sex segregation in industries, occupations, or workplaces. Sex segregation appears both horizontally and vertically. A strong sex segregation decreases the flexibility of the labor market. For example, the present care-giving crisis (lack of personnel in hospitals, municipal home care, and the like) cannot be solved by recruiting unemployed men to care-giving work because caring is labeled women's work and as such is low paying. In the society of tomorrow, there will be an excess of demand for female workers.

The great demand for women's work in the public and private service sectors strengthens women's occupational self-image. Working life must respond to these new challenges by organizing more part-time jobs and flexible work schedules, developing the quality of work and working conditions, increasing women's salaries in traditional female work areas.

Throughout the Nordic countries, men spend more time on paid work than women, whereas women spend more time than men on unpaid work. The difference is smallest in Finland because women are less frequently employed part time. Women bear the main responsibility for household work, but the proportion of married or cohabiting women who take care of daily household chores alone is diminishing.

At the macro level of societies, there is an association between women's economic equality with men and the expansion of the social welfare state. The higher the proportion of GNP devoted to social security expenditure, the more equal the incomes of men and women in a country. Women's economic equality with men is both a cause and a consequence of the welfare state. The more women work for pay outside the home, the greater the need for public services for children, the handicapped, the sick, and the elderly. On the other hand, the better the employment possibilities of women in the public and private sectors, the more women are inclined to do caring work for pay.

The increasing unemployment, tightened economic competition, and changes in the political and social structure in Europe in the early 1990s arouse concern about the future of the welfare system. Can this comprehensive social policy model survive these upheavals? This presents a challenge that must be met by the Nordic countries.

BIBLIOGRAPHY

Acker, Joan. "Welfare Policies Are Made by Men for Men." In *Worklife Research, Information from the Swedish Center for Working Life*. Stockholm: Arbetslivscentrum, 1989, 3–5.

Allardt, Erik. "Cultural Conformity in Different Types of Societies." In *Sociology in the World, Essays in Honour of Ulf Himmelstrand on His 65th Birthday*. Research Reports from the Department of Sociology, Uppsala University, no. 5 (1989): 1–16.

Allardt, Erik, Nils Andrén, Erik J. Friis, Gylfi P. Gíslason, Sten Sparre Nilson, Henry Valen, Frantz Wendt, and Folmer Wisti, eds. *Nordic Democracy: Ideas, Issues, and Institutions in Politics, Economy, Education, Social and Cultural Affairs of Denmark, Finland, Iceland, Norway, and Sweden*. Copenhagen: Det Danske Selskab, 1981.

Allén, Juovi, Päivi Keinänen, Seppo Laaksonen, and Seija Lmakunnas. *Wages from Work and Gender*. Helsinki: Statistics Finland, Studies 190, 1992.

Bergman, Solveig. "Post-War Feminism in Finland." In Solveig Bergman, ed., *Women's Worlds: Finnish Contributions to the Third International Interdisciplinary Congress on Women, Dublin 1987*. Åbo: Institute of Women's Studies at Åbo Akademi University, 1989, 71–97.

Dahlerup, Drude. *Vi har Väntat Länge nog* (We Have Waited Long Enough). Copenhagen: Nordisk Ministerråd, 1989 (in Swedish).

Darcy, Robert, Susan Welch, and Janet Clark. *Women, Elections, and Representation*. New York and London: Longman, 1987.

Eskola, Katarina, and Elina Haavio-Mannila. *The Role of Woman in Creative Cultural Work*. Research Reports, Department of Sociology, University of Helsinki, no. 221 (1984).

Esping-Andersen, Gösta. *The Three Worlds of Welfare Capitalism*. Cambridge: Polity Press, 1990.

Esping-Andersen, Gösta, and Walter Korpi. "From Poor Relief to Institutional Welfare States: The Development of Scandinavian Social Policy." In Robert Erikson, Erik Hansen, Stein Ringer, and Hannu Uusitalo, eds., *The Scandinavian Model. Welfare States and Welfare Research*. Armonk, N.Y.: M. E. Sharpe, Inc., 1987, 39–74.

Gustafsson, S., and P. Lantz. "Arbete och Löner" (Work and Salaries). *Arbetslivscentrum*. Stockholm: Almquist and Wiksell International, 1985 (in Swedish).

Haas, Linda. "Fathers' Participation in Parental Leave." In Swedish Center for Working Life, *Social Change in Sweden*, No. 37. New York: Swedish Information Service, 1987, 1–4.

Haavind, Hanne. "Förändringar i Förhållandet Mellan Kvinnor och Män" (Changes in the Relationship Between Women and Men). *Kvinnovetenskaplig Tidskrift* 3 (1985): 17–27 (in Swedish).

Haavio-Mannila, Elina. "Sex Differentiation in Role Expectations and Performance." *Journal of Marriage and the Family* 29 (1967): 568–578.

————. "Kodinhoitotehtävien Jakautuminen Perheessä" (Division of Household Tasks in the Family). *Sosiologia* 17 (1980): 185–194 (in Finnish).

————. "Gender Segregation of Paid and Unpaid Work." In Katja Boh, Maren Bau, Cristine Clason, Maja Pankratova, Jens Qvortrup, Giovanni Sgritta, and Kari Waerness, eds., *Changing Patterns of European Family Life. A Comparative Analysis of 14 European Countries.* London and New York: Routledge, 1989a, 123–140.

————. "Life Patterns of Cross-Class Families." Paper presented at the Conference on Gender and Class, Antwerpen, September 18–20, 1989b.

Haavio-Mannila, Elina, Riitta Jallinoja, and Harriet Strandell. *Perhe, työ ja Tunteet* (Family, Work and Emotions). Helsinki, 1984 (in Finnish).

Haavio-Mannila, Elina, Drude Dahlerup, Maud Eduards, Esther Gudmundsdóttir, Beatrice Halsaa, Helga Hernes, Eva Hänninen-Salmelin, Bergthora Sigmundsdóttir, Sirkka Sinkkonen, and Torild Skard, eds., *Unfinished Democracy. Women in Nordic Politics.* Oxford: Pergamon Press, 1985a.

Haavio-Mannila, Elina, Rita Liljeström, and Magdalena Sokolowska. "The State, the Family, and the Position of Women in the Nordic Countries and Poland." In Risto Alapuro et al., eds., *Small States in Comparative Perspective. Essays for Erik Allardt.* Olso: Norwegian University Press, 1985b, 69–90.

Hernes, Helga M. *Welfare State and Woman Power: Essays in State Feminism.* Oslo: Norwegian University Press, 1987.

————. "Scandinavian Citizenship." *Acta Sociologica* 31, no. 3 (1988): 199–215.

Hurri, Merja. "Naisen tie Huipputkijaksi Raskaampi kuin Miehen" (Woman's Road to Top Researcher Heavier Than Man's). *Helsingin Sanomat*, September 20, 1989, 2 (in Finnish).

Julkunen, Raija, and Liisa Rantalaiho, eds. *Hyvinvointivaltion Sukupuoli Järjestelmä* (Gender System of the Welfare State). Department of Social Policy, University of Jyväskylä, Working Paper no. 56, 1989 (in Finnish).

Kauppinen, Kaisa, and Elina Haavio-Mannila. "A Nordic Perspective: How Women's Employment Affects Women's Well-Being and Life Satisfaction." In Susan Noakes, ed., *Women at Work: Comparative Study, Global Issues.* Cornell University Press (forthcoming).

Kauppinen, Kaisa, Elina Haavio-Mannila, and Irja Kandolin. "Who Benefits from Working in Nontraditional Workroles: Interaction Patterns and Quality of Worklife." *Acta Sociologica* 32 (1989): 389–403.

Kauppinen-Toropainen, Kaisa. *Ainokaiset Työyhteisössä* (Token Men and Women in the Workplace. Consequences of Sex Segregation of Work on Job Satisfaction and Stress). Helsinki: Reports of the Institute of Occupational Health, Supplement 1, 1987 (in Finnish).

Kauppinen-Toropainen, Kaisa, Elina Haavio-Mannila, and Irja Kandolin. "Women at Work in Finland." In Marilyn J. Davidson and Cary L. Cooper, eds., *Working Women. An International Survey.* Chichester: John Wiley and Sons, 1984, 183–208.

Kauppinen-Toropainen, Kaisa, Irja Kandolin, and Elina Haavio-Mannila. "Sex Segregation of Work in Finland and the Quality of Women's Work." *Journal of Organizational Behavior* 9 (1988): 15–29.

Kiviranta, Uki, Sinikka Lonka, and Anja Tuomi. *Suomalainen mies–Hänen Työnsä, Naisensa ja Elämänsä* (The Finnish Man—His Work, Women, and Life). A-lehdet Oy:n Tutkimus Suomalainen mies 1989 (A Study of Finnish men, 1989, by A-lehdet Company). Helsinki: A-lehdet, 1990 (in Finnish).

Kosonen, Pekka. "Public Expenditure in the Nordic Nation-States—the Source of Prosperity or Crisis?" In Risto Alapuro, Matti Alestalo, Elina Haavio-Mannila, and Raimo Väyrynen, eds., *Small States in Comparative Perspective. Essays for Erik Allardt.* Oslo: Norwegian University Press, 1985, 108–123.

Kuhnle, Stein. "Welfare and the Quality of Life." In Erik Allardt et al., eds., *Nordic Democracy.* Copenhagen: Det Danske Selskab, 1981, 399–415.

Lindroos, Kari. "Isien Kiinnostus Vanhempain Päivärahakorvauksia Kohtaan on Kasvanut." (Fathers' Interest in Parental Leave Benefits Has Increased). *Journal of Social Insurance* 7 (1986): 245–249 (in Finnish).

Lonka, Sinikka, Marja-Leena Markkula, and Anja Tuomi. *Suomalainen Nainen Työssä, Kotona ja Omillaan* (The Finnish Woman at Work, at Home, and by Herself). A-lehdet Oy:n Tutkimus Suomalainen Nainen 1989 (A Study of Finnish Women, 1989, by A-lehdet Company). Helsinki: A-lehdet, 1989 (in Finnish).

Lundén Jacoby, Ann, and Elisabet Näsman. *Mamma, pappa, jobb* (Mom, Dad, Job). Stockholm: Swedish Center for Working Life, 1989.

Näsman, Elisabet. Personal communication, July 10, 1990.

Niemi, Iiris, and Hannu Pääkkönen. *Ajankäytön Muutokset 1980-Iuvulla* (Changes in the Use of Time in the 1980s). Helsinki: Central Statistical Office of Finland, Studies no. 153, 1989 (in Finnish).

Nordic Council of Ministers. *Women and Men in the Nordic Countries. Facts on Equal Opportunities 1988.* Stockholm: Nordic Council of Ministers, Nord 58, 1988.

Nordic Statistical Secretariat, ed. *Nordic Statistical Yearbook 1988, Vol. 27.* Stockholm: Nordic Council of Ministers and Nordic Statistical Secretariat, Nord 114, 1989.

Österberg, Christina, and Birgitta Hedman. *Women and Men in the Nordic Countries. Facts on Equal Opportunities Yesterday, Today, and Tomorrow.* Second edition. Copenhagen: The Nordic Council of Ministers, 1989.

Partinen, Riita, Martii Luukko, Veikko Simpanen, Ismo Luimula, Olli Saariaho, and Helena Pentti. *Palkansaajakeskusjärjestöjen Tasa-Arvotyöryhmän Raportti* (Report by the Working Group of Equality of Finnish Wage Earners' Central Organizations). Helsinki: SAK, 1989 (in Finnish).

Population Crisis Committee. "Country Rankings of the Status of Women: Poor, Powerless, and Pregnant." Washington, D.C.: Population Briefing Paper no. 20, June 1988.

Robinson, John. "Who Is Doing the Housework?" *American Demographics* 10 (1988): 24–28.

Rule, Wilma. "Why Women Don't Run: The Critical Contextual Factors in Women's Legislative Recruitment." *Western Political Quarterly* 34, no. 1 (1981): 60–77.

Säntti, Riitta. *Hoitovapaan Käyttö ja Lasten Hoitomuodon Valinta* (Use of Child Care Leave and Choice of Form of Child Care). Helsinki: Ministry of Social Affairs and Health, Development Department, 1990 (in Finnish).

Skard, Torild, and Elina Haavio-Mannila. "Equality Between the Sexes—Myth or Reality in Norden?" *Daedalus—Journal of the American Academy of Arts and Sciences* 113 (1984): 141–167.

Waerness, Kari. "Caring." In Katja Boh, Maren Bak, Cristine Clason, Naja Pankratova, Jens Qvortrup, Giovanni Sgritta, and Kari Waerness, eds., *Changing Patterns of European Family Life: A Comparative Analysis of 14 European Countries.* London and New York: Routledge, 1989, 217–247.

World Bank Atlas 1989. Washington, D.C.: World Bank, 1989.

12

Work-Family Policies in the United States

JOSEPH H. PLECK

Women's employment patterns in the United States show many commonalties with those in other advanced industrial countries. But one way in which the experience of women's employment in the United States differs markedly from that of other societies is the limited and uneven social policy response to that experience expressed in legislation, collective bargaining, and employer practices. In particular, U.S. policies concerning child care, work schedules, and parental leave do less than those elsewhere to help reduce the strains employed women with children encounter in meeting both their paid work and family responsibilities. These U.S. policies, termed here *work-family* policies, are the concern of this chapter.

Several limitations of focus should be noted. This review considers these policies primarily in terms of their impact on families with children and does not explicitly address ways that work-family policies also may help workers meet their responsibilities to the dependent elderly, an issue of growing importance in recent years. It also does not address in detail the utilization of these policies by men (see Pleck 1986, 1988a, 1989, 1990), another topic receiving increasing attention. Within these restrictions, the chapter provides an overall assessment of child care, work schedule, and parental leave policies in the United States.

BACKGROUND OF U.S. WORK-FAMILY POLICIES

Women's Employment and Well-Being

Work-family policies in the United States should be placed in the broader context of research findings about the effects of employment per se on lives of women who are married or have children. Interestingly, feminist-oriented research on these effects has been organized around two ideas that are fundamentally contradictory (see review in Pleck 1985). Some scholars have held that employment provides various rewards that enhance psychological well-being, overcoming the isolation and dependency of the full-time home-maker role. At the same time, other researchers have claimed that employment creates stress for married women who continue to have primary responsibility for housework and child care because their husbands do not increase their own performance of these family roles. Employed wives thus experience a "double day," or "role overload," resulting in their having less sleep and leisure time.

The considerable body of research empirically investigating these issues suggests three conclusions (Pleck 1985). First, employed wives do report a greater sense of time pressure or urgency, that varies directly with the total time spent in work and family responsibilities. Second, at the same time employment is generally associated with *better* mental health among wives—specifically, they have fewer symptoms of depression and anxiety. In some studies, this benefit accrues to employed wives in general; in others it is restricted to employed mothers with young children (see especially Kessler and McRae 1982). Third, employment does not appear to influence wives' psychological well-being assessed at a more global level—using measures of overall life satisfaction—either positively or negatively (Wright 1978).

Of these three general findings, most reviewers assign the greatest weight to the positive effects of employment on women's mental health (for example, Baruch, Barnett, and Rivers 1983). Although the double day has an impact on women's sense of time urgency, this effect seems to be more than compensated by the positive psychological rewards provided by employment. Further, there is evidence that the extent of employed wives' double day relative to that of their husbands' has actually decreased markedly since the 1960s (Pleck 1985), in large part because husbands' average time in family roles has increased.

The potential positive effects on women of good work-family policies rather than employment per se has begun to be investigated only recently. Two studies indicate that work-family policies may enhance the positive conse-quences of employment for wives. First, Marybeth Shinn and colleagues (1987) showed that the frequency of women's missing work due to breakdowns in child care arrangements is associated with poorer scores on measures of mental health and well-being for both employed mothers and fathers. Flex-time, a work schedule policy in which workers can modify their starting and ending times, is associated in several investigations (for example, Christensen and Staines 1990) with modest reductions in working parents' perceived conflict between their work and family roles. Although this evidence is not extensive, it suggests that good work-family policies can provide at least limited benefits to women in addition to the gains provided by employment itself. Further, evidence is starting to emerge that shows that good work-family policies promote women's retention in employment. One study found that the most important predictor of an employee's return to a job following childbirth was whether her employer offered job-guaranteed maternity leave (NCJW Center for the Child 1988). Thus, such policies help women continue to receive the psychological and other benefits provided by employment.

Some feminist scholars, however, have expressed concern that work-family policies may indirectly harm women. H. Bohen (1984) notes that women workers who use policies such as flextime may be penalized in terms of subsequent consideration for promotion. Further, by making it easier for women to combine work and family roles, these policies may actually reinforce gender inequity within the family. Barbara Ehrenreich and Deirdre English (1989) make this criticism of Felice Schwartz's 1989 proposal that large corporations create a "track" within management in which it is acceptable to take parental leave and not work long hours when one's children are young, thus permitting women who are currently dropping out of management to stay.

In essence, some feminists appear to believe that husbands' low level of housework and child care is a more important problem for employed mothers than lack of child care or rigid workplace policies. Although the husband's family role is important, overemphasis on it has caused some feminist scholars to take positions on the effects of wives' employment and work-family policies that are difficult for many to accept. For example, Arlie Hochschild (1989: 4) conveys the impression that employment has generally negative effects on women's mental health. Her position seems to be that husbands' minimal family performance dominates the lives of working wives. In her view, employment must be associated with negative consequences for wives, in spite of the considerable research literature to the contrary. Hochschild's emphasis on husbands' resistance as the main problem of employed wives seems to lead to a rather disturbing view of nonparental child care. She argues that parents use child care because husbands "pass the buck" to their wives, who then pass it to a child care provider—as though nonparental child care would be unnecessary if fathers did their fair share (Hochschild 1989: 232). More generally, Hochschild (1989: 232–235) portrays working parents who use child care as somewhat uninterested in their children.

A full evaluation of feminist concerns about the potential negative consequences of work-family policies on women is beyond the scope of this chapter; however, limited evidence concerning the impact of such policies on the marital division of labor is reviewed later. Unfortunately, there is little empirical evidence directly relevant to the effect of these policies on women's job advancement or earnings.

Recent Phases in Work-Family Advocacy

The advocacy campaign for better policies for working families has evolved and shifted in focus over time. Further, the impetus for work-family reform has come from several distinct constituencies with different and sometimes competing agendas. To generalize at a broad level, in the earliest period of contemporary work-family advocacy (roughly 1960 to 1971), the focal issue was child care. This period reached its apotheosis with congressional passage of the Child Development Act of 1971. When this landmark bill was vetoed by President Richard Nixon, the advocacy coalition for better child care seemed to disappear. Also contributing to the decline in the advocacy effort was the emergence of new data that appeared to question some of the key assumptions of liberal child care policy.

During the mid- and late 1970s, alternative work schedules emerged as a popular work-family policy issue. This new focus reached its high point in 1978 with the passage of legislation mandating greater availability of flextime and career part-time employment in the federal civil service. However, by the late 1980s, the principal alternative schedule policy—flextime—seemed to reach a saturation point in terms of utilization. Further, as described in the section on flextime below, advocates of a liberal policy began to express skepticism about how much alternative work schedules actually benefited working families.

In the mid-1980s, parental leave became the new "hot" work-family issue. A concerted effort to pass national legislation mandating employers to provide unpaid parental leave (as part of legislation mandating both temporary medical disability leave and dependent care leave) began in 1985. A Family and Medical Leave Act (FMLA) that applied to only 15 percent of all U.S. companies (those with the largest number of employees—fifty or more) was finally passed in 1990 but was vetoed by President George Bush. However, several states had already had some form of maternity or parental leave for many years, and still others—including Minnesota, Wisconsin, Connecticut, Oregon, Rhode Island, and Maine—passed legislation similar to the FMLA during the late 1980s. In spite of this success at the state level and near success at the federal level, however, many in the advocacy community privately express skepticism about the value of parental leave. Compared to child care, they note, it benefits workers for too short a time; and the fact that it is generally unpaid means that lower-income families cannot afford to use it.

As U.S. society entered the 1990s, these three policy areas began to receive relatively equal and balanced attention. A concerted national campaign for greater federal support for child care, mobilized behind the Act for Better Child Care (ABC), was introduced in 1988. Leading congressional conservatives proposed alternative legislation: The question shifted from whether there would be a new federal child care initiative to what its provisions would be. After much negotiation and struggle, ABC was enacted in 1990. Alternative work schedules are again receiving attention, but now as part of a broader concept of workplace "flexibility" in staffing and scheduling. Parental leave has become more widely available. Although the Family and Medical Leave Act passed by Congress in 1990 was vetoed, the majority of the states now have some form of parental leave legislation.

Advocacy Constituencies

The advocacy groups promoting each of these policies come from a variety of sources. The earliest and still largest impetus comes from what can be termed the child welfare movement, originating historically in the social movement on behalf of children that rose to prominence in the era of Progressive reform in the early twentieth century. This constituency views work-family policies from the perspective of children's well-being. For many in this group, child care is the first and often only priority.

Feminism has had an ambivalent relationship to the work-family reform movement. There is a widespread social perception that feminism has little concern for women in their role as mothers, for children, and for families—indeed, that feminism is fundamentally antifamily. Consistent with this perception, feminist leaders and organizations have been criticized for giving relatively low priority to child care and other policies that help working mothers (for example, Hewlett 1986), but this is not entirely accurate. Work-family issues were intellectually central to contemporary organized feminism from the beginning. The National Organization for Women's (NOW) Statement of Purpose in 1966 noted that "true equality of opportunity and freedom of choice for women requires such practical and possible innovations as a nationwide network of child-care centers, which will make it unnecessary for women to retire completely from society until their children are grown" (National Organization for Women 1966: 398). Although feminism has had a more visible role in other issues such as reproductive rights and equal employment opportunity, it nonetheless has also made an important contribution to work-family policies. One of NOW's first major federal legislative victories was the passage of the 1978 Pregnancy Discrimination Act.

At the same time, many feminists *have* expressed concerns that work-family policies may have a negative impact on women. As discussed earlier, the grounds for these apprehensions are that those using these policies (such as flexible schedules) may be penalized in terms of career advancement and that these policies may reinforce a traditional, inequitable division of labor within marriage. No doubt, these concerns have led some feminists to give less support to the improvement of work-family policies than would otherwise be the case.

More recently, groups rooted in the academic field of developmental psychology (as distinct from the child welfare movement) have taken a leading advocacy role for parental leave. This constituency's particular concern is the promotion of parent-child relationships and reduction of family stress during the first six to twelve months of a child's life. In addition, new advocacy, research, and consulting groups are advising companies that employers should improve work-family policies not only for altruistic reasons (to benefit parents, children, or families) but also because greater flexibility is in business's own self-interest, particularly in light of the increasing diversity of the workforce. Better policies, these groups argue, will improve productivity, foster worker retention, and thus promote success in the competitive market.

Finally, a conservative counter-advocacy movement has emerged. As child care and parental leave legislation reached Congress, the U.S. Chamber of Commerce, small business federations, and conservative analysts (for example, Besharov 1988; Samuelson 1988a, 1988b) have argued against these initiatives on a variety of grounds. Some of their arguments also will be considered here.

CHILD CARE

The Child Development Act of 1971

Advocacy for greater federal support for child care slowly increased during the 1960s. This rising crest of advocacy, led in Congress by Walter Mondale and John Brademas, reached an impasse with the passage and subsequent veto of the Child Development Act of 1971. Much of the funding in this legislation would have established a national system of group care centers for children in low-income families. Nixon's veto message decried this legislation as committing "the vast moral authority of the National Government to the side of communal approaches to child rearing over and against the family-centered approach" (Steiner 1976: 113).

Late 1970s Critique

The liberal pro–child care coalition had some difficulty recovering from this setback. At around the same time, research began to yield results apparently at variance with several key assumptions underlying the liberal drive for greater political support for center care. These results concerned (1) patterns of child care utilization and parental preferences, (2) the impact of child care on children, and (3) the impact of child care on mothers' employment. Suzanne Woolsey (1977), then a policy analyst in the Office of Management and Budget, brought the results of this research to public attention in a highly influential *Daedalus* article, "Pied Piper Politics and the Child Care Debate."

First, noted Woolsey, only a small proportion of working mothers with preschool children used group care—8 percent in the most recent (1971) data she cited, which was scarcely higher than the 1965 figure of 6 percent. Although the terms *day care* and *child care* were then—as now—often used synonymously with group or center-based care, such care constituted a rather small proportion of that actually used by working parents. Group care located at the workplace ("on-site"), in spite of its apparent advantages, was not only extremely rare, but many of the early centers had gone out of business due to lack of parental interest. Far more common than group or center-based care were care by relatives and "family" day care (care in the home of a nonrelative, who typically provides care for a small number of children).

Moreover, the relatively low use of group care, Woolsey asserted, was not due to its low availability but resulted from parents' preference for other forms of care, especially for care in their own homes or for informal neighborhood arrangements. Parents generally perceived group care as too impersonal and bureaucratic. Even income-maintenance experiments offering free group care found relatively few takers.

Second, data did not suggest that group care had positive effects on children's cognitive or social development. Woolsey did not argue that such care had negative effects; rather, she addressed the claim then being made by some child care advocates that group care had positive benefits for children, and she found it was not validated in research.

Third, studies suggested that even free day care had relatively little impact on women's employment, even (or especially) among welfare mothers. This was true because employment is a discretionary choice for relatively few mothers, and employed mothers prefer noncenter forms of care. Thus, concluded Woolsey, "data do not support the contention that heavy federal subsidization of institutional day care is desired by parents or would significantly promote other broad social goals" (1977: 129). The essentials of Woolsey's critique seemed to be reluctantly accepted in the 1980s by many (although not all) liberal child care advocates (for example, Feinstein 1984).

Present and Future Patterns of Utilization

Much has changed in the world of child care since the late 1970s. Despite Woolsey's argument that group care would never be used or preferred by more than a tiny minority of parents, its prevalence has risen steadily (used by 23 percent of all working mothers with a child under six in 1985, compared with 6 percent in 1965). Although care by relatives is still the single-most common form of care, it has declined (48 percent in 1985 versus 62 percent in 1965). Family day care, used by 14 percent of parents in 1965, rose to 23 percent in the late 1970s and early 1980s but appears to have stabilized at this level (22 percent in 1985). An additional 6 percent of families receive care from a nonrelative in the child's own home (see U.S. Bureau of the Census 1987; and Phillips 1989, Table 17.3, for data through 1985). Thus, use of group care actually reached parity with family day care in the 1985 data. Care provided in on-site centers at the workplace (including centers sponsored by consortia of employers) also has become more common: 5.2 percent of establishments employing 250 or more workers provided such care in 1987 (Hayghe 1988).

Many parents no doubt would still prefer care by relatives or care given at home if they could find and afford it. However, as center care has become more prevalent, its image has become considerably less negative. In more recent studies of child care preferences, parents' attitudes toward group care for preschool children appear more favorable than in the past. For example, 34 percent of employed mothers of preschoolers in a 1982 Detroit urban sample reported that they think care in centers or programs is best for children three and four years of age, compared with 31 percent for relative care, 4 percent for nonrelative care, and the remainder for parental care (Mason and Kuhlthau 1988). Group care for infants, however, was favored by only 1 percent. In a survey of low-income mothers in three cities in 1988, among those who wanted to change their child care arrangements (about one-third), the preferred alternative was a formal program in a center or preschool (Sonenstein 1991). Importantly, the lower the mother's income, the more likely she was not to have her preferred arrangement.

Only center care has the potential for expansion to meet the growing demand for child care necessitated by projected future increases in mothers' employment (Hofferth and Phillips 1987). The drop since the 1960s in the percentage of children cared for by relatives suggests that the pool of relatives available to provide care has not grown as fast as the number of employed mothers, probably because female relatives are more likely to be employed themselves. Since the late 1970s, the pool of potential family day care providers appears to be just keeping pace with mothers' employment. Group care, with its lower adult-child ratio, offers the potential for the greatest expansion of the number of child care "slots" given the number of providers available.

Effects on the Child

In the 1950s and 1960s, many were concerned—if not convinced—that nonparental child care had negative cognitive and social-emotional effects on preschool children. But by the time of Woolsey's critique, it was generally accepted that this concern had little research substantiation. A few continued to maintain that child care is detrimental (for example, White 1981), but for the majority of professionals, the debate shifted to whether the evidence suggested that good child care actually had positive effects (Woolsey, as one major participant in this debate, argued that research did not support this claim).

The debate on the effects of child care recently took a major new turn. At issue is not the consequences of child care in general but specifically of infant care (nonparental care for children under one year of age). Only recently have rates of employment for mothers of infants and the use of infant care risen high enough for this question to emerge.

Specifically, Jay Belsky (1988, 1989) has taken the controversial position that research in two areas raises serious grounds for concern about the consequences of substantial out-of-home care for children under one year of age. First, infants currently or previously receiving nonmaternal care show a higher rate of "insecure attachment" to their mothers (using an assessment procedure called the Strange Situation), which is thought to be indicative of later developmental problems. Second, infant-care–reared children show higher rates of aggressive and noncompliant behavior later in the preschool years. Belsky's concerns have had a particular impact because he earlier coauthored one of the review articles considered to have documented most definitively that for children over one, child care has *no* negative impact (Belsky and Steinberg 1978).

Subsequent reviewers of this research have agreed that when data from the available studies are combined, regular nonmaternal care in infancy *is* associated with a significantly higher rate of insecure attachment (37 percent among those receiving care versus 30 percent among those not receiving such care, in Lamb and Sternberg 1990; see also Clarke-Stewart 1989; Hoffman 1989). However, the difference in rates of insecure attachments is small, and the majority of care-reared infants are securely attached. Further, the validity of the assessment procedure has been questioned, particularly for infants who received nonmaternal care. Michael E. Lamb and Kathleen J. Sternberg (1990) make the valuable point that the real problem revealed in research on the effects of nonmaternal care on the infant-mother relationship is not what has been found to date using the Strange Situation test but rather that only this single assessment procedure has been used to assess the relationship.

The other evidence cited by Belsky is a research finding that children receiving infant care show more aggressive and noncompliant behavior subsequently in the preschool years. Interestingly, this part of Belsky's argument has received less attention. Belsky acknowledges that the social behavior effect is less consistent across studies than the attachment effect and that the social behavior effect tends to be even weaker in the later as opposed to earlier preschool years. K. Allison Clarke-Stewart (1989) points out that in addition to the inconsistency in the finding, infant-care–reared children do as well as or better than other children on measures she labels "advanced social development": sociability, social competence, language, persistence, achievement, self-confidence, and problem-solving. Because of this, she argues that the findings of greater aggression and noncompliance among children who received infant care probably signify greater independence rather than general emotional maladjustment. In addition, the same pattern of negative and positive behaviors occurs among children who enter group care at later ages, as toddlers or infants. Thus, rather than nonmaternal care specifically in the first year of life leading to emotional disturbance reflected in generalized social maladjustment, it seems more plausible that entry into group care at whatever age generates a more limited set of specific changes—both positive and negative—in the child's behavior.

Clarke-Stewart (1989) also calls attention to an effect of infant day care I have not yet discussed. Research has consistently found that compared with other children, those who have been in infant care are advanced in intellectual development when tested between eighteen months and five years. However, this acceleration of intellectual development appears to be only temporary. When children who did not receive infant care enter day care, kindergarten, or elementary school, they catch up. This pattern in intellectual development is consistent with the earlier interpretation of effects on social behavior.

Thus, the evidence that infant day care has negative long-term effects is less substantial than it first appears. At the same time, it is important to recall that in the broader policy debate about child care, the primary question about effects has not concerned potential negative consequences. Rather, the issue has been whether in addition to other possible grounds for greater public funding of child care, research shows that nonparental care has beneficial effects, particularly in the long term. Some data suggest that special child care programs designed to compensate for disadvantaged environments have such effects (Schweinhart, Weikart, and Larner 1986). But there is little evidence that nonparental care does so in general.

As far as effects on the child are concerned, the policy debate has largely focused on whether the effects of child care are positive enough to merit government subsidy and its obverse—whether these effects are negative enough to oppose government support. This focus, which views child care as a monolithic generic entity, has delayed sufficient attention to a question that perhaps has far greater relevance to the large policy debate: What constitutes quality child care? The generalization that child care does not have negative effects on children is based largely on studies conducted in university-affiliated programs, which are not typical of the nonparental care received by most children; and some surveys indicate that the majority of group care centers are only adequate in quality (Lamb, Sternberg, and Ketterlinus forthcoming).

Michael E. Lamb and colleagues (forthcoming) argue that parents have come to accept the quality and cost of currently available child care as normal and that it would have been better if higher-quality, higher-cost care—made possible by government subsidies—had been available much earlier.

Recent Policy Debate

The child care debate again reached the national political level in the late 1980s. Its major initiative has been the Act for Better Child Care (ABC), first introduced in Congress in 1988 and enacted in late 1990, providing $27 billion for child care over a five-year period. More time must pass before we can assess what made the legislation possible and what its effects will be (see *CDF Reports* 1990).

It is valuable, however, to analyze the terms on which ABC was debated. Presenting the conservative critique, Douglas J. Besharov (1988) of the American Enterprise Institute, and Robert J. Samuelson (1988a, 1988b), *Newsweek's* economics columnist, offered three main grounds for opposing the ABC proposal. Interestingly, some of their criticisms echoed Woolsey's arguments of a decade before. In evaluating their arguments below, the key features of the ABC legislation are presented.

First, Besharov and Samuelson criticized ABC as promoting only center-based care and creating needless additional federal bureaucracy and regulation. Most working mothers, they noted, do not use group care, and the cost of providing quality group care to all working families would be astronomical ($90 billion a year). Further, there is no evidence that group care is better for children than parental care.

Actually, only about one-third of ABC funds go to Head Start, other group care programs, and administrative and regulatory initiatives. Fully two-thirds of ABC funds go to tax credits directly to families. One such credit is continued funding of the Dependent Care Tax Credit (DCTC), a tax credit that two-earner couples and employed single parents can use to help offset child care costs. The second credit is an expansion of the Earned Income Tax Credit (EITC), a special tax credit for low-income households that functions as a negative income tax.

ABC opponents noted that the Dependent Care Tax Credit cannot be used to offset the cost of child care provided by relatives; in that sense, it discriminates against relative-provided care. However, the DCTC can be used for family day care, which is used currently by almost as many families as group care. Further, the other major component of ABC's tax credits—an expansion of the EITC to include more poor families—does not exclude families using relative care. Thus, the claim that ABC promotes group care exclusively or predominantly is difficult to sustain.

It also is difficult to agree with the implied claim that ABC promotes group care far out of proportion to the degree parents use or want it. The proportion of working families using group care has risen steadily since 1965 to 23 percent in 1985. As argued earlier, only group care can increase to keep up with projected increases in mothers' rates of employment. Thus, ABC's special supports for group care seem prudent. Further, the argument regarding astronomical cost also does not bear scrutiny. No liberal advocate has seriously proposed a federal initiative with the assumptions on which the $90 billion estimate is based: that *all* children of working families will or should be in group care and that the *entire* cost of group care should be borne by the federal government.

A second conservative argument against the ABC bill was that federal support for child care is really a special subsidy to the upper-middle-class minority who prefer group care and that it fails to address the far more significant needs of poor families. Conservatives point out that prior to ABC, federal support for child care had become substantial during the 1970s and 1980s, rising from $1 billion a year in 1972 to $6.8 billion a year in 1988 (Hayes, Palmer, and Zaslow 1990, Table 7–1). In more recent years, the largest share of federal expenditure for child care has been the Dependent Care Tax Credit ($3.9 billion in 1988). Other components include: Head Start ($1.2 billion), targeted to poor families; the Title XX Social Service Block Grant ($600 million), which provides funds for states to allocate for all social services, some of which are used to subsidize child care "slots" for welfare or other poor families or to support child care for the poor in other ways; the Child Care Food Program ($600 million); and a variety of small programs related to job training, welfare, teen mothers, and before- and after-school care for school-aged children ($500 million).

The Dependent Care Tax Credit is used disproportionately by higher-income families. In 1985, 64 percent of the credit was claimed by families with incomes over $20,000 and only 6 percent by families making less than $10,000 (Martinez 1989). This pattern of usage occurs in spite of the fact that the percentage of child expenses claimable for the credit declines with increased income, presumably because higher-income families nonetheless spend more on child care and because the proportion of couples with two earners (a prerequisite for the credit in two-parent families) is greater among higher-income families. During the 1980s, the DCTC expanded dramatically, whereas support for the other programs—which benefit poor families relatively more—either did not grow as fast or in the case of the Social Services Block Grant, was actually cut. Overall, the proportion of federal child care support used by poor families decreased from 80 percent in 1972 to 28 percent in 1988 (Hayes, Palmer, and Zaslow 1990: 197). As Fern Marx (1985) noted, this shift put increasing pressure on the subsidized system of care at the state and local levels at the same time that overall demand for child care was rising. This reversal of federal child care funding was not engineered by liberal child care advocates, however, but by conservatives who wanted to reduce direct spending for social services and reduce the tax burden on the middle class.

The new additional funding for child care under ABC maintains the roughly 2:1 ratio between tax credit and other child care spending. However, it shifts tax benefits away from the upper middle class and toward lower-income families by setting an income ceiling above which the DCTC cannot be used and expanding the Earned Income Tax Credit to include more lower-income families. Thus, the ABC program does respond to the concern that recent federal child care support has disproportionately benefited the upper middle class and attempts to correct this unfortunate bias.

The third conservative criticism was that federal support for child care creates economic disincentives for full-time homemaking and mothers caring for their own children. Besharov and Samuelson believe ABC is ultimately based on the assumption that mothers' being employed and children receiving group care is better than children's being raised by their parents. Conservatives assert that these assumptions are unsubstantiated and reflect only the liberal value perspective. Unless these assumptions can be validated, conservatives pointedly ask, how else can we justify spending federal funds in a way that encourages mothers to work and place their children in group care?

As noted earlier, it is true that the research does not indicate that as a general matter, nonparental or out-of-home care is better for children than parental care. But few if any liberal child care advocates make such a claim in support of greater federal funding. On the question of impact on mothers' employment, several studies do suggest that lack of adequate day care has a greater inhibiting effect than was evident in the studies reviewed by Woolsey (Hayes, Palmer, and Zaslow 1990: 34–37; Levine, Harlan, Seligson, Pleck, and Lein 1981). In a 1991 study of mothers of preschool children in low-income cities, Freya L. Sonenstein suggests that 25 percent of such mothers would work if child care were available. However, it seems likely that the availability or lack of child care has a relatively weak effect on mothers' employment decisions; family economic need has a much greater impact. The social value of greater federal support for child care is not a function of its hypothetical encouragement of mothers' employment and nonparental care, viewed as intrinsic social goods. Rather, it is a function of the extent to which mothers who *must* be employed cannot find or afford adequate child care because the child care system is underfunded at a broad social level.

To the extent that this is true, without federal support these families will place their children in inadequate or, worse, no care. Although there is no agreement among researchers that quality child care substantially benefits children, there is little disagreement that inadequate care or no care hurts them. The value of expanded federal child care support lies specifically in decreasing the number of children in the most inadequate arrangements, not in increasing the number of children in high-quality group care per se.

Now that the ABC bill has been enacted, a new era in federal policy for child care has begun. The experience of the early 1990s will be critical in determining the future of U.S. child care policies at the federal level.

ALTERNATIVE WORK SCHEDULES

After the setback to the child care advocacy campaign in the early 1970s, flexible work schedules emerged as the next focal policy issue. In 1978, at the high point of policy interest in work schedules, Congress passed legislation mandating wider use of flextime and part-time work in the federal civil service and evaluation at the end of five years to determine whether these schedules should be promoted further. It was widely hoped that in its role as one of the nation's largest employers, the federal government could act as a pace setter for other employers. These laws are still in force (*Conditions of Work Digest* 1989), although they have received little recent attention. Many policy analysts are skeptical of the actual degree of benefit to families provided by alternative schedules and are concerned about their potential negative impacts on women. Today, however, the pendulum of interest in work schedules is starting to swing back—incorporated in a new, broader formulation of workplace "flexibility."

Surveys of working parents often indicate great concern about and interest in alternative work schedules (Galinsky and Stein 1990). Although nonstandard schedules can take many forms, the two most important from a policy perspective as well as from working parents' point of view are part time (including job sharing) and flextime. The policy debates about these two schedule innovations have presented both similarities and differences.

Part-Time Work

For a significant minority of workers, part-time work can potentially be an ideal solution to the problems of combining job and family responsibilities. Many working mothers report that they want such work for this reason. Some research also finds that in certain respects, part-time work has the most favorable consequences for children's development (Bronfenbrenner and Crouter 1982).

There are fundamental concerns about part-time work from a policy perspective, however, concerning its impact on gender equity. Because women make more use of it than men, and because it can be fundamentally exploitative of the worker by generally providing lower wages, fewer benefits, less job security, and less potential for earnings mobility, promoting part-time work can increase gender inequity. For this reason, policy advocates for part-time work make clear that they support a new form of part-time work, which differs from the predominant form now available, and does not have these drawbacks. As formulated by Hilda Kahne (1985), the policy recommendation is "new concept" part-time work.

In March 1988, almost 5.5 million women with children under eighteen worked part time (according to the Bureau of Labor Statistics definition), representing over one-quarter of the 20.1 million employed (U.S. Department of Labor 1989). About three-quarters of women working part time are classified as doing so on a voluntary as opposed to an involuntary (or economic) basis—that is, because only part-time work is available (Kahne 1992). In a 1987 BLS survey of ten thousand business establishments employing ten or more workers, nearly 35 percent reported offering voluntary part-time work to at least some workers, and 15.5 percent offered job sharing—a special form of part-time work in which a single full-time job is formally divided into two part-time jobs (Hayghe 1988). By these indicators, the availability of positive forms of part-time work appears to be relatively high. However, involuntary part-time work has grown faster than the voluntary form in recent years. Kahne (1992) observes that economic part-time workers increased by over 50 percent between 1979 and 1987, whereas the number of voluntary part-time workers grew by only 14 percent.

Because of the potential problems of part-time work as it generally exists today, labor advocates for women have been reluctant to give it much policy emphasis. Among feminists, even in new concept form, part-time work is viewed as usable only by families who do not require a second full-time parental income, presumably more affluent families. Thus, no advocacy coalition is actively encouraging part-time work. However, in spite of its limitations, part-time work is nonetheless significant for women as a transitional form of employment—a step between full-time work and no employment at all. Thus, the absence of significant advocacy for better part-time work leaves an important gap in current reform efforts for work-family policies.

Flextime

Flextime is a form of schedule flexibility in which workers have some latitude in determining their daily starting and ending times. After initial enthusiasm following its introduction in the United States (it was pioneered in Germany) in the late 1960s, policy analysts soon expressed reservations about its actual benefits for the family. Only about 12 percent of the workforce reported having a flextime schedule in 1985, and this proportion had not risen since 1980 (Mellor 1986). It was not clear whether flextime could be realistically introduced on a broader basis. Further, reviewing the limited evaluations of the impact of flextime then available, Sheila B. Kamerman and Paul W. Kingston (1982: 184) concluded that "researchers, policy makers, and most importantly families themselves therefore should not expect flextime to be a panacea for the conflicts between work and family life. Any gains in quality of family life will likely be modest, although no less worth promoting for that reason." Harriet B. Presser (1989: 534, 525) more recently asserted that research has found "little or no difference in the amount of time spent with children and few differences on other family measures" and argues further that job flexibility "seems to reinforce rather than mitigate gender differences among dual-earner couples in assigning responsibility for child rearing" (see also Bohen 1984). My own reading of the past research (cf. Christensen and Staines 1990) and a major 1990 study (Staines 1990) suggest that the impact of flextime may in reality be more favorable. Among the older studies, H. Bohen and A. Viveros-Long (1981) found few differences in family time use comparing employees in federal agencies that had adopted or not adopted flextime. But the two other older studies that unlike Bohen and Viveros-Long, actually compared workers' behavior before and after the introduction of flextime (Lee 1983, restricted to two-earner families; Winett and Neale 1980) found significant increments in parents' and fathers' time with their children. In the R. A. Winett and M. S. Neale study, among parents who changed their schedules when flextime became available, time spent alone with children rose from 58 minutes per day before flextime to 82 minutes per day after flextime in one workplace and from 76 to 89 minutes per day in the second, the latter increment holding up in observations collected six months after the change in schedule policy. Among those who did not alter their schedules, there was no consistent pattern of change in time spent with children. Other data in this study suggested that the same proportion (about half) of parents of both sexes actually change their schedules when flextime is instituted.

An important 1990 study by Graham L. Staines, using data from representative samples of mothers of newborns in four states gathered in 1988, made the previously overlooked distinction between two levels of flextime: moderate flexibility (can change times, but must then keep these times for some minimum period) and high flexibility (can change starting and ending times frequently and easily). Employed mothers with the more flexible form of flextime reported higher job satisfaction, higher parent satisfaction, and lower work-family conflict compared with those with inflexible schedules. The less flexible form of flextime appeared to have little impact on these outcomes. Thus, it appears that flextime, especially forms that give workers more latitude in controlling their schedules, does have some positive impact on time spent with children and on satisfaction and stress from attempting to mesh job and family roles. The magnitude of these effects appears to be small simply because the degree of flexibility actually offered under existing policies is limited and not because schedule flexibility inherently has minimal impact.

Although flextime is associated with some increases in parents' time with children and with modest reductions of work-family stress, these do not appear to be the primary criteria used in evaluating it. Instead, many policy analysts seem to impose two other standards. First, can flextime play a significant role in meeting working parents' needs for child care? It currently does not, and it appears unlikely that it will expand to such a degree that it will do so in the future. Rather than use flextime, holding jobs with different shifts seems to be the way working parents use work schedules to reduce the need for nonparental child care (Staines and Pleck 1983).

Second, does flextime reinforce gender inequity in the marital division of labor? In spite of the concern expressed by Presser (1989) and Bohen (1984), flextime appears to have no net impact on gender equity because flextime is equally available to both sexes and has similar consequences for the family behavior of mothers and fathers, both in terms of the proportion of each group that will use it to change their schedules and of its consequences on their family time use. In order to reinforce gender inequity, data would need to indicate one or more of the following: that flextime is more available to women than to men; that when offered the opportunity to alter one's schedule, wives do so more often than husbands; or that altering one's schedule leads to an increase in time spent in family roles to a greater degree for wives than for husbands. In fact, none of these premises holds true.

Current Trends

Overall, work-family advocates are giving relatively little positive emphasis today to part-time work and flexible work schedules per se. In essence, those advocates whose work-family concerns are rooted in child welfare see these policies as having little favorable impact on children. Those whose primary interests are women and gender equity likewise view these policies as having a negative impact (a concern that does not appear to be justified for flextime). Thus, no constituency within the work-family advocacy community is actively promoting these work schedules.

At the same time, ironically there seems to be new interest in both part-time work and flextime in the corporate world. Rather than focusing on these work schedules as individual policies, corporations are now incorporating them under the broader rubric of "flexibility." Prominent recent examples include a major Conference Board report on flexible staffing and scheduling (Christensen 1989) and an American Management Association handbook, *Creating a Flexible Workplace* (Olmsted and Smith 1989).

PARENTAL LEAVE

Starting in the 1980s, the work-family advocacy campaign next turned to parental leave as a new focal issue. The publication of Sheila B. Kamerman, Alfred J. Kahn, and Paul W. Kingston's *Maternity Policies and Working Women* (1983) was a milestone event in parental leave research and advocacy. During the remainder of the 1980s, legislation mandating employers to provide varying kinds and amounts of parental leave was subsequently introduced at the federal and state levels.

In one sense, this emergence of parental leave as a policy issue was the inevitable result of the continuing evolution of women's labor force trends: As rates of women's employment continued to rise overall, dramatic increases in paid work became evident even among mothers with children under one year of age. Women workers giving birth increasingly returned to employment during the newborn's first year, and this new pattern created recognition of the need for parental leave.

Another factor in the new parental leave advocacy was the simplicity of the comparison between the United States and other industrial societies. In the case of government support for child care, what other countries were doing seemed so different from the situation in the United States as to have no applicability. Child care approaches in other societies also varied considerably from each other and thus implied no simple recommendation for the United States.

But for parental leave, it seemed more self-evident that the United States should do what other industrial countries are doing. What other countries did, although it varied somewhat, was far more uniform than their child care policies. It also was far simpler to describe, particularly in the language of rights so often effective in U.S. civic life: Women workers in almost every other industrial society had a right U.S. women lacked. This entitlement seemed so justified, in fact, that one of the early problems of the advocacy campaign was to change the common misconception that U.S. women already had parental leave benefits (Kamerman, Kahn, and Kingston 1983).

Temporary Medical Disability

The recent history of parental leave policies in the United States can be organized around three major conceptions of parental leave: as temporary medical disability, as a special protection for working women, and as child care leave. Until the 1980s, the primary issue to be resolved concerned the "pregnancy exclusion"—the then-common practice of excluding pregnancy-related disability (normal physical recovery in the period immediately following childbirth) from temporary medical disability policies. As recounted by Kamerman and colleagues (1983), in 1966 the Equal Employment Opportunity Commission (EEOC) issued an opinion that employers could exclude pregnancy-related disability from temporary medical disability benefits without violating Title VII's (Civil Rights Act of 1964) prohibition of sex discrimination. In 1972 the EEOC reversed itself, now holding that the pregnancy exclusion was impermissible. But in 1976 the Supreme Court, responding to company challenges to lower court rulings supporting the new EEOC guidelines, held in *Gilbert vs. General Electric* that the pregnancy exclusion was not discriminatory.

In response to the consternation about this decision and to intensive lobbying by feminist groups, Congress passed the Pregnancy Discrimination Act (PDA) of 1978. The PDA required that pregnancy be included if other medical disabilities were covered in benefit plans. This legislation did not mandate disability coverage where it did not presently exist but only required that pregnancy disability not be treated differentially. Thus, over a twelve-year period ending in the late 1970s, the question of the pregnancy exclusion was conclusively resolved. The motivation for this resolution, however, was the right of women to equal treatment, not the need of women (or working families) to have a benefit. The latter perspective would enter the parental leave policy debate in the next phase.

Special Protection

The next defining event in the debate was the California Federal (or Garland) case. In 1985 in a case involving Lillian Garland, an employee of the California Federal Savings and Loan Association, a federal court struck down a California law that conceptualized parental leave as a special protection for working women. The statute required employers to provide unpaid pregnancy disability leave with the guarantee of return to the same or a comparable job; California law did not specify a similar job guarantee at the end of unpaid leave for other types of temporary medical disabilities. Montana and Massachusetts had similar laws.

In 1987, however, the Supreme Court reversed the lower court and upheld California's statute (Goldstein 1988: 52–64). The test applied by the court was not whether this special protection statute was discriminatory by sex but rather whether it was consistent with the Pregnancy Discrimination Act. The court ruled that when Congress passed the Pregnancy Discrimination Act, it had not intended to prohibit employers from treating pregnancy better than other disabilities but only to prohibit them from not treating it as well.

The debate about the California Federal case caused deep division within the feminist legal and political community. The majority felt they should oppose the California statute because the principle of equal rights and equal treatment was so fundamental to feminist legal initiatives. In particular, it was the equal rights standard that had been so successful in the elimination of the pregnancy exclusion less than a decade before. A minority held that in this case, special protection was justified. Pragmatically, some also argued that if the choice was between offering leave to both sexes or to women only, the offer of leave to both was the better option. But if the choice was between leave for women only and leave for no one—the consequence of invalidating the California law—then leave for women only must be supported.

A few holding the majority (equal rights) feminist view expressed it in a rather unappealing form. Diane Feinstein, then-mayor of San Francisco, criticized proponents of the law as "asking to create a special group of workers that, in essence, is pregnant women and new mothers. I just don't happen to agree with that. I don't think the work market has to accommodate itself to women having children" (Hewlett 1986: 146). Statements such as these provided ample opportunity for Sylvia Hewlett (1986) and others critical of U.S. feminism to foster a fundamental misinterpretation of the historical role of feminism in improving work-family policies. One would conclude from Hewlett's account that the major reason the United States has poor maternity leave policies is that organized U.S. feminism not only ignores and fails to promote such policies but actively opposes them. This view is difficult to reconcile with feminism's leading role in the passage of the Pregnancy Discrimination Act. Hewlett also has an overgenerous estimate of the ability of organized feminism to influence legislation.

In retrospect, the debate over the California Federal case perhaps need not have been so acrimonious. It is important to recognize that the issue in the case was not whether the special protection approach *had* to be used or *would* be used as the primary vehicle for parental leave but only whether legally it *could* be used. Ironically, by the time of the court's affirmation of special protection, advocates for better parental leave policies were already discarding this approach. Instead, the current advocacy campaign favors a combination of temporary medical disability and gender-neutral child care leave, to which I now turn.

Child Care Leave and the Family and Medical Leave Act

In the mid-1980s, a new conception of parental leave emerged: leave as care for the child. This conception was fostered particularly by developmental psychologists active in child welfare advocacy. Especially influential was Edward Zigler, founder of the Infant Care Leave Project at Yale University, who argued that there were "compelling child and family health reasons . . . to support voluntary, part-paid, six-month leaves for infant care" (Zigler and Muenchow 1983: 91). Once this view of parental leave appeared, it seemed persuasive to many.

In the mid-1980s, child care leave was integrated in a new national advocacy initiative, the Family and Medical Leave Act. Although introduced in earlier sessions, the FMLA first came under active consideration, resulting in congressional hearings, in 1985. As originally proposed, the essence of the FMLA was that employers be required to offer a component of unpaid temporary medical disability leave (under current practice, women generally qualify for six to eight weeks of leave following birth) and a component of unpaid "family" leave. This combination elegantly integrates the principle of gender-neutrality in parental leave, with the reality that a workable policy must recognize that mothers giving birth also have a special need that is not shared by fathers. Only women are eligible for that component of parental leave intended for temporary medical disability following pregnancy (although men can make claims for other temporarily disabling conditions). Both sexes, however, are eligible for the child care component of leave.

As the lobbying for and against the bill evolved, these two components were collapsed into a unified family and medical unpaid leave period of twelve weeks, usable by workers who have newborn or adopted children and serious illnesses in themselves, their children, or their spouses. Employers would be required to continue any existing health benefits during this period. Employers with fewer than fifty workers (85 percent of all employers) were exempted. Congress passed a bill with these provisions in 1990; President Bush vetoed it.

The business community strongly lobbied against the FMLA on the grounds of the costs and inflexibility it would impose on companies, especially small ones. Pro, anti, and neutral groups produced wildly varying estimates of the total annual cost of earlier versions of this bill. The General Accounting Office (1988) estimated that the revised 1987 version would cost employers $194 million per year, almost entirely in the cost of maintaining employer contributions to health insurance. Roberta M. Spalter-Roth and Heidi E. Hartmann (1988) took the alternative tack of estimating the costs of *not* having the policies in the FMLA, including lost earnings due to childbirth and unemployment, which they calculated to be about $2 billion a year. It is in fact difficult to determine what costs and assumptions should be factored into such estimates. The principal objection of the business community, however, was not costs—likely to be quite low in light of the proportion of companies and workers exempted as well as the shortness and unpaid nature of the leave—but rather the precedent of a federal mandate for any specific leave benefit, which business saw as reducing employers' flexibility (United States Chamber of Commerce 1988). Conservatives also attacked the FMLA as "creeping socialism" and as antifamily because, they argued, it would encourage mothers to work after childbirth (Kovach 1987).

An unlikely coalition of both conservatives and liberals also opposed the FMLA on the grounds of who did—and who did not—benefit from it. Phyllis Schlafly (1988), noted opponent of the Equal Rights Amendment, denounced the FMLA as yet another example of federal policies favoring working mothers and discriminating against full-time homemakers and their families. She also asserted that it disadvantaged single-parent mothers because they could not afford to take unpaid leave. Republican Rep. Dick Armey (1987) of Texas assailed the FMLA as "yuppie welfare": Only highly affluent upper-middle-class couples could afford to use it.

Simultaneously, liberals—especially those most concerned for the poor and minorities—also objected to the FMLA because it was unpaid. The *New York Times* opposed it on the grounds that low-paid workers would be harmed more than benefited: They could not afford the leaves the FMLA provided and might lose wages as employers passed along the costs of the leave entitlement to workers in general ("Parental Leave: Leave It At That" 1990).

An additional objection of many within the broader work-family advocacy coalition was that parental leave, even under a generous policy, was so short. Thus, they said, better parental leave policies would have almost no impact on the need for child care, the most pressing need of working families. More than a few privately expressed doubts that the FMLA had any real value (Kornbluh 1991).

Work-family advocates who do not support parental leave because they favor child care more do not fully recognize that the two policies are not interchangeable. At the beginning of the current advocacy campaign, Edward Zigler and Susan Muenchow (1983) had argued for child care leave precisely because it was uncertain that nonparental care was optimal during the first months of a child's life, and it was unlikely in any event that quality infant care would ever be available on a broad scale. Although surveys show favorable attitudes toward nonparental care for older preschool children, few favor nonparental care—especially group care—for infants (Mason and Kuhlthau 1988). Thus, to the charge that parental leave will do little to reduce the demand for child care, one might respond that it also is true that better child care policies will do little to reduce the demand for parental leave. It is not that parental leave meets a need for child care or has specific positive impacts on the child. Rather, without other alternatives for mothers who must continue working, the absence of parental leave policies puts families at risk of crisis.

Although the campaign for a national family and medical leave policy appears to have paused at the national level with the 1990 veto, new parental leave legislation is steadily being enacted at the state level. As of June 1990, thirty states had some form of parental leave legislation (Women's Bureau 1990; Lenhoff and Becker 1989). States' provision of these policies has made it possible to evaluate their impact on both employers and families.

The Families and Work Institute surveyed employers participating in the state-administered unemployment insurance programs in Oregon, Wisconsin, Minnesota, and Rhode Island before and after the passage of parental leave legislation taking effect during 1988. These states' legislation mandated varying periods of disability and child care leave and included varying other provisions concerning exclusions, maintenance of benefits, job guarantees, adoption, and so forth. The majority of employers in each state reported neither serious increases in costs nor difficulty in administering and implementing the legislation. For example, between 74 and 77 percent of employers experienced no increase in training costs (due to the potential need to train temporary replacements for those on leave), and 56 to 66 percent indicated that they had no increase in administrative costs (Trost 1990).

This and earlier studies (Kamerman, Kahn, and Kingston 1983; Christensen 1989) also found that the majority of employers offered at least some leave for biological mothers during the disability period following birth. From one point of view, these data support the corporate contention that new parental leave legislation is unnecessary because comparable benefits are already being provided for most employees. At the same time, these findings put in a new perspective the criticism that mandating parental leave is "yuppie welfare," conferring a benefit only on the affluent (Armey 1987). The data suggest that rather than giving a new right to an already advantaged group, the main effect of such legislation is to extend to the minority of disadvantaged workers a benefit the advantaged already have. When the majority have a benefit, the minority who do not have it tend to be the less affluent.

Because so many states currently have some mandated parental leave, an analogous point can be made at the state level. The states that currently mandate some form of parental leave tend to be the more affluent and more progressive states. For residents of the twenty states without parental leave legislation, there still is a need for the minimum national standard provided in the FMLA, which would extend to them the benefits now enjoyed by others. In essence, the FMLA is not "yuppie welfare" because young urban professionals already disproportionately work for the employers and live in the states that currently provide parental leave (Pleck 1988b). As parental leave laws are passed by more states and their consequences are recognized to be relatively minimal in terms of actual effects on employers, passage of a minimum national standard may become substantially easier.

CONCLUSION

Before presenting an overview of the policies, it is worthwhile to reconsider the issues noted at the outset concerning the interrelationships among women's employment, women's well-being, and work-family policies. The finding in U.S. studies that employment appears to convey benefits to wives' mental health may seem remarkable in light of the limited and uneven policy response wives' employment has received. Indeed, many of the studies documenting this effect were conducted in periods when policy support for working families was far less than is the case today. There also might be grounds for questioning whether these results are fully generalizable to the present, when mothers with children under age three are a more prevalent group among all employed mothers. The absence of better policy responses might be expected to limit the gains from employment most among these women. Yet in past studies, the psychological benefits of employment were actually the most consistent for mothers of young children. In my view, the conclusion to draw is that although poor policy supports may reduce the beneficial impact of employment on women's lives, their net effect is still clearly positive. Improvements in child care, work schedule, and parental leave policies should be viewed as enhancing this overall beneficial effect.

As noted earlier, feminists such as Hochschild (1989) have viewed husband's limited family responsibility as impairing employed wives' mental health more than do problems with child care or rigid workplace policies. Some have expressed concern that work-family policies actually reinforce inequity in the marital division of labor. This apprehension seems contradicted, however, by the results of research on flextime. As argued earlier, because women and men use flextime to the same degree and using flextime increases men's family participation as much as women's, flextime appears to have no net impact on the division of family roles. Likewise, it is difficult to view nonparental child care as reinforcing women's family responsibility, unless one assumes that greater father participation in child care would make other child care arrangements unnecessary. It might be argued that because parental leave policies are used far more by mothers than by fathers, they reinforce women's traditional family responsibility. However, having no parental leave policies would reinforce women's traditional role even more because new mothers would lose their jobs.

An important analytical question that could not be taken up until the specific policies had been discussed in some detail is to what degree work-family policies have been directly linked to changes in women's employment patterns. As rates of women's employment have risen since 1960, work-family policies have become more favorable. However, as this review documents, this improvement has proceeded slowly and unevenly. It is significant that in several of the key instances of actual or proposed changes in work-family policies in earlier decades, the change resulted from concerns other than for the well-being of the growing proportion of employed women. For example, flextime was originally introduced to reduce traffic congestion at peak commuting times. The Child Development Act of 1971 was motivated primarily by concern for the well-being of low-income children, not of women.

In one of the early major works analyzing work-family policies in cross-national perspective, Kamerman and Kahn (1981) advanced the hypothesis that countries appeared to develop explicit policies in response to work-family issues when the proportion of women with young children (in particular, those under age three) in the labor force approaches and exceeds 50 percent. In the most recent figures available at the time of their writing (1979 data), this proportion was 41 percent. Thus, Kamerman and Kahn argued, because this proportion was beginning to approach 50 percent, the policymaking system was being challenged to respond more explicitly to the strains experienced by working mothers, their families, and children, just as other industrial societies currently with higher percentages of working women with young children had done much earlier.

The labor force participation rate for mothers of children under three passed the 50 percent mark in the mid-1980s, and stood at 52.5 percent in the most recent data available (1988) at the time of this writing (U.S. Department of Labor 1989). Perhaps illustrating Kamerman and Kahn's observation about

50 percent as a "tipping point," the most explicit and large-scale response to work-family issues yet to occur at the federal level—the Act for Better Child Care—was introduced in the mid-1980s and enacted in 1990. The number of states mandating some form of maternity or parental leave also jumped markedly in the late 1980s. In these recent work-family initiatives, the desire to promote the well-being of women also has been somewhat more evident than was the case in earlier decades. Thus, the particular turning point in women's employment patterns emphasized by Kamerman and Kahn has in fact been associated with significant work-family policy changes.

But important as these policy changes are, the degree of policy response to women's employment has clearly been less than in other industrial societies. U.S. policies are far less generous than those elsewhere (Kamerman, Kahn, and Kingston 1983; Kamerman 1989). Even recent progress in policies has been mixed. In the most crucial policy area—child care—supply has barely kept pace with demand, and quality and affordability have not improved overall. Federal child care support actually shifted away from the poor and toward the middle class during the 1980s, so that in some ways child care became less available and less affordable for poorer families. It remains to be seen whether the passage of the Act for Better Child Care marks the end or even the reversal of this trend.

In work schedules, involuntary part-time work has grown faster than voluntary part-time work. However, flextime has become available to a significant minority of workers. There is a continuing advocacy effort to promote a broader "flexibility" of staffing and scheduling that incorporates these and other alternative arrangements. In the area of parental leave, the veto of the 1990 Family and Medical Leave Act was a major setback. However, many states have enacted similar legislation, and the majority of states now have some form of mandated parental leave.

Just as the degree of progress has varied according to the content area of the policy, it also has varied in terms of locus. The 1990 Act for Better Child Care was enacted at the federal level, but parental leave has been more successful in the states and in collective bargaining. Schedule policies have changed most through collective bargaining and management initiatives within the private sector and in public employment (including education). The ABC legislation notwithstanding, the focus of work-family reform has shifted to some degree away from the federal level to the states and the private sector.

Why the United States exhibits such a uniquely weak policy response to work-family issues is clearly a question of fundamental importance, but it is beyond the scope of this chapter to address this question fully. Certainly one factor is the deep ambivalence about mothers' employment that appears to characterize U.S. values—an ambivalence no less evident among women than among men or corporate and governmental policymakers. In spite of high rates of employment, letters to women's advice columns in newspapers and magazines still are filled with concerns about the consequences of mothers' working. The 1990 Democratic gubernatorial candidate in a major Northeastern state asserted that "there is no question that we have a generation of neglected children, we have a generation of abused children, by women who have thought that a third-rate day care center was just as good as a first-rate home" ("Silber Laments" 1990: 1). There are undoubtedly additional reasons to explain why the United States has far less favorable policies than other industrial countries (Kamerman 1989: 108–110 provides an excellent critical discussion), but this deep-seated ambivalence must be considered a significant underlying cause.

Another factor accounting for the slow progress of the United States is that each of the three major policies provides benefits to somewhat different subgroups of working parents. Each policy thus has its own unique group of constituencies. For example, the Dependent Care Tax Credit mostly helps the middle class. Policies supporting group care differentially also benefit the middle class, but usage by working-class families is probably increasing.

By contrast, flextime and other formal alternative work schedule policies benefit lower-income workers more because these workers' schedules are generally more rigid and formalized; a large proportion of the middle class already has flextime de facto. Unpaid parental leave is used more often by higher-income families. However, having pregnancy disability leave provided on a paid rather than an unpaid basis benefits lower-income families more in terms of the value of this wage replacement to them. Parental leave policies illustrate another kind of restriction of impact because they benefit families for only a short period of time (although leave policies may have important indirect effects in the longer term).

The advocacy constituencies associated with each policy have, to some degree, pushed for their particular reform in a relatively narrow way. These groups have forged few links with each other, and there has been little development of a more holistic work-family policy perspective. One advocacy group is often unsupportive of the reforms proposed by another. The most common objection is that a particular policy does not benefit lower-income families. In this way, many in the advocacy coalition have seemed to take the position that if a particular policy does not solve all problems, then it does not solve any problems. Division among the advocacy groups promoting better policies, particularly in the context of the emergence of explicit counter-advocacy efforts, has contributed to the slow rate of progress in the United States.

BIBLIOGRAPHY

Armey, Dick. "Parental Leave Act Is Just Yuppie Welfare." *Wall Street Journal*, February 26, 1987, A14.

Baruch, Grace, Rosalind Barnett, Caryl Rivers. *Life Prints: New Patterns of Love and Work for Today's Women*. New York: McGraw-Hill, 1983.

Belsky, Jay. "A Reassessment of Infant Day Care." In *The Parental Leave Crisis: Toward a National Policy*, edited by Edward F. Zigler and Meryl Frank. New Haven: Yale, 1988, 100–119.

————. "Infant-Parent Attachment and Day Care: In Defense of the Strange Situation." In *Caring for Children: Challenge to America*, edited by Jeffrey S. Lande, Sandra Scarr, and Nina Gunzenhauser. Hillsdale, N.J.: Erlbaum 1989, 23–48.

Belsky, Jay, and Lawrence Steinberg. "The Effects of Day Care: A Critical Review." *Developmental Psychology* 49 (1978): 929–949.

Besharov, Douglas J. "The Politics of Day Care: We're About to Spend Billions on a Dubious Middle-Class 'Crisis.'" *Washington Post*, August 21, 1988, C5.

Bohen, H. "Gender Equality in Work and Family: An Elusive Goal?" *Journal of Family Issues* 5 (1984): 254–272.

Bohen, H., and A. Viveros-Long. *Balancing Jobs and Family Life: Do Flexible Schedules Help?* Philadelphia: Temple University Press, 1981.

Bronfenbrenner, Urie, and Ann C. Crouter. "Work and Family Through Time and Space." In *Families That Work: Children in a Changing World*, edited by Sheila B. Kamerman and Cheryl D. Hayes. Washington, D.C.: National Academy Press, 1982, 39–83.

CDF Reports. "Special Report: A Child Care Victory." Washington, D.C.: Children's Defense Fund, November 1990.

Christensen, Kathleen. *Flexible Staffing and Scheduling in U.S. Corporations.* New York: The Conference Board, 1989.

Christensen, Kathleen, and Graham Staines. "Flextime: A Viable Solution to Work-Family Conflict?" *Journal of Family Issues* 11 (1990): 455–476.

Clarke-Stewart, K. Allison. "Infant Day Care: Maligned or Malignant?" *American Psychologist* 44 (1989): 266–273.

Conditions of Work Digest. "Part-Time Work." Vol. 8, no. 1 (1989): entire issue.

Ehrenreich, Barbara, and Deirdre English. "Blowing the Whistle on the 'Mommy Track.'" *Ms.* 20 (July-August 1989): 56-58.

Feinstein, Karen Wolk. "Directions for Day Care." In *Work and Family: Changing Roles of Men and Women*, edited by Patricia Voydanoff. Palo Alto: Mayfield, 1984, 298–309.

Galinsky, Ellen, and Peter Stein. "The Impact of Human Resource Policies on Employees: Balancing Work and Family Life." *Journal of Family Issues* 11 (1990): 368–383.

General Accounting Office. *Parental Leave: Estimated Cost of Revised Parental and Medical Leave Act.* Washington, D.C.: General Accounting Office, 1988.

Goldstein, Leslie Friedman. *The Constitutional Rights of Women: Cases in Law and Social Change.* Madison: University of Wisconsin Press, 1988.

Hayes, Cheryl D., John L. Palmer, and Martha J. Zaslow. *Who Cares for America's Children: Child Care Policy for the 1990s.* Washington, D.C.: National Academy Press, 1990.

Hayghe, Howard V. "Employers and Child Care: What Roles Do They Play?" *Monthly Labor Review* 111 (1988): 38–44.

Hewlett, Sylvia Ann. *A Lesser Life: The Myth of Women's Liberation in America.* New York: Morrow, 1986.

Hochschild, Arlie, with Anne Machung. *The Second Shift: Working Parents and the Revolution at Home.* New York: Viking, 1989.

Hofferth, Sandra L., and Deborah A. Phillips. "Child Care in the United States: 1970 to 1995." *Journal of Marriage and the Family* 49 (1987): 559–571.

Hoffman, Lois Wladis. "Effects of Maternal Employment in the Two-Parent Family." *American Psychologist* 44 (1989): 283–292.

Kahne, Hilda. *Reconceiving Part-Time Work: New Options for Older Workers and Women.* Totowa, N.J.: Rowman and Allanheld, 1985.

———. "Part-Time Work: A Hope and a Peril." In *Part-Time Work: Opportunity or Dead End*, edited by Barbara Warme, Katherine Lundy, and Larry Lundy. New York: Praeger, 1992.

Kamerman, Sheila B. "Child Care, Women, Work, and the Family: An International Overview of the Child Care Services and Related Policies." In *Caring for Children: Challenge to America*, edited by Jeffrey S. Lande, Sandra Scarr, and Nina Gunzenhauser. Hillsdale, N.J.: Erlbaum, 1989, 93–100.

Kamerman, Sheila B., and Alfred J. Kahn. *Child Care, Family Benefits, and Working Parents*. New York: Columbia University Press, 1981.

Kamerman, Sheila B., and Paul W. Kingston. "Employer Responses to the Family Responsibilities of Employees." In *Families That Work: Children in a Changing World*, edited by Sheila B. Kamerman and Cheryl D. Hayes. Washington, D.C.: National Academy Press, 1982, 144–208.

Kamerman, Sheila B., Alfred J. Kahn, and Paul W. Kingston. *Maternity Policies and Working Women*. New York: Columbia University Press, 1983.

Kessler, Ronald C., and James McRae. "The Effect of Wives' Employment on the Mental Health of Married Men and Women." *Journal of Health and Social Behavior* 47 (1982): 216–227.

Kornbluh, Joyce. "Feminism's Failures?" *Women's Review of Books* 8, no. 6 (1991): 7–8.

Kovach, Kenneth A. "Creeping Socialism or Good Public Policy: The Proposed Parental and Medical Leave Act." *Labor Law Journal* 38 (1987): 427–432.

Lamb, Michael E., and Kathleen J. Sternberg. "Do We Really Know How Daycare Affects Children?" *Journal of Applied Developmental Psychology* 11 (1990): 351–379.

Lamb, Michael E., Kathleen J. Sternberg, and Robert D. Ketterlinus. "Child Care in the United States: The Modern Era." In *Nonparental Child Care: Cultural and Historical Perspectives*, edited by Michael E. Lamb, Kathleen J. Sternberg, Carl-Phillip Hwang, and Anders Broberg. Hillsdale, N.J.: Lawrence Erlbaum Associates, forthcoming.

Lee, R. A. "Flexitime and Conjugal Roles." *Journal of Occupational Behaviour* 4 (1983): 297–315.

Lenhoff, Donna R., and Sylvia M. Becker. "Family and Medical Leave Legislation in the States: Toward a Comprehensive Approach." *Harvard Journal on Legislation* 26 (1989): 403–463.

Levine, James, A., Sharon Harlan, Michelle Seligson, Joseph Pleck, and Laura Lein. *Child Care and Equal Opportunity for Women*. Washington, D.C.: U.S. Commission on Civil Rights, 1981.

Martinez, Susanne. "Child Care and Federal Policy." In *Caring for Children: Challenge to America*, edited by Jeffrey S. Lande, Sandra Scarr, and Nina Gunzenhauser. Hillsdale, N.J.: Erlbaum, 1989, 111–124.

Marx, Fern. "Child Care." In *Services to Young Families: Program Review and Policy Recommendations*, edited by Harriette McAdoo and T. M. Jim Parham. Washington, D.C.: American Public Welfare Association, 1985, 113–166.

Mason, K. O., and K. Kuhlthau. *Determinants of Child Care Ideals Among Mothers of Preschool Children* (Res. Rep. No. 88–126). Ann Arbor: University of Michigan, Population Studies Center, 1988.

Mellor, Earl F. "Shift Work and Flexitime: How Prevalent Are They?" *Monthly Labor Review* 109 (November 1986): 14–21.

National Organization for Women. "NOW's Statement of Purpose, 1966." In *Major Problems in Women's History: Documents and Essays*, edited by Mary Beth Norton. Lexington, Mass. D.C. Heath, 1989, 397–406 (document originally published in 1966).

NCJW Center for the Child. *Employer Supports for Child Care*. New York: National Council of Jewish Women, 1988.

Olmsted, Barney, and Suzanne Smith. *Creating a Flexible Workplace*. New York: AMACOM, 1989.

"Parental Leave: Leave It at That." *New York Times*, May 10, 1990, A32.

Phillips, Deborah A. "Future Directions and Need for a Child Care in the United States." In *Caring for Children: Challenge to America*, edited by Jeffrey S. Lande, Sandra Scarr, and Nina Gunzenhauser. Hillsdale, N.J.: Erlbaum, 1989, 257–274.

Pleck, Joseph H. *Working Wives, Working Husbands*. Beverly Hills, Calif.: Sage, 1985.

_____. "Employment and Fatherhood: Issues and Innovative Policies." In *The Father's Role: Applied Perspectives*, edited by Michael E. Lamb. New York: Wiley-Interscience, 1986, 385–412.

_____. "Fathers and Infant Care Leave." In *The Parental Leave Crisis: Toward a National Policy*, edited by Edward F. Zigler and Meryl Frank. New Haven: Yale, 1988a, 177–194.

_____. "Pro: The Family and Medical Leave Act of 1987." *Congressional Digest* 67 (1988b): 156–158.

_____. "Family-Supportive Employer Policies and Men's Participation." Paper presented at workshop held by the Panel on Employer Policies and Working Families, Committee on Women's Employment and Related Social Issues, National Research Council, Washington, D.C., March 1989.

_____. "Family-Supportive Employer Policies: Are They Relevant to Men?" Paper presented at an American Psychological Association workshop, Boston, 1990.

Presser, Harriet B. "Can We Make Time for Children? The Economy, Work Schedules, and Child Care." *Demography* 26 (1989): 523–543.

Samuelson, Robert J. "The Debate over Day Care." *Newsweek*, June 27, 1988a, 45.

_____. "Child Care Revisited." *Newsweek*, August 8, 1988b, 53.

Schlafly, Phyllis. "Con: The Family and Medical Leave Act of 1987." *Congressional Digest* 67 (1988): 145–149.

Schwartz, Felice. "Management Women and the New Facts of Life." *Harvard Business Review* 88 (1989): 65–76.

Schweinhart, L. J., D. P. Weikart, and M. D. Larner. "Consequences of Three Preschool Curriculum Models Through Age 15." *Early Childhood Research Quarterly* 1 (1986): 15–35.

Shinn, Marybeth, Blanca Ortiz-Torres, Anne Morris, and Patricia Simko. "Child Care Patterns, Stress, and Job Behaviors Among Working Parents." Paper presented at the conference of the American Psychological Association, New York, 1987.

"Silber Laments Work Vs. Family Choices." *Boston Globe*, October 26, 1990, 1.

Sonenstein, Freya L. "The Childcare Preferences of Parents with Young Children: How Little Is Known." In *Parental Leave and Child Care: Setting a Research and Policy Agenda*, edited by Janet Shibley Hyde and Marilyn J. Essex. Philadelphia: Temple University Press, 1991, 337–353.

Spalter-Roth, Roberta M., and Heidi I. Hartmann. *Unnecessary Losses: Costs to Americans of the Lack of Family and Medical Leave*. Washington, D.C.: Institute for Women's Policy Research, 1988.

Staines, Graham L. "Flextime and the Conflict Between Work and Family Life." Paper presented at the conference of the American Psychological Association, Boston, 1990.

Staines, Graham L., and Joseph H. Pleck. *The Impact of Work Schedules on the Family*. Ann Arbor, Mich.: Institute for Social Research, 1983.

Steiner, Gilbert Y. *The Children's Cause*. Washington, D.C.: Brookings Institution, 1976.

Trost, Cathy. "Survey Fortifies Parental-Leave Backers." *Wall Street Journal*, August 9, 1990, B1.

United States Chamber of Commerce. "Con: The Family and Medical Leave Act of 1987." *Congressional Digest* 67 (1988): 137–145.

U.S. Bureau of the Census. *Who's Minding the Kids? Child Care Arrangements: Winter 1984–85*. Current Population Reports, Series P-20, no. 9. Washington, D.C.: U.S. Government Printing Office, 1987.

U.S. Department of Labor, Women's Bureau. "Working Mothers and Their Children." *Facts on Working Women*, no. 89–3, August 1989.

_____. "State Maternity/Parental Leave Laws." *Facts on Working Women*, no. 90–1, June 1990.

White, Burton W. "Should You Stay Home with Your Baby?" *Young Children* 37 (1981): 11–17.

Winett, R. A., and M. S. Neale, "Results of Experimental Study on Flexitime and Family Life." *Monthly Labor Review* 103 (November 1980): 29–32.

Woolsey, Suzanne H. "Pied Piper Politics and the Child Care Debate." *Daedalus* 106 (1977): 127–146.

Wright, James. "Are Working Women Really More Satisfied?" *Journal of Marriage and the Family* 40 (1978): 301–314.

Zigler, Edward, and Susan Muenchow. "Infant Day Care and Infant-Care Leaves: A Policy Vacuum." *American Psychologist* 38 (1983): 91–94.

PART FIVE
Conclusion

13

Progress or Stalemate?
A Cross-National Comparison
of Women's Status and Roles

HILDA KAHNE

This concluding chapter returns to the questions that first sparked our interest in writing this book. What can we now say about the common work and life experiences of women in different societies, their causes, and their effects? What is distinctive about the circumstances affecting women's situation or the consequences that flow from their particular place in society? As we sift through the country studies and a wider body of confirming literature, both common and distinctive features emerge to describe women's roles and status.

The findings of our country studies suggest four general propositions: that women's economic inequality is pervasive; that a number of institutional arrangements and socioeconomic factors lead to their disadvantage; that certain distinctive national and cultural traditions bring variation to this overall picture; and that social and historical change is also at work. The chapter concludes by outlining several routes through which women's greater equality can be advanced.

WOMEN'S ECONOMIC STATUS RELATIVE TO MEN

Proposition 1. Despite women's major contributions to society and their increasing employment almost everywhere, their situation continues to be less favorable than men's in all countries and regions (International Labour Office [ILO] 1985: 204–205, 211–212; United Nations 1986: 33). An increasing number of woman heads of households are often in desperate economic circumstances. This is evident whether one examines labor market or household data.

As Francine D. Blau and Marianne A. Ferber and other chapter authors document,[1] women universally carry responsibility for most of the work involved in family sustenance and home care. Educational opportunities also are less available for women than for men, especially where education is not compulsory, per-capita income is low, and religious proscriptions constrain participation of girls and women in society. Although most governments express support for equality and have enacted legislation to promote it, job segregation is considerable (United Nations 1986: 34).

Occupational Segregation in Urban Labor Markets

In urban labor markets, the range of women's jobs is more limited than men's and is more often concentrated in occupations in which skill levels and status are relatively low. Women's work is less stable and provides less opportunity for advancement because of their socialization, girls' limited education and training opportunities, cultural factors, discriminatory practices, or sometimes women's narrowed options because of their domestic responsibilities.

Gordon Weil's chapter on sub-Saharan Africa and Helen I. Safa's on Latin America show that a majority of urban working women are employed in sales and service occupations, including domestic service or low-skill processing jobs in the export industry. In the Middle East, where Islamic tradition discourages sales and clerical work involving contact with the public, Valentine M. Moghadam describes how women are more likely to be employed in community jobs, social and personal services, or light manufacturing. Educated women in modernizing countries also are found in the female-typed professions, notably teaching and nursing.

In the Soviet Union, as shown by Gail W. Lapidus, although one-half of all industrial workers are women, they are heavily concentrated in a few sectors—notably food, textiles, and garment work—and rank low in status and pay. In the professions as in industrial employment, women are more likely to occupy the lower rungs of the occupational ladder.

The situation is similar in other Central and East European countries, where Sharon L. Wolchik finds that women make up nearly one-half of the labor force. Yet, despite political pronouncements in favor of equality, women's work has been concentrated in low-priority and low-skill areas of the economy, and only small numbers have held leading positions. Increases in technical and general education have not altered the fact that these women are still likely to cluster in traditionally feminine fields such as education, the arts, the humanities, and medicine. In the two Germanies, although women improved their occupational position in the past two decades (more so in East than in West Germany), Hedwig Rudolph demonstrates that gender equality is still far from being realized. Certificates of vocational and professional training, an integral component of preparation for paid work in Germany, are found among only 40 percent of working women in the former Federal Republic of Germany (FRG) compared with 87 percent of working women in the former German Democratic Republic (GDR). Unification is unlikely to improve these patterns. Moreover, women's access to higher positions is less than that for men of comparable ages and qualifications.

Occupational inequality of women is evident in the other advanced industrial countries as well (ILO 1985: 210–212). Occupational segregation persists in Great Britain and Japan despite legislation affirming equal opportunity as a goal (Lansing and Ready 1988). In Nordic countries, despite very high female labor force participation rates and legislation in effect since the late 1970s guaranteeing equal opportunity, occupational segregation remains high and affects women's work patterns both across occupations horizontally and hierarchically within an occupation. In the public sector, women are heavily concentrated in service occupations. Segregation also is present at the workplace level; Elina Haavio-Mannila and Kaisa Kauppinen indicate that it is reflected in the low proportion of women in top positions in both upper and lower socioeconomic categories. In fact, occupational segregation in Sweden is greater than in the United States (Moen 1989: 136–137). Here, although a declining proportion—especially during the 1970s—one-third of women still cluster in clerical work; in 1981, 62 percent of workers of one gender would have had to be redistributed among occupations in order for the occupational distribution between the sexes to reach equality (Blau and Ferber 1986; Kahne 1989; Reskin and Hartmann 1986). In Sweden a number of measures introduced to attract workers to nontraditional jobs, including financial incentives and hiring quotas, have had little effect on segregation (Ruggie 1988: 181–183).

Overall, the persistence of occupational segregation in all countries not only limits women's opportunity and restricts their mobility but also interferes with recruiting the best-qualified workers and reinforces sexual stereotyping in the society at large.

Wage Differentials

Wage differentials are a key result of occupational segregation between women and men in both developing and developed countries (ILO 1985: 224; Walby 1988). In developing regions, unreliable earnings data prevent documented comparisons for the agricultural sector in which women workers are concentrated. But data clearly demonstrate a large gender gap in industry, and its reduction since the 1970s has been minimal (ILO 1987: 129–131; United Nations 1986: 33, 91–92).

In the other countries of our study, although decreasing in recent years, a wage gap continues despite legislation or constitutional provisions supporting equality. Comparisons suggest a range in the ratio of female-male hourly earnings of between 60 percent and 90 percent. The gap is lowest in the Nordic countries and greatest in Japan. Differences in kinds of jobs, size of firm, training and education, hours of work, experience, age, and discrimination all play some part in the explanation of women's lower relative earnings (see also ILO 1985: 223–227, 1987: 146–147; United Nations 1986: 91; U.S. Department of Labor October 1990).

In the United States, sex segregation both by occupation across firms and by job within firms reflects lower relative earnings for women than men. Overall, in 1988 women's median hourly earnings were 74 percent of men's, compared with 64 percent in 1979. The diminishing earnings gap, apparent since the early 1980s, has been reflected both in "women's work" and in nontraditional occupations (Reskin and Hartmann 1986: 10–13; U.S. Department of Labor October 1990).

In the Nordic countries, the wage gap is greater in traditional female jobs; in the Soviet Union, the larger differential exists in heavy industry and construction where women are underrepresented. Women in Central and East Europe have increased their proportion in technical occupations, yet they still cluster in positions with lower-than-average wages. In Great Britain, although legislation appears to have reduced discrimination, Emma MacLennan shows that a substantial proportion of women work part time, in small nonunion firms, and without benefit of a national minimum wage. The result is low gross hourly earnings that in 1989 were about three-fourths those of men. That proportion also prevails in Germany. In the former FRG, the wage gap has been strongly influenced by job and training allocation policies.

In Japan, the gap between men's and women's hourly earnings, 40 percent in 1986, is considerably greater than in other industrial countries. Although one study reports that it is diminishing for younger women workers ages 25 to 29, in recent years the gap has increased for older women workers ages 45 to 49 (Ozawa, reference in Smith 1989: 67–68). This pay gap reflects differences in both wages and benefits. It is caused in part by differences in the firms in which women and men work but is also exacerbated by government and employer policies such as dependents' allowances, which are paid only to heads of households who are mostly men (United Nations 1986: 92). The lifetime employment system—including seniority, training, and promotion policies distinctive to Japan—also benefits men and disadvantages women (Lansing and Ready 1988: 120–123).

Women's Double Work-Family Burden

The negative consequences of women's position in the labor market are reinforced by the "double day" nature of their lives, which creates heavy time pressures for them and can interfere with job mobility and training as well as participation in public life. Women's responsibility for home care, and for family subsistence in developing nations, does not significantly diminish when they engage in paid employment. In the Soviet Union, employed women spend about twenty-eight hours a week on housework, compared with twelve hours for men. Soviet men's leisure time is 50 percent more than that of women. In East Germany women provide three-fourths of home care (Rudolph, Appelbaum, and Maier 1990: 37). In the United States, men's time in domestic work and child care has risen somewhat but does not yet approach that of women (Juster 1985). This is also true in Nordic countries. The Finnish labor force participation rate is the highest in Western Europe and most women work full time, yet their share of household work was 64 percent in 1987 (Kamerman and Kahn 1989: 25–27).

Overall, both at work and in the home, women's position is less favorable than that of men. The addition of paid work to home responsibilities has only increased the burden they carry. Improvements that have occurred have not substantially altered women's disadvantaged status.

Women as Single Heads of Households

Redressing women's worldwide secondary status in terms of economic opportunity and reward is more than an issue of equity; women not only deserve but *require* equal treatment because their work is essential to the economic well-being of their families. One-third of all households in the world are maintained de facto by a woman who is the sole provider. Except for Japan, where single heads of households are not common, most countries of the world—whatever their political orientation or economic structure—record a significant and increasing number of female-headed households; ensuring their adequate well-being is of growing concern (Goldberg and Kremen 1990; Kamerman and Kahn 1988, 1989; Rodgers 1990: 3; Seager and Olson 1986: no. 28; Sivard 1985: 17; United Nations 1986: 13, 1988).

In modernizing countries, households headed by women come into existence through death or divorce, abandonment, out-of-wedlock births, expulsion of husbands from the household, or migration of men to the urban centers in search for jobs (United Nations 1986: 13; Ward 1988: 39). Recent surveys of two groups of developed countries show the highest proportion—23 percent in 1988—and the highest growth rate of single-parent families to be in the United States (Kamerman and Kahn 1989; Sorrentino 1990). Only in Japan, where marriage rates are high and divorce rates are low, is the rate not rising. In recent times, growth of the number of families headed by women has been influenced less by death of the wage earner and more by the increase in separation and divorce, which also is highest in the United States, and the increase in childbirth outside of marriage. In each of the surveyed countries, 85–90 percent of all single-parent family heads are women. Problems of low earnings and benefits and dovetailing work and home responsibilities all contribute to the difficulties of maintaining these families. Even in Sweden, where considerable social support is available for single mothers, poverty is rising among these families (Sorrentino 1990: 49–51; Kamerman and Kahn 1989: 5, 13). Throughout the world, female-headed families are more likely to experience poverty than are other families (Kamerman and Kahn 1988: 70; Seagar and Olson 1986: no. 28; Sivard 1985: 16–17; Sorrentino 1990: 50).

In Great Britain, the policy norm is to encourage lone mothers to remain at home with means-tested income support until children reach age sixteen. As a consequence, labor force participation of these mothers is only 52 percent compared with two-thirds in other countries (Sorrentino 1990: 53). Under these circumstances, gross average income for lone mothers fell from 51 percent of income of a two-parent family with two children in 1979 to 40 percent of that income in 1984 (Kamerman and Kahn 1989: 18).

In industrial countries, where teenagers with few skills and incomplete education are most likely to become the single mothers, problems are compounded. In the United States and Great Britain, for example, where out-of-wedlock births to teenagers are 33 percent and 29 percent of all out-of-wedlock births respectively, these training and employment problems of young women added to their increased home responsibilities make it especially difficult for them to maintain their economic status above the poverty level (Sorrentino 1990: 50).

INSTITUTIONAL AND SOCIOECONOMIC FACTORS THAT INFLUENCE WOMEN'S POSITION

Proposition 2. There is a remarkable degree of similarity among all societies in our study in the factors that influence women's status and roles. These factors fall into four main categories: economic structure and conditions; the state and its policies; characteristics and rewards of women's work, particularly but not exclusively in the paid labor market; and gender relations as defined by custom, ideology, or policy.

Economic Structure and Conditions

Economic development, industrialization, and urbanization usually expand job opportunities in the paid labor market. However, although more jobs are created, this is not always so for women; and Lapidus, MacLennan, Moghadam, Safa, and Weil all note that the jobs available to women are often poorly paid and low-status positions. Changing technology in rural modernizing regions has frequently removed income-earning opportunities for women and given support to agricultural processes and resources used by men (ILO 1985: 207–208). Industrialization and technological advances in sub-Saharan Africa have increased work opportunities, but they also often have confined or displaced women's opportunities to marginal service or low-skill jobs. Women often lack the training to get skilled jobs in new fields such as electronics. Thus, although advancing technology offers potential for an improved quality of life, women do not necessarily benefit (ILO 1985: 208).

In industrialized economies, the effects of technological innovation and automation have deskilled some women's jobs and limited their access to new opportunities brought by advancing technology. Lapidus and Rudolph note that this condition is not limited to the past but is also the expectation for the future (see also Hartmann, Kraut, and Tilly 1986; Albin and Appelbaum 1988).

The State and Its Policies

The country studies also underscore the importance of the state—sometimes mediated through other institutions of religion, education, government, or the judicial system—which defines and enforces standards governing men's and women's lives and opportunities. Paid maternity and child care leaves, adaptations to a declining economy, and affirmative action policies are three examples of state policies that affect women's opportunities and economic status.

In centrally planned economies such as the former Soviet Union, the former GDR, and economies of Central and East Europe, maternity and child care benefits have been an explicit part of state policy designed to increase the birth rate while encouraging and sustaining women's participation in the labor force. The high full-time labor force participation rates for women in these societies combined with traditional gender roles in the home make maternity benefits and child care critical needs.

Family-related benefits are equally a centerpiece of the Nordic welfare societies and are based on the principle that all citizens are entitled to full social citizenship and a decent standard of living. The state is seen as an agent to influence both the market and the family, which are often major sources of social and economic inequality. According to Haavio-Mannila and Kauppinen, the Nordic countries see high rates of female labor force participation as a force for economic independence and autonomy and buttress them with an extensive array of family benefits, including maternity and parental paid leaves and a network of municipal and licensed family day care facilities, which fall somewhat short of meeting the needs (see also Kamerman and Kahn 1988: 77–80, 1989: 27–29; Sorrentino 1990: 54–55).

Such state benefits have been largely absent in other industrial countries. In the former FRG and Japan, child care facilities for young children designed to meet the needs of working mothers are available only minimally (Japan Institute of Labour 1986: 22; Goldberg and Kremen 1990). In the United Kingdom, according to MacLennan, places in public nurseries have declined to one-half their 1945 levels. Placement is available for only 1–2 percent of very young children, compared with 44 percent of children age two or younger who are attending publicly funded day care in Denmark (Sorrentino 1990: 54). Facilities for school-age children are even more scarce. Because of lack of child care, many mothers with young children do not work or work only part time. In the view of the British government, young children are better cared for at home, and when necessary, family needs should be met by the private sector as a cost of doing business. However, female but not male employees with two years of continuous employment and sixteen hours of weekly work are entitled to maternity benefits under the national insurance program (ILO 1988: 265).

In the United States, government-supported child-related benefits are among the lowest of all industrial countries. Despite the fact that 71 percent of women of child-bearing age are in the labor force, the United States has no national policy providing for parental leave (Meisenheimer 1989: 20; Kamerman 1989: 107). The Pregnancy Discrimination Act of 1978 does mandate inclusion of pregnancy disability if employers provide general temporary disability benefits. About 89 percent of full-time private-sector employees in medium and large firms work under these arrangements. Five states and Puerto Rico also provide such benefits (Meisenheimer 1989: 21; U.S. Department of Labor June 1990). In addition, 37 percent of full-time private-sector employees can take unpaid company-provided maternity leave when there is no disability, and 18 percent can take unpaid paternity leave (Cooley 1990: 61). Some form of maternity or parental leave for at least some employees also is available when there is no disability through laws in thirty states and Puerto Rico. Except for Puerto Rico, all leaves are unpaid (U.S. Department of Labor June 1990). But despite the availability of some state benefits, Joseph H. Pleck points out that without a national or state standard that provides a uniform floor of benefit support in less-affluent states, the low-income minority who lives there is apt to suffer disproportionately relative to low-income families in other states because of the absence of childbirth benefits.

Child care in the United States also is multifaceted and has major problems. A majority of children today have mothers who work outside the home. The labor force participation of women with children under age eighteen is two-thirds; it is over 50 percent even for those with children under age three (U.S. Department of Labor, cited in Rix 1990: 379). Yet, experts agree that government support for child care has been woefully inadequate, with great variability across and within states in standards of quality, forms, and costs; in low wages; and in training of child care workers (Hayes, Palmer, and Zaslow 1990). A variety of available forms of child care and company-sponsored child care assistance, applicable to 5 percent of full-time employees in medium and large firms in 1989, has not altered the fact that major deficits exist (Hayes, Palmer, and Zaslow 1990; Hyland 1990: 23; U.S. House of Representatives 1989). Pleck hopes the expanded federal support for child care under the 1990 Act for Better Child Care—the first national child care legislation in the United States—will decrease the number of children in the most inadequate child care arrangements.

Although some governments have responded positively to maternity and child care needs, in other cases governmental response to a stagnant or declining economy has often hurt women's relative economic status. Structural adjustment programs, for example, recommended by the International Monetary Fund and the World Bank to alleviate the economic crises of the mid-1970s were adopted in a number of developing regions, including those discussed in this volume. They involved a series of loans to Third World nations conditioned on the adoption of government policies reducing government intervention and increasing the role of private markets as a stimulant to growth. One of the effects of these programs has been to raise prices of imported goods due to devaluation, whereas unemployment and underemployment have increased for both men and women. Restricted public expenditures aimed at lowering debt burdens caused further distress. They reduced employment, training, and education opportunities as well as health and social welfare benefits, which had a particularly negative impact on maintaining the well-being of women and children. At the same time, women's relative position was hurt by their low mobility due to family responsibilities and their unequal access to credit and assets such as land and to information that would allow them to take advantage of new opportunities. Although gender-neutral in their formulation, the effect of structural adjustment policies—reinforcing negative effects of family burdens—has often been to make women relatively even less well-off.

Great Britain's declining economy has resulted in state policies that have had a similar deleterious effect on women. Policy has sought to increase the role of the private market, privatize public services, and adjust benefits to cut expenditures. Tax allowances have been preferred to benefit liberalization. Some aspects of the 1990 tax law, which now taxes men and women as individuals, still reinforce women's dependency status—in particular a higher personal allowance for married men payable whether or not their wives have independent incomes and only transferable to the wife if the man has no taxable income. Particularly harmful to women is the fact that the value of national insurance and welfare benefits, including birth and child-related benefits, has been cut, restricted, or eroded over time (Humphries and Rubery 1988). Publicly supported child care arrangements are among the lowest in Europe (Sorrentino 1990: 54). The government justifies its position on the grounds of expense and the claim that responsibility for child care belongs to the individual or the employer. All told, women's position has been negatively affected by recent state policy.

Finally, the effect of state policy embodied in affirmative action has been mixed. In some industrial countries, government policy has reduced occupational segregation. This has been true in the United States, especially during the 1970s—particularly for professional and managerial jobs and for younger women (Beller 1984; Blau 1988). It also has been true for Great Britain up to a point. In the former GDR, occupational disparity between men and women has been reduced both by affirmative action legislation and by technical and vocational training. But although reduced, women's unequal workplace status persists to a surprising degree (Rudolph, Appelbaum, and Maier 1990).

In Japan, legislative policy affirms gender equality for work opportunities and wages but acts largely as a guideline and carries no penalty for violation. In Nordic countries, affirmative action laws have a somewhat different purpose of stopping discrimination among individuals of either gender rather than demanding measures to assure equality for women as a group. This and related legislation have had little impact on occupational segregation, which has remained high and remarkably stable since the late 1960s (Skard and Haavio-Mannila 1984: 162; Moen 1989: 77–79).

Characteristics and Rewards of Women's Work

As shown by Blau and Ferber and other chapter authors, women's labor force participation has been rising since at least 1950 in almost all countries except in sub-Saharan Africa, where it has declined somewhat (United Nations 1986: 14), and in Japan, where the rate fell between 1960 and the mid-1970s before resuming a slightly rising trend (Bednarzik and Shiells 1989: 39). In the Soviet Union, there is evidence of a recent (1991) decline in the female labor force participation rate, possibly related to changes in the maternity leave policy and to a greater relative increase in women's unemployment rates compared with those of men (conversation with Gail W. Lapidus 1991).

General economic factors affecting product and labor demand and variables influencing worker supply, such as earnings, education, fertility, work aspirations, and need, interact with political and religious ideology, government policies, and social and cultural customs to determine labor force participation. These factors operate at different levels of intensity in different societies and even in different regions within a country. But what is important is that on balance, the effect has been almost exclusively to increase women's participation in paid work, bringing it closer to that of men. Researchers sometimes explain a dip in women's participation rates during early stages of industrialization by the decline in subsistence or family farming and the rise in educational enrollments (Psacharopoulos and Tzannatos 1989; Smith 1989). This "dip factor" helps to explain trends of women's work rates in both sub-Saharan Africa and Japan.

Among industrial countries, Japan occupies a unique position, having the lowest labor force participation rate for married women in paid market work in a business other than a family enterprise (26 percent in 1980). Primary energies of married women today, as in the past, are devoted to home and child rearing (Preston and Kono 1988: 279–280; Smith 1989: 49–51). The interaction of cultural values and employment policies negatively affects Japanese women's labor market work.

In fact, as Blau and Ferber note, whatever the level of labor force participation, women tend to experience occupational segregation and lower earnings than those of men. Even in the United States, with some movement toward greater gender equality in both occupational distribution and wages, improvement has been very gradual and the distance between the labor market positions of women and men remains considerable. In the Nordic countries, although the wage gap has decreased, occupational segregation remains high and unyielding (Skard and Haavio-Mannila 1984: 162; Moen 1989: 77). Frequently, unemployment also is higher for women than for men, although official data tend to underestimate the full extent of this difference because there are disproportionate numbers of underemployed and discouraged workers among women (Rudolph; Wolchik; see also ILO 1985: 215–216; Rudolph, Appelbaum, and Maier 1990: 38–40; Sorrentino 1989; Tilly 1990; United Nations 1986: 31; Vogelheim 1988; Kolinsky 1989).

Increasing labor force participation of women affects both the total society and individual families within it. Participation rates of the population provide a measure of the productive potential of the society, and the resulting production contributes to an increasing output per person of consumption and investment goods. Levels and patterns of work affect not only levels of employment and unemployment but also of income distribution and mobility.

At the level of the household, women's employment increases money income (Standing 1982) and hence increases consumer expenditures and improves the standard of living. It equalizes status among members of the family and gives women a stronger claim to a more equal share in family consumption, including nutrition and health care.

An important question, particularly for modernizing regions where the burdens of living are already great, is whether or not a rising attachment to the labor market adds to the economic well-being and quality of life of women. Some feminist researchers argue that women's paid work, particularly in the emerging export-processing zones in developing countries, represents exploitation of women in a new form (Ward 1988, 1990). Several chapter authors conclude, however, that on balance, labor force participation has positive consequences because it provides income for women who head families or who have become major contributors to the family when other family members become unemployed or their real wages deteriorate. Moreover, equality at work gives women greater autonomy and independence and helps to dispel the effects of patriarchal control that have been so destructive of women's status (Blau and Ferber; Moghadam; Safa).

Gender Relations

Gender relations—which have to do with the rights, responsibilities, expectations, and relationships of women and men—are amorphous. They have different forms in different regions and countries. Yet in whatever form, they permeate all aspects of national and family life. All authors refer in one way or another to the centrality of gender relations in defining women's status and roles. The roots of gender relations lie deep in the fabric of society. They may be influenced by and in turn may influence religious ideology, land rights and inheritance, labor market activities, and family and state policies. Movement toward greater equality is critical if women's societal position is to improve. At the same time, gender relations are difficult to alter.

Social support for a change in gender relations has been most pronounced with respect to the family. Legislation in the Nordic countries, enacted between 1974 and 1984, entitles fathers as well as mothers to share in benefits for childbirth and infant and child care. The benefit most commonly taken by the father is the six to twelve "daddy days" when the baby is born. But there also has been a gradual increase in the number of fathers who share in paid parental leave for care of infants, from four to fifteen months in length, that are available in all Nordic countries. In Finland roughly one-third of fathers take paternity-parental leave benefits, mostly in the form of daddy days. In Sweden by the early 1990s, taking daddy days benefits had become a customary practice. Twenty-seven percent of fathers took some parental leave in 1985, compared with only 2 percent in 1975. In addition, in some countries men as well as women can take additional unpaid leave after paid leave has expired, elect a shortened six-hour workday at reduced pay, or avail themselves of extended compensated "home care" leave for some years to care for young children. Both fathers and mothers also are entitled to some paid leave to care for a child with an acute illness. The availability of these benefits reflects a marked change in assumptions about who cares for children. The fact that fathers are slowly beginning to take advantage of such benefits is evidence that gender roles are changing. Haavio-Mannila and Kauppinen explain the hope of the policy that all family members will benefit—mothers because of reduced employment discrimination when they are no longer the only ones with extended maternity leaves and fathers and children because of their closer relationship.

Although several other countries, including the former FRG (Kamerman and Kahn 1989; Vogelheim 1988) and Czechoslovakia, have national policies that extend parental leave to fathers, the Nordic policies are the most generous and are the only ones tied explicitly to fostering gender equality (Haas 1990; Zigler and Frank 1988). But neither these nor other benefits alter the fact that in all societies of our study, as noted by Blau and Ferber and others (Haavio-Mannila and Kauppinen; Lapidus; Rudolph; Safa; Wolchik), women still bear more responsibility for and spend more time in domestic tasks than do men. Sometimes—as in the Nordic countries, Germany, and Central and East Europe—women's family burdens are reduced by government-supported child care (Kamerman and Kahn 1989; Rudolph, Appelbaum, and Maier 1990). Sometimes, as in the Middle East and Japan, the societal or personal choice is for women to focus on family as their working domain. In Great Britain, the United States, and many developing countries, support for home activities also is perceived as a private matter or, at best, as a mixed public-private sector responsibility. Even in the Nordic countries, the egalitarian policy stance is far ahead of egalitarian reality.

DISTINCTIVE SOCIETAL FEATURES
THAT AFFECT WOMEN'S POSITION

Proposition 3. At the same time that we find a high degree of commonality among the institutions and factors influencing women's roles and status, unique circumstances also often distinguish women's position in a particular country or region. Four illustrations come to mind.

Informal Labor Markets

When we talk about formal labor markets, we must not ignore the productive informal labor markets of developing countries, which are referred to by Safa and Weil. Informal labor markets function very differently from formal labor markets—without formal rules of wage and benefit contracts, licenses, or taxation. But they are not necessarily bootleg operations. Many have apprenticeship programs, and informal market workers often interact with the formal labor market as subcontractors or providers of direct services. Street-vendor retail trade, foodstuff processing, and data processing are major activities in the informal market (United Nations 1986: 170–171). These markets are expanding with rapid population growth, scarcity of resources, increasing rural-to-urban migration, and inadequate growth of opportunities in the formal labor market (United Nations 1986: 171).

Between 20 and 70 percent of the urban labor force in Third World cities works in the informal sector, with the average close to 50 percent or more. In some countries, informal market workers contribute more than 30 percent of urban regional income (United Nations 1986: 170–171). Between 46 and 70 percent of workers in the informal sector are women (Ward 1988: 33–34). In assessing the contribution of women, their role in these markets must not be neglected.

Religious Ideology and Cultural Expectations

Religious ideology, mentioned earlier as one factor that affects gender relations, also can be a strong distinctive force in society. This is especially true when the religious ideology is reflected in state legal codes, as it is in a number of Middle Eastern and North African countries. Consistent with Islam, women are viewed as the custodians of cultural values and tradition and are to be protected from the outside world. Men are expected to function in that public world and to provide for the well-being of the women in their families. In practice, this means that women's roles are more private than public—concerned with family care and well-being. Although membership in a higher social class and higher education reduce the constraining influence of Islamic tradition on women's public activities, Blau and Ferber point out that religious tradition continues to circumscribe women's choices and opportunities (see also Psacharopoulos and Tzannatos 1989: 194–195).

Cultural expectations have a similar effect in Japan where care of family is considered to be women's primary career (Preston and Kono 1988: 280). As Cordilia notes, custom—often reinforced by implicit company policy—encourages young women to leave the labor force when they marry and have children or to otherwise limit their career ambitions. The extremely low-paid market labor force participation rate for married women in Japan outside of family enterprises—26 percent compared with 56 percent in the United States—for example, is a reflection of these expectations.

Economic and Political Influences

Specific economic policies and political philosophies have particular consequences for women's status in a society. A straitened economic situation can lead to a decline in women's position because of a government policy decision to buttress the industrialized and monetized sector of the economy, which benefits men who are dominant there. An example can be seen in structural adjustment policies of modernizing countries (Dixon-Mueller and Anker 1988: 1). The same effect can result if governments seek general economic improvement by adopting measures to drastically reduce government expenditures, such as privatizing social support as in Great Britain and Latin America. Women, who are major beneficiaries of these programs, suffer as a result.

Implementation of certain political philosophies also affects women's position. In centrally planned socialist economies, the emphasis given to Marxist-Leninist philosophy concerning the centrality of women's work to the success of the socialist state has influenced the work and education policies adopted as well as the family policies that make that work possible. These policies have led to female labor force participation rates in the former Soviet Union and Central and East European countries that are the highest in the world. Almost one-half of all agricultural workers and 49 percent of employed persons in industrial enterprises in the former USSR are women (ILO 1985: 212–213). Over 85 percent of women are engaged in full-time paid work or study. Work rates are similarly high in the Central and East European countries, with the highest levels recorded for those regions that were most developed when socialism was introduced. Women's labor force participation rate in the former GDR has reached 90 percent for women ages 15 to 60. Currently, these working women represent one-half of the nation's work force. Part-time work has been virtually absent in many centrally planned societies.

The socialist states, which in the past proclaimed work-related gender equality through education, training, and occupational opportunities for women, did not simultaneously seek to advance gender equality in the home (Rudolph, Appelbaum, and Maier 1990: 33–36). Only after a falling birth rate became apparent in the 1960s did these states—concerned about possible negative economic consequences of declining fertility—respond with a range of measures supportive of women in their family roles. Women welcomed these measures and the respite they provided from the stress of combining family care with (usually) full-time employment. As noted by Rudolph, women increasingly support the right and the social desirability of reducing their "double burden" through part-time work, an expressed choice to remain at home, or other policies supportive of children or mothers (see also Rudolph, Appelbaum, and Maier 1990: 39). Wolchik reports that many women in Central and East European countries presently reject the goal of women's equality in its present form as an outmoded Communist slogan.

It is in this environment that the transition to new kinds of social market economies is taking place. Although women continue to work—often full time—in the market, many would prefer an alternative work-life rhythm. However, although this would reduce their double burden, prolonged absence from paid work or part-time work would create other problems. Family income would be reduced in societies where two earners have been essential for an adequate standard of living. And prolonged child care leave for women, without job guarantee, could create barriers to progress in occupational status and pay.

The focus of current state policy in these countries, as Wolchik comments, is not on protecting women's status or furthering gender equality but on broader issues involving a transition to political democracy and the establishment of a market economy. Yet it is likely that the position of women will be profoundly affected by the changes taking place. There is growing unemployment of women when service, retail trade, and lower-level managerial occupations become candidates for rationalization and retrenchment. An emphasis on the primacy of women's family roles reinforces the notion of women's paid work as a secondary activity, with negative consequences for their labor market status. In Germany, where transition to a market economy is further complicated by problems of unification, it is expected that the social policies of the former West Germany will prevail. This may lead eventually to a decrease in child care and other family support policies (Rudolph, Appelbaum, and Maier 1990: 33, 38–40). Women are disadvantaged when economic and political transformation fails to address very real work-family burdens.

Customs and Values

Various alternative customs and value systems dealing with what constitutes a "good life" have a distinctive effect on women's status. Some Latin American women, strong in the protection of the domestic role, have wrought a major change in the welfare of their families through community action by challenging the prevailing patriarchal gender relations of their societies. And the Nordic countries, almost alone among industrial societies, encourage equality in gender relations through their social policy, although change is taking hold only slowly and partially (Moen 1989: 135–151).

Extension of part-time work is another way in which alternative values about work are reflected. There is a desire for expansion of part-time work among women in the former Soviet Union and Central and East European countries as well as in Finland and Germany (Kamerman and Kahn 1989: 27; Kolinsky 1989: 174–188). For some of these women who now work full time in the market and for some pronatalist policymakers, the role exemplified by a majority of Japanese women who give priority to home needs has appeal. Despite the income and the sense of self-worth and contribution to society that accompany full-time paid work, its value as an unqualified good is not universally accepted.

In the United States, part-time work has strong appeal for some because of its reduced time demands, but it is criticized by others because its pay and benefits are often lower than for equivalent full-time work or because of a claim that it reduces gender equity in the workplace. Two-thirds of all part-time workers are women. About 27 percent of employed women and 11 percent of men work reduced schedules; 80 percent of these women and 68 percent of the men do so by choice (U.S. Department of Labor May 1990). Yet in the absence of a strong advocacy group, the proportion of voluntary part-time to full-time work is not growing. Although many women find that part-time work relieves stress or gives balance to the double burdens of work and family, until part-time work with prorated earnings and benefits as well as opportunities for promotion is accepted as a legitimate, committed work alternative for women and men, its potential will be limited.

CHANGING STATUS OF WOMEN OVER TIME

Proposition 4. The roles and status of women are continually undergoing change. Although life is undoubtedly better in some countries than in others, there is no guarantee that with economic development, the quality of women's lives improves. Nevertheless, there is some evidence of progress in women's relative position, shown most clearly among industrial countries and in social policy improvement.

Some Negative Influences

The rise in per-capita income that development brings may mean a general improvement in material well-being. But the loss of customary sources of livelihood without availability of new jobs, and the eradication of kinship and family supports that facilitate the functioning of a traditional society have often represented a reduction of relative well-being for women in modernizing societies (ILO 1985: 207–208). There is no automatic link between a country's rising per-capita income and the well-being of specific groups of its people (United Nations 1990).

Noneconomic factors have sometimes reinforced the tenuous nature of women's economic gains: the introduction of the male-individualized land tenure system in sub-Saharan Africa; the resurgence of Islamic ideals in the Middle East; the reduction in government social programs in Great Britain and developing countries; and unification and the move to market economies in Germany and in Central and East Europe.

In Japan the issue is less one of regression from previous gains than intensification of the conflict between accepted cultural norms about the proper role of married women and the growing aspirations of women for more autonomy in using their education in appropriate market work. Yet government and employment policies prevent and curtail women's achievement of their work goals that would move them toward greater equality with men.

Indicators of Improvement

Yet, there is evidence of improvement in women's position in some areas over time, shown most clearly among industrial countries where data are more complete.

Improving Education and Labor Market Experience. Not only does the *fact* of increasing labor force participation result in economic benefits for women but as Blau and Ferber and Safa observe, being economically active is particularly critical for women in developing countries because it legitimizes a claim to greater autonomy in decisionmaking and less dependence on men at the household level. Indirect benefits also associated with rising labor force participation rates, notes Lapidus, include decreasing fertility and slower rates of population growth, which help to raise per-capita income (see also Standing 1982). As work rates rise, so does literacy and women's level of education, due both to family decisions and to government policies that allocate schooling opportunities more equally between genders. Children tend to benefit when women, who most often are the informal as well as the formal educators of children in early years, are better educated (Standing 1982). But these effects are felt slowly and often are limited (ILO 1985: 217–218).

Improving literacy, more equal access to education and training, and a slow shift in what is considered appropriate gender work are all gradually helping to reduce occupational segregation (ILO 1985: 221–223). Women are entering traditional male occupations such as architecture, engineering, and technical occupations in both socialist societies in transition and the Nordic countries.

In the Soviet Union, despite continuing occupational segregation, women have some representation in almost all of the 290 major occupational groups, and an increasing number participate in management on an equal footing with men (ILO 1985: 223). In the United States, as noted by Blau and Ferber, the degree of segregation has been reduced—especially in the 1970s but also continuing slowly in the 1980s (see also Blau 1988; Blau and Ferber 1986; Beller 1984). The ratio of women's to men's hourly earnings rose ten percentage points from 64 to 74 percent between 1979 and 1988 (U.S. Department of

Labor October 1990). The gender wage gap in Nordic countries also has decreased over time.

Policy Support for Social and Private-Sector Work-Family Benefits. Another improvement, government support for family benefits, has been related either to an "institutional state model" that guarantees all citizens equal entitlement to an adequate standard of living or to a policy supportive of full-time work participation. An example of the former is the welfare benefit strategy used to achieve greater gender equality in the Nordic countries. An example of the latter is the work-related strategy for support of mothers in socialist societies (Rudolph, Appelbaum, and Maier 1990: 36, 39). In the former Soviet Union, there is subsidized day care and preschool education for children in addition to full pay for women during prenatal and postnatal maternity leave and, since 1981, partly paid leave until the child is one year old (ILO 1985: 228). Adjustments in work conditions to accommodate family needs also are made. Maternity leaves, financed by social insurance, are generally available in Central and East European countries (ILO 1985: 228). Hungary was a pioneer in this area in 1967 when it enacted extended leave with pay and job protection for women with children up to age three, supplementing a paid maternity leave for working mothers (Kamerman and Kahn 1989: 22–23).

In Great Britain and the United States, where women with family responsibilities have become a strong component of the labor force, debate increasingly centers not on whether there should be child care support but on whether its provision should be a public- or a private-sector responsibility and on how it should be shaped. Resistance to federal support for working women with children in the United States appears to be giving way to acceptance of a mixed system involving federal and state governments and the private sector. Policy is emerging from a broad mix of interests—political forces, feminist concerns, advocacy interests, employer and union initiatives, and individual choices. It reflects an interplay of concern for equity, the well-being of women and children and of parent-child relationships, importance of community standards, and a desire to maximize use of available labor skills and promote work force flexibility. Parental benefits are being extended, although not through federal legislation; the impact of a major 1990 U.S. federal legislative change with respect to child care has yet to be felt.

Part-time work, mentioned earlier as an example of alternative values about work, is receiving a mixed reception. For some, it is a means to perpetuate women's disadvantaged status (Beechey 1987), whereas others describe it with cautious hope as one way to reduce women's double burden (Kahne 1992). Part-time work is most common for women in some Nordic countries, especially Norway and Sweden, and in the United Kingdom and is often found in retail trade and service occupations in the United States (Belous 1989; ILO 1989). It is increasing in Germany and in Japan. Women in the Soviet Union and in Central and East European countries want to increase its availability (Agassi and Heycock 1989; Belous 1989; Green 1989; ILO 1989; Kolinsky 1989). Undoubtedly, part-time work has its limitations—as mentioned by MacLennan and Pleck—when it is intermittent or temporary, when prorated earnings are lower than those for comparable full-time work, when work-related benefits are fewer or totally excluded, or when workers do not receive otherwise-justified promotions (see also Humphries and Rubery 1988: 93–97). With careful structuring, however, these disadvantages need not persist (Sundström 1987; Kahne 1985). Until gender roles approach equality, part-time work—with modification of its shortcomings—can offer a way of reducing the double burden of work and family responsibilities (Moen 1989).

Changing Gender Roles. Although even more difficult to change than work structures, there is some evidence of changing gender roles in a way that is beneficial for women. Safa has described the changes in gender roles and in women's autonomy in Latin America that have resulted from increased women's labor force participation and educational levels and in activities in social movements designed to sustain families and communities and improve human rights. In the United States and in the Nordic countries, there is some movement toward greater gender equality in sharing homemaking responsibilities. For example, in the United States between 1965 and 1981, men's share of the total time spent by husbands and wives in housework and child care increased from 20 to 30 percent (Pleck 1985).

PROGRESS OR STALEMATE?
CAN THE FUTURE BE BETTER?

In the mosaic of similar and distinctive interacting influences that have come together to define women's status in diverse societies, both negative and positive forces are at work. Negative forces reinforce an ironic situation in which women, who are so central to the productive work of society and to family care, continue to be relegated to secondary status. Universally, they receive less acknowledgment and fewer rewards than men. General policies adopted to improve a faltering economy seem only to intensify their relatively low position.

But positive influences resulting from improved work characteristics, education and training, social policy, and slowly evolving values and customs show that forward movement also is possible. What additional steps will support and foster the frail, although real, improvements in women's position?

A major theme throughout the case studies in this book is the conflicting demands and the drain on both the time and energy of women as a result of the dual work-family burdens they increasingly carry. The evidence presented by chapter authors is reinforced by conclusions of a number of other social scientists whose research on the United States and Sweden also identifies gender roles and work-family demands as major impediments to women's equality (Degler 1980; Goldin 1990; Kessler-Harris 1981; Matthaei 1982; Moen 1989; Myrdal and Klein 1956; Okin 1989).

For the long run, it could be worthwhile to ponder the implications of assigning value to all productive contributions, both market-related and unpaid, and offering free choice to both women and men in the provision of these contributions. But within the confines of real-world social institutions, work-family structures, and reward systems, we know that free choice is constrained; families, however defined, require that time be allocated for their care and income be earned for their maintenance. The increase in families maintained by women alone and the growing recognition that for all families in both industrial and developing countries, well-being requires two incomes leads to the realization that for the short run at least, women's participation in the labor market will remain a necessity rather than a choice. Thus, solution of the problems posed by the double work-family burden must include equality of labor market opportunity, reward, and work conditions. It is noteworthy that the several indicators of improvement in women's position posed by chapter authors in this volume are all related to the issue of equality.

Unfortunately, no magic formula will ensure uninterrupted, continual improvement in women's working lives and reduction of stress and complexity associated with combining work with family care. Although some legislative progress has been made with respect to equality in the workplace, much remains to be accomplished both in providing support and encouraging adaptation of work structures and institutions to the way lives are lived. In some societies, legislation intended to bring about equality has not yet been enacted. Where it is present, the provisions of some laws need to be strengthened; others require more effective implementation. Part-time work is not yet routinely constructed so as to be an equally valued alternative to full-time work. In all societies, gender-neutral work participation, values, and behavior in work-related decisions must be encouraged.

Family support policies remain woefully inadequate in many countries. Except for the Nordic countries, there is as yet little economic acknowledgment of the desirability of enabling both parents rather than only mothers to care for infants and children. Work-family policies have resulted from a long, uneven process of interaction among a variety of political, economic, and cultural factors. To relieve the stress of women's current situation and improve care for dependents, discussions need to be carried on at all levels of social life—in the corridors and board rooms of state and private-sector policymaking as well as among the myriad community and women's interest groups. Innovative programs and institutional change based on women's preferences should be on the agenda.

The work of international agencies will play a critical role in how these forces shape the future. Only they have the resources and scope to focus an agenda of international relevance, provide cross-national comparative studies describing what is happening, and identify information gaps that need attention. They can serve as a stimulus and a forum, link research and programs, and assist governments in policy development. Their inspirational, analytic, and integrative roles are crucial.

Equally important will be the contribution of national governments. National policies that promote a sound economic structure and full employment economy are essential. Ultimately, through political debate and legislative action, it is the state that can best chart the course of social policies that address work and family environments, structures, and institutions and serve the needs of its citizens.

Although the state must provide the context and direction for improvement, private-sector initiatives of firms and trade unions can complement and supplement its work. Private-sector family benefit plans that mutually aid the firm and its employees are a potentially important advance for women.

Most important, progress toward women's equality requires strong activism by individuals at the community level. Women and men whose life experience is concerned with family well-being know well the centrality of women's contribution to the family. Their leadership in seeking gender equality at work and a more responsive environment for family care will provide a framework for forging new policy approaches. When policy innovations have been tailored to fit the cultural fabric, men and children as well as women will gain and thus, the whole of society.

NOTES

1. Much of the information in this chapter is drawn from the country studies. Only additional references are cited.

BIBLIOGRAPHY

Agassi, Judith Buber, and Stephen Heycock, eds. *The Redesign of Working Time: Promise or Threat?* Berlin: Edition Sigma, 1989.

Albin, Peter, and Eileen Appelbaum. "The Computer-Rationalization of Work: Implications for Women Workers." In *Feminization of the Labour Force: Paradoxes and Promises,* edited by Jane Jenson, Elisabeth Hagen, and Ceallaigh Reddy. Cambridge, England: Polity Press, 1988, 137–152.

Bednarzik, Robert W., and Clinton R. Shiells. "Labor Market Changes and Adjustments: How Do the U.S. and Japan Compare? *Monthly Labor Review* 112, no. 2 (February 1989): 31–42.

Beechey, Veronica, and Tessa Perkins. *A Matter of Hours: Women, Part-Time Work, and the Labour Market.* Minneapolis: University of Minnesota Press, 1987.

Beller, Andrea. "Trends in Occupational Distribution By Sex and Race, 1960–1981." In *Sex Segregation in the Workplace: Trends, Explanations, and Remedies,* edited by Barbara F. Reskin. Washington, D.C.: National Academy Press, 1984, 11–26.

Belous, Richard S. *The Contingent Economy: The Growth of the Temporary, Part-Time, and Subcontracted Workforce.* Washington, D.C.: National Planning Association, 1989.

Blau, Francine. "Occupational Segregation by Gender: A Look at the 1980s." Paper presented at the American Economic Association Meetings, New York, December 1988.

Blau, Francine, and Marianne A. Ferber. "Women's Progress in the Labor Market: Should We Rest on Our Laurels?" Proceedings of the 39th Annual Meeting of the Industrial Relations Research Association, New Orleans, 1986.

Cooley, Cathy A. "1989 Employee Benefits Address Family Concerns." *Monthly Labor Review* 113, no. 6 (June 1990): 60–63.

Degler, Carl N. *At Odds: Women and the Family in America from the Revolution to the Present.* New York: Oxford University Press, 1980.

Dixon-Mueller, Ruth, and Richard Anker. *Assessing Women's Contributions to Development.* Background Papers for Training in Population, Human Resources, and Development Planning, Paper no. 6. Geneva: International Labour Office, 1988.

Goldberg, Gertrude Schaffner, and Eleanor Kreman, eds. *The Feminization of Poverty: Only in America*. New York: Greenwood Press, 1990.

Goldin, Claudia. *Understanding the Gender Gap: An Economic History of American Women*. New York: Oxford University Press, 1990.

Green, Gretchen. "Women in Japan's Labor Force." *Journal of the American Chamber of Commerce in Japan* 26 (October 1989): 21–28+.

Haas, Linda. "Gender Equality and Social Policy: Implications of a Study of Parental Leave in Sweden." *Journal of Family Issues* 11, no. 4 (December 1990): 401–423.

Hartmann, Heidi I., Robert E. Kraut, and Louise A. Tilly, eds. *Computer Chips and Paper Clips: Technology and Women's Employment*. Washington, D.C.: National Academy Press, 1986.

Hayes, Cheryl D., John L. Palmer, and Martha J. Zaslow, eds. *Who Cares for America's Children? Child Care Policy for the 1990s*. Washington, D.C.: National Academy Press, 1990.

Humphries, Jane, and Jill Rubery. "Recession and Exploitation: British Women in a Changing Workplace, 1979–1985." In *Feminization of the Labour Force: Paradoxes and Promises*, edited by Jane Jenson, Elisabeth Hagen, and Ceallaigh Reddy. Cambridge, England: Polity Press, 1988, 85–105.

Hyland, Stephanie L. "Helping Employees with Family Care." *Monthly Labor Review* 113, no. 9 (September 1990): 22–26.

International Labour Office. *World Labour Report*. Labour Relations, International Labour Standards, Training, Conditions of Work, Women at Work, vol. 2. Geneva: International Labour Office, 1985.

_____. *World Labour Report*. Incomes from Work: Between Equity and Efficiency, vol. 3. Geneva: International Labour Office, 1987.

_____. *Work and Family: The Child Care Challenge*. Conditions of Work Digest, vol. 7, no. 2. Geneva: International Labour Office, 1988.

_____. *Part-Time Work*. Conditions of Work Digest, vol. 8, no. 1. Geneva: International Labour Office, 1989.

Japan Institute of Labour. *Problems of Working Women*. Japanese Industrial Relations, Series 8. Tokyo: Japan Institute of Labor, 1986.

Juster, F. T. "A Note on Recent Changes in Time Use." In *Time, Goods, and Well-Being*, edited by F. T. Juster. Ann Arbor: Institute for Social Research, University of Michigan, 1985.

Kahne, Hilda. *Reconceiving Part-Time Work: New Perspectives for Older Workers and Women*. Totowa, N.J.: Rowman and Allanheld, 1985.

_____. "Economic Perspectives on Work and Family Issues." In *Women and Men: New Perspectives on Gender Differences*, edited by Malkah T. Notman and Carol C. Nadelson. Washington, D.C.: American Psychiatric Press, 1989, 9–22.

_____. "Part-Time Work: A Hope and a Peril." In *Working Part-Time: Risks and Opportunities*, edited by Barbara Warme, Katherine Lundy, and Larry Lundy. New York: Praeger, 1992.

Kamerman, Sheila B., and Alfred J. Kahn. "What Europe Does for Single-Parent Families." *Public Interest* 93 (Fall 1988): 70–86.

_____. "Single-Parent, Female-Headed Families in Western Europe: Social Change and Response." *International Social Security Review* 42, no. 1 (1989); 3–34.

Kessler-Harris, Alice. *Women Have Always Worked: An Historical Overview*. Old Westbury, N.Y.: Feminist Press, 1981.

Kolinsky, Eva. *Women in West Germany—Life, Work, and Politics*. New York: St. Martins Press, 1989.

Lansing, Paul, and Kathryn Ready. "Hiring Women Managers in Japan: An Alternative for Foreign Employers." *California Management Review* 30 (Spring 1988): 112–127.

Matthaei, Julie A. *An Economic History of Women in America: Women's Work, the Sexual Division of Labor, and the Development of Capitalism*. New York: Schocken Books, 1982.

Messenheimer, Joseph R., II. "Employer Provisions for Parental Leave." *Monthly Labor Review* 112, no. 10 (October 1989): 20–24.

Moen, Phyllis. *Working Parents—Transformations in Gender Roles and Public Policies in Sweden.* Madison: University of Wisconsin Press, 1989.

Myrdal, Alva, and Viola Klein. *Women's Two Roles: Home and Work.* London: Routledge and Kegan Paul, Ltd. 1956.

Okin, Susan Moller. *Justice, Gender, and the Family.* New York: Basic Books, 1989.

Pleck, Joseph H. *Working Wives, Working Husbands.* Newbury Park, Calif.: Sage Publications, 1985.

Preston, Samuel H., and Shigemi Kono. "Trends in Well-Being of Children and the Elderly in Japan." In *The Vulnerable,* edited by John L. Palmer, Timothy Smeeding, and Barbara Boyle Torrey. Washington, D.C.: Urban Institute Press, 1988, 277–307.

Psacharopoulos, George, and Zafiris Tzannatos. "Female Labor Force Participation: An International Perspective." *The World Bank Research Observer,* 4, no. 2 (July 1989): 187–201.

Reskin, Barbara F., and Heidi I. Hartmann, eds. *Women's Work, Men's Work: Sex Segregation on the Job.* Washington, D.C.: National Academy Press, 1986.

Rix, Sara E., ed. *The American Woman 1990–91: A Status Report.* New York: W. W. Norton and Company, 1990.

Rodgers, Harrell R., Jr. *Poor Women, Poor Families: The Economic Plight of America's Female-Headed Families.* Armonk, N.Y.: M. E. Sharpe, Inc., (Rev. ed.) 1990.

Rudolph, Hedwig, Eileen Appelbaum, and Friederike Maier. "After German Unity: A Cloudier Outlook for Women." *Challenge* 33, no. 6 (November-December 1990): 33–40.

Ruggie, Mary. "Gender, Work, and Social Progress: Some Consequences of Interest Aggregation in Sweden." In *Feminization of the Labour Force: Paradoxes and Promises,* edited by Jane Jenson, Elisabeth Hagen, and Ceallaigh Reddy. Cambridge, England: Polity Press, 1988, 173–188.

Seager, Joni, and Ann Olson. *Women in the World: An International Atlas.* New York: Simon and Schuster, 1986.

Sivard, Ruth Leger. *Women: A World Survey.* Washington, D.C.: World Priorities, 1985.

Skard, Torild, and Elina Haavio-Mannila. "Equality Between the Sexes—Myth or Reality in Norden?" *Daedalus. The Nordic Experience* 113, no. 1 (Winter 1984): 141–167.

Smith, James P. "Women, Mothers, and Work." In *Women's Life Cycle and Economic Insecurity: Problems and Proposals,* edited by Martha N. Ozawa. New York: Greenwood Press, 1989, 42–70.

Sorrentino, Constance. "Adjusted Japanese Unemployment Rate Remains Below 3 Percent in 1987–88." *Monthly Labor Review* 112, no. 6 (June 1989): 36–38.

———. "The Changing Family in International Perspective." *Monthly Labor Review* 113, no. 3 (March 1990): 41–57.

Standing, Guy. *Labour Force Participation and Development.* 2d Ed. Geneva: International Labour Office, 1982.

Sundström, Marianne. *A Study in the Growth of Part-Time Work in Sweden.* Stockholm: Arbetslivscentrum, 1987.

Tilly, Chris. *Short Hours, Short Shrift: Causes and Consequences of Growing Part-Time Work.* Washington, D.C.: Economic Policy Institute, 1990.

United Nations. *World Survey on the Role of Women in Development.* New York: Department of International Economic and Social Affairs, 1986.

———. *Women's Indicators and Statistics Database (Wistat) on Microcomputer Diskettes.* Version 1, May 31, 1988.

———. *Human Development Report 1990.* New York: U.N. Development Program and Oxford University Press, 1990.

United States Department of Labor, Bureau of Labour Statistics. News Release. September 7, 1990; May 19, 1990.

United States Department of Labor, Women's Bureau. "State Maternity/Parental Leave Laws." Facts on Working Women, no. 90–1 (June 1990).

———. "Earnings Differences Between Men and Women." Facts on Working Women, no. 90–3, (October 1990).

United States House of Representatives. Children and Families: Key Trends in the 1980s. Staff Report of the Select Committee on Children, Youth, and Families. One-Hundredth Congress, Second Session, December 1988. Washington, D.C.: Government Printing Office, 1989.

Vogelheim, Elisabeth. "Women in a Changing Workplace: The Case of the Federal Republic of Germany." In Feminization of the Labour Force: Paradoxes and Promises, edited by Jane Jenson, Elisabeth Hagen, and Ceallaigh Reddy. Cambridge, England: Polity Press, 1988, 106–119.

Walby, Sylvia, ed. Gender Segregation at Work. Philadelphia: Open University Press, 1988.

Ward, Kathryn B. "Women in the Global Economy." In Women and Work, an Annual Review, vol. 3, edited by Barbara Gutek, Ann Stromberg, and Laurie Larwood. Beverly Hills, Calif.: Sage Publications, 1988, 17–48.

———. ed. Women Workers and Global Restructuring. Ithaca, N.Y.: Industrial and Labor Relations Press, 1990.

Zigler, Edward F., and Meryl Frank, eds. The Parental Leave Crisis: Toward a National Policy. New Haven: Yale University Press, 1988.

About the Book and Editors

A provocative analysis of the nature of the relation between women and paid work in both modernizing and industrial countries, this book explores the variables that shape the relationship: demographic factors, the social and cultural context, the political environment, and the level and direction of economic development. Contributors point to a number of similarities in the roles, activities, and status of women in countries with varying levels of development, but they also argue that women's productive activities in both market and nonmarket economies exhibit distinctive characteristics and have evolved in ways that reflect the particular circumstances of the country. An introductory section provides a historical and sociological framework for the analysis as well as a statistical overview of women's nonagricultural employment. A number of country case studies follow, which focus on health, education, and family roles and provide a wealth of data about the characteristics of paid work and the workplace, including occupations and earnings, technological change, pay equity, work schedules, cooperatives, and the informal labor market.

Hilda Kahne is professor of economics at Wheaton College. **Janet Z. Giele** is professor of sociology and family policy at the Florence Heller School, Brandeis University.

About the Contributors

Francine D. Blau is professor of economics and labor and industrial relations at the University of Illinois, Urbana-Champaign, and research associate at the National Bureau of Economic Research, Cambridge, Massachusetts. Within the field of labor economics, she has been particularly interested in studying the problem of labor market discrimination and the economic behavior of women. She is author of *Equal Pay in the Office* (1977) and has contributed extensively to professional journals and other scholarly publications. With Marianne A. Ferber, she is author of *The Economics of Women, Men, and Work* (Second edition, 1992).

Ann Cordilia, associate professor of sociology at the University of Massachusetts–Boston, received her Ph.D. in sociology from the University of Chicago. Initiated during a Fulbright Fellowship to Japan in 1988, her current research relates to the linkages between college life and work life in Japan, especially among women. She also has written about the transitions from high school to college to employment in Japan and the United States. She is author of *The Making of an Inmate: Prison as a Way of Life* (1981) and of numerous articles and papers on the connection between alcohol and crime.

Marianne A. Ferber is professor of economics at the University of Illinois, Urbana-Champaign, where she also was director of women's studies from 1980 to 1983. Within the broad field of the economic status of women, she has concentrated particularly on the standing of women in academia, the family as an economic unit, and international comparisons in the position of women. She has published extensively in professional journals. With Francine D. Blau, she is author of *The Economics of Women, Men, and Work* (Second edition, 1992).

Janet Z. Giele (Ph.D., Harvard University, 1961) is professor of sociology and family policy at the Heller Graduate School for Advanced Studies in Social Welfare, Brandeis University, where she is also director of the Family and Children's Policy Center. Her two main research interests are the changing lives of women and the growth of family policy. Her books include *Women: Roles and Status in Eight Countries* (with A. C. Smock 1977), *Women and the Future* (1978), *Women in the Middle Years* (1982), and *Two Paths to Equality: Women's Temperance and Women's Suffrage, 1830–1930* (forthcoming).

Elina Haavio-Mannila received a master's of social and political sciences in 1956, licensiate in 1957, and doctorate in 1958 from the University of Helsinki. At present she is acting professor of sociology at the University of Helsinki and chairperson of the Department of Sociology. Professor Haavio-Mannila's publication list includes seven books, eight edited books, and numerous articles, monographs, and reports. Her recent research has been on the position of women and men in society from a comparative perspective. Current research projects relate to social relations in the workplace and in the family and changes in intimate relations between women and men in Finland between 1971 and 1992.

Hilda Kahne (Ph.D., Harvard University, 1953) is professor of economics at Wheaton College, Norton, Massachusetts. She held the A. Howard Meneely Professorship from 1982 to 1984 and was a Wheaton College intern in Kenya in the summer of 1985. Her publications span areas of the economics of aging and social welfare, flexible work structures, and work-family issues. She is author of *Reconceiving Part-Time Work: New Perspectives for Older Workers and Women* (1985, 1987) and has contributed extensively to journals and edited books. Her current research relates to work and family issues for women and men in modernizing and industrial countries.

Kaisa Kauppinen is research scientist at the Finnish Institute of Occupational Health in Helsinki. From 1987 to 1989, she was a visiting scholar at the University of Michigan. She has a Ph.D. in social psychology from the University of Helsinki where she holds a lecturer's (docent) position. Her research covers gender roles, family and work, and women's position in nontraditional occupations. A recent article, co-authored with I. Kandolin for the ILO, is "Women in Non-Traditional Occupations—International Comparisons: Impacts on the Quality of Work, Job Satisfaction, and Stress."

Gail W. Lapidus is professor of political science at the University of California at Berkeley and chair of the Berkeley-Stanford Program in Soviet Studies. She holds a Ph.D. from Harvard University. A specialist on Soviet politics and foreign policy, Professor Lapidus has authored *Women in Soviet Society* (1979), coedited (with A. Melville) *The Glasnost Papers: Voices on Reform from Moscow* (1990), and written numerous articles on contemporary Soviet affairs and Soviet-U.S. relations. A frequent visitor to the former USSR, Professor Lapidus is working on a book on nationalism and the Soviet future.

Emma MacLennan is research officer in the Policy Development Directorate of the British Labour Party doing work on taxation and social security. She was formerly the deputy director of the Low Pay Unit, a research and lobby organization campaigning for a minimum wage, improvements in equal pay and sex discrimination legislation, and equal treatment for part-time employees and home workers. She has published on issues relating to women and employment, including chapters on Great Britain in *Women Workers in Fifteen Countries* (J. Farley, ed., 1985) and *Women, Work, and Society* (K. Saradamoni, ed., 1985).

Valentine M. Moghadam was born in Iran and took her first degree in political science in Canada. She earned her doctorate in sociology at the American University, Washington, D.C., in 1986. She taught at New York University and Rutgers University. She is senior research fellow and coordinator of the Research Programme on Women and Development at the World Institute for Development Economics Research of the United Nations University in Helsinki. Her work on the Iranian Revolution, women and work, and industrial labor has appeared in numerous journals and edited volumes. She is author of *Women and Social Change in the Middle East* (Lynne Rienner Publishers, forthcoming).

Kazuko Ohta received her M.A. in history from Syracuse University. She is now associate professor of cultural studies at Mie National University in Japan. She has written on U.S. women and feminism and has been engaged for over a decade in the study of ethnicity in North America. She is working on a book about Cajun ethnic identity and culture. In summer 1989, Professor Ohta was a resident scholar in Bellagio, Italy, where she collaborated on a project on the cultural foundations of modernity in the West and in East Asia.

Joseph H. Pleck is research associate at the Wellesley College Center for Research on Women and was formerly the Henry R. Luce Professor of Families, Change, and Society at Wheaton College, Norton, Massachusetts. His research relates to families and family policy. He is author of *Working Wives, Working Husbands* (1985) and coauthor (with G. Staines) of *The Impact of Work Schedules on the Family* (1983). He coedited (with H. Z. Lopata) *Jobs and Families* (1983). Other research interests include adolescent male sexual and contraceptive behavior and men's roles.

Hedwig Rudolph is professor of labor economics at the Technical University of Berlin and director of the Department of Organization and Employment at the Social Science Center of Berlin. Over the past decade, her research has focused on structural aspects of the educational system and the labor market and their interrelationships. She has a long-standing interest in women's employment, especially nontraditional jobs. Recently she directed an action research program on women and technology. Dr. Rudolph is coauthor of *Ungeschützte Arbeitsverhältnisse* (1987), *Ingenieurinnen-Frauen für die Zukunft* (1987), and *Frauen Gestalten Technik* (1988).

Helen I. Safa is professor of anthropology and Latin American studies at the University of Florida. She is author of *The Urban Poor of Puerto Rico* (1974) and editor of *Women and Change in Latin America* (1986), *Toward a Political Economy of Urbanization in Third World Countries* (1982), and other books. Her articles and reviews on migration, housing, race, ethnicity, education, and women in relation to national development have appeared in many scholarly journals. She is past president of the Latin American Studies Association. Her forthcoming book with Westview Press is *The Myth of the Male Breadwinner—Women and Industrialization in the Caribbean.*

Gordon Weil is professor at Wheaton College, Norton, Massachusetts, specializing in international economics and development. He is the current holder of the William C. H. and Elise D. Prentice Professorship. Most recently he has studied social market economies in transition and implications for women's roles and status. His publications include a monograph, "Exchange-Rate Regime Selection in Theory and Practice" (1983), and a paper, "Economic Reform and Women: A General Framework with Specific Reference to Hungary," presented at the 1991 UN-WIDER Conference on Gender and Restructuring in Eastern Europe.

Sharon L. Wolchik is associate professor of political science and international affairs and director of Russian and East European studies at George Washington University. She received her Ph.D. from the University of Michigan in 1978. She has written extensively on issues related to elite policies toward women and gender issues, nationality relations, and policymaking in Central and East Europe. She is coeditor (with M. J. Sodaro) of *Domestic and Foreign Policies in Eastern Europe in the 1980s* (1983) and *Women, State, and Party in Eastern Europe* (1985) and recently completed *Czechoslovakia in Transition: Politics, Economics, and Society* (1991).

Index

Abortion
  and Communist policy, 122, 126
  and Nordic countries, 229
  and post-Communist countries, 131, 133
Acker, Joan, 224, 242
Act for Better Child Care (ABC) (U.S.), 166, 251, 257–259, 270, 286
Addison, Tony, 62
Adjustment with a Human Face, 62
Affirmative action, 10, 19, 184
  cross-national comparisons of, 284, 287
  and Germanies, 170, 183
  and Great Britain, 192
Afghanistan, 89, 92, 93, 101, 102
Africa
  female labor force participation, 14, 31, 104
  and food production, 21
  gender equality in, 12
  and global restructuring, 17, 18
  See also North Africa; Sub-Saharan Africa
Age, 17
Agriculture
  and global economic restructuring, 94
  in Latin America and Caribbean, 72–73
  in Middle East and North Africa, 96, 108
  and Nordic countries, 230
  and sub-Saharan Africa, 49, 52, 53–54, 58–61
  technology and female income from, 284
  See also Food
Aidoo, Agnes Akosua, 53
Albania, 124, 126, 130
Alcoholism, 155
Algeria
  economy of, 92, 94
  female labor force participation, 104, 106, 108
  IMF riots in, 112

Islamist movements in, 92, 99–100
  male unemployment in, 106
Ali, Ben, 98
Alia, Ramiz, 126
American Enterprise Institute, 257
Animist countries, 38
Antrobus, Peggy, 22–23
Argentina
  education and employment in, 70, 84(n2)
  female employment patterns in, 96
  politics in, 80, 81
  women's movements in, 12, 81
  and women's rights, 81–82
Arizpe, Lourdes, 72, 73
Armey, Dick, 267
Asia
  female labor force participation in, 14, 17, 32, 104
  Southeast, 94, 95
Australia, 36, 37
Austria, 35

Bahrain, 33, 95
Balkans, 120, 124
Bangladesh, 40
Becker, Uwe, 174
Belsky, Jay, 255–256
Berik, Gunseli, 93
Besharov, Douglas J., 257, 259
Biryokova, Aleksandra, 159
Blacks, 70, 83–84(n1)
Blau, Francine D., 37
Blumberg, Rae Lesser, 7, 21
Bohen, H., 249–250, 261, 262
Bolivia, 70
Boserup, Ester, 5, 14, 51
Bourguiba, Habib, 98, 101
Brademas, John, 253